Global Business Management
A Cross-cultural Perspective

ABEL ADEKOLA
University of Wisconsin-Stout, USA
and
BRUNO S. SERGI
University of Messina, Italy

ASHGATE

Published by
Ashgate Publishing Limited
Gower House
Croft Road
Aldershot
Hampshire GU11 3HR
England

Ashgate Publishing Company
Suite 420
101 Cherry Street
Burlington, VT 05401-4405
USA

Ashgate website: http://www.ashgate.com

British Library Cataloguing in Publication Data
Adekola, Abel
    Global business management : a cross-cultural perspective.
    - (Innovative business textbooks)
    1. International business enterprises - Management
    I. Title II. Sergi, Bruno S.
    658.1'8

Library of Congress Cataloging-in-Publication Data
Adekola, Abel.
    Global business management : a cross-cultural perspective / by Abel Adekola and Bruno S. Sergi.
        p. cm. -- (Innovative business textbooks)
    Includes bibliographical references and index.
    ISBN 978-0-7546-7112-1
    1. International trade--Cross-cultural studies. 2. International business enterprises--Cross-cultural studies. 3. International business enterprises--Management. 4. Globalization. 5. Multiculturalism. I. Sergi, Bruno S. II. Title.

    HF1379.A34 2007
    658'.049--dc22

ISBN: 978-0-7546-7112 1

2007002939

Printed and bound in Great Britain by MPG Books Ltd, Bodmin, Cornwall.

Contents

List of Case Studies

Low-Budget Cola Shakes Up Markets South of the Border

Japan, Mexico Hammer Out Final Details on Trade Deal

Lincoln Electric's Harsh Lessons from International Expansion

Hong Kong's Economic System

The Moral and Ethical Responsibility of MNEs

Outsourcing: Jobs in Jeopardy

Euro Disney

Counselors Now Target Japanese Overseas

Transplanting Corporate Cultures Globally

Placing a US Firm in Germany

Ford, GM Fight over Brightest Labor Market

List of Boxes, Figures and Maps

List of Boxes, Figures and Maps

List of Tables

Foreword

In today's fast integrating markets, cross-cultural perspectives, especially non-European perspectives, are indispensable to the success of global businesses. Dr Adekola's and Dr Sergi's opportune work offers many such perspectives that can help enterprises the world over in understanding the complete matrix of doing business in an international arena. Many information-rich threads of management principles have been interwoven with dynamic cultural factors that influence the former in no less concrete way, serving as a vivid guide to those transacting business in the cross-cultural cosmos. This book is an expert treatise on the fundamental principles that influence cross-cultural interactions, and is thereby invaluable for those engaged in international strategy and management. The book focusses on managing transnational organizations, providing a concrete basis for understanding the influence of culture on international management, and the key roles that international managers play.

I would like to compliment Abel and Bruno on the timeliness of the book, as the new-age demands that we understand our work and its global stakeholders. The idea is not to obfuscate the differences between cultures and practices but to understand people from different ethoi to be able to make work-processes smoother. Of course, such an activity naturally enriches our understanding of people in different cultural settings, adding to our own persona.

The butterfly effect is of particular relevance. It just goes on to establish that while a product can be designed, marketed and sold with the best of brains behind it, it is finally a unique rapport with the target audience, riding on cultural understanding that will create the impact. Do people remember the vandalizing of Coke and McDonalds in Germany, and so many other similar instances? Ultimately, we are in a universe of people, by the people, and for the people. And if you must ignore cross-cultural perspectives, then you will do so at your own peril!

This book would be especially helpful for students of International Business and Management at undergraduate and postgraduate levels. It could also be used as a supplement to general undergraduate business classes, such as Principles of Management, Hospitality Management, Tourism Management, Organizational Leadership Management, and Import-Export Management.

This book is of universal appeal to students in universities and colleges, both in the US and internationally, as well as to anyone who wishes to be an international player in his or her business or profession.

Vinay Rai
President
Rai Foundation

Preface

Our intention for this new book *Global Business Management: A Cross-cultural Perspective* is to provide for readers a unique source concerning national, regional, and global economic, business, and cultural development. We began collaborating on this issue several years ago and the book is the end product of it. We expanded and edited the entire manuscript while we were both at ISM University of Management and Economics in Vilnius, Lithuania, during the autumn of 2006, when Abel was a Fulbright Scholar and Bruno a visiting professor.

Global Business Management: A Cross-cultural Perspective examines globalization and its significance, paradoxes and the interplay of cultural approaches and entrepreneurships. We have combined and used these enough to understand the entire and multifaceted phenomenon of global business management. In particular, in this book, we look at how globalization evolved, suggesting that a trend toward global interplay is not the outcome of modern times or of simple attitudes toward a firm's going abroad. We observe the role and process of financial institutions in countries and regions as well as consider globalization's impact on the world's economic system. We explore the role of entrepreneurs and consumers and how this affects globalization in its production and subsequent allocation of goods and services, and by that conclude that the significance of culture, information technology, development, and the betterment of population are the central driving forces of globalization and some of its paradoxes. In all, with this book, we offer rational and credible commentary regarding the issues that are shaping our economies and their impact on an evolving world setting as well.

Cultural perspectives have several consequences upon populations and business environments. An extended evaluation of the consequences for all of us will also emerge from reading the chapters in the book. Our approach has been to combine cultural, business, and economic issues rather than to present them separately. All regions in the world are presented to readers in a way that inspires understanding of basic governing issues and expectations concerning the future, attempting to fuse the several perspectives mentioned earlier.

Acknowledgments

While it is the authors' names that appear on the cover of the book, no book would be possible without the combined efforts of the supporting team. We would especially like to thank the students and faculty of the University of Wisconsin, Stout Business Program, where the idea of this book first started, and the Fulbright Scholars Program and the ISM University of Management and Economics in Vilnius, Lithuania. The latter two created the opportunity and academic environment for the two authors to meet during the autumn of 2005, when Abel was a Fulbright Scholar and Bruno was a visiting professor. Between the two, they have expanded the entire manuscript from a lopsided American view of global management and have given it a well-deserved European flavor.

A sincere debt of gratitude is due to Brendan George, former Senior Commissioning Editor of Ashgate Publishing, for his acceptance of our manuscript into the noted library of Ashgate Publishing. In addition, the publication of this book would not have been possible without the efforts put in by the individuals working at Ashgate Publishing who helped move this from production to the market. Therefore we would like to acknowledge and give thanks to Dymphna Evans, Publishing Director, Social Sciences and Reference, and all staff members who helped prepare this book, including Nikki Dines, Editorial Manager and Maureen Mansell-Ward, Desk Editor, both of Ashgate Social Sciences. A sincere thank you to Patrick Cole for his meticulous and thorough job of proofreading our text. We would not have noticed many of the last minute errors without his expertise, and for that we are grateful.

We would also like to pay a special tribute to Mr Vinjay Rai, President of Rai Foundation, India for his thought-provoking foreword to this book. His wisdom has set a stage for its readership.

There are numerous others, friends and family members, that are not named here for the fear of omitting any name whose hands of input have helped in the successful output of this project, and to them we say thank you.

This we dedicate to our students at the University of Wisconsin–Stout, USA, University of Messina, Italy, ISM University of Management and Economics, Lithuania and all our other global students.

Introduction

This new volume aims to probe into the interconnected process of culture, globalization of business, trade, investment, and management. We endeavor to do so under a purely cultural perspective and to take into account the increasing production and consumption that have been shaping the past decades very strongly. This work has to be formulated in a historical framework in order to give a complete and meaningful description of this interesting phenomenon. This process is dynamic because it is changing over time, and it is enterprising as business managers carry out new techniques and maximize everyone's benefit through exploiting markets at the global level and reduce production costs.

To elaborate, recalling that the process of globalization of the world economy started more than 3,000 years ago is noteworthy. From another perspective, its roots go back to the emergence of state communities in Europe after the fourteenth century and it has been expanding rapidly since the seventeenth century. Between 1870 and the First World War, the free flow of labor was impressive and capital moved freely among major countries. The US magazine *Forbes* considered Richard Cobden as a father of globalization. In fact, the nineteenth-century British liberal Cobden dedicated his life to promoting the benefits of embracing free trade, as it serves for civilizations in all the nations of the world. When free trade ideals spread throughout the world, investment flows and labor movements followed. For instance, only in the second half of the nineteenth century did 15 million people cross the Atlantic to settle in North America.

Yet, the use of the term globalization is a more recent phenomenon. It is argued that academic circles did not recognize this until the 1980s, and unquestionably after Marshall McLuhan (1960) introduced the term "global village." McLuhan's book made the idea of a global village interconnected by an electronic nervous system part of our culture. Surely, we have different definitions of globalization. We can think about economic definition, political definition, and managerial definition. For example, and in keeping with some standard definitions, globalization would be an increasing internationalization of the production, distribution, and marketing of goods and services, which causes a functional integration of national economies within the circuits of industrial and financial capital. In addition, the political definitions are not less important here. In this book, we aim to substantiate that the process of globalization is intensifying the level of interactions and interdependence between states and cultures, in which national boundaries are less important sometimes. Under a managerial perspective, which fits this book also, this process of interaction and interdependence could mean a tendency toward regionalization of people's cultures. Overall, this book approaches this considerable topic taking into account several of these perspectives and interpreting them under a cultural perspective.

In this continuing process of globalization of economics and business, it is important to recall the notion of Fordism. This goes back to Henry Ford who significantly improved the method of mass production and developed the assembly line method of manufacturing early in the twentieth century in the United States. The new method consisted of domestic mass production coupled with mass consumption and higher social stability by paying higher wages and enabled workers/consumers to purchase a larger flow of created goods. From a technical perspective, the notion built on a cycle of mass production and mass consumption, and the production of standardized consumer goods that were sold in protected domestic markets. While the standard example was post-war America, but with different varieties of Fordism across Western economies, it is believed that Fordism broke down between the late 1960s and the mid-1970s. Western economies experienced slower economic growth, rising inflation, and growing unemployment. That period after Fordism has been termed post-Fordism and neo-Fordism, the former implying that global capitalism has made a clean break from the original notion of Fordism while the latter that elements of the Fordist regimes of capital accumulation still exist. The passage from Fordism to post-Fordism or neo-Fordism is partially explained by the fact that during Ford's time workers were relatively unskilled and they could form unions which became quite strong, especially in Western Europe. But trade union strength is believed to have declined over time, while production shifted from the rich West to less developed countries where production was cheaper, and local workers could not purchase the product they produced. Such post-Fordism arose partially due to interconnectedness of countries and regions in the world and the movement of capital that is increasingly more "barrierless", and partially by governments that have reduced their invasiveness in the economic sphere. In addition and in contrast to the Ford years, Western economies have experienced a shift from traditional manufacturing toward service and the knowledge economy.

Throughout this book we attempt to prove a message: despite claims that the world between 1820 and 1913 was more borderless than it is today, nevertheless, today's world differs significantly from that of a century ago. The world economy is broader as for the number of national markets engaged, and it is deeper as for the density and velocity of interaction and flows of trade and finance; the dominant mode of organization of the world economic transactions has changed significantly from the market (trade and portfolio investment) to internationalization of production through international corporations.

In addition, several forces are paving the way for a new global economic environment. One is a clear trend toward regionalization and demographic change (for example, NAFTA and the EU). Another is the fast growth in newly industrialized countries (NICs) because of a catch-up effect and resources being transferred to more productive sectors, and the shift of labor-intensive production to low-cost countries. No less important has been the abatement of ideological conflicts and the end of the Cold War, the implosion of the Soviet bloc and the new open doors policy in China since the late 1970s, and market reforms. Also market reforms in southern America (for example, Chile, Brazil), the rising influence of the non-governmental organizations (NGOs) in addressing and regulating a wide range of international issues, mobility of capital across the globe, the expanding role of international corporations in the global marketplace should all be considered as global economic forces. It should also be noted that most of them were US-based a few decades ago, while in recent years most are no longer US-based. Moreover, the second part of the 1990s and present days have witnessed an increase in mergers and acquisitions, and ease of flow of foreign direct investment (FDI) and of labor across the globe. Trade has been expanding faster than world output and the increase in FDI has exceeded the growth of world output and the growth of international trade. Finally, FDI may have become the actual engine of world growth, replacing the role of trade. As a matter-of-fact, the liberalization and restructuring of world economies have induced international corporations to pursue an ample range of investment activities; from the protectionism of the 1920s and 1930s and the time of the Great Depression, to GATT/WTO for free trade. Technology advances have been quite important after the Soviet Union launched the first satellite, Sputnik 1, in 1957, beating the US into space. In this light, the American military became highly alarmed, and in 1958, President Eisenhower created the Advanced Research Projects Agency to jump-start US technology and find safeguards against a space-based missile attack. The US military was particularly concerned about the effects of a nuclear attack on their communications infrastructure, because they could not respond if they could not talk or regroup, making the threat of a first strike by the Soviet Union more likely.

Therefore, globalization, stimuli of technological advance, and national saving rates in the US have been other important key aspects of analysis. The marked decline in US private savings due to low inflation reduced precautionary savings by businesses and households, and eased access to domestic and foreign sources of credit. Government budget surpluses might explain this effect (Loayza, Schmidt-Hebbel and Serven, 2000). Access to easy credit helped to buy from abroad, create current account deficits, invest in high technology equipment and increase the capital stock available, bringing about not only capital widening but, recently, capital deepening (capital stock growth rates above labor force growth) too, which in turn have productivity-enhancing effects on labor productivity (and to national accounts alike) that has been remarkably high in the US, in the recent past and is now proliferating all around the advanced economies. For example, the rising trends in IT expenditures can be detected when looking at nominal expenditures on computers. Peripheral equipments tripled during the 1990s in the US from slightly less than $50 billion in 1990 to $150 billion in 2000.

That being said, a stimulus of information technology has come through a profound change in the fields of microelectronics, new and improved hardware and software, telecommunications, and the like. For example, it is easier to memorize sizeable amounts of information and share information with the rest of the world inexpensively. Two "laws" about technological advances help us to understand the occurrence on the velocity with which this process has been changing over time. The speed-up of this process is so impressive that the specialized literature refers to these two laws. The Moore law (named after the founder of Intel) predicts that the contributing power available at a given price doubles every 18–24 months. The second law, the so-called Gilder law, states that the capacity of communication may double every six months. These laws of technology improvement give us the rationale for costs to fall. Technology and further developments in nanotechnology (a nanometer is a trillionth of a meter) will lead the progress in medicine, power production, and so forth.

In addition, US domestic policies have an impact on world trends. These processes are reinforcing the process of globalization in investment and trade. Regarding foreign direct investment (FDI), after declining over the past three years, FDI rose 2 per cent more in 2004 than in 2003, states the UNCTAD's 2005 report. World investment inflows totaled $648 billion in 2004, up from $208 billion in 1990. Developing countries received roughly 36 per cent of the world total, while developed countries lost some 14 per cent over 2003. Selected rich European economies lost investment inflows. For example, FDI in Germany shrank from $50 billion in 2002 down to less than $38 billion and in France from $49 billion to $24 billion in 2004. Additionally, the FDI to Luxembourg and the Netherlands decreased. Overall, the EU-15 (that is, the current EU minus the 10 new member states) fell back by 40 per cent with respect to investment inflow data in 2003. According to UNCTAD (2005), cross-border mergers and acquisitions have totaled US$117,889 million (1990–95 annual average), increasing to $593,960 million in 2001, then decreasing to $296,988 million in 2003, increasing again to $380,598 million in 2004.

In contrast to the figures prevailing in Western Europe, Asian economies largely benefited. In addition, Latin American countries and the Caribbean countries registered a 44 per cent increment compared with 2003, and they totaled $68 billion. Africa stood at roughly $18 billion in 2004. China and Hong Kong received $34 billion (this represents a 150 per cent increase on 2003), though also outflows from these two countries reached $60.6 billion.

Table I.1 Foreign Direct Investment (millions of US dollars)

	1985–95 (annual average)	2000	2005
Inflows	182,438	1,409,6	916,3
Outflows	203,256	1,244,5	778,7
Stock–inflows	530,244	5,802,991	10,129,739
Stock–outflows	570,125	6,471,435	10,671,889

Source: UNCTAD (2005 and 2006) and FDI/TNC database (www.unctad.org/fdistatistics)

Deepening cross-border linkages create another important issue in today's global discourse concerning a flexible exchange rate regime versus a fixed exchange rate regime. If countries with fixed exchange rate regimes are more vulnerable to currency and banking crises, flexible exchange rates tend to do better on effective management of macroeconomic policy and functioning institutions. According to Duttagupta, Fernandez and Karacadag (2005), four ingredients would be necessary for moving to a flexible exchange rate system: a deep and cleaning foreign exchange market, a coherent policy governing Forex central bank intervention, an appropriate alternative nominal anchor to replace the fixed exchange rate, and an effective system for reviewing and managing the exposure of both the public and the private sectors to exchange rate risk. If many countries have switched to exchange rate flexibility recently, for instance because of fiscal dominance in Russia (1993–95) and Venezuela (2002–03), fixed and exchange rate regimes have different advantages and disadvantages. Countries have to weigh the costs and benefits in light of domestic economic circumstances and institutional readiness before moving from a fixed exchange rate system to a flexible one (see Duttagupta, Fernandez and Karacadag, 2005). Notwithstanding, flexible exchange rates could offer a better "safety belt" considering the escalation of cross-border linkages, volatile capital, and the inspiration to conduct independent monetary policy domestically. These facts could push the trend toward more exchange rate flexibility in the future.

Globalization also affects unemployment. Global unemployment rose to record highs in 2005 in spite of continued strong economic growth, reports the International Labour Organization in its latest annual global employment trends surveys (ILO, 2006). Most notably affected are those between 15 and 24 years of age. This group makes up half of the world's unemployed, and their chance to remain unemployed is three times as high as that of adults. Rising unemployment is a result of rapid population growth in some parts of the world. Since the employment growth did not match the population growth, this explains the rise. ILO (2006) makes it clear that about half of the world's 2.85 billion workers are subsisting on less than the $2 a day poverty line—the same as a decade ago. In spite of the world economy growing by 4.3 per cent in 2005, the number of unemployed climbed to 191.8 million. This represented an increase of 2.2 million in 2004 and 34.4 million in 1995. As evidence of this, the global unemployment rate remained steady in 2005 at 6.3 per cent after two years of decreases. It was down from 6.6 per cent a decade ago—employment as a share of the working age population stayed virtually unchanged at 61.8 per cent in 2004. The rate in east-Central Europe rose to 9.7 per cent from 9.5 per cent in 2004, and Asia's overall unemployment rate remained steady. In East Asia, unemployment is 3.8 per cent, the lowest in the world. In contrast, the Middle East and North Africa show a 13.2 per cent unemployment rate, the highest in the world; in Latin America and the Caribbean, the unemployed rose by about 1.3 million to an unemployed rate of 7.7 per cent (ILO, 2006). Despite these unfortunate numbers, certain countries in Europe and Central Asia have succeeded in sustaining low levels of unemployment without an acceleration of inflation pressures or a worsening of income inequality. In addition, the failure of many economies to create new jobs out of GDP growth, combined with natural disasters and rising energy prices, especially affected the world's poorest. Of the 500 million poorest people, only 14.5 million managed to clamber above the $1 a day income level last year (ILO, 2006).

Global employment and economic output naturally interact with production, and determining where to settle productive factories, where to assemble the final product, and how to market output regionally or worldwide without breaching foreign production are becoming increasingly important. The Chinese market for automobiles has been growing extensively. For example, while the demand for cars was not intended for consumers until the year 2000, the private market started purchasing cars at that time which resulted in the growth of the number of cars sold from about 719,000 cars in 2000 to more than 3,139 million in 2005. The market for automobiles in China is so promising—especially in highly prosperous towns—that experts believe it will become the biggest market in the world, and that companies such as Volkswagen, Psa Peugeot-Citroen, Toyota, Honda, Hyundai, Nissan, and Fiat are searching for more market share, even if it involves producing them through joint ventures. Note also that all cars exported to China are taxed up to 25 per cent and a truly broadminded tolerance is not yet available. Moreover, under a different perspective, the recent Chinese Chery Automobile Company, a Chinese car manufacturer that produces the QQ, a small city car that sells for less than RMB 50,000 or $6,000, is noteworthy. Founded in 1997, Chery is China's eighth largest automaker and sold about 90,000 vehicles in China in 2004. The Chinese carmaker began making the QQ in 2002, a car that the well-known US General Motors (GM) believe the Chinese are producing as a carbon copy of the GM Daewoo Matiz, a mini car developed by its South Korean affiliate Daewoo. As a result, GM filed a lawsuit against the small Chinese firm asking for a $10 million penalty, alleging that it "shared remarkably identical body structure, exterior design, interior design and key components." While the Chinese carmaker is primarily selling its cars in China—a small amount sold in Iran, Egypt, Syria, Indonesia, Russia, and Malaysia—the fact that the US could begin importing this car could represent another perspective of becoming aware of international business practices and competition.

Besides the issues that we will analyze in the text, perhaps these trends might affect inequalities, income distributions within and among countries, and future balanced economic growth alike. Not least, the global economy is a reality for companies and workers all around the world, and its impact on firm performance of developed and emerging countries is no doubt occurring. All these themes ought to be of concern to all students and the public; we hope that this book will serve mainly as a broad purpose to introduce them to think globally yet not to lose how national perspectives interact internationally and the fundamental importance of consumers and their tastes.

Chapter 1

International Management and Cross-cultural Perspectives

Introduction

International management has never been as significant as it is today. Many of the world's largest firms are truly global, and even their smaller counterparts increasingly participate in cross-border activities by subcontracting—having customers and joint venture partners collaborate with them around the globe. The arena of international management has never offered so many opportunities and challenges to individual managers, businesses, governments, and the academic community alike. The expansion of the global market has created a need for managers who are familiar with the problems of international trade and finance such as culture, political structure, foreign exchange, geographical terrain, time, food, and technology. For instance, let us recall that it has been estimated that the Asia-Pacific region could produce over half of the world's GDP by the next decade; new economic powers are an actual reality; technical countries spread production across countries; and the average GDP per capita is on the increase. In this changing scenario, which inspired Streeten (2001) to state that the world economy was more integrated at the end of the nineteenth century than it is today, there is the growing risk of amplifying misunderstanding of what is occurring worldwide, especially if one is not able to advance a proper analysis concerning the nature of economic relationships. We would need to approach this theme carefully; slogans seem to triumph over reasonable assessments (Sergi, 2005a).

There is no country in the world today, including the United States, which is economically self-sufficient without some sort of interdependence with other countries. The trend toward a single global economy is expanding markets and providing unlimited opportunities for international managers. To remain parallel and compatible to other technologies, for example, countries need to work together as more of a global economy. In addition, in order to have the greatest amount of technological expertise they need to combine their shared knowledge, which could augment this reciprocal relationship. The managerial talents within a nation are key ingredients in the economic welfare of such a nation. Being able to organize production is critically important to developing and maintaining high standards of living in any country. One can state that wise organization and governance are equal in importance to a country's natural resources and its population.

Globalization

The process of internationalization has been a gradual evolution over time. A trend toward global interplay is not the outcome of modern times. Let us think about ancient trade routes, the Amber Road or the Silk Road, which were linking various regions of the world spreading from the Baltic Sea to the Mediterranean, Central Asia, and China. Trade routes were implying international trade and also culture and civilization linkages. Global trends have always existed, and what is occurring today is nothing different from what took place during ancient times. Over the last centuries, trade, finance, and technology flew from one side of the globe to the other. Obviously, high technology did not exist, consumers' wealth is much higher today than it was even decades ago, consumers number more than six billion and they are increasingly demanding in terms of quality, supply availability, and so forth. Nevertheless, the market sells and purchases what is available at a given point in time; globalization is quite different in qualitative and quantitative terms today, but microeconomic principles did not fade away (Sergi, 2005a). Hence, merchants who traded internationally in the early nineteenth century saw themselves as agents of the progressive revolution. Ultimately, survival was difficult for these merchants because of the introduction of technological change, which was the latest novelty internationally. One significant reason a company decides to develop internationally is that they are unable to maximize their goals and objectives while operating in a closed economy context. More recently, domestic market saturation has also been making it difficult for companies to have profitable growth, and customers are simply demanding a broader base of products from which to choose. Globalization is the comprehensive solution that many companies are now exploring.

Nevertheless, as comprehensive as globalization is to companies, we would be remiss if we did not expound on globalization at the social level. Globalization has recently become a key concept in the social sciences, in particular its effect on the reduction of poverty. There is the claim that in recent years there has been a reduction in poverty in the global order, and that this development is a product of "globalization friendly" policies (DFID, 2000; World Bank, 2002a, 2002b). The World Bank (WB) (2002a) has argued that poverty and income inequality have fallen in the last 20 years. In 1980, there were 1.4 billion people living in absolute poverty, and by 1998, this had fallen to 1.2 billion. The WB has also argued that while the number of people living in absolute poverty remained constant from 1987 to 1998, taking into account population increases, this amounts to a fall from 28 per cent to 24 per cent of the world's population (World Bank, 2000).

One of the main sociological advocates of the "globalization theory," Anthony Giddens, explicitly reiterates the erroneous beliefs concerning growth and poverty reduction. In his book, *Runaway World* (1999), Giddens defines his view of global change in contrast to two commonly held views. The first view is believed by skeptics, who doubt the globalization process, and who argue that the global economy is nothing new, or that today trade remains regional rather than truly worldwide. The second view is that of the radicals, per se, who argue "that not only is globalization very real, but that its consequences can be felt everywhere," and that "The global marketplace is much more developed than even in the 1960s and 1970s and is indifferent to national borders" (1999). Giddens offers the different view that "Globalization is political, technological and cultural, as well as economic. It has been influenced, above all, by developments in systems of communication, dating back only to the late 1960s" (1999). In addition, he argues that it is equally wrong to treat globalization simply as an "out there" phenomenon, as one concerning "big systems" (such as the world financial order) which are far removed from the individual. Rather, globalization is to be understood also as an "in here" phenomenon which influences the most intimate and personal aspects of our lives (1999).

Extreme poverty is measured by counting people living on an income of $1 a day. Ray Kiely, in his article "Globalization and Poverty, and the Poverty of Globalization Theory," has concerns as to what the value of the US dollar is actually based on. Kiely states that the US dollar is actually based on purchasing power parity (PPP) exchange rates, which are adjusted to take account of the fact that the cost of living tends to be lower in poorer countries than richer ones. However, he states that claims for poverty reduction are based on two different comparative indices; the Penn World Tables, in 1985, quantified international price comparisons, in order to make its calculations, and in 1993, a new International Comparisons Project was made. Thus, because of two different measurements, there may be an unambiguously clear decline for people living in extreme poverty (Deaton, 2001; Wade, 2002)

Kiely goes on to state that he is concerned that this distortion, among others (for example, the baskets of goods and purchasing power must be comparable measures between countries to provide accurate comparisons) is likely to get worse with each successive PPP exercise, which leads to the World Bank making unjustified assertions about long-term trends in the poverty count.

Globalization does, in fact, increase trade openness, leading to economic growth; however, there are questions that examine the relationship between trade, growth and the reduction of poverty. In fact, in 1997, the trade GDP ratio for 39 of the poorest, least developed countries averaged 43 per cent, and for 22 of these 39 countries, it was approximately the same as the world average (UNCTAD, 2002a). In the period from 1980 to 1999, the share of these Less Developed Countries (LDCs) in world exports declined by 47 per cent, to a total of only 0.42 per cent of world exports in the latter year (UNCTAD, 2002).

In addition, concerning political choices, were progress on trade liberalization achieved for those countries that face rich country's protectionism in the agriculture sector, flows of final aid would have been better allocated, meaningful national policies would have started, and current Sub-Saharan Africa countries and others that are experiencing low per capita income would have grown at higher rates. Market reforms, democracy, less corruption, and the ability to attain the opportunities of the global economy are the way forward without losing sight of the fact that no issues individually are a panacea. For example, holding partially responsible regulatory institutions amid poor economic outcomes is certainly valid, yet one cannot neglect the most basic and positive forms of causality and direction of actual events since we live in a multifaceted world system (Adekola and Sergi, 2007).

The relationship between global integration and poverty reduction is not straightforward and it would be wrong to conclude in this text without further research studies mentioned and empirical data studied. Globalization and economic growth alone do not necessarily provide income to the poor, and the last 30 years have seen a general increase in inequality within countries. The most effective strategy remains the promotion of economic growth in conjunction with attainable proposals for reducing inequality. Hanmer et al. (2000; see also UNDP, 2002) argue that in order to meet the 2015 millennium targets for reducing poverty, countries with high inequality will need growth rates twice as high as those with low inequality. This argument is based on a survey of comparative economic growth from 1985 to 1990, where countries with 10 per cent economic growth and low inequality saw a fall in poverty of 9 per cent, while those with high inequality and similar growth rates saw a fall of only 3 per cent.

Nevertheless, the overall impact from globalization can be a positive sum game for all, in spite of a negative impact which may show up for some participants in the short term, and there are long-term, positive effects for all. There is no question that globalization is the direction the world is going, and that this issue will see many dynamics in the years to come.

International Management

International management requires the understanding of crossing cultures, multinational corporations' interactions, global perspectives, and corporate issues. Understanding individual values of a high ethical standard would be another asset we want to emphasize throughout this book. Not only does international management rely on core business competencies, but also it requires the knowledge and skills necessary to operate and succeed in an international business arena.

Noting that managers are multicultural is necessary not only when they work with people from other countries but also with people from the same country, who speak the same language, have the same national heritage and yet, have different ways of looking at the world. An economy per se is multicultural nowadays. In fact, international management involves planning, organizing, leading, and controlling of employees and other resources to achieve organizational goals across unique multicultural and multinational boundaries. An international manager is someone who must handle things, ideas, and people belonging to different cultural environments while ensuring that allocating and directing of human resources achieves the goals of the organization, while respecting the beliefs, traditions, and values of the native or host country (Pierre, 1980). This is a non-current definition but it still gives a revealing discernment of this complex subject.

Because the process of globalization is becoming highly competitive and deepens interactions worldwide, the international environment has created enormous challenges for managers. These challenges include analyzing the new environment, anticipating its effect on the home company, planning and managing to adapt to situational factors, while attempting to maintain an ethical climate. What is more important, international management demands a contingency approach to the ever-changing environment. This means the choice of management system and style depends on the nature of the country, and the people involved.

International Manager

When a company faces the decision of whether to become an international enterprise, they will be encountering many issues they have never before dealt with. This can be a confusing and difficult process for everyone involved especially the managers. Some companies hire consulting firms to deal with the issues involved. However, for those companies that want to do it themselves, they first need to gather some information. Companies encounter several major issues while going through the process of becoming international. The first major issue they have to deal with is exactly who is going to run this new operation and what qualification(s) this individual must possess. After they have determined the manager, the companies need to examine the roles of this manager and how these roles may differ from the local manager, the location of the new operational facility, and the relationships they need to have, to name only a few. Therefore, starting with finding the manager is only logical.

There are many aspects of international management including the need for flexible strategies and matching global scenarios with strategic options. International managers are responsible for developing strategies, deploying resources, and guiding their organization to compete in this global environment. To understand the notion of international management better, it is logically necessary to first define management and international independently. There are many viewpoints as to the definition of management and for this book we will define management as the collective functions of planning, organizing, leading, and controlling the resources of an organization within its national borders to efficiently achieve its objectives. We refer to an individual who is responsible for the realization of these objectives as a manager and his or her actions are termed managing. International, on the other hand, is synonymous with multi-domestic firms, international firms, global firms, and transnational firms, but for the purpose of this book, the word international will be used. It is any activity of an organization conducted beyond its national boundaries to exploit a potential expansion of emerging economies, earn greater return from their special competences, and realize location economies and greater experience curve economies. International management on the other hand is the collective functions of planning, organizing, leading, and controlling organizational resources across its national borders. The managerial approach that works in one country does not necessarily work in the same fashion or not at all in another one, this being explained by environmental differences (that is, cultural, political, legal, economic, and climatic) across countries. Because of these differences, a manager will need skills beyond those required to manage in his or her home country, and to be able to coordinate this type of manager at a level that goes beyond national boundaries is termed an international manager.

An international manager is "someone who has to handle things, ideas, and people belonging to different cultural environments." He or she can work either in a multinational corporation, an international organization, an institution located in a foreign country or even in a local, regional, or national organization in which people do not share the same patterns of thinking, feeling, and behaving. In referring to this broad definition of an international manager, all managers within all organizations are actually multicultural. Some managers may be more involved with intercultural issues than others, but they all have to plan, organize, direct, and lead people with different cultural backgrounds characterized by various values, beliefs, and assumptions.

Without realizing it, most international managers have been multicultural in their jobs. So far, there was not a pressing need for them to be aware of the fact that they learn many of their management decisions by utilizing their staff/personnel as resources. Many managers now have to face the fact that a lone educational background will not be enough for them to be effective and efficient managers. They must also gain a deeper understanding of intercultural relations and various cultural practices and beliefs. This goes for local, regional, national, and, of course, international managers. This means that the old style of viewing management must adjust to meet the needs of the international managerial functions. Management activities related to planning, organizing, leading, and controlling must be approached from a cross-cultural perspective if public and private organizations want to keep up their productivity both inside and outside the countries and cultures to which they belong. Today, one has placed so much emphasis on what is logical and rational, that one has become preoccupied with figuring out the right answers mentally, rather than seeing, hearing and feeling what is really going on inside and around us, and responding to it according to its demands and according to what we have to do to meet our needs. With that in mind, let us now examine what it takes to be an international manager. A successful international manager should have the following skills or qualifications:

- The ability to communicate and cooperate across cultures, including being able to develop an understanding, trust, and teamwork with people of various cultural backgrounds.
- The ability to understand and appreciate numerous different cultures.
- The ability to use more than one language to communicate effectively. This may be important when traveling to different locations or simply dealing with someone who understands better in his or her native tongue.
- The ability to build and maintain relationships at work and in the family, by supporting, growing, and learning. However, to do this, one must first understand oneself, which includes being aware of one's own assumptions and preferences.
- The ability to learn and grow from the new information just discovered by carrying out the new ideas into one's behavior, and simultaneously, the ability to maintain the health of the organization and oneself.
- The ability to coach, guide, and educate others in the organization to develop cross-cultural skills both at work and to incorporate them into their families as well.
- The ability to observe all cultures and accomplish management changes that will be most effective for the cultural mix present.

The Roles of an International Manager

International managers face a tremendously complex environment. What worked in the role of a domestic manager does not always prove effective in the international market. Like the domestic managers, international managers must also stick to the four major roles of planning, organizing, directing, and controlling.

Planning for an international firm assures that the business organization has some idea of its purpose, where it is heading and how it will achieve its objectives. International objectives may require plans that assign to each division goals that differ from what might seem appropriate from a domestic viewpoint. In preparing short- or long-range plans to achieve those goals, international managers must take into consideration not only local conditions but also overall international operations. These considerations should focus on nearby markets, servicing of regional sales divisions, transportation costs, value-added taxes, raw materials, and the purchases of the inputs from other producing divisions (Miller, 1987). However, plans must be considered and should link operations in ways that achieve global rather than local goals. Therefore, international managers need to be aware of the extent to which local customers, employees, government officials, and suppliers are likely to accept or resist changes. These changes will affect an international manager's responsibility.

The aspect of control in the responsibilities of an international manager includes ensuring that what is happening is what was intended to happen. Control applies to all levels of the organization. The organization uses control in different ways depending on the level and scope of its application. For an international manager, "control should provide managers with the information necessary to monitor the operations of the firm to help achieve its global strategy" (Miller, 1987).

International direction and leadership style is "the way in which a manager chooses to fulfill leadership, delegation, communication, and supervision responsibilities. These choices reflect both personal and cultural differences" (Miller, 1987). In some cultures, employees tend to need explicit directions and supervision from their superior rather than from someone who is considered an equal. In other cultures, the employee's leadership needs to come from relationships and communication built between co-workers. In addition, a leader should demonstrate a mix of competence in technical, interpersonal, and conceptual skills. A leader understands that people do the work and must interact effectively if they are to work well.

Secondly, Hal Mason states (1987), "a leader gets organizational work done by motivating people, getting commitment, by energizing behavior, and by creating personal interests and excitement in the organization's goals. A leader is keenly aware of what decisions and events mean to the others of the organization." Mason (1987) continues to say that an effective leader is able to direct others without dominating all decisions and can achieve goals by overcoming all obstacles while utilizing resources efficiently. A leader develops subordinates by sharing the power and responsibility with them. By delegating the power, the leader is creating opportunities to challenge people to go beyond the limits they have set for themselves and give them a chance to be creative. A leader also represents the values, goals, and visions of the organization. However, in order to do this correctly, the leader must be active as opposed to reactive, by taking educated risks and seeing opportunities. Lastly, a leader sets the standards, not only for performance but also for the basics such as conduct. An effective leader must be able to recognize good performance and reward it accordingly, yet they can act on poor performance.

International managers' roles can be very effective when a manager can learn and develop leadership functions such as completing organizational work through employee motivation, getting commitment, energizing employees' behavior, and by creating personal interests and excitement in the organization's goals. However, not all these leadership roles will work in every aspect of a different cultural environment, because it ultimately depends on the employees or workers in that country.

Characteristics of Effective and Efficient International Managers

As one could observe in the above information, effective and efficient international managers possess all of the characteristics that effective and efficient domestic managers possess. International managers, however, have to be willing to adapt to a new culture and the new ideas that come with it. An international manager must be willing to research the new lifestyles and cultural norms before entering the new operational facility.

For example, an international manager should discover how to motivate his or her new employees. Just as often happens domestically, not the same things have motivated everyone. For instance, in Western culture, "choice" is highly motivating. There are many utilized theories that demonstrate that choice enhances employee job satisfaction, motivation, and how an employee performs. We know that the United States often encourages and promotes employee autonomy. The option of having work-related choices is a driver for employee satisfaction and his or her efficiency and output. Having the freedom to choose their hours worked, to participate in decisions made, and to contribute to their future career planning, enhances employee satisfaction and performance of both American and Hispanic employees. By contrast, Asians enjoy how much responsibility they have.

This predicts their job satisfaction and performance. For example, while Americans perform better at and are more satisfied with work activities that they choose to do, some Eastern countries and employees perform better at tasks that trusted others have chosen for them; for instance, their manager. On the other hand, Asians are motivated by the tasks collectively decided upon by their entire group of colleagues—unlike the independent and autonomous Americans. Job satisfaction, success, new challenges, and self-respect motivate United Kingdom employees. Indian employees are motivated by their individual contributions and movement "up the ladder," recognition, job security, and the image of the company for which they work. No two cultures are alike. Each has its own beliefs and value systems. As a result, different things motivate different people. Not only this, but different things motivate different people at different points of time. It is just another challenge that the international manager must be prepared to handle. Giving adequate thought and being able to delegate effectively are other key characteristics that effective and efficient international managers must have. However, international managers need to understand when and where to use this as well. For example, Mexicans do not like it when an authority figure gives up his or her power. Yet in other cultures such as in the United States, employees do not like to be highly supervised and they prefer not to be given explicit directions for every task. They rather enjoy the freedom to tackle a task the way they see fit.

Conclusion

International business includes a variety of perspectives. Culture, economics, finance, technology, marketing, ethical decision-making, politics, strategic planning, and human resource development are equally important and mutually reinforcing in this global environment. Managers attempting to manage this process must learn the fundamentals and significance of international trade theories and systems, understand the various issues, opportunities, and related problems in order to conduct business in today's dynamic global economy, examine how governments and legal systems affect international business, and investigate the social and ethical roles of business in today's global society.

Today's international managers face the challenge of creating work environments that address the needs of a culturally diverse workforce. For that to happen, international managers need to be involved and move beyond their own cultural frame of reference to a multicultural one. The international manager needs to know that to be successful in the global business world, he or she must know their particular field of functional expertise and act on that. Knowing the culture they are working with proves more important. Since every culture has its own perceptions about the proper roles of the manager and the employee, there is nothing instinctively natural about the way the two groups interact. Individual culture shapes the ideas and norms for both parties and it is critical that the international manager be aware of this. Characteristics of an effective, efficient international manager are hard to define. The key to being a good international manager is first learning about the new culture and then adapting one's "old" ways to fit in with the new culture and employees.

Case Study

A Low-Budget Cola Shakes Up Markets South of the Border

Summary Kola Real (pronounced RAY-AL) is giving Pepsi and Coca-Cola some heated competition in their critical Latin American markets. Kola Real entered the Mexican market adopting aggressive pricing and marketing tactics. Kola Real is a significant threat to Pepsi and Coca-Cola because Mexico represents an important source of revenues. Kola Real was a product created by entrepreneurs whose farm was razed by the Shining Path guerrillas in Peru. The family realized the guerrillas were hijacking Coca-Cola trucks and disrupting supply to Ayacucho. The Ananos family decided to develop and market their own cola brand.

After success in Peru, the family decided to sell their product in other countries including Ecuador and Venezuela. A major decision involved moving into Mexico to compete with Coca-Cola and Pepsi. Kola Real is produced inexpensively compared to the Pepsi and Coca-Cola brands. The upstart company does not advertise extensively or provide incentives like life insurance, business classes, or cooking oil to those who sell it in their stores. What Kola Real does have is a very low price as compared to Pepsi and Coca-Cola. This forces Coke and Pepsi to lower prices to remain competitive.

Mexico City The Ananos family was in a tough spot. Shining Path guerrillas had just razed their family farm in southern Peru and were slowly strangling the nearby city of Ayacucho, where the family had retreated to its second home. However, while the rest of Peru despaired at the Shining Path's campaign of terror in the late 1980s, Eduardo and Mirtha Ananos spotted an opportunity. Rebels routinely hijacked trucks bringing Coca-Cola to the city, so the couple decided to start making cola in their backyard and sell it to locals. Together with their five sons, they took out a mortgage on their home and started the business with $30,000.

Today, Kola Real is emerging as an unlikely threat to both Coca-Cola Co. and PepsiCo Inc. in a region where the two soft-drink giants enjoy some of their fattest global profit margins. By cutting out frills and skimping in areas such as advertising, Kola Real, officially called Industrias Ananos, offers ultra-low prices that appeal to the region's poor majority. As a result, the company has captured almost one-fifth of the Peruvian market and has made inroads into Ecuador and Venezuela.

Now Kola Real is shaking things up in Mexico. Mexico is a crown jewel in Coke's international operations and the world's second-biggest soft-drink market after the US, with annual sales of roughly $15 billion. In less than two years, the Mexican version of Kola Real, called "Big Cola," has captured roughly 4 per cent of the market. Coke and Pepsi have cut prices in response, denting their profits. At the Sam's Club warehouse store in Mexico City's upscale Polanco neighborhood, Big Cola is the fifth-best-selling product, narrowly trailing Coke.

Kola Real has put a new twist on globalization. As trade barriers have dropped in much of the developing world, foreign-owned behemoths such as Wal-Mart Stores Inc. have squeezed local incumbents unaccustomed to competition and raised local people's price sensitivity. The Ananos family has turned the tables on two US giants by undercutting their prices and adapting their aggressive marketing tactics to local conditions. "Not bad for having started out in the backyard, don't you agree?" says Carlos Ananos, 37 years old, one of the family's two sons who moved to Mexico last year to direct the upstart's expansion. The family-owned company does not release sales or profit figures. Analysts estimate the company's revenue is more than $300 million a year and growing fast. Kola Real's success also illustrates how the cola wars are changing in many markets around the globe.

Coke and Pepsi once vied primarily with each other. Today both are fending off down-market alternatives—either so-called B-brands such as Kola Real or private-label drinks sold by Wal-Mart and other big retail chains. These cheaper rivals can cut into Coke and Pepsi's profits and make it harder for them to raise prices to offset slowing sales. The trend goes beyond Latin America. Big retailers in Germany, Great Britain, and other European markets are selling more private-label cola, and B-brands are aggressive in Poland and Hungary. One big reason this is happening: the switch to plastic. In the 1990s, plastic bottles largely replaced glass, offering a cheaper alternative that lowered newcomers' cost of entry into the soft-drink industry.

Plastic also allowed larger bottles that could be sold cheaply in supermarkets. Supermarkets provide an important outlet for new competitors since Coke and Pepsi often dominate smaller stores.

Big Sizes, Low Prices Kola Real's strategy is simple: offer big sizes at low prices. In a Carrefour supermarket in Mexico City, a large display of Big Cola beckons shoppers with a price of about 75 cents for a 2.6-liter bottle. Nearby, bottles of Coke go for about $1.30 for a slightly smaller 2.5-liter bottle. On a recent day, housewife Lourdes Avila put four of the Big Cola bottles in her cart and said, "For that price, I'll try it." To keep prices low, the Ananos family runs a lean operation. While Coke and Pepsi bottlers spend nearly 20 per cent of their revenue on beverage concentrate from Atlanta-based Coke and Pepsi, Purchase, N.Y., the Ananoses make their own. Instead of maintaining a fleet of trucks as most Coke and Pepsi bottlers do, Kola Real hires third parties for deliveries—even individuals with dented pick-up trucks. The company also does little advertising beyond an occasional radio spot, relying on word of mouth from penny-pinching housewives.

So far, Kola Real has hurt Pepsi more than Coke, in part because the upstart competes more directly with Pepsi as a lower-cost alternative. Coke has more than 70 per cent of the Mexican market, based on volume; Pepsi has about 21 per cent, Kola Real, 4 per cent. Pepsi's biggest bottler, Pepsi Bottling Group Inc, Somers, N.Y., said its Mexico volume fell 5 per cent in the third quarter and it warned that full-year profits from Mexico would be more than 40 per cent lower than expected due to the escalating price war and a weak economy. That is a disappointing result after Pepsi Bottling spent more than $1 billion last year to buy Mexico's biggest Pepsi bottler, Grupo Gemex S.A.

However, Coke has much more at stake in Mexico than Pepsi. Ever since Coke arrived south of the border in 1926, Mexico has been Coke country. Mexicans drink more Coke per capita than anyone on earth, and countless small restaurants and mom and pop shops are awash in the company's red and white colors. Mexico's current president, Vicente Fox, is a former head of Coke's Mexican operations.

Coke gets about 11 per cent of both its global profits and sales volume in Mexico. Fomento Economico Mexicano S.A., or Femsa, the biggest bottler in Mexico and the number two Coke bottler in the world, has recorded an average annual return on invested capital—a broad measure of profitability—of about 20 per cent during the past decade, two to three times what Coke's other big bottlers earn.

Earlier this year, Femsa, one of Coke's most assertive and best-run bottlers, bought Miami-based Panamerican Beverages Inc. for $2.7 billion, the biggest purchase of a foreign entity by a Mexican company. The purchase put Coke's two biggest Latin American bottlers under the same management team. Still, the increased competition in Mexico could threaten Coke's high returns there. Last week, Femsa said its cola sales in Mexico were flat for the first nine months of the year.

"Coke cannot afford to see the Mexico system unravel," says Carlos Laboy, a Bear Stearns beverage industry analyst. Kola Real's foray into Mexico has put the two beverage giants on the defensive. Jose Bustamante, owner of the small Santa

Cecilia store in Mexico City's middle-class Roma neighborhood, says his local Coca-Cola salesman recently threatened to stop delivering Coke unless Mr Bustamante removed Big Cola from his shelves. Mr Bustamante says the salesman also offered two free cases of Coke a month. "I agreed," Mr Bustamante says. "I can't afford to stop selling Coke."

Earlier this year, two Mexico City stores lodged a complaint with Mexico's antitrust commission, alleging similar tactics by Coke. Authorities are investigating the allegations. Last year, the antitrust commission ruled Coke was abusing its dominance of Mexican retailers and ordered it to stop certain sales practices designed to keep out competitors, such as exclusive contracts. Several Coke bottlers in Mexico have challenged the government decision in court.

Jose Octavio Reyes, president of Coke's Latin American division, says accusations of bullying are "urban legends" and "simply not something that we would do." He said Coke abides by Mexico's rules and welcomes competition. Coke officials concede the price gap with Big Cola has grown too wide at times. Nevertheless, they plan to compete with smaller, inexpensive bottles and do not intend to match Pepsi's recent price reductions, says Xavier Tercero Quintanilla, a sales executive at Coke bottler Femsa.

Pepsi Bottling this month instituted its second price cut of the year. Others have joined Kola Real's march into Mexico. This year, an Ecuadorian company, Fiemex SA, launched a cut-price cola called El Gallito, or Little Rooster. Mexico's popular Guadalajara soccer club has its own Chiva Cola. Toronto-based Cott Corp., which supplies the private-label drinks for Wal-Mart in North America, expanded to Mexico last year.

One risk for Coke and Pepsi is that Mexico will go the way of Brazil, the world's third-largest soft-drink market. There, B-brands went from 3 per cent of the market in the early 1990s to about 30 per cent of soft-drink sales. Soft-drink sales in Brazil are also less profitable than in Mexico, because more than half goes through supermarkets. Supermarket chains use their buying influence to squeeze suppliers.

In Mexico, supermarkets account for less than 5 per cent of soft-drink sales, but they are the fastest-growing sales channel in Mexico. As Kola Real got its start in 1988, Jorge, the eldest son, used his agricultural engineering degree to develop the drink's formula. The family kept distribution costs low by using old beer bottles and pasting labels on by hand. The operation grew slowly, with the family reinvesting profits and looking for cost-saving ways to grow, such as buying plants abandoned by other bottlers. The company expanded to the Peruvian capital, Lima, in 1997. When Peru's economy stalled in 1998, Kola Real's low price appealed to cash-strapped consumers. By year's end, Kola Real and other B-brands more than doubled their market share to 21 per cent.

The Ananos family next targeted Coke and Pepsi bottlers in Ecuador and then Venezuela. Within a year after entering Venezuela, Kola Real had nearly 10 per cent of the market. Coke's biggest bottler there at the time, Panamerican Beverages, was forced to cut prices. The Ananos sons, who now largely run the business, saw the promise of Mexico. Last year both Carlos and Arturo moved to Mexico to oversee the company's $7 million investment—its biggest yet—in a state-of-the-art plant near the central city of Puebla. Previous B-brands in Mexico tried to compete against

Coke solely in the supermarkets. Coke's stronghold in Mexico has been the nearly one million mom and pop stores and family-run eateries that account for more than 75 per cent of the country's soft-drink sales. Kola Real's 800 salesmen have attacked that market and gotten their drinks in more than a quarter of those outlets in Mexico City, Guadalajara and other big cities. Kola Real has also attacked Coke and Pepsi on price, something other independent brands failed to do.

Taking on Coke's well-oiled distribution machine has been tough for the Peruvian firm. Coke woos shop owners by buying them life insurance policies or cooking oil and offering free classes on how to run a business. Fernando Garcia Tapia, who runs the Abarrotes Casa Conchita bodega in Mexico City, says he twice rejected a sales pitch from Big Cola for fear of losing the valuable perks he receives from Coke.

Mr Garcia says Coke gives him 100 free cases three times a year and he personally has received a free refrigerator, 29-inch television and compact disc player from Coke because his sales earned enough points in a rewards program. "The free cases are like oxygen for me," he says. Mr Garcia does not carry Big Cola.

Coke for Breakfast In his cramped store, packed with snacks and daily staples, Coke and Pepsi coolers are squeezed in the back. His low-income clientele of construction workers, maids, and waiters clearly prefer Coke. "I even have Coke for breakfast," says construction worker Raymundo Perez. Coke is Mexico's only soft-drink maker offering returnable plastic bottles, a competitive advantage over all rivals because they cost consumers about 20 per cent less than disposable bottles.

Coke says it does not sign deals forcing the shops to carry only Coke, a practice forbidden by last year's antitrust decision. But, most Coke salesmen forbid shop owners from putting rival products in Coke's 850,000 coolers across the country. The ruling against Coke made some of the mom and pops more aware they have a choice, helping Big Cola get a foot in the door. While Coke can still prohibit stores from selling rival drinks in its refrigerators, Big Cola salesmen, such as Fernando Mejia, point out that they can chill Big Colas in the refrigerator where shops usually keep meats and cheeses.

Only about 10 per cent of Mexican mom and pop stores do not have a Coke cooler. La Roca de Oro in Mexico City is one. Pamela Medina, the owner, uses her own cooler to stock a variety of drinks, including Big Cola. "Customers ask for it," she says. Still, it can be hard to match the manpower of Coke and Pepsi. Juan Chavez, manager of a giant Comercial Mexicana grocery store in a Mexico City suburb, recently berated visiting Big Cola officials about their sloppy service. He said Coke and Pepsi employees constantly tend to their products in the store, keeping them stacked and clean. The Big Cola display, Mr Chavez said, was a mess.

"We can't afford to pay a guy to sit and tend to our display all day long," says Roy Morris, marketing director for Big Cola in Mexico and a former executive at Ambev, Brazil's biggest Pepsi bottler. Kola Real is now trying to keep pace by rolling out more sizes and flavors. This summer, the company introduced a new grapefruit-flavored soda and its first individual serving-size bottle.

It is all a long way from the jungles of southern Peru. Carlos Ananos recently showed a visitor an old family photo taken a few years before the Shining Path destroyed their farm. "Life is odd," said Mr Ananos. "If it weren't for the Shining Path, we would have never lived our dream."

Reprinted with permission: D. Luhnow and C. Terhune (2003), "A Low-Budget Cola Shakes Up Markets South of the Border," *The Wall Street Journal*, October 27, A1.

Case Questions

1. How did the Ananos family decide to make and market Kola Real? What business strategy did the start-up company adopt? Was it successful? Explain.
2. What motivated Kola Real to expand into Mexico? Who are its major competitors? How have those competitors been affected by Kola Real? Why could competition hurt the profitability of Pepsi and Coca-Cola even if the two companies were able to maintain their market share?
3. Compare and contrast Kola Real's distribution strategy, advertising, and its relationship with retailers as compared to Pepsi and Coca-Cola. How is Kola Real's brand image perceived in comparison with Pepsi and Coke?
4. Sometimes companies face barriers to entry in marketing and manufacturing a product. Why was the use of glass bottles a significant barrier to entry? How can exclusive contracts with distributors act as a barrier to entry? Are there any other barriers to entry illustrated in the article? How did Kola Real benefit when some of the barriers to entry were removed?
5. Despite its lean operation, what challenges does Kola Real face as it tries to compete with Pepsi and Coca-Cola? Do you think the major companies should be worried? Explain.

Chapter Review

Because globalization is becoming highly competitive, the international environment has created enormous challenges for managers. International managers must apply theories, tools, and insights in their new positions. Not only must they understand the similarities and differences among the people of our world, and how these cultures and people affect business management, but they must also handle issues related to management such as finances, leadership, strategic management, and motivational techniques that arise in an international context. International managers must understand the effects of world events as they unfold, and they must know how to handle the various areas such as culture, economics, and politics that can affect business behaviors and attitudes.

International managers face a tremendously complex environment. What worked in the role of a domestic manager does not always prove effective in the international market. Like the domestic managers, international managers must also adhere to the four major roles of planning, organizing, directing, and controlling. In preparing short- or long-range plans to achieve those goals, international managers must consider not only local conditions but also overall international operations. Effective and efficient international managers possess all of the characteristics that effective and efficient domestic managers possess, and in addition, today's international managers face the challenge of creating work environments that address the needs of a culturally diverse workforce.

One of the most beneficial things an international manager can bring to a global organization is the transfer of knowledge he or she will impart on the other country. Most often, there are technical or operational situations that are in dire need of an experienced and skilled global manager. An international manager will provide the human components necessary in the operation that the industrial and business aspects cannot provide.

Chapter Questions

1. Why are there different definitions of globalization?
2. Discuss the roles and characteristics of an international manager. How do these roles differ from those a manager would possess while based in the US?
3. How can a company develop managers to acquire international skills and perspectives?
4. What are the unique issues and concerns an international manager will face globally? Economically? Politically? Legally?
5. As a US manager based in Taiwan or in Hong Kong, explain the specifics you would need to be aware of to be successful.

Chapter 2

Changes and Growth in the International Marketplace

The Global Market

The global market is a number of profit-related business activities conducted across international boundaries. The makeup of many products sold throughout the world today reflects the international character of business. It is extremely difficult in today's business environment to identify where specific products are manufactured. Frequently products are becoming hybrid; they contain parts from many different countries. For example, slogans such as "Made in the USA" or "Made in Germany" might have a much less precise meaning today than it would have in the past. The increasing number of businesses operating across international boundaries makes this idea more evident.

In order to compete overseas, businesses should analyze and assess the countries with which they intend to conduct business. Simply, countries differ in the ability to produce goods efficiently and consumers to spend. It is not easy to choose the best path to a foreign expansion in a world made up of hundreds of economies and regional blocs. We ask the reader to think about the many economic risks, political risks, and other types of barriers, and it proves extremely hard for a manager to assess long-term profit potential. There are many ways for a company to conduct such analyses, but the best way is to look at the country's market and economic conditions. Economic conditions according to per capita Gross National Product (GNP) and levels of economic development vary widely around the world. The economy and the individual standards of living have a huge impact on the size and affluence of a particular target market. Furthermore, managers must educate themselves on any trade agreements existing between countries as well as on local and regional economic conditions. Therefore, being aware of economic conditions and the likely direction that those conditions will take can help companies better understand the profitability of their potential markets.

Company managers must be trained in facets of international business that are not normally the concern of domestic managers. On a broad scale, these issues include knowledge of other country infrastructures, balance of trade (the difference in a country's exports and imports) and balance of payments (account of goods and services, capital loans, gold, and other items entering and leaving a country). International managers must be knowledgeable of exchange rates, legal–political, and social–cultural elements of other countries.

Individual Country Economics

There are three types of countries with which there are potential business opportunities—developed, less developed, and newly industrialized. A fourth possible type of market that the former communist economies of the former Soviet bloc and China have represented is the business novelty of the end of the past millennium and today. Once managers have assessed to which group a country belongs, they must then analyze the country's infrastructure.

Besides certain statistics, international managers must look at the country's consumption of goods and services, and likely developments. Knowing what type of goods or services the country consumes is very important as well as what consumers will do as long as their disposable income changes. One problem Americans face is that they push their products abroad without considering the differences in environment, tastes, and use-patterns in the foreign markets. A few big companies that have reported suffering from problems of consumer acceptance are Campbell's Soups, General Mills, and the Ford Motor Company.

In recent times, the end of the Cold War inspired a significant number of consumers to partake in international consumption of goods and services. A good example is how Russia, Eastern Europe, and China are now flooded with international sales of goods and services. They have been so flooded that there is now a black market for basic items such as shoes and other clothing. This is not all bad for Russians and the like: they are now able to strengthen their economy and introduce their new markets to the world.

The Growth of the International Marketplace

The growth of the international economy over the past 40 years has occurred because of many driving forces, which include but are not limited to the following.

Market Needs

Most global products and markets exist because marketing phenomena create them. For example, society and individuals do not need soft drinks, but the industry, with its marketing suaveness, created the need by making individual's "wants" become his or her "needs." Any industry that can serve a global need is a candidate for globalization.

Technology

Technology is a universal factor across the global market. Once we develop a particular technology, it immediately becomes available to the world.

Cost

The enormous cost and risk of new product developments have made companies look across their borders for low-cost factors of production.

Quality

To satisfy their home customers, marketers cross their national boundaries to find the best quality products and services at the most limited cost.

Communications and Transportation

The information revolution has played a large role in the evolution of global markets. Everyone wants the best and most modern products. Because consumers travel in many areas, managers must bring products and services to them in almost every regional market.

After the Second World War, the global economy experienced tremendous growth and the following factors emerged.

The World Trading System

The restrictive trading process of the 1920s and the 1930s needed to change in order for a global economy to develop. In addition, the rapid growth and investment following the Second World War created a need for international liquidity. Before 1969, gold and foreign exchange were the only means of international payment. In 1969, the International Monetary Fund (IMF) made an international reserve asset available and the emergence of the European Community has made the world increasingly liquid. Henceforth, companies could continue financing trade and investments between nations by allowing the growth of the global community. At the time of the creation of the International Monetary Fund and the World Bank, international actors were seeking to establish a third institution, an International Trade Organization (ITO) as a specialized agency of the United Nations. The role of this agency would include not only world trade subjects, but also rules on employment, international investment and services, commodity agreements and restriction of business practices. The goal was to create the ITO at the UN Conference on Trade and Employment in Havana, Cuba in 1947; however, events of previous years would have some effect on the outcome.

In December 1945, 15 countries had begun talks regarding customs tariffs. With the recent end of the Second World War, they wanted to reduce tariffs in order to improve trade liberalization, and attempt to right the legacy of protectionist measures, which had been in place since the 1930s. The first round of negotiations resulted in a package of trade rules and 45,000 tariff concessions affecting $10 billion of trade, about one-fifth of the world's total (World Trade Organization, 2006). Additionally, by the time the deal was signed on October 30, 1947, the group of 15 had grown to 23. The compromises took effect by June 30, 1948 through a "Protocol of Provisional

Application." Thus, the new General Agreement on Tariffs and Trade (GATT) was born, with 23 founding members.

These members were part of a larger group who were working on the ITO Charter. One of the provisions of GATT stated that some of the trade rules of the draft should be accepted swiftly and "provisionally" in order to protect the value of the tariff concessions they had negotiated (World Trade Organization, 2006). The Havana conference began on November 21, 1947 but it was not until March of 1948 that the Charter was finally agreed upon. However, ratification was difficult. The US Congress, although one of the initial driving forces, announced it would not see Congressional ratification of the Havana Charter, thus, in essence, ending the ITO.

The General Agreement on Tariffs and Trade (GATT) of 1947, that is, the international forum of less than 20 members at that time, came into operation in January 1948. The GATT became the only multilateral instrument governing international trade in order to promote expanded trade among its members and to avoid protectionism practiced during pre-war depression years. This provided a set of rules to promote liberalized trade. The GATT principle stipulates that each country extend the same favorable negotiation terms to every country. It is a guarantee of non-discriminating or equal treatment in trade relations.

Several conferences marked the systematic liberalization of international trade, the abolition of trade barriers, and finally the liberalization of services. It began with the Geneva Round of 1947, the Annecy Round in 1949, the Torquay Round in 1951, and again the Geneva Rounds in 1956 and 1960–61 (the latter known as the Dillon Round). Three major negotiation rounds followed: the so-called Kennedy Round (1964–67), the Tokyo Round (1973–79), and the Uruguay Round (1986–94). The Kennedy and Tokyo Rounds brought industrial tariff levels down (see Table 2.1 that reports date, place, and subjects covered).

Table 2.1 GATT Trade Rounds

Year	Place/Name	Subjects covered
1947	Geneva, Switzerland	Tariffs
1949	Annecy, France	Tariffs
1951	Torquay, UK	Tariffs
1956	Geneva, Switzerland	Tariffs
1960–61	Geneva–Dillon Round	Tariffs
1964–67	Geneva–Kennedy Round	Tariffs and anti-dumping measures
1973–79	Geneva–Tokyo Round	Tariffs, non-tariff measures, and framework agreements
1986–94	Geneva–Uruguay Round	Tariffs, non-tariff measures, rules, services, intellectual property, dispute settlement, textiles, agriculture, creation of WTO

Source: World Trade Organization (www.wto.org)

However, since the Tokyo Round, world trade recession and larger unemployment brought about concerns and calls for safeguard measures and more protectionism. In addition to deteriorating trade policy environment, world trade had become far more multifaceted than it had been 40 years before: the globalization of the world economy was progressing, trade in services, which was not covered by GATT rules, was of increasing interest to countries, and international investment had expanded, hence the General Agreement was no longer as relevant to the reality of world trade in the 1980s as it had been in the 1940s. The expansion of services trade was also related to further increases in world merchandise trade. However, in other respects, GATT desired more. In agriculture, loopholes in the multilateral system were heavily exploited, and efforts at liberalizing agricultural trade met with little success. In the textiles and clothing sector, an exception to GATT's normal disciplines was negotiated in the 1960s and early 1970s, leading to the Multifibre Arrangement. Even GATT's institutional structure and its dispute settlement system were causing concern (World Trade Organization, 2006). It required a ministerial meeting in 1982 to reaffirm the notions of free trade that were the inspiring notions of the GATT and to improve the logic of the GATT.

Although no practical agreement was taken in 1982, except studies to examine financial support for domestic enterprises, and farm export subsidies, the eighth round of negotiation was launched in September 1986 in Punta del Este, Uruguay, and became known as the Uruguay Round. This multilateral global trade negotiation aimed to consider the aspects of restrictions of trade in services, agriculture export subsidies, and restriction of foreign direct investment. After that, the Uruguay Round led to the establishment of the World Trade Organization (WTO) as an entity, coming into effect on January 1, 1995. This new World Trade Organization is based on the principles of the GATT, a multilateral trade and labor mobility agreement applying to the international trade in service (GATS, General Agreement on Trade in Services) that was signed in Marrakesh, Morocco, in September 1994. The Uruguay Round was implemented under the WTO. Annexes to the above agreements were the agreement on trade-related aspects of intellectual property rights (TRIPS); dispute settlement understanding (DSU) for resolving trade quarrels and ensuring that trade flows smoothly; and agreement on trade-related investment measures (TRIMS) which apply to any measure that discriminates against foreigners or foreign products by trying to avoid certain measures that can restrict and distort trade, such as those measures that require particular levels of local procurement by an enterprise (local content requirements) or that limit a company's imports or set targets for the company to export (trade-balancing requirements).

Note that according to the principle of single undertaking, all countries adhering to the WTO must accept the GATT, GATS, as well as the previously mentioned agreement obligations.

The World Trade Organization

The World Trade Organization (WTO) is the only international body dealing with the rules of trade between nations. WTO agreements, which are negotiated and signed by the majority of the world's trading nations, provide the legal boundaries for international commerce. They are contracts, binding governments to keep their trade policies within agreed limits. Although negotiated and signed by governments, the goal is to help producers of goods and services, exporters, and importers conduct their business. There are three purposes of the organization:

1. Free flow of trade
2. To provide a forum for trade negotiations
3. Dispute settlement.

The five principles of the trading system are:

1. Without discrimination—a country should not discriminate between its trading partners. They are all, equally, granted "most favored nation" or MFN status; and it should not discriminate between its own and foreign products, services or nationals.
2. Freer—with barriers coming down through negotiation, lowering trade barriers is one of the most obvious means of encouraging trade. The barriers concerned include customs duties (or tariffs) and measures such as import bans or quotas that restrict quantities selectively.
3. Predictable—foreign companies, investors and governments should be confident that trade barriers (including tariffs, non-tariff barriers and other measures) should not be raised arbitrarily; more and more tariff rates and market-opening commitments are "bound" in the WTO.
4. More competitive—by discouraging "unfair" practices such as export subsidies and dumping products at below cost to gain market share, the WTO is sometimes described as a "free trade" institution; however, the system does allow tariffs and, in limited circumstances, other forms of protection. More accurately, it is a system of rules dedicated to open, fair, and undistorted competition. The rules on non-discrimination—MFN and national treatment— are designed to secure fair conditions of trade. So too are those on dumping (exporting at below cost to gain market share) and subsidies.
5. More beneficial for less developed countries—by giving them more time to adjust, greater flexibility, and special privileges (WTO, 2006).

The benefits of the WTO are the following:

- The system helps promote peace
- Disputes are handled constructively
- Rules make life easier for all
- Freer trade cuts the costs of living
- It provides more choice of products and qualities
- Trade raises incomes
- Trade stimulates economic growth
- Governments are shielded from lobbying
- The system encourages good government.

As of November 2006, 150 states are WTO members, with Vietnam becoming a member 30 days after the Hanoi Parliament ratified entry. In addition, 28 countries are seeking membership. Whereas GATT had mainly dealt with trade in goods, the WTO and its several agreements now cover trade in services, and in traded inventions, creations, and designs (intellectual property).

Saudi Arabia's dairy industry and the associated changes in relation to the country's acceptance to the WTO is an example of how the organization can affect an economy. After more than 13 years of negotiations, on December 11, 2005, Saudi Arabia became the 149th member of the WTO. The terms of the accession included agreements to undertake a series of important commitments to liberalize its trade regime. These included agreements on agriculture to provide market access, remove subsidies and protection, eliminate non-tariff and quota barriers, and reduce tariffs.

The agriculture sector in Saudi Arabia has always been striving for prosperity. The generous support from the government was substantially intensified with more than two decades of interest-free loans and subsidies. Until 2002, the Saudi dairy market was growing by less than 5 per cent annually, which is well below world standards ("Saudi Milk Processors Merge," 2002). With many market entries, the supply of dairy products exceeded the demand. Additionally, many dairy producers were confused because of the inconsistent pattern of consumption and lack of solid market knowledge.

This resulted in two price wars. The first lasted for six months and ended in May 2000. The other price war broke out towards the end of 2001 and lasted for two years ("Saudi Milk Processors Merge," 2002). Prices dropped by up to 25 per cent at one stage; this price war reached such proportions that it became almost impossible for small companies to survive. The big companies who have a major market share of the domestic market and export their products to GCC (Gulf Cooperation Council) countries slashed their prices to such levels that smaller companies, in order to match their price tag, lost millions of Riyals. The products of some companies never reached the market and perished in warehouses. Eventually, the Saudi Ministry of Agriculture intervened and the price of many products including milk and buttermilk (laban) has since then stabilized ("Future of Dairy Product Companies in the GCC," 2004).

The outcome of the above-mentioned price wars was good. The results of these price wars reduced average prices of the dairy products to more realistic levels, prompted smaller dairy producers to discuss joining forces and consider merger into bigger companies, there was more diversification in dairy-related products offering larger variety of such products to the market, dairy companies penetrated in more markets available in the region, and some dairy companies diversified their business even to dairy-unrelated products such as juices, which would help these companies to survive and prosper their business if the dairy market became sluggish for any reason (Najran Dairy, 2004).

Saudi Arabia consumes around $1.5 billion worth of dairy products annually. In 1998, Saudis consumed 630,000 tons of liquid milk, an increase of 2 per cent over 1997 consumption rates. Per capita consumption increased from 34 kilograms in 1975 to an estimated 58 kilograms in 1995 (*The Saudi Arabian Economy*, 2005).

Total consumption of liquid milk amounted to 335 million liters in 1999, increasing to almost 600 million liters if laban is included (Al-Otaibi and Robinson, 2002). Per capita consumption is therefore around 30 liters per annum based on the current official population figure of approximately 20 million. In value terms, the market for milk and laban is worth an estimated US$675 million at the retail level.

By the end of 2005, the Saudi milk market was expected to grow by an estimated Saudi Riyal (SR) 200 million to reach SR 3.6 billion ("Saudi Dairy Market...," 2005). By the year 2007, the market value of domestic demand is expected to reach SR 10.10 billion. An expected value of exports would be around SR 3.0 billion. Thus, the combined market value of dairy products will reach SR 13.10 billion by that target year ("Estimated Volume of Investments in the Saudi Dairy Sector...," 2003).

While government policy remained supportive for the dairy industry, gradual elimination of all forms of subsidies according to WTO agreement would expose increasing challenges to this local industry. The government decision to lower custom duties to 5 per cent on the import of dairy products would induce competition from foreign suppliers, especially in the area of cheese and other solid dairy products where Saudi capacity is still lacking.

The direct effect of globalization on the dairy industry in Saudi Arabia is the increasing competition. This increase in competition would be the result of the following:

1. Foreigner investment accession into the Saudi dairy market due to lifting of restrictions by the Saudi government and the growing and attractive opportunity that the Saudi markets possess.
2. Lowered tariffs (which would be eliminated gradually) would attract new foreign products to penetrate the Saudi market, as a market development strategy is approved by foreign dairy firms.
3. Existing foreign products in the Saudi market would maximize their profit margin because of reduced or absence of tariffs. Therefore, these foreign products would possess a greater competitive advantage position in the market.
4. One of the effects of globalization is the lowering of the cost of national dairy products due to, for example, the low price of imported resources such as machinery and materials (Griffin, 1999).

Now that Saudi Arabia has joined the WTO, the Saudi dairy industry may temporarily suffer an unbalanced situation and therefore require them to regain their balance. However, after regaining the balance, Saudi firms would seek strategies to penetrate and develop new markets. Short life-cycle dairy products would be more available to close GCC countries as well as Jordan and Yemen representing existence in these markets. Furthermore, Saudi dairy products would have great opportunities to penetrate European and US markets because of their competitive advantage driven by the low cost of production, more specifically in labor cost and increased efficiency. The penetration and development of European and US markets require the Saudi dairy firms to stress quality in addition to maintaining competitive price strategies. Due to the high competition subsequent to joining the WTO, many Saudi dairy firms would implement differentiation strategies by producing high quality dairy products (for example, producing non-diluted milk products). In addition, many firms would implement low price leadership by being extremely efficient in their operation (Al-Ghamdi, 2006).

Al-Ghamdi goes on to state that increasing competition and increasing demand on dairy products worldwide would therefore force dairy firms to improve efficiency. Moreover, dairy firms would also seek additional capital through having stocks traded (for example, family dairy firms would go public). In addition, firms would invest more in the Research and Development sector.

The globalization effects on the Saudi dairy industry after Saudi Arabia has joined the WTO are that the agreement included many commitments to free trade, reducing tariffs, and eliminating subsidies to local Saudi industries. Mergers, acquisitions and joint ventures could take place within Saudi dairy organizations, and between Saudi and foreign organizations. If this occurs, the dairy industry could concentrate more on product development and diversification strategies as well as investments in R&D. Furthermore, the Saudi dairy industry would have greater opportunities to penetrate European and US markets because of their competitive advantage driven by the low cost of production specifically in labor costs; in addition, it would strengthen its current market share in the GCC market (Al-Ghamdi, 2006).

With these extra measures including mergers, use of technology, of R&D, and diversifications it is believed that the ascension of Saudi Arabia to WTO membership and the related future of the Saudi dairy industry will be successful operations locally and competition globally (Al-Ghamdi, 2006).

Global Peace

There is currently a relatively stable foundation for rapid growth of the global market. We live in a world that is constantly in bitter conflict, but on a global basis, we are at peace.

Domestic Economic Growth

Managerial skill and technology enable companies to become international. When a country is growing rapidly, it is possible for an outside company to enter and establish itself without taking away business from the local firms. The international business is not doing business at the expense of others, but actually enlarges the total gains to be distributed. Without economic growth, international business would become much more difficult. It would mean taking business away from the local businesses. The existence of market opportunities is a major reason for the internationalization of a business.

The Internet and Transportation Technology

The cost of transmitting voice, television, and data has declined since the end of the Second World War. The use of the Internet has been beneficial and this especially took place when penetration into the markets reached a 50 per cent level, and so it starts to reduce production costs all across the economy. The US economy reached this critical value in 1999. And if we want to focus on total factor productivity (TFP) growth, computer investment accelerated early in the 1990s. It is believed that between 1987 and 1994, the use of computer capital generated about one-fourth to a half of TFP growth at the firm level, which grew nearly 25 per cent per year. If we translate the firm-level results to the overall economy with a time lag of about seven years, the gains in TFP growth from the 1995–99 flows of computer investment growth (which exceeded 40 per cent per year) should peak around 2006. For 20 years, productivity in the US grew at a rate of 1 per cent a year; starting in 1995, productivity has grown at 3 per cent per year, while between 1990 and 2000, the average annual growth rate of real investment in computer capital was about 33 per cent. The growth in the sector of the Internet has had beneficial effects on production (some 25 per cent of the increase in production is because of the Internet). The impact could be substantial if the use of computers simplifies a broad collection of complementary innovations within firms and the benefits of computers become apparent when we combine new technologies with organizational aspects. There is evidence that the benefits from computer use persist long after firms have undertaken the investment. The use of computers increases TFP in the manufacturing and service sectors also by way of changes in the organization of production. Telecommunications has allowed the world to function in a more global manner than ever before. In addition, traditional trade has benefited from technology advances, such as the cases of commercial jets, super freighters, and containerization. This has made it possible to manage in the more distant geographical areas. Transportation technology has only improved over the past 60 years. The cost and time of shipping internationally have become less expensive and quicker than ever before.

The Global Corporation

The global corporation has taken advantage of the expanding communications and technologies, and the corporation serves the population on a truly global scale. Global corporations' true managers look at the opportunities and use the international world resources to satisfy global needs.

Foreign Exchange Market

The Foreign Exchange Market (FEM) is a worldwide network of financial establishments that assists international business transactions by trading (buying and selling) foreign exchange. It is the process of exchanging currency between countries. Foreign exchange allows international transactions to occur. The FEM is the largest financial market in the world with a volume of more than $1.5 trillion dollars. The FEM is unique in that it has neither a physical location nor a central exchange; instead, it operates through an electronic system of banks, corporations, and individuals. Like many other markets, foreign exchange includes both dealers and customers. Foreign exchange consists of several types of financial instruments: instruments like national currencies, and deposits in commercial banks to name a few. Foreign exchange consists of a relatively small number of large banks that are located in the major commercial and financial centers of the world.

The foreign exchange (FX) rate, or an international exchange rate, is defined as the price of one country's money (currency) in relation to another country's currency. For instance, if the Euro is quoted as 0.772, this means that $1 will buy 0.772 Euros. Supply of and demand for foreign currencies determines exchange rates. Several factors influence these rates, such as inflation, interest rates, GNP, dependency on outside energy sources, central bank, government stability, and the perception of world strength in currency. FX has emerged as the world's focus point. The FX estimated turnover rate is over one trillion dollars daily. The largest users of FX are commercial banks. Corporations also use the FX to trade currencies in order to secure foreign currency. FX has now become the center or "nucleus" of the world economy.

Stock Exchanges

There are many other exchanges throughout the world. One of the largest is the New York Stock Exchange. This is usually the trendsetter in the world markets. Most analysts evaluate the New York Stock Exchange and then predict future trends in other world markets. Other giants of the world market are the Nasdaq Exchange, London Exchange, Warsaw Exchange, Tokyo Exchange, and Johannesburg Stock Exchange, just to name a few. These exchanges for the most part run many countries' economies, not to mention the world economy.

In America, the best way to follow international stocks domestically is the use of the *Wall Street Journal* (WSJ), in Europe the *Financial Times* (FT). Both the WSJ and the FT have a list of all the companies that invest in foreign and domestic markets. Using these daily sources is another way to follow international business and trade. It is definitely a main source of international news. Other sources are business magazines such as *Forbes* or *The Economist*, the UK magazine. Each month, *Forbes* lists the World Markets Review, given by top financial analysts.

Companies Becoming Global

Many well-known companies are becoming global. We are going to discuss three of them and explain in which of the three stages these companies currently operate.

Nike

Nike sells its sportswear in over 80 different countries and operates over 60 retail outlets. Nike has administrative offices in Austria, Canada, Hong Kong, the Netherlands, and the US. It manufactures its product in host countries at over 40 different locations, mostly in East Asia. Since the 1970s, Nike's manufacturing locations have gradually changed from Japan to Korea and Taiwan, and most recently to China and Indonesia, who currently produce 60 per cent of Nike's shoes. It carries out all product development and marketing at the headquarters in Beaverton, Oregon.

In addition, the little air bags that cushion the heels of its shoes are produced there as well.

Generally, companies go through three stages to become global companies. The first stage is when companies simply move goods internationally. This is what is widely known as importing or exporting goods. At this stage, there is no production being done in the foreign countries. The second stage is when firms have strategic corporate offices in the foreign countries and goods and/or services are produced in one country, and possibly transferred to another country for additional assembly. Ultimately, they are distributed to other countries where they are sold because demand starts to grow. This is referred to as multinational enterprising. The third stage of globalization is when firms' strategic corporate offices in other countries interact with each other and headquarters. To better exploit countries that have differences in factor endowments, technologies, and consumer preferences, certain functions are performed in the different countries depending on specialization. For example, marketing may be done in one country, research in another country and production in yet another country. During this stage, people and products are moved significantly across country borders to meet company demands. Companies are referred to as global firms at this stage. Global firms attempt to create a global culture that unites people to the organization and helps coordinate the scattered offices.

Before the 1970s, Nike was in stage one of globalization, which means that they manufactured in the US and then exported all of the products to other countries. However, in the 1970s, Nike began to produce its products overseas, which pushed them into the second stage. Now Nike is a global firm. They have numerous offices throughout the world, all of which talk with the corporate headquarters as well as each other. They are also becoming more specialized in each location. For example, the Beaverton, Oregon headquarters is the only place that makes the cushions; therefore, they are specializing.

Exxon

Exxon is vertically integrated and the corporation carries out four major types of activity—exploring, production, refining, and marketing.

Vertical integration refers to a style of ownership and management of the company. Vertically integrated companies are related via a hierarchy, and the companies have the same owner. Generally, each member of the hierarchy produces a different product, and the products combine to satisfy a common need.

Exxon Company International is located in New Jersey, and controls activities of its affiliates who conduct oil and gas operations outside the US and Canada. Exxon affiliates operate in more than 55 countries, with about 21,000 service stations, interests in 24 refineries, and oil and gas production in 12 countries. In some countries, Exxon does all four of the activities, yet in others, just one. Exxon has support companies to maintain its refining and distribution and its exploration and production.

Exxon has well surpassed the multinational enterprise stage and is well into the global stage. The fact that four different countries carry out all four of the major activities is a prime factor. There are still some characteristics of a multinational enterprise present in the Exxon Company, however. Brazil is still specializing in marketing, while Nigeria solely concentrates on exploration.

Nestlé

Nestlé makes infant formula, powdered milk, instant coffee, chocolates, and other food products, which are sold in over 100 countries. It has almost 500 factories in 74 nations. Nestlé engages in manufacturing and wholesale distribution but it is not vertically integrated into farming or retail. Although about half its sales come from Europe, only 2 per cent come from Switzerland. It has 12 factories in Canada, the same number as in Switzerland. In Africa, it has offices in 17 countries and factories in 12.

Nestlé might be a multinational enterprise, since none of its various locations are specialized. However, it also seems like they are trying to become global since they have factories in so many different locations.

Recent Theories and Research on Trade Patterns

Theories of international trade explain trade patterns by differences in the factor endowments and cross-country differences in industry productivity. Recently, it has been recognized that only the most productive firms will become exporters. Bernard, Jensen and Schott (2003) have studied the factors leading to the exit of manufacturing firms, including competition from low-wage countries and declining trade barriers. Exits occur less frequently at multi-product plants, at exporters, and at plants paying above average wages. In addition, productivity growth is faster in industries with falling trade costs, and plants in industries with falling trade costs are more likely to die or become exporters.

Hummels and Klenow (2002) decompose the growth of world trade into an extensive margin (that is, that part attributable to countries exporting new products) and an intensive margin (that part attributable to countries exporting more of the same products). They find that extensive margin accounts for two-thirds of the greater exports of larger economies, and one-third of their imports.

Feenstra and Kee (2004) estimate the impact of new goods on productivity growth for the exporter, and find that export variety accounts for 13 per cent of within-country productivity growth. Conversely, Broda and Weinstein (2004) measure the impact of new goods on the welfare of the importer. For the United States, they find that upward bias in the conventional import price index (because of ignoring product variety) is approximately 1.2 per cent per year, implying that the welfare gains from cumulative variety growth in imports are 2.8 per cent of GDP in 2001.

Antràs (2003) finds that capital-intensive industries are more likely to engage in intra-firm trade across borders, and he offers an incomplete-contracting explanation for this finding.

Helpman, Melitz and Yeaple (2003) model the decision of heterogeneous firms to serve foreign markets either through exports or FDI. Concerning investment in a subsidiary, exporting involves lower sunk costs but higher per-unit costs. In equilibrium, only the more productive firms choose to serve the foreign markets, and the most productive among this group will further choose to serve the overseas market via FDI. Testing their predictions on data of US affiliate sales and exports, they confirm that having more productive firms leads to much more FDI on export sales. Head and Ries (2003) confirm this prediction for Japanese multinationals.

The most direct empirical evidence on the ownership structure of foreign affiliates comes from Desai, Foley and Hines, Jr (2002) using data on foreign affiliates of US firms, in which they study why partial foreign ownership has declined markedly over the last 20 years, in favor of complete foreign ownership. They argue that there is a complementarity between whole ownership and intra-firm trade, suggesting that reduced costs of coordinating global operations, with regulatory and tax changes, caused the sharply declining propensity of American firms to organize their foreign operations as joint ventures over the last two decades.

In empirical applications, Trefler (2004) investigates the 1989 Canada–US Free Trade Agreement, and finds results consistent with the heterogeneous-firm models discussed earlier. Trefler used the experience of Canadian manufacturing industries over 1989–96 to examine the short-run adjustment costs and long-run efficiency gains that flow from trade liberalization. For industries subject to large tariff cuts, the short-run costs included a 15 per cent decline in employment and a 10 per cent decline in both output and the number of plants. Balanced against these large short-run adjustment costs were long-run labor productivity gains of 17 per cent or a spectacular 2 per cent per year. Surprisingly, this growth is not attributable to rising output per plant, increased investment, or market share shifts to high-productivity plants. Instead, half of the 17 per cent labor productivity growth appears to be caused by favorable plant turnover (entry and exit) and rising technical efficiency.

Romalis (2005) also investigates the impact of the Canada–US and the North America Free Trade Agreements on trade between Canada, the United States, and Mexico. He argues that these trade agreements increased North American output and prices in many highly protected sectors by driving out imports from non-member countries.

On the measurement of real GDP and growth, Feenstra et al. (2004) argue that previous measures from the Penn World Tables conflate productivity growth with terms of trade changes. We distinguish real GDP measured on the expenditure side from real GDP measured on the output side: the current measure of real GDP reported in the Penn World Tables is the former. The difference between these two is the terms of trade, in other words, an index for each country of actual export and import prices relative to average world export and import prices. Countries that earn lower than average prices for their exports, or pay higher than average prices for their imports, will have some low terms of trade, and for that reason will have real GDP on the expenditure side less than on the output side.

Why are the export prices low for poorer countries? One possibility is that they are selling lower quality goods, as discussed by Hallak (2004). Then, the export prices used to construct real GDP should be quality-corrected. Alternatively, it may be that poorer countries face higher than average trade barriers in their export markets, as found by Anderson and van Wincoop (2004): both higher trade costs and remoteness reduce the prices that countries receive for their exports. Redding and Schott (2003) describe the relationship between countries' distance from global economic activity, educational attainment, and economic development. Firms in remote locations face greater trade costs on both exports and intermediate imports, reducing the amount of value-added left to remunerate domestic factors of production. Redding and Schott show that remoteness depresses the skill premium and therefore incentives for human capital accumulation. Empirically, they find that countries with lower market access have lower levels of educational attainment, and that the world's most peripheral countries are becoming increasingly remote over time.

Conclusion

As globalization has developed, living conditions have improved significantly in nearly all countries. The strongest progress has been made by the advanced countries and to a lesser extent, by the developing countries. Yet, it is evolving. The global market is a profit-related business with activities conducted across international boundaries. Without economic growth, international business would become much more difficult. Global corporations' true managers look at the opportunities and use the international world resources to satisfy global needs.

The Foreign Exchange Market is a worldwide network of financial institutions that simplifies international business transactions by buying and selling foreign exchange. Foreign exchange allows international transactions to occur. The foreign exchange rate, or international exchange rate, is the price of one country's currency in terms of another country's currency. There are many other exchanges throughout the world. Other giants of the world market are the New York Stock Exchange, Nasdaq Exchange, London Exchange, Warsaw Exchange, Tokyo Exchange, and Johannesburg Stock Exchange, just to name a few. The technology in these exchanges is a universal factor across the global market, allowing trading to be completed with ease.

Globalization offers extensive opportunities for worldwide development. Those companies most interested in succeeding are taking the route of globalization. It is the source of the future world's economic development and it is inevitable for those companies wanting to compete. Although some believe that globalization is widening the gap between the rich and the poor and some regard it with apprehension, due to its impact on employment, living standards, and social progress, it is unavoidable.

Case Study

Japan, Mexico Hammer Out Final Details on Trade Deal

Summary This article describes the near completed trade agreement between Japan and Mexico. This deal encourages expansion of Japan's auto and electronic giants into North America. Farmers in Japan, who are heavily protected by the government against foreign competition, closely watch the planned trade agreement. The Japanese government has looked upon this pact as a potential blueprint for other bilateral trade pacts with other nations such as South Korea, Thailand, and Taiwan. The obstacle to the Mexican pact is a 4.3 per cent tariff on pork imports. Mexico has an agreement similar to NAFTA with EU-15 member nations. Nissan Motor Co. stands to benefit from the Japan–Mexico agreement because of its current presence in the country.

Tokyo Japan and Mexico are hammering out the final details of a proposed free-trade pact that could pave the way for similar agreements between Japan and other countries and encourage the expansion of Japan's auto and electronics giants in North America.

The two countries had hoped to agree Thursday to coincide with a visit to Tokyo by Mexican President Vicente Fox, but negotiations stalled over Japan's unwillingness to eliminate its pork tariffs. Still, Mr Fox said he hoped an agreement could be reached before he leaves Japan Friday.

"We have run a long distance, and only a little bit remains for us to come to the final conclusion," Mr Fox told reporters.

They are watching the planned trade deal because it would be the first that Tokyo makes with a country that sends significant volumes of agricultural products to Japan. Farmers in Japan are heavily protected against foreign competition. The thorny issue of agricultural trade also lurked behind the collapse of last month's World Trade Organization negotiations in Cancún, Mexico, between developed and developing nations.

A pact with Mexico would not just bolster trade between the two countries but could also be a blueprint for a string of pacts Japan hopes to seal with large trading partners including South Korea, Thailand, and Taiwan, trade experts said. Some Japanese manufacturing executives worry that Japan's industry will be at a disadvantage to competitors in the US and European Union, which have been more aggressive in seeking trade deals.

"A deal with Mexico would create a very good atmosphere for approaching other agreements," said Masayoshi Honma, a Tokyo University professor who specializes in trade. However, he warned that other possible deals could also founder over agricultural tariffs.

The obstacle to a Japan–Mexico deal is Tokyo's 4.3 per cent tariff on pork imports. Mexico wants it eliminated. Japan fears that Mexican pork imports will hurt Japanese farmers, an important political constituency of Prime Minister Junichiro Koizumi's Liberal Democratic Party, now campaigning for November 9, 2003 parliamentary elections.

The absence of a free-trade agreement with Mexico has put Japanese exporters and multinational companies at a disadvantage to companies in the US and Europe. The North American Free Trade Agreement (NAFTA) lifted most barriers to trade between Mexico, the US, and Canada. Mexico has similar agreements with members of the 15-nation European Union.

One beneficiary of a Japan–Mexico pact would be Nissan Motor Co., the largest carmaker in Mexico. While Nissan gets more than 75 per cent of the parts for its Mexican plant from within the NAFTA region, its Mexican operation buys from Japan some auto parts that are now subject to Mexican tariffs. A pact "would be saluted by Nissan," said the company's chief executive, Carlos Ghosn.

In addition, Toyota Motor Corp. is building a plant to make pick-up truck beds outside Tijuana and another big plant in San Antonio, which will also depend on free-trade ties with Mexico.

Reprinted with permission: T. Zaun and J. Millman (2003), "Japan, Mexico Hammer Out Final Details on Trade Deal," *The Wall Street Journal*, October 17, A9.

Case Questions

1. Discuss the potential implications of a trade pact between Mexico and Japan for NAFTA.
2. Would Mexico or Japan benefit most from this potential trade deal? Explain.
3. Why is a 4.3 per cent tariff on pork imports from Mexico an obstacle in the deal?
4. Do you agree that the absence of a free-trade agreement with Mexico has put Japanese exporters and multinational companies at a disadvantage to companies in the US and EU?

Chapter Review

The global market consists of several profit-related business activities conducted across international boundaries. We reflect the international character of business in the make-up of many products sold throughout the world today. Economic conditions such as per capita Gross National Product (GNP) and levels of economic development vary widely around the world. Company managers must be trained in many facets of international business that are not normally the concern of domestic managers. International managers must be knowledgeable of exchange rates, legal–political and social–cultural elements of other countries.

International managers must also look at the country's consumption of goods and services. Most global products and markets exist because marketing phenomena create them. Without economic growth, international business would become much more difficult. It would mean taking business away from local businesses. The managers of true global corporations look at the opportunities and use international world resources to satisfy global needs.

The Foreign Exchange Market is a worldwide network of financial institutions that facilitate international business transactions by trading (buying and selling) foreign exchange. It is the process of exchanging currency between different countries. Foreign exchange allows international transactions to occur. Like many other markets, foreign exchange includes both dealers and customers. Foreign exchange consists of several types of financial instruments. The foreign exchange (FX) rate, or international exchange rates, is the price of one country's money (currency) in terms of another country's currency. Corporations also use FX to trade currencies in order to secure foreign currency. There are many other exchanges throughout the world. Most analysts evaluate the New York Stock Exchange and then predict future trends in other world markets.

Chapter Questions

1. What is the definition of globalization? Do you know additional definitions of globalization? What limits are there to globalization?
2. What are the differences in the business environment across borders? What implicit and informal differences exist?
3. How do these differences affect firms, customers, and trade?
4. Why do firms invest directly in foreign countries? When do they do so?
5. How do managers select foreign markets to enter?

Chapter 3

An Introduction to Multinational Enterprises

The Oxford English Dictionary (OED) Second Edition defines multinational as relating to, consisting of, or involving several or many countries or nationalities. It is of a company or other organization, operating in several or many countries. The OED goes on to define enterprise, the noun, as a design of which the execution is attempted, a piece of work taken in hand, a bold, arduous, or momentous undertaking. Enterprise, as a verb, is defined as to take in hand (a work), take upon oneself (a condition), attempt or undertake (a war, an expedition, and so on), run the risk of or venture upon (danger) (*Oxford English Dictionary*, 1989). As shown, a multinational enterprise is literally an attempt of several countries or nationalities to venture or take in hand the organizations and operations in a bold way. This chapter will explain multinational enterprises, their purpose, importance, and future.

Multinational enterprises (MNEs) have many of the same activities and functions that ordinary non-multinational enterprise companies have. However, many factors make these activities and functions significantly different. When looking at multinational enterprises in conjunction with other businesses, the three-cost strategy framework, fixed costs, distance costs, and location costs still works. You can still analyze your business and that of your competition by examining the framework. However, when it comes to competing internationally, things change.

A multinational enterprise is a company that owns a significant part of and operates facilities in nations other than the one in which it is based. As noted in Chapter 2, there are three stages companies go through to become global companies. The first stage is when companies simply move goods internationally. This is what is widely known as importing or exporting goods. In this stage, there is no production being done in the foreign countries. The second stage is when firms have strategic corporate offices located in the foreign countries and goods and/or services are produced in one country, and possibly transferred to another country for additional assembly. Ultimately, they are distributed to other countries where they are sold. This is referred to as multinational enterprising. The third stage of globalization is when firms' strategic corporate offices in other countries interact with each other and headquarters. Certain functions are performed in the different countries depending on specialization. For example, marketing may be done in one country, research in another country and production in yet another country. During this stage, people and products are moved significantly across country borders to meet company demands. Companies are referred to as global firms at this stage. Global firms attempt to create a global culture that unites people to the organization and helps coordinate the scattered offices.

Multinational enterprises are also defined as firms that engage in direct investment, in which the firms acquire substantial controlling interest in foreign firms or set up subsidiaries in foreign countries. Multinationals are important in industries and firms with four characteristics: high levels of research and development relative to sales, large shares of professional and technical workers in their workforces, products that are new and/or technically complex, and high levels of product differentiation and advertising.

Characteristics and Functions of Multinational Enterprises

MNEs are entities that have operations in a home country, where the headquarters is based, and one or more host countries. These host countries may employ only certain divisions of the company (for example, production) or the offices may be separately run from the headquarters. The factors that face any corporation are multiplied when the company is diversified into more than one country. The challenges increase with the number of countries involved (Hodgetts and Luthans, 2002).

Functions of the company are done where cost is the lowest for the quality they desire, not necessarily where the product is going to be sold. A good example is the current outsourcing of US companies to India, China, and many other economically developing countries, though 65 per cent of the sales of foreign affiliates of US MNEs went to the local market and another 24 per cent shipped in the local region in 2002, the latest year for which data are available. Note that in the case of China, 71 per cent of US affiliates' production was sold domestically. Moreover, the largest part of workers employed by US corporations are located in other high-wage countries, though declining from roughly 68 per cent in 1987 to slightly over 61 per cent in 2001. In addition, foreign firms in the US employ 5 per cent of all private industry jobs and this is another example of why wages are not necessarily the key factor driving investment abroad. If we think that a manager does not only has to look at wages per se, but also at labor costs of production, which take into account the productivity of workers, and the geographical location of where to go and invest, it would result in a complex task.

Sending American jobs overseas, referred to as outsourcing or offshoring, is perhaps the most talked about corporate strategy of the twenty-first century. What is most discussed are the savings that can be realized by outsourcing products or services such as computer coding, credit-card-balance retrieval, document scanning, customer-service call-center staffing, and payroll processing. Anything that can be outsourced is considered a potential candidate for emerging economies like India and China.

By outsourcing their work, American and multinational companies can reduce their labor costs and increase or decrease their workforces quickly to reflect peaks and valleys in production. For instance, Meisler (2004) states that college graduates in India earn one-tenth to one-fifth the salaries of their American or Western European counterparts. Other low-wage countries/regions include the Philippines, China, Russia and Eastern Europe, and Central and South America. Companies have found they can also reduce their investment in equipment and increase or decrease their workforces quickly to reflect fluctuations in demand. Finally, yet importantly, because the overseas workday begins when the American workday ends, companies can conduct activities, like software testing, both at home and abroad and save valuable time by having the work continually done.

According to Lemon (2002), China had 200,000 IT professionals employed in the software export industry, with an additional 50,000 entering the workforce each year. Chinese IT employees, who include project managers and software engineers, are also less costly to employ than their US counterparts, typically earning one-sixth of the salaries paid in the US. In addition, many Chinese information technology professionals have some experience working overseas.

However, there is more to outsourcing than finding experienced employees willing to work for less. There are numerous economic, managerial, political, and cultural problems to navigate along the way. For example, some professionals still lack in areas such as language and cultural compatibility. A large problem is that many managers do not appreciate the vulnerabilities until it is too late, and the company fails in its endeavors. There can also be failure if a company is set up in the wrong location, or they do not get the funding and staffing they need.

In America, offshoring may seem like a restructuring of its economy, much like the industrial revolution or the Rust Belt migration to service and information jobs of the last three decades, but it has generally angered Americans who feel that this will endanger their jobs in an already declining economy. The Rust Belt is the heavily industrial area of the north-eastern United States, which contains the older industries and factories.

MNEs gather feedback from the communities in which they are located and they typically use expatriate managers sent from headquarters to oversee the foreign operations. These managers coordinate between subsidiaries and headquarters to implement strategies that will ensure the quality and effectiveness of organizational control systems, and manage global information systems. The managers gain expertise in international business skills that are critical to ensuring them top executive positions.

A multinational enterprise establishes operations in a host country only when it brings with it some firm-specific advantages that more than offset the advantages that host country firms have. For example, the establishments of accounting firms and computer subsidiaries in India and China deliver cheap labor, while the establishments of Exxon/Mobil, British Petroleum, and Chevron in Nigeria and Venezuela provide crude oil resources. Multinational enterprises usually possess a special advantage such as superior technology or lower costs due to economies of scale and they bring inherent advantages, such as technology, that potentially constitute an important gain for the host country. A disadvantage for MNEs is the cost to shift production to other global markets. It costs billions of dollars to expand and grow. The more growth a company has into different countries, the greater the number of knowledgeable managers that are needed.

Managers of multinational enterprises must be very knowledgeable in many areas. It is of great importance for these managers to learn the appropriate language and culture of the host country. Human resources management skills are key factors in being a good manager in any corporation, but are especially important when working cross-culturally. Treating people as individuals and avoiding stereotypes are just a few of the precautions a global manager must take. They should effectively understand, analyze, measure, and manage their division and face the increasingly numerous challenges that take place in the world economy.

Current trends such as globalization, leaner organizations, and product/service alliances have made an impact on multinational enterprises. These trends are predicted to grow and the corporations involved must keep pace.

The number of competitors for MNEs includes not only those domestically, but also those producing in the foreign market. This brings challenges of market share and product nationalism. In addition, if the competitor is a domestic company in a market, while the corporation is a foreign entity, taxes, duties, and trade restrictions come into play for only one of the two competitors. This may raise prices and cause competing in that market to become more costly.

Customers also differ between countries. Everyday culture can control many aspects of consumer attitudes. These attitudes can determine what kind of product the customer will buy, how much they will pay for the product, and what type of material the product will be made of. The degree of nationalism in a country can also determine how an MNE must be run. If nationalism is high, the consumers are more likely to buy products produced in the home market. They will also tend to favor management techniques that are similar to their own, and may prefer that management positions be given to a citizen of that country.

To illustrate, suppliers can put additional stress on an MNE. For example, the suppliers in the foreign country may not have the specific material a corporation needs to make a technical part, and because the idea of time may differ, this may cause production backups. For example, a supplier from Mexico may say that the product will be "rush delivered," and mean that the material will get there within a month. An American company could get continually aggravated with the lead-time on the order. However, the American supplier would have a "rush" order out in three to four days. Depending on the purpose of the company, these differences could determine when the supplies will be delivered.

Governmental "red-tape" can also cause problems for an MNE. Trade restrictions and embargoes that are put into effect during the time that the corporation is already in production can become costly and time-consuming. Political changes that alter a relationship between a multinational corporation's home and host country can become a difficult obstacle to overcome.

All of these challenges are met by MNEs all over the world on a daily basis. The obstacles and operations differ from one company to the next, but they share a number of characteristics. One of these characteristics is centralized ownership. Although joint ventures and stock options are often used to expand the company, the entity is always centrally owned. This is what ties the company together. Although the operations may be located in different countries, the company is one company because of the ownership (Hodgetts and Luthans, 2002).

Another characteristic is that these companies use one resource base. Information, money, legal documentation (for example, patents and licenses), and credit are all shared between the different branches of a multinational corporation. This helps keep the company more effective and reduces the need to repeat certain aspects of business life.

A multinational corporation extends its strategy to all parts of the world. This global strategy is the backbone of any MNE. This maintains the cohesive nature of the company and keeps all branches working smoothly with the others. It also helps define objectives of the corporation and allows all subsidiaries to focus on the same goals.

Functions of MNEs differ between companies, but looking at the characteristics, we can draw a few conclusions. Multinational enterprises take advantage of the functions that each different environment offers. For example, if one environment has cheaper labor costs, it is easier to become involved in that country. It may be costly to start up, but the benefits far outnumber the disadvantages when the cost advantage is obvious. In addition, using an environment that may have natural resources that the home country does not have is advantageous to MNEs.

Multinational enterprises also function as a way to capture new markets. Name recognition becomes easier when the company is located in a local area. The company can also understand more about what products and/or services the area is lacking when they are located in the area.

Advantages and Disadvantages of Multinational Enterprises

Engaging in foreign direct investment as a multinational enterprise has advantages as well as disadvantages in the areas of employing host-country locals for employees, the location that the firm decides on, exchange rate fluctuations, and convertibility of currency.

First, the main advantage of using a host-country local is that they are familiar with the local environment, language, culture, and customs. This may be good because they would require less training. Because they are local, they may be able to be productive right away; they do not need time to adapt to the local environment, where someone coming from the home country would need this adaptation period. If you hire a host-country local into an upper level management position, it may enhance your company's image in the host country. This person may be vital to establishing important relationships with customers, clients, employees, and the public. Host-country locals are usually cheaper to employ than an expatriate due to cheaper labor costs overseas.

Along with the advantages of using host-country locals, there are also some disadvantages. It is important when hiring a host-country local, that they are loyal to the company. Sometimes, their loyalty may be with their country, not with the company. Due to lack of education, and differing levels of the economy, it may be quite difficult to find someone from the host country who is qualified to perform the duties that the position may require. This may also make it more difficult to assess their abilities. Although they may be quite capable of performing certain tasks in their country, they may not be able to perform adequately the differing levels of technologies and education. Host-country locals may not understand the typical corporate culture of US or other home country companies; they may do things very differently in their companies. They may not be able to communicate effectively with the home office in the domestic market, they may not know the other language, or there may be certain parts of the language that do not translate into the other language the way that it was meant. A host-country local may not be mobile because of family in or around the area. Some cultures that have strong family values ensure that the family's needs come before the needs of the corporation. A firm must also be careful when hiring a host-country local to ensure that they do not have ulterior motives. A local may be hired that is currently employed with the competition, and they are serving as a spy and selling the secrets of the foreign firm, keeping their loyalty with their country. A firm may have to spend more money on training them to get them acquainted with the customary corporate culture of the firm, language training, and so on.

The advantages of the location that the firm chooses in other countries could be to lower the basic costs of the goods and/or services provided to customers. There may be access to critical supplies, natural resources, and lower labor costs. The firm must be managed effectively in order to gain the full benefits of the advantages of the location chosen.

Some factors that affect multinational enterprises are exchange rate fluctuations and the convertibility of the currency. When exporting to or importing from another country, the export terms must be established. These may include which country's currency will be used, when the payment is made, and the shipping terms. A firm should be sure to make the export and receive payment relatively quickly. If the exchange rate happens to fluctuate during that period, they may lose money. Money may also be gained from exchange rate fluctuations. A firm can protect itself by stating a certain payment amount no matter what the current exchange rate is at that time. With the convertibility of currency concern, a country with soft currency that is hard to exchange, barter, or counter trade may be considered for terms of payment instead. This could also prevent loss from exchange rate fluctuations if a certain amount of goods is agreed upon for the trade or payment.

Multinational enterprises may help the economy of the host country. They may employ locals for positions in the firm or in production plants if they also manufacture the products in the same country. It may also help because it will create more taxes for the foreign government. The firm may have to pay extra taxes or duties for certain products, but will have to pay taxes to the government of the host country. However, the presence of another firm will cause more competition for the local businesses. It could also put local firms out of business.

The Relationship Between Multinational Enterprises and the Economy

MNEs benefit from both vertical and horizontal economies of scale and the resulting power of monopoly that this permits. Many firms choose to merge rather than grow internally as it is often cheaper to do so. It is easier and quicker to become much larger and the company can experience lower average costs through economies of scale. There are two common types of integration of firms, horizontal and vertical.

Horizontal integration involves the merger of two firms in the same industry, both at the same stage of production. An example of horizontal integration would be the merger of two car manufacturers such as Chrysler and Daimler Mercedes-Benz in 1998, or Ford and Jaguar in 1989. When two car manufacturers merge to create one large company, it is likely to experience all sources of economies of scale to a greater extent. This is because fewer managers would be required as the two original firms produced similar products.

An example of vertical integration is a corporate merger that involves firms that are involved in forwardly or backwardly related production stages, that is, they buy each other's inputs or outputs. Two adjacent production stages are vertically integrated when they are brought under common ownership and control. Using the same industry as above, an automobile company may own a tire company, a glass company, and a metal company. An example of this is General Motors' relationship/ operation with Allison Transmissions, a manufacturer of heavy-duty automatic transmissions. Control of these subsidiaries is intended to create a stable supply of inputs and ensure a consistent quality in their final product.

Technical expertise, experienced personnel, and tested strategies are also a major benefit to MNEs. Opponents of MNEs usually view an MNE as an economic and political means of foreign domination. Small developing nations are particularly vulnerable to having their societies changed drastically by MNEs. Proponents of MNEs see it as the triumph of global capitalism. MNEs bring advanced technology to poorer countries and low-cost products to the wealthier ones.

To understand the enormous impact of MNEs on the world, one must first understand their sheer economic size. MNEs account for nearly one-half of the world's industrial output, dominating industries such as automobiles, electronics, pharmaceuticals, chemicals, and machinery. MNEs command two-thirds of the world's trade in industrial products (Vernon, 1995). More than 90 per cent of the 500 largest MNEs in the world are based in the European Union, the United States, and Japan. Ninety per cent of the world's automobiles are produced in North American factories owned by Japanese/European MNEs, and the big three US auto companies (General Motors, Chrysler, and Ford). Over 90 per cent of the steel and heavy electronic equipment produced in the world is produced by MNEs. In North America, nearly 70 per cent of service sector positions are through an MNE. A recent study of the 200 largest MNEs shows Japan with an average return on foreign assets of 1.25 per cent, USA 6.24 per cent, Europe 5.49 per cent, UK 7.8 per cent (Rugmanand Hodgetts, 1998).

Technology is an integral part of today's MNEs. MNEs use technology in a variety of ways. The most successful MNEs use technology to help gain competitive advantage in their industry. Companies that provide networking solutions have been impacted greatly by technology and the information age. MNEs would not be able to communicate as efficiently as they do today without networking technology. The networking companies also owe their growth to technology. The large advances in technology have made it more affordable and accessible to smaller firms. Some smaller firms in low and medium technology sectors are using sophisticated information technology to coordinate regional production networks.

The lower cost of technology and its ease of use have prompted a new wave of business called electronic commerce or e-commerce. E-commerce expands the reach of a company to every corner of the globe. E-commerce penetrates most conventional boundaries (language, political, and so on). E-commerce is business transacted over the Internet. E-commerce is reaching new heights in both business-to-business and business-to-public consumer sales.

The Internet is a major technological breakthrough that allows companies to communicate much quicker and more effectively. Many MNEs use the Internet to hold "virtual meetings." Virtual meetings allow the parties involved to converse with one another via their home or office Internet connection. Virtual meetings can save thousands of dollars on travel expenses alone, not to mention the savings in time. The Internet has the ability to change the way business is conducted around the globe by giving businesses the opportunity to operate globally no matter their size. It is now possible for a small Internet company to sell their goods all over the world without following the traditional business model of "brick and mortar." E-commerce can generate new sales for companies that know how to harness the power of the Internet. Companies who do not have an Internet presence are losing market share and sales at an incredible pace—the time it takes to click a mouse. It should be noted that most analysts feel that the Internet is not an answer to all business questions, but a major part of modern business activities. Internet companies must continue to have "brick and mortar" facilities for their customers to visit in the physical world. At the same time, "brick and mortar" companies must have an Internet presence in order to be competitive and keep up with the changing times. The perfect balance of cyberspace and mall space is often referred to as "click and mortar." The Internet should not be ignored, yet it should not be the gospel.

As MNEs grow more dependent on the Internet, more time will need to be spent on policy-making. There are wide ranges of policies that arise from the information age: intellectual property, privacy, culture, regulatory principles, consumer protection, fraud, crime prevention, liability, auditing, and taxation. The US government is currently in a very heated debate over the taxation of e-commerce. Some feel it should be taxed so the government does not keep missing tax revenues. Many traditional business firms would like the playing field leveled between the physical and the cyber world.

Impacts and Relationships of MNEs with Home and Host Countries

Multinational enterprises need to have good relationships with their home countries. However, often this is not the case. When a company decides to become global, it must turn to its home country for support and for some much-needed advice. It is easy to find experts on international laws within the home country that are willing to help. With their help, the company will be able to decide which country would best suit their needs and will best mesh with their operations and policies. Yet when a company decides to become global, it is also deciding to take away many of the jobs that are being held by home country citizens. This creates a negative image that the company must be ready to reverse. For example, in the US, the labor unions are always against any action of corporations to set up a subsidiary overseas, knowing its implication. When the company eliminates all of these current jobs, they are also increasing the unemployment rate.

In addition, by leaving the home country, multinational enterprises are taking away the much-needed capital inflow that they are creating. In time, this can be created by other sources; however, it is the initial absence of the inflow that harms the home country's economy. The home country will also lose all of the taxes that were once collected from the company's production and sales. However, these can be recollected, just at different times. Instead of collecting taxes on the sales, they can implement tariffs and importation/exportation quotas that would limit the company's activities or create capital inflow.

The home government remains important to the MNE. It provides its main operating environment, helps negotiate its international affairs and incentives, and provides its own incentives for foreign investment to targeted areas.

Multinational enterprises also produce many benefits for their host countries. One of the benefits is creating capital inflow for the host countries if all the returns from investments are not repatriated to the companies' home countries. Another major benefit is the creation of numerous jobs in different educational and skill levels as well as technology transfer. Oftentimes, the locations that companies tend to establish their subsidiaries in are those with less cost of operation. Many of these countries are less developed with mostly lesser or inadequate technologies. When a multinational company moves to these countries, it usually brings along all the necessary technology to run its business. This would include computers and their applications, telephones, fax machines, copy machines, and so on. For a less developed country, this translates to technological inflow. For the host country, MNEs are an important—if not the main—vehicle in manufacturing sector restructuring and productivity growth. Foreign enterprises show a better structure, faster and more promising restructuring trends than do domestic enterprises. Besides productivity growth correlated with technological intensity and the level of foreign penetration, it is plausible to detect significant improvements in the output quality, changes in management style, and the overall reshaping of organizational culture.

Organizations work closely with governments and the political players in a pluralistic environment. Frequently, business objectives require the cooperation of political authority, and managers find themselves working with government officials and ministries to clear the way for operations. The ease of this work depends on the institutional context they face in their negotiations. Managers sometimes work with governments that are similar to their own. This makes the work easier, due to the similarity between the company and the political players, with common understanding of how a system works. However, occasionally managers find themselves working with governments that are very different from their own. This sometimes presents an animosity of systems that makes the work a great deal more frustrating and difficult.

Relationships between governments in the home and host countries are an important issue facing MNEs. Governments can affect the economic and legal environment in many ways. For instance, they set monetary and tax policies, price controls, and intellectual property regulations. They also influence labor relations, trade policies, capital and exchange controls, and transfer pricing policies. Ultimately, the government can be a regulator, a legislator, a competitor, a customer, a distributor, and a potential partner.

The political objectives in the host country involve favorable trade and investment for the host country, ready access to markets, lessened regulatory hurdles, legitimacy of the business and other local government objectives. While the political objectives are important, the real bargaining power of the MNE and the host government come from the following:

- Technologies or products of the home company
- Potential tax revenue
- Increased exports
- Employment
- Complex management requirements
- Political/economic alliances.

The opportunity for investment abroad can be very risky for a company that chooses to locate a subsidiary within another country. The risks of differing cultures should always be examined but, more importantly, possible complications with the host government need to be expected in advance. When a corporation decides to venture into foreign markets, it is necessary to conform to the laws and regulations of the country involved. Although countries welcome foreign investment to further their economic growth, they must require guest companies to adhere to the same rules that local firms follow. With increasing free-trade agreements between countries, companies are looking to expand more than ever. Companies realize the challenge mounted by expansion and virtually every company will experience setbacks when entering foreign countries.

Examining a brief history of US corporations who have gone multinational, the ability to identify the distress between host governments and home country companies is visible. The adversities faced may be easily resolved or can completely cause a barrier of entry for the company involved. Examples of such problems include the use of suggestive materials, use of banned ingredients and violations of antitrust laws. Corporations attempting to expand into these markets need to cross these barriers or they will be forced out of the highly competitive global marketplace. The issue of host governments and multinational corporations can be seen through the research of several high profile companies and the countries involved. Coca-Cola's difficulty with expansion in France and Peru's fears of Shell Oil's impact on their environment will be explored. In addition, Sony Music's attempt to combat piracy in Singapore and Gerber's difficulties with transitional government in Poland will be discussed.

Coca-Cola and France

When Coca-Cola witnessed the For Sale sign go up in the window of the second-leading soft drink producer in France, they were ready to buy. With Coke controlling nearly half of the French soda pop market, the addition of the popular orange-flavored soda, Orangina, would allow Coke to take over nearly 9 per cent more of the market. The very popular Orangina was developed in the 1940s, and had been under the control of the firm Pernod-Ricard. Pernod-Ricard was now ready to sell Orangina to the highest bidder. The asking price of $840 million dollars seemed steep to Wall Street insiders, but Coke felt it was necessary to expand into the non-cola sector of the global market. Coca-Cola envisioned the potential for Orangina, an all-natural product, in the health-minded American market. In addition, the esthetics of the product, including its bubbly shaped bottle and easily pronounced name, attracted Coke to the idea of purchasing Orangina. Pernod-Ricard on the other hand viewed Coke as its chance to establish its presence around the world, taking advantage of Coke's advertising budget and extensive distribution channels.

France is a friendly country that enjoys the simple things in life. It is a country rich in culture, a gastronome's paradise, and breathtaking and beautiful from its architecture in Paris, to its cultivated land in the north, to its plateaus in the west. France has the fourth largest economy in the world, with the US, Japan, and Germany being the top three. When doing business in France, it is an advantage to have knowledge of the French language; however, it is considered impolite to begin a conversation in French and then revert to English. Although French is the official language, English is widely spoken. Speaking and marketing in French do provide a distinct advantage over those who use only English. Business entertaining usually takes place in restaurants. The CEOs of French companies frequently have similar backgrounds and often come from the same choice group of colleges and universities. In France, meetings and business discussions are often lengthy debates, with much data to back up the business or sales presentations. The meetings are formal, and the emphasis put on detail, especially in the proposals and business dealings, is likely an indication of the rigid French class structure of days past. The French seem more relaxed now than in the past; however, structure still plays an important role in business. High-pressure sales tactics are not advisable since the French tend to be more receptive to an unassuming, logical presentation that explains the advantages of a proposal in full. If an agreement is reached, the French will likely insist that it be formalized in a comprehensive, accurately worded contract.

Box 3.1 Country Profile 1— France
Source: Going Global, *Country Export Issues* (2004)

The deal that would transfer Orangina's ownership from Pernod-Ricard to Coca-Cola would have gone through almost immediately until questions were raised by Pepsi, Coke's archrival in the soda industry. Pepsi challenged the merger, stating that Coke would have a near monopoly, possessing over 60 per cent of the French soda beverage market. For months, competition authorities appointed by the French government did analysis and crunched the numbers, pros, and cons. In September of 1999, the French government handed down their ruling that the Orangina buy-out would indeed give Coca-Cola an unfair competitive advantage in the soda market. Citing the French antitrust regulations, the merger was seen as a partnership that would be able to influence an entire market, hurting the economy of France. Pepsi was thrilled; the French Finance Minister seconded the decision, yet left the door open for a revised proposal.

One of the largest obstacles for Coke's proposal was that the main distributor for Pepsi products was currently Orangina. With the takeover of Orangina, Pepsi would be left without a distributor and would lose much of its share of the French market. Coca-Cola tackled this with a second proposal, for a lesser amount of $762 million and a 10-year plan to distribute Orangina through a third-party vendor. Despite the revised plan, in late November of 1999, France once again denied Coke's bid to buy Orangina. France retains the idea that the merger would allow Coke to have an anti-competitive advantage.

France's decision illustrates the authority and stance a host government can yield if a multinational enterprise is unable to conform to the laws of the land. Much like the United States, France maintains a capitalistic market structure and the establishment of trusts are viewed as illegal. The decision by France has been viewed as fair by Wall Street officials and has been accepted by Coca-Cola, which will no longer pursue the purchase of Orangina. The interference by Pepsi disallowed Coke's bid and now presented Pepsi with the opportunity to bid for Orangina. If Pepsi chooses to do so, their bid would not violate France's antitrust laws and would allow Pepsi to expand their global share of the soda pop market.

Sony and Singapore

We have seen that the relationship between governments and companies attempting to establish themselves in the host country can be very difficult and sometimes impossible to establish. However, once a company is able to set up for business in a foreign company, a rocky association may develop immediately or in the future. The problem which is being encountered by many music companies in Asian countries illustrates the dilemmas that can be faced after an alliance has been established.

Sony Music is experiencing just that: after years in the international market, the issue of piracy has become an immediate issue. The black market for illegally copied compact discs (CDs) in Singapore alone accounts for approximately 30 per cent of the market (Cheah, 1987). An outcry from Sony Music to foreign countries has resulted in a response from Singapore. An investigation called by the government of Singapore resulted in their first raid of a pirated CD manufacturer in July of 1997. More than 78,000 CDs worth over half a million dollars were seized and 13 people were arrested, facing fines of $100,000 and five years in prison. With growing evidence that CDs are being exported from Singapore to European countries, the raid has come at a skillful time, serving notice to piracy chains.

The government of Singapore is proposing stricter techniques to control the pirating of CDs. These methods include such things as the use of identification codes, police investigations beyond the retail sector, and the restriction of convicted pirates founding new operations. In the past, Singapore has been reluctant to get involved with the music industry, electing fruitless counsels, and dismissing lawsuits quickly. With the threat of major investments leaving with Sony Corp., Singapore was forced to listen. The government has acted with raids and investigations into piracy manufacturers, plus a reward fund of $750,000 to thwart illegal copying. Without the direct involvement of the Prime Minister and the government of Singapore, Sony Music would be forced to take losses and possibly avoid the widespread market that Singapore has to offer. In addition, due to stricter export restrictions, the dealings of Singapore will directly affect the sale of illegal compact discs in other Asian countries and Europe.

The relationship between Sony and Singapore has not limited the impact to just the music industry. Such participation is causing other countries to pass laws and enforce copyrights for both music and video game enterprises. This case shows that entering a foreign market may be just the beginning of the process and problems can arrive at any point. If resolve cannot be met, it may result in a once-prosperous alliance ending due to a lack of goodwill and loyalty.

Singapore is a very tiny island at the southern tip of Malaysia, close to the equator. The total land area is about 640 sq km, which is about one-fifth the size of Rhode Island. Singapore is known as the Lion City. "Singapura" in Malay means "Singa" (lion) and "pura" (city). The official languages of Singapore are English, Mandarin, Malay, and Tamil. Malay is considered the national language; however, English is the language used in business organizations.

Singapore is the top convention city in Asia and ranks among the top ten meeting destinations in the world. Singapore is a very conservative society and its citizens are agreeable and obedient. The country enforces fines and punishment for public smoking, spitting, littering, jaywalking, and unsanitary restroom use. As a result, Singapore is proud to be able to say it is one of the cleanest cities in the world.

Singaporeans prefer to consider the collective good to the good of the individual. In Asian cultures, it is rare to boast about one's personal good luck. Asians will not call attention to themselves; they are typically much more prone to humility than the American. A Singaporean is generally much more reserved than an American. The Singapore businessperson may speak directly and will take pride in being pragmatic and realistic. They often do not discuss business at social events.

Business and office attire is formal, yet can be adjusted to fit the warm, tropical climate. In these climates, women will often wear a skirt/slacks and blouse, and men will wear a shirt and tie. Suits and coats should always be worn to official functions. Introductions are often followed by the exchange of business cards, using both hands. Americans and Europeans may find it beneficial to have a Chinese translation printed on the reverse side of their business cards if they are meeting with Chinese Singaporeans. Gift-giving is not obligatory, yet it is appreciated. Any items received as gifts should not be opened immediately.

Box 3.2   Country Profile 2—Singapore
Source: Going Global, *Country Export Issues* (2004)

Shell Oil and Peru

When researchers discovered 11 trillion cubic feet of natural gas and 600 million barrels of liquid natural gas below the forests of Peru, Shell Oil looked to exploit the opportunity (Chatterjee, 1997). The first round of drilling began in 1986 with a loosely signed agreement between Peru and Shell, which was ended soon after it began. According to Charles Chatterjee, "Accusations of Shell workers abusing local women and outside loggers who brought diseases that killed a major part of an indigenous community of Nahua people who have lived in isolation for centuries forced Shell to halt operations" (Chatterjee, 1997). The Peruvian government, under pressure from environmentalists, ended their association with Shell Oil immediately. The relationship between Shell and Peru seemed to be ended by Shell's insensitivity to the people and ecology of Peru. Over ten years later, in mid-1999, Shell still had their foot in the door of Peru's vast natural gas resources. Chatterjee goes on to say, "This time around the company says it will obtain the permission of local people before doing any work, it will not build any roads, and will forbid any hunting and fishing by all staff. Also the use of the best available technology to combat pollution will be used along with the promise to clean up every last scrap of waste" (Chatterjee, 1997).

Peru is a country on the Pacific coast of South America, with border countries of Ecuador, Colombia, Brazil, Bolivia, Chile, and the Pacific Ocean. It is a large mountainous area; the Sierra contains the Andes, and the Selva, which is an area of fertile, subtropical uplands. The country's ethnicity is comprised of native Indians and Caucasians, who are mostly of European descent. In addition, there are those of mixed race, called mestizos. There are also some Peruvians of African descent and in Lima and other coastal cities, the Chinese and Japanese are establishing communities. Peru's current President, Alberto Fujimori, is of Japanese ancestry.

Despite this varied ethnic makeup, more and more a consistent culture is emerging. One will see this primarily in the large cities because of the effects of standardized education, a developing economy, and the trend of residential movement from rural to urban areas. Peru has two official languages—Spanish and Quechua. Spanish is spoken in almost every city and town in the country, while Quechua is mainly spoken in a few places in the Andes. When conducting business in Peru, outsiders will see the formal, proper, and reserved dealings known to emanate from their Spanish/European roots. It is important that appointments be set well in advance, and confirmed in writing. Titles are used if the title is known and when those in superior positions are addressed, their title is followed by their last name—Licenciado (for a man with a university degree), Ingeniero (engineer), and Doctor (advanced degree or a lawyer) are all commonly used titles. A welcome and courteous gesture is to possess bilingual business cards in Spanish and English.

Executives and professionals in Peru often speak English, so although this is not a necessity, it will show respect and consideration of their culture. Negotiations may advance slowly, which is yet more evidence of the characteristic European self-discipline. This allows Peruvians to feel comfortable with a prospective business partner on an individual as well as corporate basis. Personal trust and confidence are hard to win with Peruvians, but are long-lasting.

Box 3.3   Country Profile 3—Peru
Source: Going Global, *Country Export Issues* (2004)

Shell has made many promises, including gifts, compensation, and the replanting of trees, yet have not extracted one drop of gas from the ground. The Peruvian government, willing to deal with Shell Oil again, believed that a compromise could be met. The obstacle for Shell remains the local people and vocal environmentalists. The tactics of Shell hiring Peruvian experts and lawyers to assure the people that minimal damage will be caused leaves these groups unconvinced. Without the support of the local groups, petitions and protests are destined to hold up the Peruvian government's ability to approve Shell's plan to drill oil. Eventually, after over 12 years of negotiation, research, and investments, Peru and Shell ended their relationship in July of 1998. With preliminary work amounting to over 250 million dollars from Shell's pocket, the project has amounted to a huge disappointment. What is seen as the largest oil reserve in America will go untapped due to the failure to strike a balance between the multinational Shell Oil Company and the government of Peru. Peruvian law put a stop to what was seen as "the contract of the century." It is felt that the pricing means proposed for gas used in electricity plants would have broken laws, which govern the power industry. Peru's Finance Minister, Jorge Baca, felt there were irreconcilable differences over distribution, the price of gas for generating electricity, and exports. Shell Oil and the gas industry do not only feel the loss; Peru is reeling from the effects of the failed pact. This was seen as their largest foreign investment, the development of industries, bringing over 6,000 jobs alone to the drilling operations.

A traumatic impact on the Peruvian economy and the loss of foreign investment was not enough incentive for this deal to go through. Even though the results would amount to prosperity, the violation of their own laws closed the doors between Peru and Shell.

Gerber and Poland

When Gerber agreed to purchase a struggling food manufacturing plant in the growing market of Poland, they did not foresee the government changing hands within months of striking a deal. Gerber's goal of expanding into the European market, introducing packaged, safe, baby food products, became possible with the purchase of the government-owned Alima packing plant. Paying out 11 million dollars in hard currency for ownership, Gerber felt they had successfully entered the market. Because Gerber signed a Purchase and Sale agreement, formally committing to the deal while promising to work with the government on property ownership and taxation issues, it seemed that the issues would be resolved within months and the sale could continue without a hitch.

Intervening in the Gerber purchase from the government of Poland, surprisingly, was the government of Poland. Poland's first democratic election, which took place within a month of the Gerber deal, forced control of the country from a solidarity state to more of a communist regime. While Poland had been witnessing vast economic reform from government-owned business to a more capitalistic market structure, it was possible that the country could revert to government-controlled firms. With a signed agreement on the table, Gerber was committed to the deal and committed to the new government, which promised to be stricter and was unable to deliver promises of the past government control. What seemed for Gerber to be a solid entry into the European market, and sound foreign investment, was turning into more of a gamble, not knowing what the future had in store. The evolution of the Polish environment could prove costly for a multinational company in the country. Losing control of their plant and not being fully compensated were just a few of the risks.

Gerber was left with two choices: to struggle through and stick with the original plan or to abort the plan due to fear of total loss and failure. By aborting the plan, Gerber would not be able to enter the European market, as it had planned for years. It would be impossible for Gerber to attempt to ignore the risk that was at hand with the new government. The Polish government might not comply with the contract laws and commitments, and this might force Gerber to re-bid for the plant, which they had already committed to purchase. That which Gerber felt they had already owned might be taken from them without recourse.

Gerber's final decision was to maintain its original plan, demonstrating that the opportunity outweighed the risk. The usual risks involved with enterprising into foreign markets did not apply to Gerber here. The obstacle encountered by Gerber is highly unlikely and mostly unforeseeable. Transition in governmental control is possible in many countries that contain several powerful political parties, and the risk of one losing control of the government is a risk that can be discovered.

The obstacles experienced by the multinational companies reviewed are both common and uncommon. The violations of antitrust laws between Coke and France, and the environmental concerns of Peru regarding Shell Oil are typical concerns when companies move to multinational. The control of piracy in another country's borders and the transition of government in a country like Poland are fears a company cannot always forecast, yet they feel the impact of these changes. The use of such cases illustrates that barriers may not always be visible and that all possibilities need to be explored before any attempt is made to expand outside the domain of the United States or any other home countries.

Poles are very formal and therefore it is beneficial to plan well in advance of a business trip, giving the Polish company ample notice. This formality can be seen in government and state organizations, where the employees often do not take a lunch break. It is customary to greet a Pole by shaking hands. In business, a woman should not be offended if a Polish man kisses her hand during an introduction, consequent meetings, or upon saying goodbye. Men wear a suit and tie at business meetings and women wear a skirt and blouse or dress.

Business cards are generally given to each person at the meeting, and since the Polish tend to bring more than one person to their meetings, when doing business in Poland it is wise to bring a good supply of one's business cards. Unlike some other countries, it is not necessary that the cards bear the Polish language. Titles carry prestige in Poland. In the past, a title represented a Pole's nobility or status as a landowner. More recently, a title refers to one's academic achievement, his or her profession, or administrative position. Once a person's title is known, it is used, especially in work situations, on formal occasions, and in any written communication. Gift-giving for business or a special occasion is appropriate and common gifts are candy, flowers, and liquor. It is considered bad luck to give flowers in even numbers, so if giving flowers, ensure that you give them singly or in odd numbers.

Box 3.4   Country Profile 4—Poland
Source: Going Global, *Country Export Issues* (2004)

Influence of MNEs in the Developing Countries

As MNEs continue to spread across the world, they have begun to influence developing countries largely. MNEs control the power of technology, which has adversely affected many cultures and societies. These problems are seen all over the world from the US to China. MNEs along with government and politics have a close tie in many countries. For example, in 1993, the US-based Hoover Corporation, a producer of household appliances, planned to move a plant with 600 jobs from France to Scotland. The French were furious and the British government was forced to get involved. MNEs usually play by the rules of their "home country" government, which poses a problem much of the time (Vernon, 1995).

For example, during the mid-1950s, the Central Intelligence Agency (CIA) supported local forces to overthrow the Mohammed Mossadegh regime in Iran and Jacobo Arbenz in Guatemala. In 1973, the CIA also aided locals in destabilizing the Chilean government, which was overseen by Salvador Allende. Some MNEs were seen "cheering" from the sidelines, so to speak.

Situations such as those above demonstrate how strong MNEs' home-country governments can interfere in the internal affairs of neighboring countries (Vernon, 1995). Many governments use manipulation, putting governments in a position to influence MNEs. MNEs often have to dissuade their home-country governments from taking action against other countries. This was the case in the 1960s and 1970s when MNEs sought to persuade the US government not to take drastic measures against Peru for nationalization of US-owned oil properties and its seizure of US-owned fishing boats. The US also played a role in quarrels with Japan's Toshiba Corporation. Toshiba was selling illegal military technology to the Soviet Navy. Political scientists believe that situations as discussed above are not the result of MNEs. They believe MNEs can only be of marginal influence since governments are generally guided by the nation's best interest. This statement poses two problems. First, MNEs are not an inconsequential force in international economic relations. Second, MNEs pursue their business interests and not those of the host country (Vernon, 1995).

The governments have sensed the need for some redefinition of rights and responsibilities of MNEs. In the 1970s, governments throughout the world had nationalized foreign-owned oil fields and mines. In 1976, the Organization for Economic Cooporation and Development (OECD) was established to create a set of standards to which governments and enterprises needed to adhere (Vernon, 1995).

International agreements affecting MNEs have been numerous, but these have been typically confined to relatively narrow issues. For example, governments have negotiated hundreds of bilateral treaties designed to prevent double taxation of corporate profits as well as numerous other agreements intended to ensure non-discriminatory treatment of subsidiaries in foreign countries.

While there are numerous horror stories of MNEs overtaking developing countries, there are also examples of MNEs helping countries. For example, the Chinese government is opening up China to foreign investors, little by little. China is no longer the "iron rice bowl," which is a Chinese phrase referring to the system of guaranteed lifetime employment in state enterprises. The Chinese government used to be more concerned with how foreign companies affected the bottom lines of the government. Now, the Chinese government is more concerned with what foreign companies bring into China in terms of jobs, technology, and foreign exchange. The desire and need for technology in China is the main reason the government has loosened its "iron-fist." However, foreign firms are somewhat reluctant to give away more proprietary knowledge of technology than is necessary to their Chinese business partners, for fear that it will be copied. This is particularly important due to China's reputation of not enforcing intellectual property rights (Vanhonacker, 1999).

One of the largest home bases for MNEs is the United States. The United States plays a huge role in developments, and no new international regime relating to MNEs is likely to emerge if the US government is not involved. This is because the United States government is highly active in any international economic issue. Governments constantly have to decide whether a proposed international agreement will best serve their national interests. Governments regulate everything from cross-border liability and border taxes, to the capital structure. The need for this regulation is to control MNEs from dominating countries. This is why government intervention is very important; government intervention takes into account what is good for the host country and if an MNE would benefit the country.

The Demand for Skilled International Managers

As the need for global managers increases, a list of qualities an international manager must possess is starting to take shape. The overwhelming quality is the ability to deal with uncertainty and change. Effective global leaders should enjoy the challenge of ambiguity.

Below are a few of the qualities it is suggested that a global manager possess:

- Ability to handle complexity and uncertainty
- Ability to relate well with diverse groups of people
- Good listening skills
- Good communication skills
- Ability to think "outside the box"
- Acceptance that there is more than one way to do something
- Willingness and desire to travel
- Ability to deal with complex information
- Ability to deal with multiple languages
- Willingness and desire to relocate to another country for at least three years.

In addition, in an international organization, companies are subjected to multinational risks. The concept of risk management includes examining all exposures of possible calculated loss, and subsequently, establishing how to manage those exposures. Once a company identifies the risks, the process of risk management endeavors to lessen their effects. It does this by employing a range of management techniques, such as avoiding, reducing, or transferring the risk, usually with insurance. This process of identifying, managing, and eliminating indeterminate events that may affect system resources is a necessity to international managers when faced with mergers, acquisitions, and joint ventures.

For an international management career, the global economy means that a manager will have to deal with nationally and culturally diverse teams, understand foreign competitors, and spend more time studying the culture, politics, and operating style of the global economy.

The Future and Multinational Enterprises

The big issue for multinationals today is how to tailor the global marketing concept to fit each business. Companies must consider their objectives through all phases of their business. When determining whether to standardize a product or keep it similar to the domestic version, several conditions must be taken into account. It is possible that the product is beneficial to the host-country customers just as it is in the home country. However, some products must be changed for cultural or functional reasons. For example, many packages from the United States must be altered to include measurements in metric units before being shipped out of the country to many countries in Europe and Asia. In addition, a number of products suffer if there are changes of certain types. For example, colors of logos may prove offensive to foreign consumers; however, the product would not be recognizable without those colors. Not only should the product be considered, but also, when a product is altered, it changes the entire marketing mix. Moreover, these variables may change from one country to the next, which leaves hundreds of possibilities.

In order to stay competitive, multinational corporations will have to enter the emerging markets of China, Indonesia, India, and Brazil, where a vast consumer base is rapidly developing. As powerful corporations compete in these markets, both the companies and the markets themselves will be affected (Rugman and Hodgetts, 1998). The transformation that multinationals must undergo includes reconfiguring their resources base, rethinking their cost structure, redesigning their product development process, and challenging their assumptions about the cultural mix of their top-level managers.

There is evidence that globalization is the wave of the future. Today, most multinational corporations are subsidiaries of strong domestic companies. However, these companies will have to develop more to rely on than name recognition in the twenty-first century. In order to take full advantage of all markets available, multinational corporations will have to become global corporations (Hale, 1998). This includes expanding to a larger number of countries and taking advantage of the possibilities that exist there. All of this takes time and money, but globalization is becoming a more pertinent decision for the future. The difference between being "multinational" and "global" is that a "global" company has a product/service that is acceptable in many countries around the world. A "multinational" company has subsidiaries in certain countries developing products and/or services for specific countries. Although the difference may seem small, the changes for multinational corporations to global corporations will be drastic. In becoming globally integrated, companies must balance the tension between the headquarters and the almost equally powerful subsidiaries. They must focus their functions specifically to the subsidiary while keeping attention on the organizational objectives.

The globalization of business still has a long way to go, but in the future, corporations will have to become global enterprises operating under worldwide rules and regulation following a global code of conduct. One thing that will help this globalization phase is the advancement of technology. The Internet has already introduced a number of people to companies that they will never visit in person. This expands a corporation's market by thousands of consumers. In addition, video-conferencing makes negotiations between companies in different countries much more feasible. There is less travel involved and it provides a more productive means of communication with minimal cost.

The only complication in relying on technology is that not all countries are technologically advanced or compatible. As time progresses, more countries will become so, but for the time being, technology is a privilege that not many countries have. An MNE must consider the choice of country and the access to technology that the business may have. This may influence where the company chooses to become involved. A manager must keep updated on the changes in technology in all countries in which they are involved, or are planning to becoming involved.

Conclusion

Multinational enterprises are by no means a new phenomenon. For decades there have been companies that have taken advantage of the economies of scales and cheaper production costs. However, the impact of these types of corporations has become more evident. Competing in what is becoming a more global society starts with becoming a multinational enterprise.

Expanding into new markets is always costly and dangerous, but in a multinational environment, the risks are even more numerous. Different cultures, customs, and ways of doing business all influence the transactions between the two countries. A marketing strategy must be formulated for each different product/service for each different country. Although it may be costly, some companies can benefit beyond measure from these endeavors.

There are many reasons that a corporation may decide to become a multinational enterprise. Taking advantage of economies of scale, locating new resources, and capturing new markets are just a few. All of these are focused on one main organizational goal: earning profit.

Overall, multinational enterprises are taking an increasingly important role in the world economy. They have great financial and technological resources, seasoned management, and powerful brands. Tailoring the global marketing concept to fit each business may not be easy, but in doing that, multinationals are guaranteed success.

Case Study

Lincoln Electric's Harsh Lessons from International Expansion

MNEs are a special breed. They are large, well funded, and very ambitious. Many MNEs make the mistake of trying to force their home-country culture, philosophies, and operations management to their foreign subsidiaries abroad. Forcing their home-country values and beliefs is often viewed as beneficial to the host country, which is true in some cases. However, in most cases forcing home-country culture can have disastrous results.

Take the example of Lincoln Electric Company, a US-based manufacturer of business and consumer arc-welding machines. Lincoln was extremely successful in the US (# 1 in the domestic market). After experiencing the US recession of the early 1980s, Lincoln decided to make their company a global one in order to weather future US recessions. From 1986 to 1991, Lincoln invested heavily in foreign markets: Japan, Venezuela, Brazil, Germany, Norway, Britain, the Netherlands, Spain, Australia, Canada and Mexico. Lincoln assumed that their very successful US operations guaranteed them success anywhere in the world. Lincoln management teams saw great opportunities to reduce costs by applying their manufacturing expertise, equipment, and incentive system. Much to Lincoln's dismay, the European culture was very much set against the incentive system of piecework. Because of Lincoln's hasty decisions and incompatible culture, the company was losing money for the first time in its 97-year history (Hastings, 1999).

Another sore spot of Lincoln's global expansion was due to inexperienced international managers. As Lincoln CEO, Donald Hastings (1999) put it, "Our managers didn't know how to run foreign operations; nor did they understand foreign cultures. Consequently, we had to rely on people in our foreign companies who we didn't know and who didn't know us." Before 1993, Lincoln's head of European operations had never even taken the initiative to relocate in Europe for any substantial length of time. Several of Lincoln's international executive officers did not even have passports. Lincoln had a tradition of promoting top line executives from within. It became glaringly important for Lincoln to hire new managers with international knowledge. Lincoln realized that they had reached the limits of their management styles and skills. Lincoln's domestic management skills had enabled the company to prosper but they were not up to international standards.

Lincoln's executives could not understand why their foreign subsidiaries were failing. When Hastings traveled to visit the European facilities, he was shocked at what he saw. During an unannounced visit to Lincoln's German facility, Hastings observed three employees sleeping on the job. Even with Lincoln's piece-rate incentive and sizeable bonus, the German workers did not respond. This was unfathomable to the Lincoln executives. After all, the piece-rate incentive raised US workers pay by nearly 50 per cent of their annual salary. Hundreds of the US workers have made $70,000–80,000 in a year and some as high as $100,000, allowing them to be among the highest paid "factory workers" in the world (Hastings, 1999). Lincoln executives researched their piece-rate incentive system and found that it was most easily transferred to countries that were settled by immigrants. Immigrant-settled countries have hard work and upward mobility ingrained in their society and culture.

At Lincoln's German facility, the average workweek was 35 hours. In contrast, the average workweek in Lincoln's US plants was 43–58 hours per week. The fact remained, the incentive system required workers to stay for longer periods and work on short notices. Europeans seemed to lack the flexibility needed to prosper under the piece-rate incentive system (Hastings, 1999, p. 164).

Lincoln's Japanese plants were not fairing much better than the European ones. Much thought had been put into the construction of the Japanese plants. Lincoln went as far as having the plant blessed in a Shinto ceremony (religious ceremony). Virtually none of the Japanese would buy the American products because the Japanese felt "insulted" by the American firm not having the decency to invest with a Japanese partner (Hastings, 1999, p. 180).

Before making the foreign acquisitions, Lincoln had cash reserves of nearly $70 million and zero debt. By 1992, their debt soared to 63 per cent of their total equity. Something had to be done to save Lincoln from sinking. Lincoln decided to shut down the very unprofitable operations in Japan, Germany, Brazil, and Venezuela to avoid further losses. The closures were the first in the company's history. Hastings headed up a training and goal-setting session with the remaining European operations. The US employees trained the Europeans in assertive sales and marketing techniques. Lincoln thought that the training and goal-setting had gone well. To their surprise, the European goals were never met. The Europeans had a tendency to overestimate revenues and underestimate expenses. The poor budgeting enraged Hastings. He later found out that it was standard practice for European firms to be optimistic about operating budgets instead of realistic. Lincoln felt they could never light a "fire under the bellies" of the European management (Hastings, 1999, p. 168).

Lincoln did not want to downsize in the US. They felt downsizing would drastically affect workers' morale. Hastings could not bring himself to make cuts in the US workforce because he knew many of the workers and their families. Hastings regarded his employees as resources not liabilities. Hastings was forced to call upon his American workforce to bail out the company for the mistakes it had made abroad. Lincoln made videotapes for the employees to take home to their families. The tape explained the reasons for their financial predicament. They admitted to their mistakes and asked the American workers to work harder than they ever had before (Hastings, 1999, p. 168).

The American employees responded very well to Lincoln's need for increased output. Hiring new employees reduced bottlenecks; however, new employees can take as long as two to three years to learn to run some of the more complex machinery properly. With the great number of new employees, the veterans were asked to postpone vacations and work on holidays. Overall, 450 employees sacrificed 614 weeks of vacation for the sake of the company. Some people worked seven days a week for months on end. The hard work paid off and the output goals were achieved. The record output combined with the foreign closings was enough to get the company in the black within a year's time (Hastings, 1999, pp. 180–81).

Eventually, Lincoln was able to change a few of their foreign subsidiaries' business practices for the better. Lincoln's European plants had a very large presence at a European trade show. Traditionally, the exhibitors used the eight-day event as a vehicle to entertain customers and for public relations opportunities. The company had never used the trade show as a vehicle for making sales. There were no laws or rules against selling, but tradition prevented it. In Lincoln's view, it did not make any sense to spend a couple of million dollars on a trade show and not use it to gain desperately needed sales. Desperate times called for desperate measures. Lincoln flew three plane-loads of product to Europe. The objective was to sell 1,200 units of semi-automatic welding equipment. With much hard work and many strange looks, 1,762 units were sold during the span of the eight-day trade show. Finally, conventional American wisdom and perseverance paid off for Lincoln (Hastings, 1999, p. 170).

Case Questions

1. What was Lincoln's strategy for overseas expansion?
2. How would you evaluate Lincoln's management structure?
3. What circumstances surrounded Lincoln's decision to expand?
4. What changes would you recommend for Lincoln at the time it decided to expand?
5. How does culture influence entry mode and international strategy?
6. How does a host country's culture influence organizational culture and the effectiveness of management?

Chapter Review

Multinational enterprises are becoming stronger and more prevalent each year. MNEs have many of the same activities and functions that ordinary non-multinational enterprise companies have. MNEs are entities that have operations in a home country, where the headquarters is based, and one or more host countries. An MNE establishes operations in a host country only when it brings with it some firm-specific advantages that more than offset the advantages that the host-country firms have. Although the operations may be located in different countries, the company is one company because of the ownership.

Multinational enterprises need to have good relationships with their home countries. The home government remains important to the MNE. Relationships between governments in the home and host countries are an important issue facing MNEs. The political objectives in the host country involve favorable trade and investment for the host country, ready access to markets, lessened regulatory hurdles, legitimacy of the business and other local government objectives.

If you hire a host-country local into an upper level management position, it may enhance your company's image in the host country. It is important when hiring a host-country local that they are loyal to the company. Host-country locals may not understand the typical corporate culture of the US or other home countries' companies; they may do things very differently in their companies.

MNEs often help the economy of the host country. MNEs bring advanced technology to poorer countries and low-cost products to the wealthier ones. MNEs, along with the home-country government and political arena, have a close tie with their host countries. MNEs usually play by the rules of their "home-country" government. While MNEs may overtake developing countries, there are also examples of MNEs helping countries. The need for regulations arises to control MNEs from dominating countries. This is why government intervention is very important. Government intervention takes into account what is good for the host country and if an MNE would benefit the country.

The profit and income flows that MNEs generate are part of the foreign capital flows moving between countries, which increase economic growth and development for all parties involved. The increasingly free movement of capital allows corporations to transfer production without regard to national boundaries to wherever costs are low. Some of the most important benefits of MNEs are significant job additions in the local economy, and training and education for local employees, thus creating a higher skilled labor force, which in turn may transfer to other areas of the host country. In addition, MNEs will contribute tax revenue to the government and other local revenues if they purchase existing national assets. Generally, some of the disadvantages of MNEs are home and host employees adapting to the other's culture, loyalty to the home company, and training costs.

Today, most multinational corporations are subsidiaries of strong domestic companies. MNEs are the key actors in the world economy and globalization process. The structure and dynamics of the global economy rely on this economic integration process in our contemporary world.

Chapter Questions

1. Discuss the characteristics and functions of a multinational enterprise.
2. Discuss the stages companies usually go through to become global.
3. Explain the importance of MNEs in terms of international trade, technology transfer, and foreign direct investment.
4. Explain the nature of multinational enterprises and their role in the globalization process.
5. What are the challenges of working in countries whose legal systems are different from that of the MNE's home country?
6. What levels of influence and control should an MNE be concerned with?
7. How do laws regarding competition, product liability, and the like affect the MNE's operations and competitive advantage.

Chapter 4

The Impact of Economics and the International Monetary Framework on International Management

The international manager's knowledge of economics and the monetary framework plays an important role in a multinational enterprise. Knowledge of these functions is important because the economy in each country is constantly changing. To make decisions in the rapidly changing global economy, managers need to have background knowledge of key economic and monetary fundamentals, and how these fundamentals affect multinational corporations.

International managers need to have a global economic perspective and the ability to learn its trends. These managers need the ability to be able to decide which project in one country is more important than in another country. Furthermore, international managers have to know how to reduce delivery costs to take advantage of economies of scale and reduced transport costs and tariffs. They also have to know how to substitute lower cost foreign suppliers and reduce delivery costs. Similarly, managers need to have an understanding of changing economies and the implications of this change for the strategy and operations performance of their business.

In a market system, individuals or organizations trade in order to benefit or realize profit from the exchange. As a result, trading occurs in nations as well as among regions within a given country. Trading among nations involves the Foreign Exchange Market (FEM). The FEM is a network of financial institutions around the world. The FEM facilitates trade and assists international businesses by buying and selling (trading) foreign exchange. The foreign exchange rate, also known as the international exchange rate, is the value of one country's currency in terms of another country's currency. This section will discuss the origins of money, monetary systems, monetary issues, and the measures of value of the economy. An international manager must have basic knowledge of how the following key fundamentals affect an economy in relation to the multinational corporation.

Money Supply

Money is any medium universally accepted in an economy both by sellers of goods and services as payment for those goods and services and by creditors as payment for debts. Money is an asset that accounts for part of personal wealth; money by definition is the most liquid of any asset there is.

The United States has a fiduciary monetary system because its money is not convertible to a fixed quantity of a commodity such as gold or silver. In a system such as this, in which the government issues money, the currency's value is based on what the public believes the currency represents. Changes in the total money supply, and changes in the rate at which the money supply increases or decreases, affect important economic variables such as the rate of inflation, interest rates, employment, and the equilibrium level of real national income.

An example of money supplies gone wrong happened to Indonesia during the 1990s, when its currency lost over 80 per cent of its value, its banking system was seriously shaken, businesses shut their doors, and foreign capital packed up and went home. To get the country back on its feet, the government increased its global integration into foreign markets. Indonesia allowed international capital to move in and out freely. New private banks were allowed to open, and reserve requirements were minimized.

More and more of the world's earnings depend on foreign trade. Indeed, international exchanges have exploded; at least $1.5 billion worth of goods is traded each day. Widening market opportunities are for international integration to increase its economic dynamism and to lead to faster income growth. As shown by the Indonesia example, the benefits of foreign trade are not only limited to rich, developed countries; it can also benefit developing countries. In recent years, even China, a non-free market has received a third of all direct foreign investment in developing countries.

Historical and Current Monetary Systems

The history of credit and banking goes back much further than the history of coins, while the origin of money goes back even further. To discuss the current monetary system, one needs an understanding of the origin of money. Many items have been used as currency or money over time. Items such as rice, amber, beads, eggs, vodka, ivory, and even feathers have been used for money. Knowing this, it is nearly impossible to define money in terms of its physical properties. It is, however, more practical to define money on its functions. The several functions on how money is used worldwide are as follows:

- Unit of account
- Common measure of value
- Medium of exchange
- Means of payment
- Standard for deferred payments
- Store of value
- Liquid asset
- Framework of the market allocative system
- A contributing economic factor
- Financial manager of the economy.

Money originated largely from non-economic causes such as tribute, as well as from trade, bride-money, ceremonial, and religious rites and barter. In a practical sense, a spark for the development of money was purely economic, thus that resulted in bartering. As Glyn Davies (2002) states, archeological, scholarly, and linguistic evidence of the ancient world and the tangible evidence of actual types of primitive money from many countries demonstrates that barter was not the main factor in the origins and earliest development of money. Thus, the use of money evolved out of deeply rooted customs and the clumsiness of barter that provided an economic impulse (Davies, 2002).

Primitive Forms of Money

The use of primitive forms of money in the developing world and North America is more recently and better documented than in Europe and its study sheds light on the probable origins of modern money. For example, manillas were ornamental metallic objects worn as jewelry in West Africa and used as money as recently as 1949. In Fijian society, gifts of whale's teeth were a significant feature of certain ceremonies. The potlatch ceremonies of Native Americans were a form of barter that had social and ceremonial functions that were at least as important as its economic functions (Davies, 2002). Even after the invention of coins, the use of commodities as means of exchange continued in some societies for hundreds of years (Davies, 2002).

Figure 4.1a Primitive Forms of Money—Katanga or "Wife Buying" Cross

These crosses were made of copper mined in the Katanga region of the Congo. Their principal use as currency was in making part payment of the "bride-price" or dowry.

Figure 4.1b Primitive Forms of Money—Manilla

Open bronze rings called "manillas" were in use as money along the west coast of Africa as late as the mid 1900s.

Global Business Management

Figure 4.1c Primitive Forms of Money—Pu (Spade Money)

Bronze cast in the shape of miniature household tools and farm implements became a widely accepted form of Chinese currency as early as the tenth century BC. Some of these metallic pieces were still in use in the second century AD.

Figure 4.1d Primitive Forms of Money—Shell Arm Ring

Multiple–strand arm rings made from the shells of giant clams were widely used as Currency in the Solomon Islands.

Source: Federal Reserve Bank of Richmond. Retrieved July 7, 2004 from http://www.rich. frb.org/research/econed/museum/1a.html.

The History of the United States Monetary System

For most of the history of Western civilization, silver rather than gold has been the principal means of payment/standard of value. As Ben Best states,

> The United States used bimetallism beginning with the Coinage Act of 1792. Gresham's Law states that when two or more media of exchange are being used, one that is legally or otherwise overvalued will drive the others off the market. At first gold coins were driven-off the market until gold discoveries, several decades later, reversed the process and drove silver coins off the market (Best, 1990).

In 1821, Britain became the first country to adopt a gold standard, and other countries followed beginning in the 1870s. A gold standard, as an international monetary structure, was most inclusive from the mid-1890s until 1914. This was a time of powerful economic activity and international trade. In the 1880s, iron ore doubled in production, redoubled in the 1890s and again doubled by 1910. Due to the war in the 1920s, many countries went off the gold standard to help finance the war effort. Nonetheless, in the interest of "economizing," most nations in the 1920s adopted a "gold-exchange standard" based on a limited reserve of gold for their country.

By the 1930s, there was a common belief that the gold standard was not working. Many countries suspended gold convertibility and made gold ownership illegal for their citizens. Trying to replace aggressive nationalist monetary policies with deliberate international monetary cooperation, 44 nations met in Bretton Woods, New Hampshire. The International Monetary Fund (IMF) was established in July of 1944 and began operations in June 1946. The IMF was designed to promote international monetary cooperation, produce international monetary stability through a system of fixed exchanged rates to be supported by loans from the Fund, and to facilitate the development and growth of international trade. It established a multilateral system of payments, and shortened the duration and lessened the degree of disequilibria in the international balances of payments of members. The IMF will be discussed further in the International Monetary System section below.

European Monetary Union (EMU)

A special case in international monetary and financial markets is the European Monetary Union (EMU). During the Madrid European Council (in the composition of Heads of State or Government) on December 15 and 16, 1995, the scenario for the changeover to the single currency in Europe was adopted. It was then confirmed unequivocally that this stage would commence in 1999. The European Council meeting in Madrid decided to name the currency the "Euro." (A unique name, the same in all the official languages of the European Union, taking into account the existence of different alphabets and able to symbolize Europe.) It was also confirmed that January 1999 would be the starting date for Stage Three of the Economic and Monetary Union, in accordance with the convergence criteria and procedures laid down in the Treaty of Maastricht, that entered into force on November 1, 1993.

The implementation of the EMU has followed a three-stage process:

Stage One (1990–94). This stage began July 1, 1990. Regulations hindering the free movement of capital were eliminated. There was some increase in the coordination of economic policy, with closer discussions between the member states based on convergence programs in which the countries described economic developments. The central banks also stepped up their cooperation during this period.

Stage Two (1994–98). This stage commenced January 1, 1994, when the European Monetary Institute (EMI) was established. The purpose of the EMI was to take measures in tandem with the national central banks in the EU countries to prepare for the common monetary policy and the activities of the European Central Bank (ECB). The EMI also supervised EU exchange rate cooperation in the Exchange Rate Mechanism (ERM). On June 1, 1998, the EMI was replaced by the ECB and cooperation between the member states' central banks continued under a new system designated the European System of Central Banks (ESCB). During this stage, the member states were further required to implement necessary changes in their national legislation, one major purpose being to make their central banks more independent. The effect of these legislative changes is to prohibit the central banks from requesting or accepting instructions from the governments of the member states, the EU institutions or any other body, in the performance of their duties. In addition, member states' economic policies came under enhanced monitoring to ensure that their public finances were sound. To this end, and notably to ensure greater fiscal judiciousness, at the Amsterdam Summit in 1997, the decision was taken to establish the Stability and Growth Pact, which entered into force the following year and was somewhat revised in 2005, which characterized Stage Three of the EMU and economic policy overall in Europe.

In Brussels in May 1998, the heads of state and government determined that 11 countries met the necessary conditions for membership of the monetary union. These countries were Belgium, Germany, Spain, France, Ireland, Italy, Luxembourg, the Netherlands, Austria, Portugal, and Finland. Sweden, Denmark, and the UK have not introduced the Euro. In particular, on examination in May 1998, Sweden was not considered to meet all the conditions, since the Riksbank Act was not compatible with the Treaty and the krona had not been sufficiently stable in relation to other EU currencies. (However, the year before, the Swedish Riksbank had taken the position that Sweden would not take part in the monetary union from the outset.) Denmark and the UK kept purposely out of the Euro.

Stage Three (1999–). This stage started on January 1, 1999 and brought to the establishment of the monetary union the part of the process that most people associate with EMU. This stage began the irrevocable fixing of conversion rates among the currencies of participating countries and against the Euro, and it was at this point that the Euro was designated the common currency of the 11 members of the monetary union. From that date, monetary policy and foreign exchange rate policy were conducted in Euros, and the use of the Euro was encouraged in foreign exchange markets and the participating member states issued a new tradable public debt in Euros. By January 1, 2002, Euro banknotes and coins were circulating alongside national notes and coins. The dual circulation period ended on February 28, 2002, when the national currencies were completely replaced by the Euro. Thereafter, national banknotes and coins were still exchanged at the national central banks. In fact, as from March 1, 2002, the Euro is the sole legal tender in the countries participating in the monetary union. In addition to the decision taken at the afore-mentioned Brussels 1998 meeting, not until June 2000 was it decided that Greece fulfilled the criteria for membership of the monetary union, thus Greece subsequently joined the monetary union on January 1, 2001, becoming its 12th member, while the European Central Bank (ECB) took over responsibility for monetary policy from the national central banks.

Clearly, the Euro simplified operations of some businesses that interact with EMU participants and eliminated the need for many currency-risk protections such as option and forward contracts in those currencies. Of course, the elimination of the need for these services will adversely affect the financial intermediaries that offer these services, such as banks. US money centers may also find their status as leading financial markets sliding in the event that the Euro edges out the US dollar as the dominant international currency.

As for the concept of time consistency in monetary policy, Sergi (1998), using the Bohn (1991) time consistency model of monetary policy, calculated the external component of inflationary incentives of nine European countries. Sergi's research adds up domestic and external incentives to analyze the European economics during the 1980s and 1990s and shows that we must allow for external incentives in the formulation of economic strategy. Both the 1980s economic recession and the early European Monetary System (EMS) troubles in the 1990s may explain why countries were resetting their "fundamentals" before standing for the single currency. At first sight, it would appear that countries were resetting their fundamentals before standing for a common currency. Two facts become apparent. First, the EMS fluctuation band was enlarged to ± 15 per cent; second, the deadline for a single currency (stage III of EMU) was postponed to a time frame set not before 1999 as agreed at the 1995 ECOFIN summit and the Cannes meeting. These facts relied on the widespread perception that the policy of readjustment then needed a much longer time and the least economic constraints (Sergi, 1998). Note that the ECOFIN Council is comprised of the Economics and Finance Ministers of the EU member states.

Background of the European Monetary Union

The origins of the monetary union date back to the 1960s, when the Europeans were seeking to respond to changes in the international monetary system. In 1970, Pierre Werner produced a well-known report that was intended as a blueprint for monetary union in Europe, and it was based on a three-stage process to be achieved within a decade. Besides requirements for fixing exchange rates and implementing free mobility of capital, the first stage would ensure that the economic infrastructure was suitable and could prepare the way for institutional progress. The second stage would build on the economic and institutional developments of the first. The third stage would be the irreversible fixing of exchange rates and possibly the implementation of a single currency.

Despite delays, the EMS was set up was set up on December 5, 1978 and its operating procedures were agreed on March 13, 1979 between the central banks of the member states of the European Economic Community. The objective was to prompt monetary policy cooperation between Community countries, leading to a zone of monetary stability in Europe. It ceased to exist on January 1, 1999, when the Euro was introduced, and was replaced by ERM-II (for a detailed analysis, see Jovanovic, 2005). The 1980s saw further progress towards monetary union and the Delors Report (1989) gave the impetus and the finalization of the monetary union culminating in the Maastricht Treaty or Treaty on European Union. (Note that although the Treaty is mostly on the monetary union, it also includes two other main pillars of the European Union, that is, defense and foreign policy, and justice and home affairs.) The policy was signed in Maastricht on February 7, 1992, with an effective date of November 1, 1993, in which the plan put forward was very similar to the original Werner proposals. The establishment of a single currency zone was conceived and five economic criteria were required to be eligible for Euro monetary qualification. The five Maastricht Treaty criteria, which we can assume as partially arbitrary, are as follows:

1. An inflation rate within the margin of 1.5 per cent of the three best performing EU countries
2. Long-term interest rate levels within 3 per cent of the three best performing EU countries in terms of price stability
3. A budget deficit of less than 3 per cent of GDP
4. A public debt of less than 60 per cent of GDP
5. No devaluation within the EU exchange rate mechanism for at least two preceding years.

However, these criteria have been applied in a rather relaxed way, especially as concerns the level of debt over GDP criterion. The Treaty stated that the final eligibility to the Euro zone had to take into account good progress on this issue made by the country toward convergence in case a country failed one or two conditions. The Euro itself was launched on January 1, 1999, irrevocably fixing their exchange rates, and subsequently the ECU (the official accounting unit of the EU until the end of 1998, a basket currency made up of the sum of fixed amounts of the twelve national currencies of the member states of the EU) ceased to exist and national currencies were replaced by the Euro. On January 1, 2002, the Euro currency became the common currency of the following 12 countries:

1. Austria
2. Belgium
3. Finland
4. France
5. Germany
6. Greece
7. Ireland
8. Italy
9. Luxembourg
10. The Netherlands
11. Portugal
12. Spain.

Note that the creation of the European Central Bank in Frankfurt, which is at the heart of the EMU, has created the basis for having a sole issuer of the Euro with the main objectives of overseeing the Euro as a common currency, ensuring price stability, and reducing uncertainties and conflicts over national monetary policies among the countries in the Euro zone. In addition, it has the power to set short-term interest rates in order to meet its objectives. National central banks in Europe remain and are set to continue playing important roles. Starting in January 2007, Slovenia became the 13th member country of the Euro zone. This is the first country among the ten new EU members to adopt the Euro after the acceptance by the European Commission and final approval by the European Parliament; after that, the Council of EU economic and finance ministers of the member states (the so-called

ECOFIN council) fixed the exchange rate between the Euro and the Slovene tolar. The Euro finally became legal tender and this was the first country to adopt a "big bang" scenario characterized by the absence of any transitional period. (Note that Lithuania was denied membership by the European Commission due to an inflation rate above the current target for inflation.) It is also worth mentioning that while new EU members were strongly aspiring to join the Euro area as soon as possible, there is emerging now among these same countries a propensity to rethink the hasty Euro adoption that they had manifested in 2004; yet, it is likely now that other candidates for the Euro area will follow Slovenia by the end of this decade or so.

Besides monetary policy in Europe, individual governments retain control of fiscal policy, although governments are expected to keep national deficit and debt within the guidelines of the Maastricht Treaty, and countries willing to adopt the Euro must comply with economic performance criteria, set out in the Maastricht Treaty, which is the proper legal basis for the Euro. The surveillance economic policy provisions of the Maastricht Treaty and the ensuing Stability and Growth Pact that came into force in 1998 (slightly revised in 2005 with the aim to clarify the excessive deficit procedure of the Maastricht Treaty) make budgetary discipline the most remarkable feature of the new monetary system in Europe, although authors such as De Grauwe (2002) maintain the idea that the control by European institutions goes well beyond even what the IMF does not impose on "banana republics." Despite this criticism, the European approach, to coordinate fiscal policy and commit all member states to keep below critical values of deficit to GDP ratio, would in fact restrict the room for maneuver of national fiscal policy-makers; this is widely understood as the price to be paid for the creation of the Euro.

This new fiscal policy coordination at the European level has been compared in terms of importance to the founding of the Bretton Woods system (Artis, 2002) and in fact, designs a medium-term budgetary objective of close-to-balance or in surplus. This would work by calculating a safety margin against breaching the 3 per cent deficit ceiling enough to ensure that budgetary balance movements due to business and cyclical fluctuations would leave the deficit below 3 per cent in all cases except a few rare episodes of deep economic recession. To this end, national governments started submitting to EU headquarters in Brussels stability programs (countries that are Euro area members) and convergence programs (those states that are outside of the Euro) that cover a minimum of three years ahead, that is medium-term budgetary strategies to show their fiscal strategies toward the aforementioned close-to-balance or in surplus objective. A budgetary position complying with safety margin would allow for the full working of the built-in stabilizers without triggering the sanction procedures originally set by the Stability and Growth Pact.

This Pact, however, was very partially reformed in 2005 to take into account medium-term objectives and country-specific circumstances. There were two major changes introduced in 2005: on the preventive side, changes concerning the medium-term target and the adjustment path that should be differentiated from country to country in light of different debt ratios and potential growth rates; on the corrective side, the application of the excessive deficit procedure it should operate through; a more specific definition of exceptional cyclical circumstances and the Commission should also take into account a number of factors ranging from cyclical conditions to the Lisbon Agenda, debt sustainability, and so on.

Notwithstanding recently adopted adjustments, the original rationale of fiscal coordination in Europe—introduced at Maastricht and although with that greater discretion left to the Council now—has not changed. Note in addition that on the specific public debt ratio and the threshold of 60 per cent as introduced by the Maastricht Treaty, this should assume greater prominence in European-type fiscal coordination but agreement was not found—at the time of the reforms to the Stability and Growth Pact in 2005—on a minimum debt reduction for the countries that exhibit very high debt ratios.

The European Union originated due to the effects of the Second World War. The smaller nations feared that enormous war reparations would impoverish Germany and would refuel national resentment. They argued that they needed an economically strong Germany as a market for their produce and trade. Because of this, in 1951 the Economic Coal and Steel Community started, only to be overshadowed in 1957 by the European Economic Community (EEC). The EEC was made up of six countries—Italy, Belgium, Holland, Luxembourg, Germany, and France. Their purpose was to remove internal trade and customs barriers in order to promote a free flow of capital and labor within Europe.

Table 4.1   Old and New European Union Member States Delegation to the United States

Pre–May 1, 2004 EU Members	May 1, 2004 Acceding Members	New Member Countries as of January 1, 2007
Denmark	Cyprus	Bulgaria
Ireland	Czech Republic	Romania
Greece	Estonia	
Portugal	Hungary	
Spain	Latvia	
Austria	Lithuania	
Finland	Malta	
Sweden	Poland	
Belgium	Slovakia	
France	Slovenia	
Germany		
Italy		
Luxembourg		
Netherlands		

Source: Retrieved April 22, 2004 from http://www.eurunion.org/legislat/agd2000/agd2000. htm.

During this time, the only social policy was one that was confined to the Steel and Coal Community. The European Social Fund funded this policy. It mainly served Germany because of Germany's large steel sector and the fact that the Fund was financed through direct national contributions, of which Germany paid the most. Toward the end of the 1960s, social protest and unemployment began to rise, which created pressure for more social policies. This was the start of the 1974 Social Action Programme. Since funding was not limited to subsidizing existing programs anymore, the Social Fund was now being financed out of the total EEC budget. This provided difficulties for member states in demanding financial support. Therefore, the poorer regions of Western Europe became the major beneficiaries.

Together the EU and the Social Action Programme came up with three objectives to help with these problems. The three objectives were full employment, improvement in labor conditions, and more worker participation. In order to decrease the rapid growth of the unemployment rate, new programs were developed with the input of the three new memberships into the union—Great Britain, Ireland, and Denmark. Even with the implementations of the new programs, the unemployment rate still increased. Some of the member states recorded two-digit unemployment rates while some non-members such as Sweden and Switzerland had low unemployment rates. This raised the question, could the effects of the EU be a contributing factor in the unemployment rate, by reducing the options for national social and economic policies? To determine this, the EU set up the European Foundation for the Improvement of Living and Labor Conditions (FILLC). This helped them incorporate the second objective of the Social Action Programme. The FILLC helped raise equality in labor conditions as well as encouraging labor mobility by ensuring equal treatment for the subjects of any member state in other states.

Because of recent world oil crises, governments started to look for national solutions to the recession and the free market. This brought a new wave of EU through Western Europe, a Single European Market. A single monetary policy would be expected to work well for the members of the EU only as long as those countries had similar rates in inflation and unemployment and therefore needed approximately the same monetary conditions (Dunn, 1999, 29). Despite these problems, the Single European Market had some advantages:

- Price stability in Southern Europe. For example, countries such as Italy and Spain had a history of excessive inflation, and would be better off not managing their own monetary policies.
- Reduced transaction costs. A single currency would end the need to exchange one currency for another within the EU, which would reduce costs.
- Transparency in pricing. A single currency would make it difficult for European firms to charge different prices for the same products in various EU countries. It would make uniform pricing almost universal.
- Rivalry with the dollar and New York. The Euro could emerge as a widely used international currency, which might allow it to supplant the dollar. This would also result in Frankfurt and Amsterdam becoming successful competitors with New York as world financial centers.
- Ease of management for other EU institutions. For example, a common

agricultural policy would be more manageable with a single currency rather than many different currencies.

• Advancement of European unity. The EU is a large step in making sure that the chaos and pain can be avoided, even if it causes some economic pain, it is argued, and the political gains will make it worth it.

The EU has also been very beneficial to Spain. Since Spain joined the EU in 1986, it has had growth approaching 4 per cent and inflation at just one-half of that. They now benchmark themselves against the US rather than France as they used to. In the past two years, the country has produced 691,000 jobs, more than half of all new jobs in the EU. The Union, whose membership has now increased to 25 as of May 1, 2004, now accounts for over one-third of world trade.

In 2003, the US dollar reached a record low against the Euro. A weak dollar at times could be considered a deliberate policy of the US government since the new US Secretary of the Treasury who replaced Snow is in favor of a weak dollar compared to other major currencies such as the Euro and the pound Sterling, which creates a growing concern about the exchange rate uncertainty.

Overall, the change to the Euro has had a positive effect on companies operating in Europe. For American exporters, the Euro created much transactional efficiency, as the elimination of 12 currencies now allows the countries to handle their financial transactions in one currency. There is also greater price simplicity, which allows companies, both US and non-US, to see how prices of goods and services compare to companies in the Western part of Europe.

For small and medium-sized companies unable to use funds to circumvent business dealings, the stabilizing effect of the Euro will have the benefit of lessening exchange rate risk. Regarding investment, American investors have found it easier to make investment decisions, as they are better able to compare and assess the financial situations of European companies in which they want to invest, either by acquisition or through purchase.

Figure 4.2   Japanese Currency
Source: http://home.att.net/~fukuoka/notes-1.htm

The History of Paper Currency in Japan

The origin of paper currency can be traced back to the Yamada Hagaki, a private note that first appeared around 1600. The Yamada Hagaki's issuance system and organization clarified its historical significance, as well as the development of the Japanese currency system in the early modern times. The Yamada Hagaki was issued without interruption for 300 years until the beginning of the Meiji Era, an era that ranged from 1868 to 1912. This is when Japan began its modernization, went through economic reforms, and rose to world power status (Seno'o, 1996).

Although it was issued privately under the control of a local autonomous organization, the Yamada Hagaki gained strong acceptability as a national currency. The Yamada Hagaki is recognized as having close connections with the modern bank notes of Japan in the sense that it is the prototype of paper currency.

Figure 4.2 shows an example of Japan's first nationally accepted paper money. It is called the Dajokan satsu and it was issued in 1868, after the Meiji Restoration. Following the Meiji Restoration, 153 national banks issued paper money. These looked very much like US currency of that time, which are also pictured here. The Japanese bank note is in the middle and was issued in 1873; the US 10 dollar bill of 1868 is on the right.

The Yen (pronounced "en") became the official unit of currency in 1871. The name en was used because it means round, as opposed to the oblong shape of previous coins. There are four kinds of bills (10,000 Yen, 5,000 Yen, 2,000 Yen 1,000 Yen) and six kinds of coins (500 Yen, 100 Yen, 50 Yen, 10 Yen, five Yen, one Yen) used. Japanese currencies are all sized differently. This was done to make it easier for people with sight impairments. The 1,000 Yen is the shortest, the 5,000 Yen bill is next in length, by approximately 1 cm, and the 10,000 Yen bill is yet anther 1 cm longer than the 5,000 Yen bill. In addition, to assist, if looking at the currency from the front, each bill can be seen to have raised bumps in the bottom, left corner (Seno'o, 1996).

International Monetary System

In essence, the international monetary system consists of the regulations and procedures by which different currencies are exchanged for other currencies in world trade. Gold was the first international monetary currency to be accepted by the world as a whole. The gold standard declined and by the 1930s, it was almost abandoned. At this time, most nations around the world fixed their currency relative to that of the United States dollar.

As previously mentioned, the IMF was formed after the Second World War, in July of 1944 at the Bretton Woods Conference in Bretton Woods, New Hampshire, to manage the system of fixed exchange rates. It was also created to promote cooperation among the world's countries in the monetary policy market. The Bretton Woods Conference also brought forth the International Bank for Reconstruction and Development, which was originally meant for the nations involved in the Second World War to recover their devastated homelands. Later, it became an organization helping developing countries. Since the collapse of the system in the early 1970s, the IMF has been on a quest to find its mission, and that mission has still not been established. Many countries are able to receive loans from the IMF and this activity has seemed to lead to an extensive debate on the appropriateness of the organization's activities. A question that has been raised frequently is what the mission of the IMF should be. It will be some time before a conclusion is ever reached about its mission.

Major concerns for countless multinational companies have been the measuring, managing, and reduction of the risk and exposure that is intrinsic in international operations. Since the early 1980s, global companies have been establishing international cash management systems to manage their worldwide cash flows as effectively as their domestic treasury.

The IMF today is not as strong as it was a few years ago. Multinational companies, world leaders, and individuals alike are trying to determine the outcome and the future of the IMF. In recent years, we have seen the fall in the value of the Yen in Japan and the Euro in Europe. With Russia defaulting on its debt in mid-August of 1998, interest rates in the new emerging markets have skyrocketed and there has been the concern of a world recession. Promoting cooperation among our world's countries was a goal of the Bretton Woods Agreement, but today many in the developing world increasingly see globalization as a form of colonialism and imposition by the Western world.

In 2004, amid the backdrop of a worsening global economic crisis, the World Bank and the IMF worked on a plan to prevent a worldwide financial descent. A framework, along with strong policies to promote economic growth, is a prerequisite to eradicating poverty in all its forms by 2015. The proposed framework will consider the following when determining how much money may be lent to a country: the quality of policies and institutions in a country, potential upsets that could make repayment difficult, and the level of debt. This framework, which has been discussed by the Boards of both the World Bank and IMF, is a forward-looking approach that will involve using a more complete examination of a borrowing country's ability to repay debt before loans are approved. In 1998, James Wolfensohn, president of the World Bank, stated in an interview with Jim Lehrer of PBS's NewsHour, that this crisis is not something that will be solved by money alone, but by good programs in the countries and in the world financial system. Wolfensohn is one of many subjects in the 2004 book titled *The World's Banker*. This book recounts the struggles of Wolfensohn and the other heads of the global development world—making decisions that millions of peoples' destiny hinges on every day.

In the past decade, the IMF has accomplished a great deal; however, the IMF must keep up with the evolving world economy. Maintaining international financial stability is an ongoing process and the global economy is changing at a more rapid pace than ever before. Although the IMF can help strengthen the multilateral framework that has brought economic growth, rising living standards, and poverty reduction, it will require constant monitoring and adaptation as well.

The impact of the IMF has been immense. According to Hale (1998),

First, the IMF offers macroeconomics policy advice that politicians can sell to voters as their own; although the fund remains heavily influenced by the United States and other G-8 countries. It still offers a semblance of autonomy that makes its policy proposals more politically acceptable to borrowers. Second, the IMF acts as a global lender of the last resort during a liquidity crunch, similar to the role played by national central banks during domestic banking crises. In this capacity, the fund can step in when market panic prevents a troubled economy from receiving necessary credit. Third, the IMF promotes macroeconomic reforms that might otherwise be politically unacceptable. Such reforms have generally helped promote non-inflationary economic growth (Hale, 1998).

There is one great difference between the modern market economy of a century ago and today's economy, and that is the speed and frequency with which money moves across borders of nations.

Monetary Issues

Within the global market, three main monetary issues have a dramatic effect on the overall market itself. The three factors worth discussing are inflation, foreign exchange, and the interest rate. Every one of these has its own adverse impact on the global market in some way or another. In some cases, the effect may be more devastating to the country than to any certain individual, while in other instances it may affect an individual person and not really have any effect on the country at all.

Inflation

Inflation is a situation in which the average of all prices of goods and services in an economy is rising. Inflation occurs when there is an increase in money supply and an increase in the price level. This decrease in money value occurs when too much of the country currency is in circulation at one time. This is also known as an inflationary gap. To solve this problem the government will instigate a Contractionary Fiscal Policy, which will increase interest rates and taxes in order to discourage consumers from spending. This also has an effect on business, as it is harder to borrow money and expand into new products and markets. However, a Contractionary Fiscal Policy decreases the demand for dollars, thus depreciating the dollar against other currencies, which leads to more exporting. In other words, other countries will buy more goods since the price is cheaper. The opposite of an inflationary gap is a recessionary gap. A recessionary gap occurs when there is not enough spending or growth in the economy. To solve this problem the government will instigate an Expansionary Fiscal Policy, which increases output by increasing spending and lowering taxes. In this situation, there is an increased demand for dollars, and the dollar appreciates, thus there is less exporting and more importing. An international manager must keep abreast of the prices of goods and services, as well as the government policies that are enacted to stabilize the economy. This is because such policies directly affect imports and exports.

Foreign Exchange

When two countries trade goods for money, one thing that must be considered is the value of the currency being traded. Most recently, the top currencies are the Yen, Euro, and the US dollar. In the early years of the foreign exchange market, the dollar was highly regarded as one of the highest valued and recognized forms of money for trade. Recently, the dollar has been pressured by other currencies like the Yen and the Euro, which are causing the value of the dollar to drop.

Exchange rate Exchange rates play a large role in determining how a corporation decides to become a multinational corporation. The value of the corporations' home-country currency could make a corporate expansion abroad unrealistic if the rate is not favorable. There are several ways to globalize the corporation though.

If a corporation wishes to globalize its operation, but the market it has identified with may not have an ideal rate of exchange, building a production facility may not be cost-effective. If the exchange rate is still good enough to allow the corporation to develop a profit in the market, then exporting from the home country may be more attractive. The corporation may wish to handle all of the facets of this through direct exporting, which is, being directly involved in the marketing chain from beginning to end. If the corporation notices too much risk in the new market, for example, a potentially hostile foreign country, they may choose to find another company that is willing to take the export risk. This could be a company based in that new market willing to import the goods. This indirect exporting does have disadvantages though. It may reduce the ability of the multinational corporation to control such things as product marketing and price structures.

Another option for multinational corporations is the use of a licensing agreement where another company located in the target market is allowed to produce and sell the originating company's product. This can be an advantageous way to guarantee a specific amount of return that may be immune from exchange rates due to contract amounts (Greider, 1987, 246). The advantages of a guaranteed return can be overshadowed by the drawbacks though. First, if you are just breaking into the market, you may not be able to have a type of marketing consistent with your corporate philosophy. Second, you may be giving technology to a future competitor.

As far as exchange rates, franchising may have some of the same advantages as well as the ability by the multinational corporation to have more control over quality and marketing.

Yet another way for a corporation to expand into a multinational corporation is the strategic alliance. This can glean some advantages for both companies' economic abilities. The companies may be able to generate capital into different country's currencies to benefit from changes in the world markets.

When a multinational corporation decides that it truly wishes to globalize and place a subsidiary on foreign soil, it needs to be mindful of the exchange rate. Building a factory can be cost-effective when rates are good, but it may not be financially viable to operate if rates change. This could be caused by a change in the cost of raw materials, shipping, and of course, the purchasing power of customers. A good example of how rates can be advantageous is the Japanese move to put

Japanese manufacturing in America in the 1980s. Due to the Yen's high value against the dollar and other factors such as trade tariffs, it became viable for the Japanese to build up a large amount of manufacturing in America. Some of the economic advantages gained include saving on purchasing raw material in America versus Japan where they would have been much more expensive.

Interest Rate

Interest is the cost of borrowing money while interest rate is the percentage of such cost. As a rule, interest rates rise with inflation and in response to the Federal Reserve raising main short-term rates. Rising interest rates have a negative effect on the stock market. This is because investors can get more competitive returns from buying newly issued bonds instead of stocks. Interest rates can have a large effect on how a corporation manages its affairs and operates on a global scale. In the past, interest rates were generally nationalized and somewhat stable, but with the globalization of world markets, interest rates, like almost all things involved in modern businesses, have changed and changed rapidly. These changes in interest rates can greatly affect a multinational corporation's ability to grow and redesign itself. Even a small movement in an interest rate can mean billions of dollars in adjustments for multinational corporations.

Money Measures

Gross National Product

The Gross National Product (GNP) is the total dollar value of all final goods and services produced for consumption in society during a particular time. Comparing GNP from year to year is to measure in constant dollars the difference of a country's overall production and how well off its economy is. Thus, some economists can look to the size and growth of the GNP to know how healthy the country's economy is. There are at least two ways to measure GNP, but they have the same result. One is from the buyer's point of view and another is in terms of total demand. Both methods are the sum of the four components of GNP expenditures: consumption, investment, government purchases, and net exports.

In the late 1980s, rapid economic growth occurred in the newly industrialized countries (NICs), which has caused the international competitive environment to change dramatically. An example of rapid growth economies can be seen in the Japanese economy. Japan's real per capita GNP was less than one-third of American real per capita GNP. However, by 1992 Japanese real per capita GNP exceeded US GNP by over 10 per cent. Moreover, Hong Kong and Singapore's economies had also reached about one-half the Japanese level by 1992. GNP continues to grow in the newly industrialized countries and continues to slow in other industrialized countries, such as the United States. As of September 2004, Japan's annualized economic growth of 6.1 per cent outpaced that of the United States, which was 4.4 per cent in the same period. GDP in Japan rose 1.5 per cent in the first three months of

2004, and has risen for the last eight quarters, indicating that Japan's economy may be improving.

A country's gross domestic product (GDP) is similar to its GNP, except that GDP excludes net income from foreign sources. Like GNP, GDP is a measure of the value of a country's production of goods and services for a specific period, usually one year.

Many companies think of globalization in terms of only Europe and the Far East. This way of thinking is changing. During 1997, Intel decided to set up a 300-million-dollar operation in Costa Rica instead of in Ireland. In addition, Chrysler decided to build a major new plant in Brazil and Mercedes did the same in Argentina. Those companies made this same decision because they estimated a 30–35 per cent annual revenue growth from their Latin American markets. Thus, this change has brought and reflected the improvement in the South American region's economic fundamentals. The GDP has been growing steadily and significantly since 1990 for Chile, Peru, Argentina, Venezuela, Brazil, Columbia, and Mexico. At the same time, both inflation and trade barriers are falling (Luengo, 1998).

Budget Deficit

A budget deficit happens when a government is spending more than it is recovering via taxation of its citizens. A short-term effect of the budget deficit is an increase in the level of aggregate demand because the government is spending more each year. However, as the level of government spending continues to increase, the level of taxation increases, more taxes discourage consumers from spending money, thus demand goes down, production goes down, and the economy is depressed. A budget deficit can also indirectly affect the growth of money supply. The kind of influence exerted by a budget deficit depends on how the deficit is financed. If the deficit is financed entirely by issuing new government bonds to households (through the sale of savings bonds) the monetary effect is small. What happens is that idle money balances previously held by households are now borrowed and spent by the government. In other words, the quantity of money remains unchanged, but its average rate of circulation is increased.

However, the government can also finance the deficit by borrowing from the banking system. If that is done, and it frequently is done, it will automatically produce an increase in the supply of money. This increase in turn tends to stimulate private spending some time later. In short, large budget deficits can have a powerful expansionary effect on the money supply. A disadvantage to having a large budget deficit is that an excessive amount of money supply can cause inflation. An international manager must be aware of how large a budget deficit a country has and how the government finances its budget deficit. A budget deficit affects the supply of money, therefore affecting consumer consumption.

Trade Deficit

A country gets involved in foreign trade for many reasons, some of which are to sell surpluses in production, because they have a need for products and resources that can only be provided by foreign countries, or to expand markets for overall profit. Trade with foreign countries promotes competition and a more efficient industry. If a country imports more than it exports, a trade deficit occurs. A trade deficit is not necessarily a bad thing. For example, the United States has been prospering from a trade deficit. A trade deficit can be a good sign for an economy when it reflects growing demand for imports. When an economy expands, consumers are able to afford more goods, both domestic and imported. Returns on investment also increase, attracting foreign capital. The combination of incoming capital and increased demand for imports tends to widen the trade deficit. That explains why every recent US economic expansion has been accompanied by an expanding trade deficit (Center for Trade Policy Studies, 1998).

The United States is in a unique position with its trade deficit. In most cases, if a country has a trade deficit (importing more than exporting) it is likely that prices and inflation would be high, and in case of high government budget deficit to the so-called twin-deficit identity, a term that should describe a link between a country's government budget deficit and a simultaneous current account deficit. Although twin deficits need not always appear together on these two national accounts, this identity became commonplace in the US during the 1980s and 1990s because the country experienced deficits in both of these accounts. In either case, an international manager must be keep abreast of the competition and trends, and price sensitivity.

International Stock Exchanges

One of the most important goals of any stock exchange is liquidity. The success with which the market meets the functions of raising capital for new investments is dependent on it. Today, there are many countries whose economy will support a stock exchange. The rationale and advantage of stock exchanges are abundant. Stock exchanges enable large sums of capital to be raised for expansion, for the financing of new businesses, and the creation of new employment opportunities. For the individual in society it represents one of the best means of investment, in the medium- to long-term. Stock exchanges are a benefit to the economy as a whole because there is not a bias towards any particular business operating in the economy or any particular social community. The rich, poor, or middle class can all participate in the stock exchange.

Tokyo Stock Exchange (TSE)

The TSE maintains markets for securities and related futures and options, and secures the fair and smooth trading of securities in order to protect public and investor interests. In this way, the TSE resembles a public institution. In addition, the TSE's role as an international stock exchange has recently expanded due to advances in international capital flow (Tokyo Stock Exchange, 2004).

In the 1870s, Japan introduced a securities system and the trade of public bonds commenced. As a result, the need for a public trading institution arose, and the Stock Exchange Ordinance was enacted in May 1878. The TSE was founded on May 15,

1978 with trading beginning two weeks later. This history of the exchange notes that the TSE became a controlled institution during wartime. In 1943, 11 exchanges throughout the country came together and the Japan Securities Exchange was established. Unfortunately, the war was having economically depressing effects on Japan, and the economy was such that the market suspended trading from August 10, 1945 until December 1945. The Japan Securities Exchange dissolved in 1947.

The TSE functions as a self-regulated and non-profit association and is maintained and managed by its members. The functions of the TSE are sophisticated and varied; therefore, it is appropriate that management and administration are delegated to a self-regulated body of members, which is involved with the operations of the market.

The TSE is a central institution in the secondary market and its major functions are as follows:

- Providing a market place. Trading in the market moves continuously throughout each trading session, on the trading floor, and in compliance with exchange rules. The TSE also monitors all trading; transaction prices are available to the public.
- Monitoring trading. Real-time trading exists on the exchange floor and transactions are carefully observed in order to uphold exchange rules and properly determined prices. If any rule violations, improper conduct, or unfair trading is discovered, appropriate measures are taken.
- Listing and monitory securities. The TSE also lists securities. Securities adhere to the listing criteria established and approved by the TSE. Once listed, the securities are monitored in order to maintain high listing standards. The TSE has the option and authority to suspend the trading of, or delist, a security, if certain listing criteria are not met. In order to ensure investor protection and a fair, transparent transaction, the TSE necessitates the accurate, swift, and fair disclosure of company and security information. Such rules relating to the disclosure of corporate information are stated in the Securities and Exchange Law. The TSE also maintains guidelines for the timely disclosure of important corporate information resulting from business activities.
- Monitoring members. As noted above, the TSE is a membership organization of securities companies. As constituents of a prominent, public exchange, members are expected to maintain the highest of standards. Therefore, the TSE continually inspects the business and financial conditions of applicant companies as well as current members (Tokyo Stock Exchange, 2004).

Today the mission of the Tokyo Stock Exchange is to be a global financial exchange with a significant international presence by providing domestic and international investors, issuers, and intermediaries with a liquid, reliable, and fair market (Tokyo Stock Exchange, 2004). The exchange assumes responsibility as a public infrastructure for the principal markets of Japanese securities. The TSE is an important institution that contributes to the strong development and growth of the Japanese economy and financial markets. The TSE actively works to fulfill its role as a forerunner towards the improved standing of Japanese capital markets in the international marketplace.

London Stock Exchange (LSE)

The London Stock Exchange has a history all the way back to the eighteenth century. In 1760, 150 brokers left the Royal Exchange to form a club in a cafe named Jonathan's Coffee House. At that time, people who wanted to sell or buy shares in joint-stock companies could do so through brokers. These brokers then joined to form a club, which they named the "Stock Exchange." In 2000, the shareholders agreed to go public and rename it the London Stock Exchange. Today, this stock exchange not only occupies the leading position on British soil, but in Europe too. It is also the most internationalized. It handles share, bond, and account receivable listings for share issuers. Shareholders also have the opportunity to buy and sell interest in the companies with whom they invest. The London Stock Exchange also provides a complete information service, made up of price indications, company histories, and their market position. As centuries passed, the technology grew, making it quicker and easier for people to buy and sell their shares.

Today the London Stock Exchange is the world's third largest market for the buying and selling of corporate shares. They seem to have almost total control of the market by accounting for almost 97 per cent of the shares sold in the UK. Even with this large control, the exchange still has worries about rival competitors. Since changing to the electronic trading system in 1986, the London Stock Exchange has continuously been trying to find new and better ways to complete their stock exchanges. They must continue to do this in order to stay on top of the market.

The LSE lists almost 3,000 depository receipts, Eurobonds, and company shares, with nearly 500 of these based outside the United Kingdom. After 200 years as a regulated exchange, the LSE has eliminated floor trading in favor of an electronic system called Stock Exchange Electronic Trading Service (SETS).

New York Stock Exchange (NYSE)

The NYSE was founded in 1792. It registered as a National Securities Exchange with the US Securities and Exchange Commission on October 1, 1934. Throughout the years, the NYSE has become the largest equities marketplace in the world. It is home to over 3,000 companies worth more than $15 trillion in global market capitalization. It represents approximately 80 per cent of the value of all publicly owned companies in America. Over two-thirds of the companies have listed in the last 12 years. These companies include a combination of leading US companies, both mid-size and small capitalization companies. Non-US issuers are playing an increasingly important role in the NYSE. As of August 20, 2004, 457 non-US companies from 47 countries were listed. Some of the US companies that have listed in 2004 are Dominos Pizza, Inc., Albertson's, Inc., Life Time Fitness and General Motors Corporation.

Every transaction made in the NYSE is under continuous scrutiny during the trading day. Stock watch is a computer system that searches for atypical trading patterns. NYSE transactions need to be monitored carefully because it is the most active self-regulator in the securities industry. Transactions valued at billions of dollars flow through the exchange each day. An exchange listing provides international companies with access to the world's largest group of investors and is the world's most resourceful, competitive, and equitable marketplace for trading. The quality of the NYSE, its range of investors, its visibility, and its capital-raising process are one of the major reasons companies choose to list.

Johannesburg Stock Exchange (JSE)

The JSE, one of the larger stock exchanges in the world, is based out of Johannesburg, South Africa; it is the largest stock exchange in Africa today. Founded in 1887, the JSE came into existence to provide a market place for the mining and financial companies of South Africa. In 1963, the Federation International Bourses de Valeurs (FIBV) accepted the JSE as a member. However, today non-mining organizations make up the greater part of companies that are listed on the JSE. In recent years, South Africa has undergone changes from white minority rule of a black majority population to the majority population ruling the country. With this new conversion of power, there has been a wave of new business listings on the JSE. One hundred and one new firms became public in 1998 alone. Since the African National Congress-led government (ANC) came to power in 1994, efforts to transfer economic ownership have taken two directions. The first, led by the private sector, transferred equity in South African companies to black business through financially engineered arrangements. The second, led by the state, made black empowerment a condition for government licenses, tenders, and procurement contracts. In 1995, requirements that all stockbrokers be South African citizens were removed and an organization was put into place to examine, admit, and discipline stockbrokers. Instead of the stockbroker being the member, it is now the trading entity. Corporate membership is available but is subject to limitations of the appropriate capital requirements. The BusinessMap Foundation noted in its recent report on BEE (Black Economic Empowerment) that while the market capitalization of black-controlled companies listed on the JSE increased from R44 billion ($6.7 billion) at the start of 2003 to R58 billion ($8.9 billion) by the end of the year, black control of total market capitalization on the JSE remained at 3 per cent. The number of companies owned by blacks listed on the JSE also dropped from 22 to 21 during 2003, which is far below the peak of 38 in August 1999. This means that less than 10 per cent of business senior managers and executives are black. The color of a person's skin is still being examined in the business world in South Africa and the new government is not helping the majority population particularly well (10 years Down the Line, 2004).

In June of 1996, a new era of trading was established in South Africa giving way to high-tech computer trading. Since then, all trading was and will continue to be conducted on the Johannesburg Equities Trading system (JET) which was also introduced together with dual trading and negotiated brokerage. The JSE has also become available to individuals by introducing an Internet-based support system that matches providers of capital and seekers for small and medium-sized enterprises. The system is known as the Emerging Enterprise Zone (EEZ).

Every country needs to stay abreast of technology, not only to keep up to speed with innovations but also to have the same competitive advantage as other countries and their markets since countries are trading with each other. If countries are unable to do this, trading may dwindle. This new era continues to show how important it is for countries and their trades to keep up with the ever-changing technology. The Johannesburg Stock Exchange even took precautionary steps against a possible disruption from the Y2K bug by closing on December 30–31, 1999.

All stock exchanges have their problems and the Johannesburg Stock Exchange is no exception. The problem at the JSE ties in with international trading and setting standards. Insider trading has historically been a dilemma at the JSE with no one ever being successfully prosecuted. Legislation has finally been put into place to review this issue in hopes to align South Africa with the international standards.

Trading is the livelihood of the JSE and in recent years, volumes of trade have been immense. Of the companies quoted on the JSE, over 150 have dual listings on foreign bourses, which are stock exchanges, especially ones in a continental European city.

China and Hong Kong

The changeover in sovereignty of Hong Kong on July 1, 1997 made it clear that China has become a country that the international business community cannot afford to ignore. Because of economic reforms during the Deng Xiao Peng era, there has been a dramatic increase in the standard of living of the Chinese people. For example, between 1978 and 1996, personal savings in the banking system rose from US$3 billion to US$470 billion. During the past 20 years, China has averaged an almost 10 per cent compound growth. Such growth will bring many benefits to Hong Kong, and ensure that China will be a major participant in the international economy.

In the field of international trade, China and Hong Kong total trade with the rest of the world was some USD $22 billion when Deng came to power in 1978. By 1996, that figure increased to USD $290 billion. Currently, China is the fourth largest trading nation in the world.

There is a natural increase in the labor force by 10 million people every year. At the same time, the commercialization of state-owned enterprises will affect some 40 million people. In the workforce, there will also be a significant shift from the agricultural sector towards better-paid positions in industry. The challenge of the government is to create millions of new jobs over the next decade. The only way to achieve this will be through rapid economic growth. This, in turn, will only be accomplished if international trade expands and foreign investment continues to flow.

East Asian executives consider that with the failure of communist regimes, businesses and government in the China of today cannot be called, by any standards, communist. Deng Xiao Ping's successors' modern China is transiting towards a new emerging subsidized, socialistic, protected capitalism.

With China being a member of the World Trade Organization, the world's most populated country takes a step toward free enterprise and away from a centrally planned economy. China is now ready to accept the WTO's requirements to eliminate tariffs restrictions and provide a better foreign investment atmosphere. This shows a distinct shift in the thinking of the Communist Party. In the area of economic reform and growth, China is in the midst of an economic explosion that will continue if the government continues in its quest for economic freedom. These economic improvements were brought about by a total renovation of China's economy.

Currently, government leaders in China have begun an even more aggressive release of the economy. While some improvements are necessary now that China is a member of the WTO, many are a result of internal pressure from China's many entrepreneurs and businesspeople. Increasingly, these pressures are the motivation behind the country's growth and political reformation. For foreign companies endeavoring to gain access to a market of over 1.2 billion people, there is a complex set of rules, laws, and regulations to deal with. While some criticize global capitalism and the WTO, the people of China recognize that it is through the freedom of a market economy that genuine benefits will come to the Chinese people. As the obstacles to economic freedom are unleashed, the energy and potential of China will be realized.

Modern times are evident by much greater individualism and globalization. While in most countries the social fabric of family and church is weakening and politics cannot make up for the loss of transference of values or the way in which values are perceived, society is showing their own recent ways of purpose and the acceptance of values. They are often attracted by global values, as seen by the enormous interest in Amnesty International, human rights, Médecins Sans Frontières, and in a number of environmental organizations. Amnesty International (AI) is a worldwide group of citizens who crusade for internationally recognized human rights. Médecins Sans Frontières (MSF) is an international organization that provides humanitarian aid and emergency medical support to people in danger. There seems to be a renewal of value awareness—only in a new way.

Conclusion

In a market system, individuals or organizations trade in order to benefit or realize profit from the exchange. Trading among nations involves the Foreign Exchange Market. The Foreign Exchange Market is a worldwide network of financial institutions that facilitates international business transactions by trading foreign exchange. The foreign exchange rate or international exchange rate is the price of one country's money in terms of another country's currency. In essence, the international monetary system is the rules and procedures by which different national currencies are exchanged for each other in world trade. Gold was the first international monetary currency to be accepted by the world as a whole.

Today there are many countries whose economies support stock exchanges. The rationale and advantage of stock exchanges are abundant. The largest stock exchanges are the Tokyo Stock Exchange, the London Stock Exchange, the New York Stock Exchange, and the Johannesburg Stock Exchange.

In recent years, the competition has increased for the use of capital. There are many needs for capital in the global economy, such as major building projects in South America or the industrialization of Asia and the Pacific Rim. The returns from the investments have been large but there continues to be an ever-increasing supply of capital in world markets. With supply still exceeding demand, you would expect the price of capital to decrease overall, but this is not the case. The true cost of capital, that is the nominal interest rate discounted by inflation, has actually gone up. The true cost is the percentage of your income it takes to pay for your debt. This will force you to speed up just to keep up with old obligations or if times are bad to borrow more, causing a never-ending cycle of repayment (Greider, 1987, p. 234). Some explanations for this could be the heightened risk of the global market, the upward pull for competing returns, or the government removal of rate ceilings (Greider, 1987, 234).

All of these effects have to be closely watched by multinational corporations because they can have serious effects on operations. These effects may determine whether you can afford to expand into new markets or purchase a new technology that will help you stay competitive in current markets. For example, the investment in a new subsidiary in a foreign country may not be possible if the environment is such that an investor may not want to take on that risk. There may be other profitable opportunities out there for them to acquire.

This works in other ways too. It may not be the multinational corporation attempting to receive investment. They may be trying to invest past revenues to generate new capital. When this is the case, they will have to be extremely careful in the ever-changing, fast-pace world economy. An investment that is very profitable today may not be a good choice tomorrow.

The multinational corporations can use these trades in the currency and stock of other countries to improve their ability to merge or form strategic alliances in those foreign entities. This can give a non-multinational corporation the extra capital it may need to become international by purchasing other companies with home country stock. Investment in foreign stock exchanges has proven very profitable for many multinational corporations. Conversely, these markets can prove to be a pitfall to the multinational manager that is not familiar with their operation. Managers need to be familiar with these markets and how their changes can have far-reaching effects on the business, corporation, or the economy in other countries.

The global economy is growing. Competition is increasing as money supply increases and new consumers emerge. As the competition continues to grow stronger, business must use every resource efficiently and effectively in order to maintain a competitive advantage. How these resources are used efficiently and effectively depends on an international manager's skill in assessing the trends in an economy. Knowledge of the key economic fundamentals outlined in this book is a tool that an international manager can use to determine the state of a country's economy and how they affect the multinational corporation.

Case Study

Hong Kong's Economic System

Hong Kong is one of the world's major economic accomplishments. Its progressive telecommunications are excellent and its air and sea facilities are functional and modern. Its financial system is responsive and receptive, with its banks providing the diverse services that modern business and consumers need and expect. The region's free market economy has few tariffs and continues to move forward.

However, it has not always been this way for Hong Kong. Britain returned Hong Kong to China on July 1, 1997. BBC News reported that on October 23, 1997, three months after the handover, the Hong Kong stock market crashed. Millions of dollars were quickly lost and the government struggled to defend the Hong Kong currency's linkage against the US dollar. High interest rates contributed to a drop in Hong Kong's property market, with prices falling steadily. Although Hong Kong's economy had been steadily growing in the 1990s, it fell into a recession in 2001. Housing and residential property prices decreased dramatically, while unemployment in 2003 rose to a record high of 7.9 per cent, and in addition, the annual growth rate over the last four years has averaged just 1.9 per cent. It seemed the more Mainland China developed, the more Hong Kong's future seemed to darken.

A 2004 article in *Time Asia*, "The Ties that Bind," states that until the last decade, almost 70 per cent of China's exports passed through Hong Kong's ports and airport; in the last ten years, as other Pearl River Delta cities have begun to develop their own ports and transport links, this has decreased to 28 per cent. Beijing began to become concerned, not wanting Hong Kong, a once dominant city, to slowly deteriorate. This would be seen as an international embarrassment, a demonstration that one country but two systems does not work. China needed a strong Hong Kong because it played a crucial role as a financial center for the mainland economy, and China could not afford to have Hong Kong perceived as unstable in the international trade arena (Shyman and Gough, 2004).

However, since the handover in 1997, Hong Kong's economy is brightening due to Chinese tourists and closer links with the booming Pearl River Delta. Guangdong province dominates most of the Pearl River Delta and is quickly becoming the workplace of the world, with thousands of factories making everything from toys to tennis shoes. Hong Kong, located outside the river's mouth, is placed perfectly to benefit from the growing China trade. The Pearl River Delta is one of China's most dominant economic powers, with its export volume accounting for one-third of the total in China.

In addition, the government began lifting travel restrictions so that millions of mainland tourists could visit the city. Beijing also approved the Closer Economic Partnership Arrangement (CEPA), which granted Hong Kong-based businesses preferential treatment over other foreign firms in investment and trade with the mainland (Shyman and Gough, 2004). As a result, it appears that Beijing's economy, along with a global economy which is also improving, is reviving Hong Kong. The city's GDP is the strongest it has been in over three years, spending is up, and housing and residential property prices have risen as much as 45 per cent since August 2003. If Hong Kong is deteriorating, Beijing is there to assist in its rejuvenation.

Tourism, which has always been an economic strength for Hong Kong, has been the most obvious benefactor of the central government's assistance. According to the Hong Kong Tourism Board, about 2.9 million visitors visited in the first three months of 2004, a 37 per cent increase over the same period in 2003 and more than twice that of 2002. This increase is a direct result of Beijing's decision to let Chinese tourists from cities such as Guangzhou and Shenzhen travel to Hong Kong as individuals rather than as part of organized tour groups. The number of visits made by mainlanders has risen even further since Hong Kong Disneyland opened in 2006 (Shyman and Gough, 2004).

In addition to tourism and government intervention, to add even more intensity to Hong Kong's economy, the Pearl River Delta is the site of a massive bridge, which is scheduled for completion in 2007. The bridge will bring exports from Mainland China to Hong Kong's lively ports quickly, and will open up the weak and less developed region west of the Pearl River to new ventures. The bridge starts on the western edge of the Pearl River at Zhuhai, moves through Macau, and into Hong Kong. The construction of the Hong Kong/Zhuhai/Macau Bridge will introduce the Pearl River Delta area in southern China into an economic zone equal to that of any in the world.

Economists believe that the bridge which links Hong Kong, Macau and Zhuhai will not only be an important traffic route in the Pearl River Delta, but also a lifeline to the future economic development of the whole south of China, not to mention adding goods to Hong Kong's air and sea transportation.

According to the Shyman and Gough article, despite this windfall, it is not yet clear whether Hong Kong's recent recovery will last. One problem is the territory's relatively high wages; it is difficult to generate new jobs in meaningful numbers. While the labor force has grown slowly from 3.2 million to 3.5 million from 1997 to 2003, the number of unemployed has almost quadrupled from 71,000 to 277,600 (Shyman and Gough, 2004).

China and Hong Kong may ultimately depend on each other. Hong Kong's economy will be expanded by the opportunities in the region and Hong Kong's contribution to Mainland China is financially rewarding. In February 2005, the banks of Hong Kong became the first foreign banks that were allowed to offer renminbi accounts, opening freer trade in the Chinese currency. It is a win–win situation. Hong Kong is rescued from a stumbling economy, but it will trade political autonomy for this prosperity. With the two countries' economic success tied to the other, and with the mainland's support so crucial to Hong Kong's economic role, Hong Kong must adapt itself to a changing Chinese economy.

Speculation may be that in time Hong Kong's economy would change somewhat under Chinese control; however, the prospect of that is doubtful since the Chinese will prefer Hong Kong to maintain its own economic strength. To stay strong, Hong Kong's economy must adhere to free market principles, be governed by strict yet flexible financial policies, and be assisted by a disciplined government that can make rapid external adjustments. China's Special Administrative Region (SAR), Hong Kong, is adhering to these principles and the outlook for the economy is for a strong domestic recovery.

Case Questions

1. What are the underlying economic factors that contributed to the current relationship between China and Hong Kong (for example, trade, technologies, economy, wealth, poverty, and so on)?
2. Analyze the interactions between the Hong Kong and Chinese economy.
3. What problems may China face as it tries to govern Hong Kong and keep the rest of China under communist rule?

Chapter Review

Understanding international trade and finance and the effects of various international economic policies on domestic and world welfare is just one more area that an international manager must be knowledgeable and skilled in. Things such as sources of comparative advantage, gains and losses from trade, the impact of trade on economic growth, and effects of trade policy interventions such as tariffs, quotas, and export subsidies are critical to an organization's bottom line. International agreements on regional trade liberalization (such as EU and NAFTA) and on multilateral trade liberalization (such as WTO) are as important and relevant as international finance itself, which includes balance of payments, determination of foreign exchange rates, and the international monetary system. The primary objective of an international manager should be to develop an understanding of international economics, explore gains from trade, the mechanisms necessary to capture these gains and the incentives to avoid them, and explore globalization as a system.

In summary, trading among nations involves a worldwide network of financial institutions that smoothes the progress of international business transactions by trading foreign exchange. The foreign exchange rate is the price of one country's money in terms of another country's currency, and changes in the total money supply and changes in the rate at which the money supply increases or decreases affect important economic variables, such as the rate of inflation, interest rates, employment, and the equilibrium level of real national income.

Doing business with foreign countries promotes competition and a more efficient industry. Competition increases as money supply increases and new consumers emerge. When two countries trade goods for money, one thing considered is the value of the currency that is traded. Managers working in an international realm will come to understand the sources of comparative advantage, exchange rates, and international labor practices. They will become familiar and understand the concepts of national income accounting and balance of payments accounting practices. Finally, international managers will develop an appreciation of how the globalization of international capital markets can affect international trade, and be able to compare capitalist systems and a United States economy.

Since the Second World War, the nature of the international economy and the interactions that nations experience have changed significantly. Globalization and the global economy have become commonplace in the news and media. Influential changes in technology, finance, markets, and trade have contributed to the economic forces that have led to an ongoing integration of economies worldwide over the centuries. This chapter examined the nature of those changes and the premises that tried to explain them. The international economy consists of the exchanges of nations in an increasingly interdependent and technologically complex global economy. Understanding the consequences of the new global economy will benefit the international manager and increase his or her knowledge of economic inequality on the world scale, economic integrations (such as the creation of NAFTA and the European Community), and the outlook for the global and dynamic economy.

Chapter Questions

1. Discuss the different monetary measures currently used (GNP, budget, and trade deficit).
2. Explain the growth and shift of the economy since the Second World War.
3. Explain the goals and impact of the International Monetary Fund.
4. Why is the NAFTA trade agreement so emotionally contested?
5. Identify the main tenets of the international economic systems.
6. In the global economy, discuss how jobs, resources, and trade are allocated. Are the needs for these jobs, shelter, and food being met?
7. Discuss the unique approach of fiscal and monetary policies in the European Union and the special role of the Stability and Growth Pact.

Chapter 5

The Impact of Domestic Politics on International Business

In the highly developed and affluent United States, the well-oiled machine of international business flows seamlessly, seldom thought about by the average citizen. Yet, in this world of consumption, we are completely dependent upon a multinational business and trading system to provide us with our requisite daily dose of cheap, plentiful goods. Rarely do we contemplate the international economic aspects, except when political concerns surface: awareness of sweatshops, child labor, dictatorships, apartheid, and the suspicious behavior of dictatorial leadership around oil wells that threatens oil flow to the world market. The political aspects of international business are expansive. Evidence was provided at the 1999 World Trade Organization Conference in Seattle and the raging protests surrounding its agenda, when more than 50,000 people turned up in the pouring rain to protest current issues. This challenge of harmonizing economic and political goals is one the world community will continue facing in the twenty-first century, if not until the end of time. This chapter will discuss general elements and ramifications of politics in international business and the management of it.

Foreign Trade Regulations

There are many regulations and laws set up by different countries to help them establish their political initiatives. In addition, countries have bonded together with allied countries and trading partners to form commissions and boards such as the WTO, the European Union/Community (EU/EC), and Organization of the Petroleum Exporting Countries (OPEC) to facilitate their political and economic goals. In exploring the existing tax laws, rulings, regulations, and political attitudes, it is evident how economic issues function autonomously and contradict political doctrine. Further exploration of international trade laws reveals some of the ways countries circumvent political restrictions to benefit their monetary goals.

In the United States, the US Department of Commerce and the Customs Office enforces the majority of regulations concerning trade. There are laws and taxes, which govern both the import and export of goods and even their manufacture and distribution. One such tax is the value-added tax (VAT), which is mostly applied to imports but can be used on exported materials as well. The value-added tax functions effectively as a trade restraint in that the corporation or manufacturer must pay the tax in addition to established customs duties. This causes the tax to be highly significant in determining whether or not competition in a global market is a feasible alternative or if the costs outweigh the market potential. Another preliminary concern is that of export or import licensing and establishment of an international sales agreement. In this agreement, the laws of either the country of the buyer or that of the seller will govern the rights of the parties. If the bargaining advantage of the parties is approximately equal, it is adequate to say that it is more customary for the buyer to agree that the seller's law will govern the agreement.

International Trade Rulings

In 1988, the Convention on the International Sale of Goods was enacted. Forty-three countries including the United States signed this multinational treaty, and in subsequent years, other countries have followed suit. In the Convention, over 100 articles concerning international trade and laws were discussed. This agreement has served to facilitate trade between diverse political nations that cannot agree and is serving as the default conditions by which a transaction will be governed. This can prove disadvantageous for the US seller because the Convention reinforces the rights of buyers in various ways. Politics has a negative connotation in this view of world trade because as a country becomes more politically developed, it generally seeks a higher standard of living, which brings new rights and conditions that raise the cost of labor and trade. How this affects the global manager will vary depending on which side they are on, but having a trade agreement with many countries allows trade to continue more autonomously of political issues.

Countries wishing to import goods into the US may have to apply for a customs ruling from the US Customs Service to ensure they are abreast of all current regulations, quotas, and taxes. Similar or more stringent requirements are for US goods entering other countries. If there are further problems, litigation may be necessary. It is the desire of all global managers to avoid these proceedings, as they are costly and can cause damage to the sometimes fragile relations between current or potential trading partners.

In the global marketplace, it is beneficial to establish neighborhoods in an effort to streamline the flow of commerce and avoid political conflicts. It was for this attempt to eliminate borders between countries of different political systems for which the North American Free Trade Agreement (NAFTA) and the EC/EU were established. The North American Free Trade Agreement (NAFTA) was a major step in carrying out free trade between the United States, Mexico, and Canada. These multinational organizations affect the way that limits on amounts or values of imports (tariffs) and country-specific protection against market dumping and flooding (quotas) are implemented and administered.

For instance, NAFTA provisions call for the elimination of all quotas between Canada, the United States, and Mexico—except for those that apply to the agricultural, energy, textile, and automobile industries. Another example is the GATT, which in 1995 became the WTO. While GATT did not eliminate all quotas, it did restrict their use and included provisions that called for greater simplicity and clearer guidelines in the rules governing quotas.

Managing the costs attributed to trade barriers such as quotas, tariffs, and duties is a key issue in global management for companies struggling to capitalize on markets in countries and zones that facilitate rather than restrict trade. In a restrictive environment, the manager must negotiate carefully to try to attain the most favorable conditions such as duty refunds, temporary status and tariff reductions, or eliminations. To achieve this goal, communication is essential; today's global manager must be able to communicate effectively between culturally and politically diverse nations to cultivate the fragile cooperative trade relationship into solidarity.

Attitudes in Foreign Trade

Measures such as the above are established by the government to protect not just the economy of national industries, but also the citizens involved. In a democratic system, the citizens' concerns are reflected in political opinion. This is conveyed into governmental regulations, which can in turn affect the way an international business markets itself abroad. There are varieties of marketing tools available to deal with or influence the individual behavior, but established government regulations are far more difficult to change. Even economic integration efforts have not been very successful in harmonizing these differences because every nation has its own national attitude in different areas. Standards that are acceptable for one nation may be morally offensive to another. These differences can range from large to small but have a significant effect in promoting or dissuading world trade. For example, the European Community was formed to do away with the regulatory differences within the community. Thirty years later the community still struggles in socio-political-based issues such as the Euro and even "jam vs. marmalade." Currently, the regulatory ban on hormone-treated meat products adopted after much public pressure is a contentious trade issue between the United States and the EU. This debate displays the intimate relationship between politics and economics in international business (Hassan, 1999).

Economically, the US would like to capitalize on the British market segment, while Britain is also closely tied to the US in terms of trade dollars. Often, global managers are faced with this challenge of being successful in the sales department at the expense of being chastised (or in Seattle, demonstrated against!) by the public. A huge challenge for the global manager is to be both economically correct (not in the red) and politically correct. Controversy develops when trade restrictions against a nation are loosened while its political environment continues to contradict with the economic, cultural, and social standards of the host country. Two of the biggest issues in this arena are the environment and human rights.

An example of politics in international business can be seen in the developing Asian markets, which became prominent world players in the 1980s and 1990s. Significant changes in government policy were necessary when these markets emerged as a driving force. Despite undemocratic governments, corruption and human rights atrocities such as the Tiananmen Square massacre and child slavery, developing Asian and other Far Eastern markets could no longer be ignored as international business partners. For example, during the period of 1975–85, France,

West Germany, and the United Kingdom had ten-year gross domestic product changes of 24 per cent, 26 per cent, and 18 per cent, respectively. At the same time, South Korea reported growth rates of 107 per cent, Pakistan 89 per cent, and Thailand 84 per cent. Overall, the GDP of the world grew by 34 per cent while Asian developing countries grew by 71 per cent (Hassan, 1999).

In early November of 2001, in Doha, Qatar, and after 15 years of negotiation, the World Trade Organization members formally approved the accession package for the People's Republic of China. China became the WTO's 143rd member on December 11, 2001. China's economy began to open up in the late 1970s, and entry to the WTO has seen China's immense production power and potential market finally brought into the mainstream of world trade. China already has the world's tenth largest economy and the deal is expected to boost economic growth further. China, as a major partner in trade and a WTO member, was not able to have a greater influence and say in the international and multilateral trading system.

China was motivated to join the WTO by the realization that it needed an external force to help overcome domestic obstacles if it was to sustain the rapid economic growth of the 1980s and 1990s. However, many of its trading partners were worried. Some developing countries feared that global demand for their exports would shrink due to China's ability to generate an enormous supply of labor-intensive exports. There were also concerns that China's WTO succession might lead to a deflation of the renminbi. Some industrial countries worried that China's exports might inundate their domestic markets. However, these countries—notably the United States and Australia—found they had improved access to China's agricultural markets and could increase their exports to China in the areas of capital and technology-intensive manufactures. Eventually, the release of China's services sector provided industrial countries with large trade and investment opportunities (Adhikari and Yang, 2002).

In response to these concerns, China's commitments are substantial, exceeding most expectations. China's WTO accession agreement will aid companies in the US to do business in China by addressing many of the trade restrictions and problems the US firms have experienced. China has committed to reduce its tariffs on many items including cosmetics, distilled spirits, medical equipment, motor vehicles, paper products, scientific equipment, and textiles. China will also eliminate its tariffs on beer, furniture, and toys ("What Does China's WTO Accession Mean for Foreign Industry," 2004). In addition, all companies in China will be granted full trading rights within three years after accession—by December 2004. China is also subject to more anti-dumping actions than any other country. A circumvention program closely monitors imports from China in several key sectors. In addition, in accordance with the WTO Technical Barriers to Trade (TBT) Agreement, China cannot use technical regulations, standards, and conformity assessment procedures as unnecessary obstacles to trade. China will now base technical regulations on international standards. China has agreed to eliminate all subsidies on industrial goods that are forbidden under WTO rules, that is, export and import substitution subsidies ("What Does China's WTO Accession Mean for Foreign Industry," 2004).

According to a 2002 article in *Finance and Development*,

the newly industrialized economies of Asia are likely to gain the most from China's WTO accession. They have already invested heavily in China, and their exports are now competing with China's to a lesser extent. In particular, low-income Asian countries will benefit if their exports are complementary to China's goods and services. India, for example, now has the potential to export computer software and other information technology-related services to China (Adhikari and Yang, 2002).

An important factor in the success of the US economy is its trade with China. In 2000, China was America's fourth largest trading partner, with imports and exports totalling $116 billion, and it is fully expected that this growth in exports will increase quickly with China's WTO membership ("What Does China's WTO Accession Mean for Foreign Industry," 2004).

When political issues stand in the way of world trade, the restricted country often goes to the regional trade commission seeking a trade ruling on the issue. For example, in the European Community, it used to be GATT and in the Caribbean, it used to be the Caribbean Basin Initiative (CBI). Now, the majority of trade concerns go to the WTO, which is a panel of several people from European nations—in itself an issue with many who feel that the WTO is an autocratic decision-making body that represents only monetary gains.

Issues such as environmental degradation in the Brazilian rain forest and impoverished standards of living have been ignored by the WTO in the pursuit of furthering trade. At the 1999 conference in Seattle, the US was seeking an agreement on labor standards so the US could compete with countries in the developing world that are increasingly producing more and more for an extremely low labor cost. There was no such accord on labor and the WTO concluded that nurturing the economies of the emerging markets was of equal or greater importance than protecting the economies of the US and other developed nations. Proponents of totally free trade argue that the standards of living and political systems are already established and cannot be changed through trade restrictions.

A good example of this point of view is Cuba. The US has completely restricted trade with Cuba for years in an attempt to rally the population against dictator, Fidel Castro. Throughout the trade restrictions, embargo and sanctions, Castro has remained in power and the Cuban standard of living has changed little. A growing number of US firms argue that Cuba is a lost market and restrictions should be lifted.

Politically speaking, the source of international business was Japan in the 1980s, Asian markets (China, Taiwan, Korea, and Hong Kong) in the early 1990s and the developing world in recent years. The issue of child and sweatshop labor in apparel production has served to bring many Latin American countries to the forefront of international business controversy. Attitudes amongst international managers have shifted due to public sentiment on humane manufacturing processes.

Conditions and economies that were acceptable norms are now subjected to increased scrutiny and can change the political relationship between nations. The world community finds some standards of living accepted by citizens unacceptable, and attempts to raise such issues via trade restrictions, rulings, and protest. The success of these attempts is often poor, as evidenced by the fact that apparel still continues to be produced primarily in Asian and developing world markets and shows little signs of a shift.

Literature on Tax Policy

There are two elements of tax policy literature; one focusses on the impact of changes in taxes on foreign investments and the other concentrates on the relationship between taxation and economic freedom.

Firms discriminate against location advantages and disadvantages (Dunning, 1993; Devereux and Freeman, 1995; Caves, 1996) and foreign investors resort to a country's tax advantages or move away from highly taxed location (see, for example, Devereux and Griffith, 1998; Grubert and Mutti, 2000; for a synthesis of empirical research, de Mooij and Ederveen, 2003).

Desai, Foley and Hines (2003, 2004) found that both direct and indirect taxes exert strong impact on location investment by multinationals and that the tax rate elasticity found is 7.7 concerning Europe and 2.3 for other countries for the direct taxes.

The tendency to encourage investment decisions based on fiscal policy might escalate over time (for example, Zodrow, 2003; Kubicová, 2004) due to high capital mobility. Experts believe intergovernmental tax competition is desirable to enhanced domestic efficiency (for example, Blankart, 2002), though it is not clear whether distortions from fiscal competition actually do arise and eventually to what extent do they exist in the case of asymmetric competition between small and large countries.

This latter case, known as the hypothesis of central–peripheral regions which is promoted by Baldwin and Krugman (2004), suggests that central regions tend to agglomerate, thereby having the chance to levy higher taxes with no risk of losing investment in the direction of peripheral regions, seeing that agglomeration might compensate for the tax advantages that peripheral countries offer to investors (Baldwin and Krugman, 2004).

Egger and Winner (2004) find a link between economic freedom and taxation. A large part of the literature has already suggested with positive arguments that economic freedom fosters growth (for example, de Haan and Sturm, 2000). Egger and Winner estimated the impact of economic freedom on the national tax policy (corporate tax revenues to GNP) for 46 developed and less developed countries between 1980 and 1997 and found that firms would be willing to pay more in exchange for economic freedom. Economic freedom attracts investors and enables governments to levy higher business taxes. Egger and Winner's work reveals that changes in economic freedom have equalized the international distribution of corporate tax revenues to GNP; Huizinga and Nicodeme (2003) have shown that the countries that witness foreign investment tend to have higher corporate taxes than other countries.

Under a different perspective, increasing economic integration among countries may lead to strategic statutory tax setting. This has been found by Devereux et al. (2002a) in selected OECD countries in the 1980s and 1990s, and would have similar effects on corporate income tax ratios in GDP (Besley et al., 2001) as found in 29 OECD countries.

Decreasing taxation rates have been found by Devereux et al. (2002a). Statutory corporate tax rates and effective tax rates (note that the statutory tax rate does not mirror the effective tax rate) fell for the two last decades. Grubert (2001) observed that average effective tax rates shrank by ten per cent between 1984 and 1992 in a sample of 60 countries.

In addition, Devereux et al. (2002b) experimented with tax competition with each other to attract investment and calculate a "fiscal reaction function" for 21 OECD countries in 1983–99. They developed two models with firm mobility and capital mobility, and countries would compete only over the statutory tax rate or the effective average tax rate in the first case, while countries competed only over the effective marginal tax rate in the other case with capital mobility. Devereux et al. (2002b) estimated the parameters of "fiscal reaction functions" and proved that countries compete over all the three measures, particularly over the statutory tax rate and the effective average tax rate. In contrast to the aforementioned issue, Grubert (2001) maintained that tax rates shrank over time but tax rates did not converge; this implies that tax competition has been absent.

Sergi (2006b) studies the linkage between tax competition and foreign investment in Europe. Although a link between these two phenomena is unambiguous for the majority of economists, the literature ignores its long-term implication. To gauge the economic rationale of this issue, Sergi (2006b) considers the experience in Western and Eastern Europe, which he understands as central versus peripheral regions, and distinguishes between short- and long-term. As long as policy-makers want to attract foreign investment and have incomplete information over optimal taxation policy, these facts may inspire one country to initiate cutting tax rates. Because other countries would respond similarly, a dynamic tax policy response would cause methodical tax rivalry among peripheral regions as they aim at the same tax purpose on one side, and between them and central regions on the other side. The current reality in Europe shows that tax competition benefits peripheral regions in the short-term but that a continuing tax competition would make current short-term tax advantages to peripheral regions either disappear or exert negligible weight on international investment decision in the long term, posits Sergi (2006b).

In addition to the above, some suggest that the EU should harmonize corporate income taxes. But it is claimed that tax competition requiring corporate tax rate harmonization is not yet compelling (Zodrow, 2003) or that peripheral regions have to compensate for missing agglomeration that is present in the central regions and harmonization would aggravate the central–peripheral relationship (Baldwin and Krugman, 2004). When facing the trade-offs between tax autonomy and fiscal neutrality in coordinating taxes on consumption, labor, and capital, EU member states' tax reforms should precede tax harmonization, because the costs of distortions within member states may be greater than the gains from reducing intergovernmental tax competition, states Cnossen (2003).

From the Irish Tax Friendly Strategy to Recent Tax Competition in Europe

Internationally, major ruptures with a rising tendency of governments to spend have been taken in the US when as part of the Tax Reform Act of 1986 the US cut the corporate income tax from 46 per cent to 34 per cent, a move that happened nearly concurrently with rate reductions in the UK and Canada. Does current tax competition in Europe resemble Ireland's strategy? Ireland had adopted a friendly tax regime on income, capital, and corporations in the 1980s. This resulted, with other investment incentives to prospective investors, in a foundation stone of economic success, becoming one of the wealthiest countries in the European Union. The overall tax burden in Ireland is now one of the lowest in Europe, and the tax on trading income is down 12.5 per cent from 24 per cent in 2000. This rate has been agreed with the European Commission to replace the ten per cent tax rate on manufacturing profits in place since 1981. A phasing-out regime applies to industrial manufacturing until 2010 and other services operations.

The debate that followed the Irish experience concerned tax policy, and several countries have adopted the idea of competing on taxation. Few figures substantiate occurrences in Western Europe during the first part of the 2000s:

- Austria cut the tax rate on corporation profits from 34 per cent in 2003 to 25 per cent in 2005
- Portugal from 33 per cent to 27.5 per cent
- Belgium reduced its corporate income tax from 40.2 per cent to 33 per cent in 2003
- Denmark agreed upon slashing corporate income taxes from 32 per cent in 2000 to 30 per cent in 2001
- Greece to 35 per cent in 2003, from 40 per cent in 2000
- Iceland cut corporate tax rates to 18 per cent in 2002 from 33 per cent
- Luxembourg to 30.4 per cent from 37.5 per cent.

Recently, the Spanish Prime Minister Zapatero is taking into consideration a flat tax rate on incomes following the recommendations of Miguel Sebastian, one of the government's advisers (that is, 30 per cent instead of the current tax bands, which tops out at 45 per cent; the corporate top rate is 40 per cent). To face unemployment, that was 6.75 per cent of the workforce in the mid-2000s, the Dutch government wanted to offer tax breaks and boost spending for education and the environment. The Prime Minister Jan Peter Balkenende's attempt faces low approval rating ahead of general elections in 2007 and he plans to reduce taxes for middle-income families with children and reduce corporate taxes. The budget was proposed on September 20, 2005 and calls for the corporate tax rate to fall to 29.6 per cent from 31.5 in 2005 and 34.5 in 2004. Also, the Swedish Social Democratic government was facing high unemployment rates and the former left-wing oriented government of Prime Minister Goran Persson wanted to reduce taxes on lower- and middle-income workers as well as lower payroll tax on new hires by small, one-person firms. What was then the Swedish political opposition wanted to curb taxes and jobless benefits and, as of September 2006, Sweden's right-wing won the general elections.

Germany is a very enlightening example, being the largest European economy suffering from companies that are shifting production to countries in Eastern Europe where corporate taxes and labor costs are comparatively competitive. Germany's unemployment rates hit a post-war high in March 2005, with a 12 per cent jobless rate (according to seasonally adjusted figures), compared with about 5 per cent in the UK and the US (the non-seasonally adjusted figures are even worse). Former Chancellor Schröder announced in March 2005 an extension of the labor market reform known as "Agenda (2010)" in such a way that he would push through tax reforms and drop federal tax on profits from 25 per cent to 19 per cent. Note, however, that this slashes the current 38.3 per cent to roughly 32 per cent when taking into account local business taxes and the solidarity tax. Closing tax loopholes and raising taxes on dividends will mostly offset Germany's tax cut rate, and this fact represents a key issue to debate next. The former opposition leader, Angela Merkel—who did not obtain a solid majority in the September 18, 2005 general elections—was strongly considering revising the country's tax policy, and her main adviser Paul Kirchhof, who could have become the country's Finance Minister, is a supporter of a 25 per cent flat tax for individuals and corporations (Sergi, 2005b). However, while it was widely expected that the new government would be able to introduce businessperson-oriented tax reforms, and after the election which proved inconclusive, and due to the country's budget troubles, the new Chancellor Angela Merkel and the "Grosse Koalition"—or the "grand coalition" of the center-right and center-left parties—did not introduce any fiscal cut. In contrast, the new government increased tax brackets for higher income (for example, in early May 2006 it agreed on a top 45 per cent rather than the current top rate of 42 per cent starting in 2007). In addition to the above, there was a range of measures to reduce government spending by closing tax loopholes, a gradual raising of the retirement age to 67 from 65 and a rise in the value-added tax from 16 per cent to 19 per cent from 2007, also keeping in mind the intent of reducing overall labor costs, that is, tax wedge.

Overall, the unweighted average for corporate income taxes decreased from 33.6 per cent in 2000 to 30.8 per cent in 2003 in OECD countries, from 35.1 per cent to 31.7 per cent in the EU-15 (Sergi, 2005b; Owens, 2005). Whatever is slashing corporate taxes in Europe, however, the US corporate tax rate is still at 39.4 per cent, even after major corporate tax reductions in the 1980s. To clarify the gap between Europe and the US, the effective tax rate for US companies operating in Europe in 2002 would have been 9 per cent in Portugal and the Netherlands, 12 per cent in Belgium and 13 per cent in Spain, according to Martin A. Sullivan (2005) (quoted in *The Wall Street Journal Europe*, January 28–30, 2005, A9). By way of comparison, the effective tax rate in the US has been calculated at some 32 per cent in 2001 by Jane Gravelle of the US Congressional Research Service, or approximately 10 per cent higher in the US than the European average, as calculated by Margie Rollinson of Ernst & Young (quoted in *The Wall Street Journal Europe*, January 28–30, 2005, A9).

Nevertheless, a comparison between statutory corporate tax and the average effective tax rate across the Atlantic is not straightforward. This is a result of the American system that taxes less labor and consumption than the practice in vogue in Europe. Second, the distribution of tax revenue among major taxes explains differences between the two sides of the Atlantic. While Europe relies more on social security contributions, the United States collects more money from personal income and property taxes. Third, the tax-to-GDP ratio was 25.4 per cent in the US while 40.6 per cent in the EU-15 in 2003. In fact, the US tax base is narrowly defined and our reported figures and tax policies should be judged with more care when making comparisons.

Some Revealing Cases

In a larger international context, a few more cases are informative. For instance, Saudi Arabia cut the corporate tax rate on August 15, 2004. The country's tax system had remained unchanged since 1948 and the new flat tax rate of 20 per cent applies to all industries, except gas projects that remain at 30 per cent, and oil and hydrocarbons at 80 per cent. Perhaps this also eased the country's entry into the WTO as well; surely, the main purpose of slashing corporate tax burdens was to trigger foreign investment, though taxpayers should also benefit from a new defined set of tax rules. Singapore has embarked on a policy of tax reduction since the 1960s, when the top personal rate was 55 per cent in 1961. The Singapore government's Economic Review Committee recommended in 2002 a further step: 20 per cent for both corporate and personal income tax within three years. The top personal and corporate tax rates now stand at 22 per cent. Hong Kong has a dual income tax system under which individuals are taxed between 2 per cent and 20 per cent or at a flat rate of 16 per cent on their gross income, depending on which liability is lower. The top corporate tax rate is 17.5 per cent.

Recently, Switzerland is an example of strategic tax setting. The country has some of the lowest corporate tax rates in the world, attracting multinational companies to set up holdings in one of its 26 cantons, or regions. A recent survey showed that 18 cantons intended to lower their taxes in 2006 in order to slash the levy on wealth and share dividends to attract wealthy residents and businesses. This gained momentum in cantons such as Zug, Schwyz, Nidwalden, and Obwalden, to attract wealthy people and international investors with the lure of low taxes heated up on January 1, 2006, when Obwalden introduced the lowest corporate rates among cantons, and to introduce a regressive income tax system that reduces rates as income rises, especially for those earning over $233,000 a year. Empirical evidence shows that Swiss taxpayers reside where income taxes are low and that there is a strategic tax setting by cantonal governments: the result is that the income tax rates in cantons are lower tax rates than their neighbors (see Schmidheiny, 2004; Feld and Reulier, 2005).

The lessons we can draw from this section are that Singapore and Hong Kong have grown impressively. Ireland is one of the richest countries in Europe today. Finally, Western Europe is enjoying lower effective tax rates on corporations' profits than the US, Central, and Eastern European countries, and is accelerating on having an even more friendly tax system than its Western counterparts have.

Tax Policies in Central and Eastern Europe

Central and Eastern European countries have campaigned for slashing taxes since the mid-1990s, particularly implementing a national level flat type tax rate. This is understood to reduce red tape and discrimination among taxpayers, to counterbalance tax dodging and cheating, to create more incentives to work, save, and invest. The success of the flat tax type depends on the actual level of the tax rate: the lower it is, the more efficient it will become to swell tax revenue and spark off economic growth. The first country to implement a uniform flat tax for personal and profit incomes (26 per cent) was Estonia in 1994, although a decisive step toward lower rates was adopted in 1991. This country started a highly favorable attitude toward foreign investment, which was governed by new legislation striving to maintain liberal policies in order to attract investments. Estonia set further tax reduction in stages to be introduced by 2007, but surely as important has been Estonia's decision to eliminate the tax on retained earning in 2000. Latvia followed and together with Lithuania, both have a corporate tax of 15 per cent, and tax rates on personal income at 25 per cent and 33 per cent, respectively.

Surprisingly, Russia moved towards a new tax model effective January 1, 2001. President Putin's first step has been to introduce a 13 per cent personal income flat tax rate, which replaced three-bracket tax with a top rate of 30 per cent. Effective January 1, 2002, a 24 per cent corporate flat rate was also introduced, down from 35 per cent. Since January 1, 2003, small business enterprises have been granted either a 20 per cent flat tax on profits or an 8 per cent flat tax on revenues. Small business enterprises have also been exempted from value-added tax, sales tax, property tax, and social insurance tax. Recently, in September 2005, both Vladimir Putin and the Prime Minister Viktor Khristenko were seriously considering introducing tax breaks for oil companies to encourage exploring new fields (Sergi, 2005b).

Other countries took up this new trend recently. Serbia and Ukraine adopted new tax codes in 2003. Serbia introduced a comprehensive 14 per cent flat tax on personal income and corporate profits, though the country is setting up a 10 per cent flat tax for most forms of personal income. Ukraine implemented a 13 per cent tax on personal income (replacing five brackets, 10–40 per cent) and a 25 per cent tax on profits (down from 30 per cent). Moldova is bringing its corporate tax rate down to 20 per cent from 25 per cent and lowering the top tax rate on personal income to 22 per cent from 32 per cent. Hungary lowered corporate taxes to 16 per cent; Poland cut the rate by 8 percentage points to 19 per cent, Slovakia from 29 per cent in 2000 to 25 per cent in 2002 and 19 per cent effective January 1, 2005.

In 2005, comprehensive tax reforms took effect in Georgia and Romania. In Georgia, a 12 per cent flat tax on personal income has been inaugurated by parliament. In Romania, the new government of Prime Minister Calin Popescu Tariceanu has introduced a flat corporate and personal income tax of 16 per cent to be enforced starting January 1, 2005, which aims at preventing tax evasion and time corruption, and attracting foreign investment. The new system, enforced with a special ordinance on December 29, 2004, replaced the previous personal income tax, which consisted of five brackets (top of 40 per cent), and top business profits rate of 25 per cent. Romania was simply trying to prevent tax evasion, time corruption, and

Global Business Management

Table 5.1   The Index of Fiscal Burden, Europe and North America

Rank	Country	Fiscal Burden
1	Cyprus	1.8
1	Slovak Republic	1.8
3	Estonia	2.0
3	Hungary	2.0
3	Macedonia	2.0
6	Latvia	2.1
7	Armenia	2.3
8	Bulgaria	2.4
8	Georgia	2.4
10	Ireland	2.5
11	Iceland	2.6
11	Canada	2.6
11	Moldova	2.6
11	Bosnia and Herzegovina	2.6
11	Ukraine	2.6
16	Lithuania	2.8
16	Albania	2.8
18	Poland	2.9
19	Switzerland	3.0
19	Croatia	3.0
21	Russia	3.1
22	Luxembourg	3.3
22	Romania *	3.3
24	Slovenia	3.4
24	Belarus	3.4
26	Finland	3.5
26	Germany	3.5
28	Denmark	3.6
28	Czech Republic	3.6
28	Turkey	3.6
31	Norway	3.8
32	Sweden	3.9
32	Portugal	3.9
32	Mexico	3.9
35	United Kingdom	4.0
35	United States	4.0
35	Greece	4.0
38	Belgium	4.3
38	Italy	4.3
38	Malta	4.3
38	France	4.3
42	Austria	4.4
42	Spain	4.4
44	The Netherlands	4.5

Note: * The index does not take into account tax changes adopted by the government in late 2004.

Source: 2005 Index of Economic Freedom

attract foreign investment. In addition, the Bulgarian Parliament has unanimously passed a law to cut the corporate tax rate from 15 per cent down to 10 per cent from January 1, 2007. Macedonia enjoys a 12 per cent flat tax on profits and personal income and the country will cut both to 10 per cent as of January 2008.

In other countries, tax burdens are already low though a definitive move towards a flat tax is advocated. Poland's former Finance Minister, Mirosaw Gronicki, was proposing a flat tax rate of 18 per cent on personal income, business profits, and value-added tax, attempting to win back voters in September 2005 and overcome the proposal made by the opposition Civic Platform party to introduce a 15 per cent flat tax on personal income and profits. Since the general elections took place and two major right-wing coalition parties won the majority, we should expect a major change in Poland's tax policy. The former Czech opposition Civic Democratic party is suggesting a 15 per cent flat tax on individuals and corporations.

In Table 5.1, we give a broad picture of fiscal burdens in Europe, reporting the index of fiscal burden for 44 European and North American states. This index is part of that calculated by Miles, Feulner and O'Grady (2005) on behalf of the Heritage Foundation and the *Wall Street Journal* in 2005, to form the overall Index of Economic Freedom. The fiscal burden of government is made up of three components:

1. The top marginal income tax rate
2. The top marginal corporate tax rate
3. The year-to-year change in government expenditures as a share of GDP.

The lower is the calculated score, the lower is the involvement of the government in the economic sphere. It is unambiguous that apart from the notable exceptions of Cyprus, Ireland and Iceland, all Eastern and Central European economies are in the highest position in the index, while all remaining rich Western European economies follow. Belarus and the Czech Republic are in the middle rank.

Tax Dumping and Unfair Tax Competition in East–Central Europe

If Central and Eastern European countries jump on the flat tax bandwagon, this could be a magnet for investment and economic growth, and could lead to the accusation of unfair "tax competition" and "tax dumping," and that some governments are strategically setting their tax rates at the expense of other countries' attractiveness (on the theory of international tax competition and Europe's experience, see, for example, OECD, 1998; Sorensen, 2001; Zodrow, 2003; Egger and Winner, 2004; Kubicová, 2004; Sergi, 2005b, 2006b). In summary, statutory corporate income tax rates in the EU-15 declined from 35.1 per cent in 2000 to 31.7 per cent in 2003, partially to face tax rate competition and avoid losing further business activities because of "an unequal corporate tax burden in Europe," stated the former German Chancellor Schröder (Sergi, 2005b). Germany is the largest European economy that is suffering from many companies that are shifting production to countries in Eastern Europe where corporate taxes and labor costs are comparatively lower. Fears of negative effects on labor markets are scattering in Europe as new EU member states could lure companies, jobs, and investment flows. To thwart risky tax competition, a tax corridor has been proposed through which minimum and maximum corporate tax rates would be put in place. In addition, European Commissioner for Taxation, Laszlo Kovacs, recommended harmonizing the corporate tax base (in line with the recommendation made by the European Commission in 2001) aimed to skip unfair competition for foreign investment and prevent uneven foreign investment distribution. In fact, some complain that their contributions to the EU budget to support structural and cohesion funds towards new members could end up paying for tax cuts. Some former leaders of Europe's strongest economies (for example, former German Chancellor Gerhard Schröder and former Swedish Prime Minister Goran Persson) were afraid that transition economies can cut taxes not least because any lost revenue is more than compensated by subsidies from Brussels. According to Schröder, it is unacceptable that his country, being the EU's biggest net payer, finances "unfair tax competition." If the German Chancellor dubbed this practice a dangerous "tax-dumping," the former French Finance Minister Nicolas Sarkozy expressed the same as Schröder and indeed suggested cutting European transfers to states practicing it. In addition, new EU member states with below-average tax regimes should not receive aid funds from Europe, stated Sarkozy.

The transition states that could undergo negative effects have repeatedly refuted this argument (Sergi, 2005b). Overall, tax burdens on corporate profits are approximately 15–20 per cent in the East, compared to tax rates in the Eastern European states that can be twice as high. In addition, the East has also been proffering several investment incentives. Nevertheless, this reveals nothing about the effective tax burden and the ways in which the tax base is formed (that is, a company's debt, machinery depreciation, and so on), and indeed can be deceiving when comparing countries. First, despite the statutory corporate income tax rates that have fallen in the European Union countries during the 1990s, we must recall that these are broadening the base rate. Second, several European governments grant deductions, exceptions, and various kinds of tax relief, such as relief for research and development, or investment in poor areas. As a result, effective tax rates vary from the statutory tax rate. For instance, in Germany's complicated tax system, the effective corporation tax rate is estimated to be only half of the statutory rate, and some of the country's largest companies enjoy so many tax breaks that their effective tax rate is zero (Barysch, 2004).

Toward a New Form of Competition in Europe

It is well known that effective tax rates on corporate profits have been a significant tool to attract foreign investors in Central and Eastern Europe; this will be equally important over coming years. Investors and policy-makers, however, should focus more on the importance of the overall investment climate, as several other factors besides taxes determine a country's competitiveness over the long term. In actuality, competitiveness in an interacting and multifaceted international business environment asks for continuous efforts to keep costs in labor markets apace with workers' productivity growth, to eliminate regulatory restrictions whenever possible, to reduce the high tax wedge and payroll taxes in order to cut the cost of hiring, and further overhauls.

These changes could have consequences for many aspects of the economy and for investors' long-term strategies, as Sergi (2006b) posits. By way of example, Hungary's experience is very revealing: the country has witnessed close to ten foreign investors, such as IBM and Philips, moving some or all of their Hungarian operations to cheaper places further East and South in Europe. In a short-term attempt to lure further resources and to compete more strongly with other neighboring markets, Hungary cut corporate tax rates to 16 per cent from 18 per cent and dropped the top tax rate on personal income to 38 per cent from 41.5 per cent.

Perhaps less valued is the fact that international and regional competition depends on the strength of several factors that drive the business process. As fierce competition is growing increasingly important, decision-makers in Europe introduced the cutting of tax rates, and other incentives such as cash grants, fixed-term tax relief, and labor subsidies, to keep attracting investors. Because policy-makers do not have complete information on optimal tax rates, cutting tax rates has become a systematic policy in Europe where a country's first move is followed by another country's reaction.

However, the combined implication of this action–reaction tax policy has been less considered. Although we have not calculated whether FDI is or is not highly elastic to tax changes, the tax competition argument is central when confined to a short-term horizon, much less when we shift the analysis from the short term to the long term. Decision-makers in peripheral regions keep competing against each other because they emphasize tax breaks as a long-term panacea, or rather, they simply fail to spot the optimal tax rate: both these facts push them to initiate an endless tax game (Sergi, 2006b). That is, long-term effects from tax competition have been emphasized, but the rationale behind these occurrences could steer the business environment toward a convergence of investment opportunities when they are based on tax advantages only. Starting a tax competition between central and peripheral countries in Europe could likely maneuver national business environments toward tax equalization. In the long term, resorting to systematic tax slashes necessarily makes peripheral European regions work with a fiscal tool that would exert no impact on investors' international strategic decisions in the long term simply because effective tax rates would converge on the same level.

Additionally, buoyant economic growth in Europe's peripheral regions is helping maintain state revenues adequate for a budget in equilibrium. Nevertheless, what would happen to public finance should the economic growth slow down sometime in the future without a serious restructuring of policy priorities and public revenues? Therefore, the debate has to be firmly based on the long-term wisdom of tax strategy among peripheral and central regions, without overlooking competitiveness taken as a whole. If competition in Europe calls for innovative policies, rejuvenating peripheral regions in Europe rests also on technological innovation, less rigid labor regulations, and the smallest tax wedge. At present, if it seems that the most important challenge for the European Commission is to introduce a more rational course of action based on a definitive tax policy harmonization, the tax competition race could hit a new level. To thwart risky tax competition, a tax corridor has been proposed through which minimum and maximum corporate tax rates could be put in place. During the hearing of Laszlo Kovacs, the 2004 designated European Commissioner for Taxation, he expressed in favor of the creation of a common consolidated corporate taxation base (European Parliament, 2004). Recently, Kovacs told a gathering of the Irish Business and Employers Federation, the Irish Bankers' Federation and members of the European Parliament that formal plans for a common EU corporate tax base will be unveiled soon and the Commission will present revised proposals on a Common Consolidated Corporate Tax Base (available at: http://www.tax-news.com/asp/story/Ireland_Prepares_Defences_Against_European_Tax_Harmonisation_xxxx27087. html). This would be in line with the suggestions made in the Bolkstein Report and published by the European Commission in 2001 aimed to skip unfair competition for foreign investment and prevent uneven foreign investment distribution. Commissioner Kovacs hopes the proposals will be in place by the end of 2008. This move is intended to bring transparency and simplification, and a significant reduction in compliance costs for businesses operating within the EU. Should the latter be the case, short-term fiscal policy advantages would become vague among peripheral regions in the medium and long term (Sergi, 2006b).

To help understand this point, one appealing property of any tax system to be the major factor contributing to significant increase in FDI is that tax advantages are "generous" and "persist" over time: these two characteristics secure the attention from foreign investors. While it is difficult to get a precise measure of the relative contribution of tax advantages to FDI, recent statistical figures indicate that changes in the tax system in European emerging markets may have been one of the key factors contributing to this. However, as long as tax competition hits a new level in Europe, the interest of international investors in one particular country or another tends to vanish. That is, tax elasticity could equalize among these peripheral regions and a tendency toward equalization in turn would happen between peripheral and central regions. It follows that the probability that a multinational enterprise prefers one country or another within the same peripheral area upon mere tax advantages fades away.

If tax advantages could have been advantageous in the recent past, unit labor costs, other financial incentives, and geographical locations are equally important, and laying emphasis on tax advantages would be an oversight in the long-term. In addition, shifting profits to tax havens is another way to skip national tax disadvantages; this could induce big corporations to have plants in several countries. It follows that tax advantages may not be enough to attract FDI in the end because big corporations could still exploit a specific country's tax legislation while having a plant somewhere at the same time. Simply, the phenomenon of FDI, outsourcing, and international business in Europe requires a comprehensive rather than a narrow tax-policy scrutiny in the end.

The Politics of Most Favored Nation Status

Through Asian markets, many international managers have recently learned the impacts of politics on international business, specifically, concerning the trade status known as Most Favored Nation (MFN). MFN is the term used to describe the favorable tariff prices that almost all countries receive from the United States. The only exceptions to this trade status are Afghanistan, Cambodia, Cuba, Laos, North Korea, and Serbia/Montenegro (Kapp, 1998).

In 1997, President Clinton ended a several-year conflict concerning the status of MFN with China. Most Favored Nation status had been granted to China since 1980, per a commercial agreement. Controversy ensued when human rights activists began to lobby to end MFN with China until the human rights abuses are brought to an end. Threatening the end of MFN status has been seen as the strongest way to persuade the Chinese government to move closer to democracy, but the price of that threat to the US is potentially more damaging to US businesses than it is to the Chinese. By 1991, China had a $15 billion trade deficit with the United States, had exported $19 billion worth of products, and had stated they would increase tariffs on US goods. It was obvious that millions of jobs would be lost in both countries if MFN status were not continued.

The first to face the issue of renewing China's MFN status in light of their flagrant human rights abuses was President George H. W. Bush. The Chinese United Nations veto power, its trade issues, and its increasing nuclear power all contributed to its importance in world affairs. Bush's strong foreign policy background seemed to give him an advantage in this area. When the massacre of students occurred in Tiananmen Square, the event went unacknowledged by Bush. Suddenly, revoking MFN status seemed the only way to communicate to China that a continuous disregard for human rights was not acceptable. However, President Bush went on to veto every bill placed before him, which linked the Chinese human rights issue to that of their MFN status.

This trend later haunted President Clinton in his foreign policy dealings. President Clinton's view of China was much different from that of President Bush. He believed that progress should be made on human rights in China before MFN status was continued. By this time, special interest groups, political action committees, and business lobbyists were all strongly vocalizing their opinions. In a White House press briefing, Winston Lord (1993), Assistant Secretary of State, who had been extensively involved in the MFN situation, was quoted as stating, "It would be very helpful if the business community could make progress … as effectively as they are lobbying the congress and the President."

Despite all the pressure, there continued to be no progress on either side of the issue. Clinton began to consider the economics of de-linking the two issues. Ultimately, it was seen that continuing MFN status with China was imperative to keeping American jobs and normal trade relations between the two countries.

The impact of the outcome in this particular example was monumental for global managers. Consider for a moment that China's MFN status was not continued; for companies without Chinese subsidiaries it still would have meant the loss of jobs, exports, and potential markets. For companies with Chinese subsidiaries, all of the same would be potential disasters in addition to having to contend with China's changing economic environment. A situation like the one ending China's MFN status could threaten expatriates living in China and have adverse effects on their businesses. It is also important to realize that MFN is a two-way street.

While the US may be the one granting the trade status, it also means that China gives us that status in return. The United States would never suddenly solve a complex social, economic, or political problem simply because one of our major trading partners told us to. China is the largest country in the world and one of the United States' largest trading partners yet we would expect this action from them. The outcome of this issue, and whether or not it continues to draw attention, is a cause for concern amongst international managers. These issues have become an ongoing difficulty of doing business in the global marketplace. Big business can ill afford to not be involved with China; to have to face the MFN issue every year would become very troublesome and would consume a great deal of time that could be spent productively on other key areas of operation.

Politics of Joint Ventures

While an international manager's response to a country's MFN status is more of a reactive management style, when it comes to joint ventures a proactive strategy is pursued. Joint ventures can be the best way for two diverse companies to maximize the strengths of each other's business acumen while mutually profiting through the shared knowledge. However, the politics involved in joint ventures causes them to be a complex business dynamic that should not be entered into lightly.

Many considerations need to be thought of before a joint venture can even begin to materialize. Along with the decisions of who and where are the problems that arise when dealing with distances, travel, currencies, language barriers, laws and customs, the global manager must consider the country's culture; for instance, is it orientated towards small, family businesses or is it urban and open to industrialization? Once two companies decide to form a joint venture, they must decide a demographically correct region in which to locate their business.

A good example illustrating the complications of this decision can be seen in the case of Denmark's Carlsberg and Holland's Heineken breweries. Both are top ten breweries in terms of total production. Carlsberg and Heineken were both considering joint ventures in the country of Myanmar. They planned to set up distribution centers to supply their beers to Myanmar and other Southeast Asian countries. A military government rules Myanmar and it was ultimately that military rule that reversed the decisions of both Carlsberg and Heineken in their potential joint ventures in the region. Some human rights organizations had pressured Heineken to withdraw its investment in Myanmar, and Heineken, fearing a consumer boycott, decided to withdraw its Myanmar investment. Similar to the Heineken Beer Company of the Netherlands, the Carlsberg Beer Company from Denmark was also facing pressure from the Danish Burma Committee, a new anti-Myanmar government expatriate group. The human rights groups protested that the companies' joint venture in Myanmar would be construed as support of the military government and in some way would contribute economic assistance to that regime. As a result, the government stopped the import and sales of these beers.

As an international manager, it seems an enormous job to find a country that would be appropriate for a joint venture. Weighing the social, economic, and political aspects of a country is a critical issue whose costs can be high, but ultimately can determine the success or failure of the venture. In the case of Carlsberg and Heineken, their international managers must now deal with the loss of sales to Myanmar and other Southeast Asian countries.

No company wants to choose between political and economic factors and have a potential market cut off from sales of their product. What if the Southeast Asian countries represented one of Carlsberg and Heineken's most profitable potential markets? The next choice for an international business would be to deal with the prospect of finding new markets or increasing sales in existing markets. It is easy to see the difficulty that can be involved in the preliminary stages of the joint venture process.

Both of the companies involved in joint ventures must also be cautious of their actions during the time of the commitment. People by nature are very concerned with fairness and trust, and these concerns become accelerated in joint ventures. It is important that the two parties involved trust each other and that fairness exists in equal profit sharing.

Pepsi-Cola and Lipton Tea formed a joint venture on October 14, 2003, which exemplifies trust in business. This joint venture was formed in 1991 between the two beverage companies in order for Lipton to make their iced tea using Pepsi's production processes for sales of iced tea in glass bottles. A year later, the project was going nowhere, but the trust between the two companies kept them searching for new ideas. This is how Lipton Brisk was formed. The leader in its market, Lipton Brisk is iced tea sold in cans and plastic bottles like most soft drinks today. By utilizing this manner of production, Brisk could also be produced and distributed using Pepsi's existing facilities. This is an excellent example of the promising results that are possible with joint ventures if a good working relationship is fostered.

It is also very important to recognize that not all joint ventures are going to be as mutually advantageous as that of Lipton and Pepsi-Cola. In today's complex global marketplace, a myriad of conflicting issues and agendas frequently present themselves. Unfortunately, when this happens it is not as easy as a handshake and a "better luck next time." A joint venture is often a contractual relationship that is binding.

Withdrawing from a Joint Venture

There are many considerations to be accounted for before parties can withdraw from a joint venture. Most of the complications seem to fall on the shoulders of the withdrawing party. It may become impossible to restrict the remaining company from using trademarks, company secrets, and expertise or any disclosed information vital to the life of the joint venture. There is also the possibility of the remaining company enforcing a non-competition covenant, thereby prohibiting the other company from competing in the future. While this type of restriction is not always enforceable by law, it is still worth recognizing as a possible outcome of a joint venture.

Other problems that can arise are complications with distribution or research and development, particularly if any patents involved in the joint venture are held in the name of the joint venture. Perhaps all of the former have been discussed and a consensus reached; now a decision must be made on what path to follow in ending the joint venture. There are three ways to go about this: the two companies may have a buy-out, a shoot-out, or a complete dissolution.

In a buy-out, the remaining company simply buys out the withdrawing company. Buy-out presents several complications. First, if the company that has chosen to withdraw is the local company, it may be impossible by law for the foreign company to buy out the local company. Even where it is legal, there is a possibility that it will be ill received by the local population. In addition, the value of a business in one country may not be the same as its value in another country, so some agreement must be met on the value and price, if conditions exist.

A shoot-out is a situation where one party offers to sell its shares to the other party for a stated amount. If the other party does not buy the shares, then they must sell their shares to the first party for that amount. This option is much more of a gamble and becomes increasingly complicated when government involvement is necessary.

The final way a joint venture may be ended is by complete dissolution. Potential conflicts can occur if the laws of the country in question do not permit this type of action. This type of action is usually a last ditch effort to end a joint venture when a compromise cannot be reached.

It is also very important to keep in mind that it is possible for two companies to destroy the current or potential value of a joint venture by ending the relationship. Aspects such as name recognition, quality, and standardization are ways in which a complete dissolution can damage a joint venture. From an international manager's standpoint, complete dissolution is to be avoided. No manager or company would want to invest the time, personnel, and numerous other assets in a joint venture that could prove to be unbeneficial in the end, or that puts the company further behind than they were previously.

Politics of Employment Law

When conducting international business, the global community uses the law in many different ways. The use of the law varies according to the system of government in place. It is easy to assume that democracy is the norm rather than the exception; while this is increasingly true, new democracies sometimes find themselves on politically shaky ground. While the definition of democracy means governed by the people, in different countries this has many connotations. For instance, in South Africa, if the law fails to produce the desired outcome, many believe that it should be set aside, manipulated, or ignored (Gibson and Gouws, 2002, 188). This presents problems if the nation ever decides they may need some or all of the law's provisions in the future. In this case, it would prove quite difficult to reenact the law. This fits into employment law because changing countries or ones governed by an unstable or military government tend to be prone to rapid shifts in law, often decreed one week and repealed the next. It is important for global managers to assess accurately the state of the law abroad; sometimes lenient employment laws represent an opportunity for the foreign investor and other times they can be the preliminary conditions to social revolt among laborers.

The right of workers and employers to establish and to join organizations of their own choosing without previous authorization is an important democratic right. It has the same significance as the right to associate freely in the political sphere and is closely linked to basic political rights such as freedom of expression, of assembly, and from arbitrary arrest (Lee, 1998, 313). It is considered a high priority in the US and other developed nations that people have the right to free thought and speech in the workplace, and that they should not have to get permission regarding how they think and in what they believe. Yet, when the public learns of opposite conditions that exist where their consumer goods are manufactured, a public outcry ensues. However, very seldom does the social pressure lead to any real change in employment law.

In many countries, legislation now requires equal pay for women who perform work of equal value or of comparable worth to that performed by men in the same organization. If all countries adapted the same wage gap as the United States, the ratio of male to female pay would be reduced significantly. Sweden and Australia are two other countries that have a small wage gap. There are other countries that have a very large gap, which results in the worldwide gap being quite significant.

Women receiving a lesser amount of education than men mostly caused the wage gap in the United States before the 1975 law, because women sometimes did not have an opportunity to go to school. There are still many jobs that have a large pay gap between men and women, but there are also jobs that are very competitive between the pay for men and women. Affirmative action and gender quotas have contributed to the rise of females in positions of power and in access to universities. Today, the American working women's average pay is 76 per cent that of men's average pay.

Another breakthrough for women is starting to break through the glass ceiling—the invisible barrier to upper management that does not allow for certain types of people, which includes women and minorities, to progress in the workplace. For example, in 1999 the first woman to be Prime Minister was appointed in New Zealand. In Finland, for the first time a woman became President of the Central Bank; the United Nations had its first woman Commissioner for Human Rights, who was the former President of Ireland; and the World Health Organization had as its first woman Director-General, a former Prime Minister of Norway (Wirth, 1998). When Madeline Albright became the highest-ranking woman in any American Executive Administration, there were concerns that she would not be respected around the world, especially in the Arab world that usually relegates the role of women as a supporting role to men. As the US Secretary of State, she was very successful in the role of the Chief US Foreign Diplomat. While Wirth stated these might be extreme cases, there may be a starting pattern that will continue to grow through the years and will cause the wage gap to grow smaller. This is a good sign for women in the workplace and should be recognized as a growing trend by international managers. These women may be exceptional cases, reflecting strong individual motivation and ability combined with lucky circumstances, which allowed them to rise to top positions (Wirth, 1998).

Politics of Environmental Protection Laws

Although the preventive principle has found its way into at least 15 multinational agreements since making its debut in the 1980s, its application remains highly controversial, especially in the United States. The United States is looked upon by other countries to take the first step in environmental clean-up and pressures others to follow suit. The status of the United States as a highly developed nation causes the world community to look to her for the technology to do so and an expectation that it will use and share such technology.

Some countries, most notably the countries in the developing world and those that are not as advanced as the United States, are not looked upon to make the first step in the clean-up. In fact, these countries have been derided in recent years for their excessive damage to the environment, such as in the Brazilian rain forest and the air quality in Mexico City. What comes of this sentiment is an altogether different thing. For fear of hurting trade relations, the US refused to sign the agreement forged at an environmental summit in Rio de Janeiro, as well as opting out of the Kyoto agreement by President George W. Bush's administration.

The laws around the world are different in some manners but the same in some unifying areas. There are some laws, like laws against nuclear waste, that are in effect worldwide and there are other laws, such as a ban on pouring chemicals down the sewer, that are in effect in a few countries. In less developed countries a foreign company often actively seeks out lax environmental policies and laws, as the taxes, fines and penalties in their home countries can be quite costly.

When looked at, the United States is one of the biggest polluters in the world, but it goes further than most other countries to help clean up the mess that has been created. While environmental damage has been reduced, it is still happening, and the United States wants to look better as a whole in this area. The government has done much in the way of public education on environmental responsibility and recycling, but corporate environmental degradation remains a tough issue. Sometimes a large company opts to pay the fine rather than investing in more advanced, environmentally friendly manufacturing processes. This is an issue that global managers face—the technology is out there, but is it cost-effective?

Politics of Ethics and Social Responsibility

With only a small percentage of the world's population in the Arab Middle East, remarkably this part of the world has seen almost 25 per cent of the world's wars since 1945. Most of these conflicts have been ethically based. This statement alludes to the fact that most barriers between countries exist because of deeply rooted national ethics. These ethics tend to result in many disagreements that lead to conflicts, economic and sometimes violent with other countries. A broad definition of ethics is the system of beliefs held by people of different races and religions in one group. The system grows very complicated when the ethics stem from religious conviction. The Arab region has a significant number of people who lay claim to the same holy-land, share many characteristics, but are of different highly secular religions (Muslims, Christians, Jews, and Copts) that influence almost every act of society. This is what causes the majority of the conflicts. Countries with a variety of people, cultures, and religions can deal with the ethics of another country in a better manner.

Despite the predominance of ethnic conflicts in the Arab world, Arab social scientists and political activists alike have not given the observable fact its due share of attention. If this were done, there might be a chance that there would not be as many conflicts in the future between the Arab world and the other countries which deal with them. If this matter was given some consideration, then it just might be resolved to the point that their role in conflicts would be greatly reduced in the world. Participatory political systems have proven to be the most effective modality for peaceful management of social cleavages in general and ethnic conflict in particular (Ibrahim, 1995). When the weight of the problem is put on the political system and the problem represents the people's concerns fairly and effectively, the state of affairs will be more peaceful and, as a result, not as many conflicts will arise in the end.

Smelser (1998) states: "There has been a general increase in the pattern of international economic interdependence during the past three decades, revealing a thirty-fold in volume of world trade. The same decades have seen a remarkable redistribution of economic activity throughout the world" (Smelser, 1998, 175). This statement means that smaller countries are not depending on larger countries for trade and economic stimulation but are seeking to establish themselves as emerging markets in world trade.

Corporate social responsibility (CSR) is having an impact on where and with whom major multinational corporations do business. CSR factors include business ethics, corporate accountability, sustainability, and corporate citizenship. A study, called Race to the Top, prepared in October 2003 for the World Bank and the International Finance Corporation, has confirmed such.

Among the observations and findings were that 88 per cent of participating companies report that these factors are of great influence in determining where they source and invest in—more so than such factors were five years ago. In addition, 52 per cent of participating companies have chosen one developing-country partner over another based on their CSR policies (Study Reveals Corporate Social Responsibility a Major Factor in Overseas Investment and Purchasing, 2004).

The report (Study Reveals Corporate Social Responsibility a Major Factor in Overseas Investment and Purchasing, 2004) also included recommendations such as:

*   Addressing CSR concerns of potential investors early in their evaluation of new ventures
*   Identifying CSR-ready partners for international firms
*   Evenly enforcing strong laws on CSR-related issues, such as environment, health, safety, and corruption
*   Reaching out to large multinational corporations as public–private partners, focusing on the company's stated CSR goals and programs.

The project, which included more than 100 MNEs, was specially made by the World Bank Group to determine whether a business' social responsibility affects the international decisions of the major companies in the world. The study determined that global companies are committed to establishing lasting social and economic value in their host communities, and that the investment and purchase decisions are influenced by where they can meet those commitments.

Whether it is service to stakeholders or good citizenship, it appears that ethics and social responsibility are becoming more important and visible. Doing what is socially and ethically correct gives companies a better chance of succeeding in the long term. According to *Business Ethics* magazine (Spring, 2004), the following companies have been on the list of 100 Best Corporate Citizens for the past five years:

1. Fannie Mae
2. Procter & Gamble
3. Intel Corporation
4. St. Paul Companies
6. Deere & Company
7. Avon Products
8. Hewlett Packard
10. Ecolab Inc.
12. IBM
14. Herman Miller
17. Timberland Company
19. Cisco Systems
22. Southwest Airlines
24. Motorola
27. Cummins Inc.
31. Adolph Coors
32. Modine Manufacturing
33. Clorox
43. AT&T
44. Pitney Bowes
45. Starbucks Coffee
48. Merck & Company
49. Graco
53. Brady Corporation
57. Medtronic
63. New York Times Co.
74. Golden West Financial
89. Sonoco Products
98. Whirlpool

Politics of Importing and Exporting

Politics plays a large role when importing or exporting to or from a country. It sets which tariffs will be placed on the items imported or exported and it affects which items may be imported or exported, and from where.

One of the ways that politics affects trade is by imposing trade restrictions. There are many political reasons a country would impose trade restrictions. One reason to impose a trade restriction is to protect national defense. Some industries need protection because they are vital to national defense. Competition from a foreign firm could drive the domestic firms out of business, and then in times of need, such as wartime, these imports may not be available.

Another reason to impose trade restrictions is to help an infant industry grow. In order for an industry to grow, it needs to be protected from foreign competitors so that they do not drive the growing industry out of business. Allowing a growing industry to be killed may harm competition or the host country. This protection is meant to last for only a limited time, although many companies will not admit when they have matured and will want to continue to receive protection.

The governments of most developing countries accept the end of protection as a valid reason to invoke a trade restriction. The first firm in a new industry to a new country will usually get protection for an unspecified amount of time. Some of the larger developing countries, however, have been reducing their protection for companies like these so the companies are forced to lower their prices and become more competitive. Many international businesses seek out developing markets to receive this kind of protection and to establish themselves while the market is new.

Scientific tariffs or fair competition is another way to invoke trade restrictions. This simply imposes a tariff on the imported good to bring it up to the cost of similar domestic goods. This eliminates any unfair advantages that a foreign competitor might have because of cheaper labor costs, better technology, lower materials cost, or lower taxes.

Retaliation often occurs when trade restrictions are imposed on an industry. The industry may ask its host country's government to impose a similar trade restriction on the country to which it is trying to export.

There are many benefits of international trade; however, many nations will put limits on trade for various reasons noted below. The main categories of trade restrictions are quotas, tariffs, standards, subsidies, and embargoes:

- A tariff is a tax put on goods imported from overseas. Tariffs raise the price of the imported product and help domestic producers of like products to sell them at higher prices. The domestic government collects the revenue received from the tariff. Tariffs imposed on goods being imported may also be politically motivated. Tariffs are usually levied on imports for raising the selling price of the imported goods. This is utilized for either reducing the competition for domestic products or discouraging the importation of other products. Some small countries use tariffs to raise revenue for their country.
- Quotas. When referring to imports, a quota designates the maximum quantity and can have a significant impact on certain industries and companies. A quota

will create a shortage of that particular good, which causes the price to rise. Domestic producers then raise their prices and expand their production.

- Standards are regulations and/or laws that countries use to restrict imports. Nations may establish health and safety standards for imported goods that are higher than those for the goods that are produced domestically. These standards have become a major form of trade restriction and are used differently by many countries.

- Subsidies are grants of money given by the government to the domestic producers to encourage exports. Those companies who receive subsidies can use them to pay production costs and as a result can charge less for their goods than foreign manufacturers.

- An embargo is an edict or order of the government prohibiting the departure of commerce from some or all of the ports within its dominions. An embargo stops imports or exports of a product to or from another country. There may be times that all trade with a country is stopped, usually for political reasons.

The theory of parallel import has received wide attention in the study of international trade and its practice. This form of import takes place when someone starts importing a particular product in competition with the exclusive authorized dealer in the same country for that product. In the case of software, a parallel imported version should be referred to as a perfect substitute for the version that the official dealer officially imports into the market. While this fact creates a conflict between the third party importer and the property right proprietor of the official distribution channel, the basic rationale for this phenomenon to occur is that someone else from the official importer could buy something in a cheaper foreign country and import what has been purchased into the dearer country. It could resemble an international free trade notion, but the basic issue here is that the price for some similar goods that differ among destination countries—different mark-ups of prices over marginal costs of exports—could be explained by transport costs, disparities in demand elasticities across countries, imperfect competition in international markets, barriers to arbitrage, and protection provided by the parallel import ban overall (see Skoko, 2005). This parallel import would harm the higher price in the targeted country and trouble the official dealer there, resulting in redistribution from manufacturers to intermediaries. If producers could attempt to set a uniform high price for all markets, at the same time, the producers would enjoy not destroying the parallel import totally as it could exploit the heterogeneity of markets and find a compromise between setting uniformed prices and country-specific prices. However, it is worth mentioning that the processes of globalization, IT development, a business culture more open to internationalization, and Internet-driven electronic commerce (note that it has been estimated that the value of Internet-transacted goods and services at the global level is over $200 billion per year at the beginning of the 2000s) have been hastening over the past decades, this fact envisaging the end of such a territoriality idea of export/ import, that is, exactly the opposite of what parallel imports are based on. This reality will be blurring geographical barriers (see Skoko, 2005) and steer toward a diminishing differing mark-up to negligible numbers so the phenomenon could disappear eventually. This new global market reality could lead to reduced price differences between markets and make difficult the same notion of parallel import.

Politics in Expropriation and Confiscation

Expropriation occurs when a government seizes property within its borders that belongs to another country and compensates the owner of the seized goods promptly and adequately. Many times, countries that are unstable will use expropriation to prevent money from leaving the country. International law states that compensation must be given for expropriation of another country's goods. If compensation is not given, it then becomes confiscation.

Many times this procedure becomes almost a game between two countries. This took place between the United States and the former USSR during the Cold War. The former USSR confiscated property belonging to the United States. In retaliation, the United States confiscated the Soviet Union's property in the United States. Indirectly, this makes the former Soviet Union's confiscation of US property an expropriation. American firms or individuals who had property seized by the former Soviet Union could then file a claim with the United States government in order to receive a percentage of the property seized by the Soviet Union, providing their claim could be substantiated.

Another well-known example is US relations with Cuba. Soon after Castro came to power in 1959, relations deteriorated. Cuba expropriated large areas of land from Cuban nationals and US citizens. The following year, Cuba confiscated American and British refineries when they refused to process Soviet oil. The US retaliated by cutting off imports of Cuban sugar. In October of 1960, Cuba confiscated most US businesses on the island, and as a result, the US separated from all relations with Cuba. Finally, in February of 1962 the US imposed a trade embargo (Strayhorn, 1995).

Conclusion

The dynamics of globalization have altered our environment and the fundamental requirements of businesses. As technological advances and international trade continue to shrink the world in which we live, cross-cultural experience and understanding becomes not an advantage toward success, but a prerequisite. Businesses wishing to be integrally involved in the globalization process must not only consider different cultures, but the political, ethical, and legal practices and dilemmas faced within the realm of international business. The impact of politics, government, laws, ethics, and social responsibility on businesses is no less significant than it is on individuals; and it may be even more significant. Often there are billions of dollars of revenue at stake, resultant from trading and investing abroad. For a business, the political risks associated with political change are intricate and complex. This section examined regulations, laws, social responsibility, ethics, and politics as they apply to business in the global environment.

This chapter has proven the validity of a saying by a former US Congressional Lumina, the late Tip O'Neill, who was the House Majority Leader, that "all politics are local." It is also evident that domestic politics affects international trade.

Case Study

The Moral and Ethical Responsibility of MNEs

For a multinational enterprise (MNE) it can be difficult to determine what acceptable behavior all over the world is. Because MNEs are dominated by a parent company, typically in the developed world, the highly centralized nature of these corporations is often the cause of international concern. They are criticized for not having a sense of loyalty to, or responsibility for, the citizens of the underdeveloped countries in which their subsidiaries reside. MNEs are criticized for their environmental, labor, and economic behavior. Critics of MNEs base much of their issues on social concerns, such as income differentials, environmental impacts, or unwelcome changes in the host culture.

Kathie Lee Gifford was charged with sweatshop allegations at her factory in El Salvador in 1996. She later pledged to help end labor abuses in the apparel industry. Kathie's husband, Frank Gifford, said that his wife was working hard to improve conditions at the factories, and that his children are sometimes driven to tears by people who criticize their mother for permitting workers to toil in sweatshop conditions ("Kathie Lee Goes on Defense," 1999).

However, this is little comfort for those sweatshop workers who earn as little as 50 cents per hour, states Charles Kernaghan of the National Labor Committee ("Kathie Lee Goes on Defense," 1999). It is nothing in comparison with how thousands of young women must live, trapped in factories throughout the world, behind barbed wire and armed guards. They are paid starvation wages, go home to one-room homes without running water, and raise their children on coffee because they cannot afford milk, while Ms Gifford has reaped millions from the sweatshop in this country in the developing world. Production workers get no sick pay and their bathroom visits are restricted and monitored. Every new employee must pay for a mandatory pregnancy test, and if the results are positive, they are fired immediately, Kernaghan says ("Kathie Lee Goes on Defense," 1999) .

Similarly, companies such as Reebok, Nike, and Levi-Strauss have exploited human labor, having workers live in deteriorating conditions and only earning a mere pittance a month. Although the MNEs were not directly involved in the local operations, bad publicity and loss of business naturally resulted.

Another ethical responsibility is that of the environment. For example, the dramatic environmental damage from the Union Carbide gas leak in Bhopal, India that killed thousands of people or Shell Oil's leak in Nigeria, are grave situations that have demonstrated the negligence of the parent company. As a result, MNEs, which produce products in countries in the developing world or operate in environmentally susceptible areas, have taken steps to control operations more closely. MNEs must follow industry-wide codes governing both labor and environmental standards, and they must insist on compliance by their contractors.

However, the counter arguments to the criticisms are the benefits that these relationships can bring to the world. For instance, MNEs contribute to world prosperity by enhancing development and trade, providing useful products for the country as well as human productivity and friendship between the nations. Specifically, the benefits to the host nations include access to foreign capital, development of people and existing resources, technology improvement, economic alliances, and improved relations with the governments of these countries.

Benefits to the individuals of the country include employment, skills, and products or services available to the consumer that may not have been available in that country before. For instance, many of the new jobs may require technical training that the foreign investor could now provide. New jobs are created within local companies, which then provide additional goods and services to the economy. These effects of the new business could create even more employment and income in the local economy. There is even the chance that this new economy will satisfy some of the human needs that are lacking and improve the quality of life. MNEs can have a socially helpful role in the production and distribution of products that contribute to the ease and convenience of modern life, both home and abroad.

Competition is more intense and markets are more efficient, thus MNEs will continue to be an important factor in the development of world trade and in the resulting improvement in the conditions in which we all live and work.

Case Questions

1. Does an MNE have moral or ethical responsibilities to ensure a safe, fair, and legal working environment in developing nations at the cost of American wealth and access to low-cost goods?
2. What would happen if US companies changed their overseas labor practices and stopped using underpaid labor?
3. Do sweatshops, in general, promote economic stability? Are they inhumane?
4. What constitutes exploitation? What values do you use to support your answer?
5. Does culture matter in an ethical decision? How?

Chapter Review

The political aspects of international business are expansive. Managing the costs attributed to trade barriers such as quotas, tariffs and duties is a key issue in global management; struggling to capitalize on markets in countries and zones that facilitate and not restrict trade. Further exploration of international trade laws reveals some of the ways countries circumvent political restrictions to their monetary goals.

Controversy develops when trade restrictions against a nation are loosened while its political environment continues to conflict with the economic, cultural, and social standards of the host country. When political issues stand in the way of world trade, the restricted country often goes to the regional trade commission, seeking a trade ruling on the issue. Proponents of totally free trade argue that the standards of living and political systems are already established and cannot be changed through trade restrictions.

As an international manager, it seems an enormous job to find a country that would be appropriate for a joint venture. Weighing the social, economic, and political aspects of country after country is a critical issue whose costs can be high, but ultimately determines the success or failure of the venture. When conducting international business, the global community uses the law in many different ways. In less developed countries, a foreign company often actively seeks out lax environmental policies and laws, as the taxes, fines and penalties in their home countries can be quite costly. International tax competition is a common outcome today, as the European experience especially suggests. Overall, tax burdens on corporate profits differ among countries since they are engaging in offering tax and other investment incentives to lure international investors. As noted, the sizeable flow of international investment has been reported in the Introduction of this text.

One of the ways politics affects trade is by imposing trade restrictions. There are many political reasons a country would impose these restrictions. The governments of most developing countries accept the end of protection as a valid reason to invoke a trade restriction. The industry may ask its host country's government to impose a similar trade restriction on the country to which it is trying to export. Some small countries use tariffs to raise revenue for their country. Many times countries that are unstable will use expropriation to prevent money from leaving the country. International law states that compensation must be given for expropriation of another country's goods.

Chapter Questions

1. Discuss the effects of international regulations and trade rulings on exports and imports.
2. How should one evaluate the foreign economic policies of a nation?
3. Explain the importance of foreign trade and the dilemmas posed by trade policies. What is the general attitude of your country's labor force toward foreign trade?
4. Discuss the role of tax burdens on corporate profits and investment incentives in East–Central Europe and Western Europe.
5. What does effective tax burden mean?
6. Explain how a joint venture operates. What are the positive and negative results of a joint venture? Other than those mentioned, name an international joint venture with which you are familiar.
7. What does it mean to act ethically in international politics? Are there laws regulating this?
8. What does unfair tax competition mean? What are the positive and negative effects of engaging in an international tax competition race?
9. Where do human rights originate? Does their content differ across national boundaries?
10. In the case of "sweatshop" labor, who is responsible for addressing it? Home countries, host countries, corporations, laborers, consumers, or a combination of the above?

Chapter 6

Information Technology and its Impact on International Management

In this era of globalization, rapid technological changes, and significant shift in wealth creation, international managers must remain at the forefront of information technology in order to achieve global competitiveness. From Europe to Asia to Canada, nations recognize the importance of information technology innovations, economic growth, and international competitiveness. The competitors are making ever-increasing investments in basic and applied information technology strategies of government–industry–academic collaboration to stimulate technology-based growth, trade, and investment. An important focus of some nations is to target the acquisition of US information technology uses in key industries to supplement their own efforts to foster innovation, rapid commercialization, and value-added production. In this way, these nations seek to increase both their international and US market share.

With the growing complexity of the economic world, particularly with the economies of India (43) and China (13) growing so dramatically, it is important that one recognizes and understands the key factors which determine economic growth. These factors help to explain why some countries are much more successful than others in raising income levels and opportunities for their citizens. The World Economic Forum (2006) has recently published its global competitiveness index, which contains 125 countries. The Growth Competitive Index (GCI) names nine factors that are critical to driving productivity and competitiveness. They are:

1. Institutions
2. Infrastructure
3. Macroeconomy
4. Health and primary education
5. Higher education and training
6. Market efficiency
7. Technological readiness
8. Business sophistication
9. Innovation.

The US was first in 2005; however, it has dropped to sixth place in 2006. Now in first place is Switzerland followed by Finland, Sweden, Denmark, and Singapore. The US has reported the most dramatic drop by falling five places. Similar to our findings regarding e-readiness, we see that the Scandinavian countries are leading not only in technology but also in global competitiveness:

1. Switzerland
2. Finland
3. Sweden
4. Denmark
5. Singapore
6. US
7. Japan
8. Germany
9. The Netherlands
10. UK
11. Hong Kong
12. Norway
13. Taiwan, China
14. Iceland
15. Israel
16. Canada

This year, over 11,000 business leaders were polled in a record 125 economies worldwide.

To compete effectively in global markets and to hold their own in the domestic market, US companies and researchers similarly need to track and remain current with foreign information technology developments. This is critical as US corporations increasingly collaborate with foreign firms as a way of addressing new opportunities while sharing technical strengths and financial resources. However, very few nations have open access to information technology as in the United States. American companies may find that their efforts alone are not fully effective when it comes to monitoring foreign information technology. To address this need, additional resources are available through the US government and various private sector organizations that monitor and acquire foreign information technology on behalf of their interests. The importance of continually reevaluating the global market implications of foreign information technology applies to the whole spectrum of US industry and research activities. With the advancement of information technology, US companies and researchers will be able to broaden their opportunities for international business.

The Role of Information Technology in the US

The sweep of digital technologies and the transformation to a knowledge-based economy have created a robust demand for workers highly skilled in the development and use of information technology. In the past ten years alone, employment in the US computer hardware and software industries has grown more than any other employment sector. The demand for workers who can create, apply, and use information technology goes beyond these industries, cutting across manufacturing and services, transportation, healthcare, education and government. Information technology has contributed to almost 50 per cent of the nation's long-term economic growth since the Second World War. In addition, information technology is the most important enabling technology in the world today. It is responsible for new products and services, new companies and industries, revitalizing existing products, services, and industries, providing new venues for commerce, enhancing our ability to manage information and to innovate, and improving our productivity, quality of life, and national standard of living (Meares and Sargent, 1999).

Information technology is altering the way we live and work, and changing the economy at a fundamental level. The substantiation is located in the following information noted by Meares and Sargent.

According to the US Department of Commerce, information technology's share of the US economy nearly doubled between 1977 and 1998, growing from 4.2 per cent to 8.2 per cent. Information technologies contributed more than one-third of real US economic growth between 1995 and 1997.

In 1994, three million people used the Internet. Year-end 1998 figures indicated more than 147 million people worldwide were accessing the Internet at least once a week from home or business. The number of Internet users grew to approximately 320 million by 2000, and was predicted to be 720 million by 2005. Traffic on the Internet is doubling every 100 days. This rapid growth in traffic is generating demand for both hardware and software, as well as for skilled IT workers to implement and manage these systems. The Department also states that IT industries accounted for 35 per cent of US real economic growth between 1995 and 1998.

Between 1998 and 2003, US business-to-business commerce over the Internet was projected to grow from $48 billion to $1.3 trillion, with an additional $1.8 billion to $3.2 billion in global e-commerce; and US consumer sales over the Internet were projected to rise from $3.9 billion to $108 billion.

These numbers show the world's overwhelming response to technology. When computers and people are networked, their power multiplies. Not only can people share all that information inside their machines, but also they can reach out and instantly access the power of other machines and people, essentially bringing the entire network to their computer; in essence, bringing the world closer to them.

The Experience of Technology in the US

For 20 years, productivity grew at a rate of 1 per cent per year; starting in 1995, productivity has grown at 3 per cent per year. Note that between 1990 and 2000, the average annual growth rate of real investment in computer capital was about 33 per cent.

The growth in the sector of informatics (hardware, software, and Internet) has had beneficial effects on production (some 25 per cent of the increase in production is because of informatics).

The impact could be substantial if the use of computers facilitates a broad collection of complementary innovations within firms and the benefits of computers become apparent when new technologies are combined with organizational aspects. There is evidence that the benefits from computer use persist long after firms have undertaken the investment.

The use of computers increases total factor productivity (TFP) in the manufacturing and service sectors also by the way of changes in the organization of production.

Table 6.1   Sources of US Productivity Growth, 1959–2003

	1959–73	1973–95	1995–2003
Average labor productivity	2.85	1.49	3.06
IT capital deepening	0.21	0.40	0.92
Non-IT capital deepening	1.19	0.49	0.83
Contribution of labor quality	0.33	0.26	0.17
IT Total Factor Productivity	0.09	0.24	0.53
Non-IT Total Factor Productivity	1.03	0.10	0.61

Note: IT capital includes computer hardware, software, and telecommunication equipment.
Source: Jorgenson, Ho, and Stiroh (2004), Table 1, p. 3.

According to Brynjolfsson and Hitt (2003):

* Computer use accounts for a substantial share of TFP and output growth
* Computer investment has its maximal impact on productivity after about seven years
* Between 1987 and 1994, about 0.25 to 0.50 per cent of TFP growth at the firm level was generated by the use of computer capital, which grew by about 25 per cent per year.

However, why has this not influenced Europe and Japan? According to experts (for example, Brynjolfsson and Hitt, 2003; Jorgenson, Ho and Stiroh, 2004) the beneficial effects of Internet and computers happen when their penetration into the markets reaches 50 per cent, and so it starts to reduce production costs all across the economy. This critical value has been reached in the US in 1999.

Others say that if we focus on TFP growth, computer investment accelerated early in the 1990s. If the firm-level results are translated to the overall economy with a time lag of about seven years, the gains in TFP growth from the 1995–99 flows of computer investment growth (which exceeded 40 per cent per year) should peak around 2006.

The Role of Information Technology Outside of the US

One of the hottest debates recently is that of outsourcing or offshoring. The transfer of millions of manufacturing jobs and hundreds of thousands of service jobs over the past few years, with millions more to come, is clearly an area of national debate. While the US is losing millions of jobs and the associated economics, India and China's economies are booming with information technology leading the way. The advantages of outsourcing include:

- Cost savings—can get labor cheaper at the same quality
- Highly skilled staff at lower cost
- Economies of scale
- Often it is the country's core business.

The disadvantages of outsourcing include:

- Possible culture issues
- No competitive advantage to your firm
- May affect the corporate image
- Cost-savings may not materialize
- Data and information security may be at risk
- Vendor longevity cannot be guaranteed.

Often the common factor of the countries either sending or receiving work is a large population that speaks and understands English. In India, the new giant of the outsourcing industry, more than one billion citizens speak 26 different native languages, including its one unifying language—English.

Outsourcing, or what Bhagwati (1984) termed the "long-distance" purchase of services abroad, is a trade phenomenon, and can lead to gains from trade. Outsourcing can be either goods or services that are shipped or sent over the Internet or telephone from one country to the next. Its effect is positive and brings about a benefit to all economies over time since the process could result in higher-value jobs replacing low-wage jobs (see also Bhagwati, Panagariya and Srinivasan, 2004; Mankiw, Forbes and Rosen, 2004). While its effects on jobs and wages are not different from traditional trade in goods, it has been a small phenomenon in the US labor market and Bhagwati, Panagariya and Srinivasan (2004) affirm that those who "profess that this phenomenon causes a shrink in information technology jobs seems especially far-fetched" (p. 111) and who "contend that all or most service jobs will be outsourced to India and China are both empirically and theoretically mistaken" (p. 109).

Groshen, Hobijn and McConnell (2005) have observed employment changes that have been caused by bilateral trade flows and the significant job implications for the US. They substantiate that offshoring has been a limited phenomenon and has contributed little to the labor markets' poor performance in recent years (Groshen, Hobijn and McConnell, 2005). In fact, they have calculated how many US workers at current wages, prices, and productivity levels are needed to produce the goods and services that the US imports, minus how many jobs are required to produce the goods and services that the US exports. They found that the jobs embodied in recent net trade for the entire private economy is small—at most 2.4 per cent, and sometimes less than zero. They have also found that the maximum value of the jobs lost in the US did not exceed 2.4 per cent of its total employment in 2003, which is the maximum value for the entire period observed, that is, from 1983 through year-end 2003. Moreover, they found that jobs lost to net trade flows grew at a slower pace after the recession, dropping from approximately 45,000 jobs per month in 1997–2001 to 30,000 jobs per month in 2001–2003. These facts do not support the claim that the transfer of US jobs to workers abroad is to blame for the jobless recovery (Groshen, Hobijn and McConnell, 2005).

In a poll taken in 2003, by the consulting firm A.T. Kearney, India has the best reputation as an outsourcing destination among top US companies. A potential challenger is the Philippines, which has a large pool of English speakers thanks to its American occupation in the twentieth century. Despite the language handicap, Eastern European countries such as Hungary, the Czech Republic and Russia also have potential, particularly for outsourcing from Western European countries like Germany and France.

The country to watch, however, is China. With a population of 1.3 billion and an exploding industrial base and educational system, the only downfall at this point is its amount of English-speaking citizens. However, that is quickly changing. Recently, when the Premier of China visited India and realized the competition, he returned home and ordered that English be taught as a required subject to every child in school.

Information Technology Transfer

The business environment in which an organization operates affects the techniques with which international managers make use of the labor market, including hiring and training workers. Today, the business environment for information technology product and service providers is having a significant effect on management approaches to the recruitment, retention, and training of highly skilled information technology workers.

In the decades following the Second World War, government spending in defense and space dominated the US high technology enterprise. In the article, *The Digital Workforce*, authors Meares and Sargent (1999) state:

> Dominant employers of highly skilled technical workers resided in industries characterized by product life cycles measured in years, such as the defense and aerospace industries. Later, with the development of commercial computers, new information technology industries began to play important roles in the labor markets for highly skilled technical workers. This came about with the growth of computer hardware makers such as IBM, semiconductor manufacturers such as Texas Instruments and Intel, and service companies such as Electronic Data Systems. These large and stable firms had the time and incentive to serve as the training grounds for highly skilled technical workers. Many of these workers brought their knowledge and skills to small and medium-sized high technology firms that are connected to these industries.

Currently, the US information technology industry is a grand conglomerate in comparison with its humble and meager beginning. In comparison with the defense and aerospace industries that have been downsized and are experiencing slow or no growth, the US hardware manufacturers have globalized. In addition, the computer and data processing services industry is experiencing an extraordinary period of growth. This growth is a direct product of the extraordinary demand for information technology-related products and services that augment the productivity of current operations and create new firm capabilities. Computer software, and its applications, is often the critical driver of these improvements. Today, the computer and data processing services industry yields an astonishing amount of workers, as will be studied in other chapters of this book. This field is also most vulnerable to outsourcing as the industry explodes globally.

Time is one of the most unfavorable competitive factors for companies whose information technology is their core business. While product and technology life cycles have decreased markedly across all industry sectors, the pressure of time is most intense for these information technology products and service producers. These companies confront life cycles or project deadlines that are measured in Internet years or months.

For example, at Hewlett Packard, new products earn their greatest revenue in their first year on the market and, by their second year, revenues are already tapering off. Nearly two-thirds of the company's revenues are generated from products less than two years old. Moreover, early market entry provides a critical competitive edge. In many cases, the first competitors to the market with a new product are likely to capture most of the market share (Meares and Sargent, 1999).

An example of this is the key area of packaged software, such as word processing, spreadsheet, and page layout software, as well as Internet browsers and e-mail services. Those manufacturers who are among the first to the market will secure the flow of funds generated by those markets that are needed to pay the costs of developing the next generation of technology and products. If a company cannot get its product into the market in a timely manner, the lack of revenue that would have been generated is a serious loss to the development of future products. Inevitably the competition will persevere. These time pressures are felt most by smaller firms, due to a smaller product portfolio from which to generate revenues and a smaller staff who are often multi-tasking and not available for deployment to projects.

It is important to note that the development of software is a highly labor-intensive manufacturing task. A primary way to increase software development is to devote more human resources to the process. However, rapid technological change makes it more difficult for international managers to predict future resource requirements and introduces greater hesitation in the business environment. Therefore, international managers may find it difficult to develop their specific skill needs very far into the future.

Information Technology and its Effects on the Labor Market

Another major competitive factor concerns the production of hardware versus the production and application of software. Developing and producing high-tech hardware is capital intensive, requiring expensive manufacturing plants and other facilities. This is a relatively high barrier to entry into the business—a barrier that tends to limit the number of competitors. In contrast, software development and applications can be carried out from a home basement, with a couple of computers and desks. This low barrier to entry has allowed many competitors to enter the market with a rapidly growing array of products and services for different industries and consumer markets (Meares and Sargent, 1999).

The pressures of time, product, and service proliferation play an important role in the labor market of the information technology industry. The critical element of time is the argument for hiring workers who already possess the needed technical skills and experience and who can work productively. Product proliferation creates the need for information technology workers to specialize in particular technical skills and their applications. Time taken together with product proliferation produces the demand for the right worker, with the right skills, at the right time.

The information technology industry is advancing at a rapid pace, with the lifetime of product delivery to market periods shortening, and demands for continued creativity and innovation growing daily. What we will offer next year has not been invented today. In this environment, it is critical to have competent employees who can do the job and keep the company in front of the rest of the competition.

Some Effects on International Trade

The high-tech manufacturing sector has been the area of international trade showing the higher growth rates, and now it is about 20 per cent of total international trade.

In addition, traditional trade has benefited from "technology advances," such as the cases of commercial jets, super freighters, and containerization.

Table 6.2   Growth of High-Technology and Other Manufactured Exports, 1985–2000

	High-tech manufacturing	Medium-tech manufacturing	Low-tech manufacturing	Resource-based manufacturing
World	13.19	8.45	8.85	6.60
Developing countries	19.21	13.36	11.69	11.00
Developed counties	11.13	7.57	6.86	5.18

Sources: Lall (2004), World Bank (2004).

Research and Development

Upon the onset of going international with businesses, the international manager should begin by having a vision that will integrate strategic planning. Brainstorming and major discussions between senior managers will bring the planning procedures together. For example, New York Life Insurance Company included their plans for global service in their mission statement. As New York Life Insurance Company began globalizing, they had to provide excellent information concerning their customers to agents in the field. Some questions that should be asked in the information technology industry are how a business can stand out above the competition in the marketplace, what is needed to make ends meet, and how it can be achieved. Some major impacts which information technology has made on the world today are very crucial. Instead of insurance agents carrying all detailed information on paper and written by pen, they possess electronic notepads or computers that will connect with the office modem.

When integrating technology with international management, centralization/decentralization is a major issue, as is the need for integration. In the 1980s, microprocessors had chips that provided the "dumb" terminals with processing and data management facilities entered into the computer scene. Then, in 1989, IBM made more revenue from sales of micro-based technology than from the sales of mainframes. Internationally, this caused problems for the users of computers. The users would often buy various hardware and software without consulting their personal needs of the computer.

Daniels (1994), the author of *Information Technology: The Management Challenge*, found that not all companies become global in the same way. That statement proves that different companies start their globalizing process in different ways. In order for technology to become successful internationally, the current mindset has to be changed, and the configuration of resources and management practices.

Management based both nationally and internationally is very dependent upon technology. Mrs Field's Cookies, a small chain that started in 1977, has approximately 500 stores located in shopping malls all over the world. The structure of Mrs Field's Cookies consists of two parallel organizations. One has a traditional span of control while the other has a very broad span of control. Until recently, every shop was owned by the company rather than franchised. Debbie Fields and her husband, Randy Fields, centralized the control. This unique structure allowed the owners maximum flexibility in adapting what they were offering. In 1988, this hierarchical organization was changed into 500 store managers, 105 district sales managers, 17 sales managers, four regional directors, a vice-president of operations, and Debbie Fields. The span of control changed to a 1:5 ratio. For the second organization, it consisted of 500 store managers that reported to six store controlers, who reported to the vice-president. This span of control went from a 1:35 to a 1:75 ratio. This represents a very flat organization structure.

Before Randy Fields came into the cookie business, he was an IBM systems engineer. Information technology instantly became part of Mrs Field's structure. Each store is connected online to a central database, and there is extensive automation of production quotas, sales volumes, and so on, based on recent daily sales records for each store. The store is then given hourly sales projections and it reports hourly sales results. The ordering is done directly through the online service and directly delivers the supplies. Through voice mail and electronic mail, each manager has direct contact with Debbie Fields. Announcements worldwide for the company can be frequently broadcast. This example of management has created a level of technology through which an organization structure feels flat despite having many layers of management.

Financial and organizational problems occurred when Mrs Field's made its products and market mix internationally. They lost money for the first time in 1988, and its stock fell extensively on the London Exchange. Mrs Field's was planning on buying out La Petite Boulangerie and gaining control of it. The company had allowed themselves to spend $50 million on the bakery chain in the early 1990s, closing 100 of its 700 stores and making them into combined bakeries and cookie stores. Randy Fields was confident that this was the way to go because of the success of their new computer systems. To make a long story short, consequently, Mrs Field's had a net loss of $8.8 million in 1990. In 1992, Mrs Field's and Pasteleria el Molino announced a leasing agreement to open 50 new stores in Mexico over a five-year period. In addition, in 1992, Jesse Ewing became the first franchiser of Mrs Field's. Then in 1993, Debbie Fields left Mrs Field's Cookies and sold her share to four lenders led by Prudential Insurance Company.

Today's technology is linked together by several factors. The trend today is in personal computers, workstations, and mainframe computers linked together in numerous corporate databanks, databases, electronic filing systems, and specialized servers connecting them to private and public telephone lines. Having these conveniences, simplicity in creating new kinds of organizations and economic systems has come much easier. These are then defined by technology and the architects that make growing opportunities happen. The systems created will allow managers to interact, communicate, and organize their affairs internationally in an organized manner. Managers are able to make decisions and have them transferred to the designated people and/or businesses within minutes. The transferring through technology has the ability to strengthen their competitive products and reorganize their strategic operations. To have access to these forms of communication, authority and responsibility can be delegated downward so that management layers of control and planning can be decreased.

The transformation from hardware to software is the biggest investment ever made. This change came about because of the reduction of semiconductor devices and the use of intelligent machines and intelligent infrastructures for the design, production, distribution, and operation of all products and services. The software is needed today to run more intelligent, high-tech, multi-use computers. Since software has the ability to contain more information, hardware is being condensed onto these disks to make the accessibility of numerous programs and information easier (Estabrooks, 1995).

The Level of Technology in Less Developed Countries and How it Affects International Managers

The level of technology in less developed countries and developed countries is different in many ways, yet there are some similarities. Development of the global Internet has been phenomenal. It has grown from a small, closed, text-based computer network of a few thousand scientific and government users in the early 1980s to hundreds of millions of users by 2005. During 1998, the last remaining unconnected countries established links to the Internet, turning it into a truly global network. Petrazzini and Kibati (1999, 31) noted, "A closer look reveals great disparities between high- and low-income regions in terms of both Internet hosts and users.

More than 97 per cent of all Internet hosts are in developed countries that are home to only 16 per cent of the world's population" (Petrazzini and Kibati, 1999).

Even though there are differences in developed and developing countries with the Internet, there is a problem that a developed and a developing country both share and that is the high cost of Internet services. There are two different costs, the set-up cost, and the operating cost. Set-up costs are the costs incurred when the company receives the Internet service from the provider. These are going to be the same in both developed and developing countries. On the other hand, the operating costs differ between developed and developing countries because of many factors. The main reason for this difference is the manner in which the user accesses the Internet. Some parts of the country are able to receive the Internet for longer periods at cheaper costs and some do not have this ability because of their location. For example, in Cameroon, dial-up services as local call rates are available only in Yaounde and Douala, the country's two biggest cities. Elsewhere in the country, it is necessary to make costly long-distance calls to reach the Internet service providers (ISP). The lack of adequate infrastructure in the interior is also a major hindrance. In 1997, over 60 per cent of the people in developing countries lived in rural areas, yet over 80 per cent of the main telephone lines were in urban centers (Petrazzini and Kibati, 1999).

The operating costs hurt developing countries because they are not able to receive the Internet for long periods. Therefore, the Internet is not used as frequently, and if the Internet is used for long periods, the cost is expected to be extremely high. This affects the role and decision-making of international managers for many reasons.

The first reason is communication. The international manager will not be able to make contact with other managers concerning orders, shipments, and supplies. This affects managers because some managers will not be willing to wait and take the time to get in contact; therefore, they will go elsewhere for their orders, shipments, and supplies they need.

A second reason why the level of technology in less developed countries affects international managers is the organization of the company. Organizational functions, such as quality control and sales that have a direct impact on organizational performance, are primary candidates for computerized support. Information systems can be effective in collecting and analyzing data, in order to enhance and maintain the quality of a product or service. This can help an organization's competitive position in national and global markets. Likewise, using information systems to integrate sales, production scheduling, and material requirements data can help streamline operations, minimize costs, and generate customer satisfaction and goodwill (Azad et al., 1998). The international manager must be accustomed to these types of organizational functions and when managing in a country where a company does not use these systems, it may be more difficult for the international manager to cope with the confusion.

A third reason why the level of technology in less developed countries affects international managers is time. With many different countries, there are different time zones. These time zones affect the way companies work. Without being able to connect to the Internet, they may use the phone or mail, and this takes a longer amount of time to establish what the companies may need.

Table 6.3 World Internet Usage and Population Statistics

World Regions	Population (2006 Est.)	Population % of World	Internet Usage, Latest Data	% Population (Penetration)	Usage % of World	Usage Growth 2000–2006
Africa	915,210,928	14.1 %	32,765,700	3.6 %	3.0 %	625.8 %
Asia	3,667,774,066	56.4 %	394,872,213	10.8 %	36.4 %	245.5 %
Europe	807,289,020	12.4 %	308,712,903	38.2 %	28.4 %	193.7 %
Middle East	190,084,161	2.9 %	19,028,400	10.0 %	1.8 %	479.3 %
North America	331,473,276	5.1 %	229,138,706	69.1 %	21.1 %	112.0 %
Latin America/Caribbean	553,908,632	8.5 %	83,368,209	15.1 %	7.7 %	361.4 %
Oceania/Australia	33,956,977	0.5 %	18,364,772	54.1 %	1.7 %	141.0 %
WORLD TOTAL	**6,499,697,060**	**100.0 %**	**1,086,250,903**	**16.7 %**	**100.0 %**	**200.9 %**

Source: Internet World Stats Usage and Population Statistics. Retrieved September 28, 2006 from http://www.internetworldstats.com/stats.htm

One of the many reasons why the level of technology in less developed countries affects international managers is the relatively slow growth of a skewed Internet market, with small number of users concentrated in a few large urban centers. Table 6.3 depicts the abundance of Internet use in developed countries as opposed to less developed countries. As shown, Europe, Asia, and North America overpower Africa, the Middle East, Latin America, and Oceania.

Technology and Inequality

The skill premium in the US kept approximately constant in the pre-1970 era. Successively, the economy has witnessed sharp increases in wage and income inequality. In the US, the college premium (the wage of college graduates relative to the wages of high school graduates) increased over 25 per cent between 1975 and 1995 and overall, earnings inequalities soared: in 1971, a worker at the 90th percentile of the wage distribution earned 266 per cent more than a worker at the tenth percentile. By 1995, this percentage had risen to 366.

Why did the demand for skills accelerate over the past decade? Why has new technology favored more skilled workers throughout the twentieth century, but not during the nineteenth century and what are the implications of technical change for the labor market? It is certain that technical change in the US and the OECD over the past 60 years has been skill-biased. Some economists trust that what happened over the past few decades is a matter of "technology–skill complementarity." The consensus among experts is that technical change is able to privilege more educated workers, to replace tasks previously performed by unskilled, and to increase the demand for skills. However, how can we rationalize the large increase in the supply of skilled workers with the increase in the college premium? Simple microeconomics would suggest to us that the relative demand for skills must have increased and this because of the changes in technology (for "tech" it is intended not only the machines available to firms, but also the organization of production, of labor markets, consumer tastes, and so on). That is, the acceleration in the skill bias begun in the 1970s and 1980s has been steered by advances in information technology or a sort of "Third Industrial Revolution."

For the economist Daron Acemoglu (1998), it can be argued that the increased skill bias of technology throughout the twentieth century and its acceleration during the past 30 years resulted from the changes in profit opportunities which were, in turn, a consequence of the steady increase in the supply of skilled workers over the past century and its surge starting in the early 1970s. That being said, technology advancements have an impact on the business sector and labor markets, as well as increasing businesses' desire to hire skilled workers, and increasing skills are driving technological change. However, the information revolution, aided by the revolution in telecommunications and business innovations, had initially promised to change the nature of the market altogether, but we are far away from a homogeneous degree of penetration of Internet technology and the progress of technology all around.

The acceleration of skill bias in the US means that returns to schooling rose over the past 30 years despite the unusually rapid increase in the supply of educated workers. Because of the entry of the large and well-educated baby-boom cohort starting in the late 1960s, and the Vietnam-era draft laws to increase government support for higher education, the educational attainment of the US labor force increased sharply starting in the early 1970s.

Why is the Skill Bias of Technology Related to the Supply of Skilled Workers?

Technical changes privilege more profitable areas, and two factors determine the profitability of new technologies:

1. The price effect: in light of relative price changes, also the relative profitability of different types of technologies changes. Technologies used predominantly in the production of goods that are now more expensive will be demanded more. The invention and improvement of these technologies will become more profitable.
2. The market size effect: it is more profitable to introduce machines that will be used by a large number of workers because greater market sizes will enable greater sales and profits for the producers and inventors. That is, it is through this effect that an increase in the supply of skills induces technology to become even more skill-biased. Therefore, when there are more skilled workers in the labor market, this effect will make the production of skill-complementary machines and technologies more profitable.

In the end:

* The market size effect can be so strong that the relative demand curve for skills can be upward sloping, this in contrast to the standard downward sloping relative demand curve for labor
* The skill premium and returns to education will be higher when there are more skilled workers in the economy
* As the market size increases, it becomes more profitable to create and introduce more such technologies.

The Case of Inequality in the US in Light of Greater Trade with the Less Developed Countries (LDCs)

Under a different perspective, it is also possible to disregard the role of globalization and trade for the following reasons:

* The volume of trade is small
* A large increase in the relative prices of skill-intensive goods because of greater world demand for these has not in fact been observed
* A straightforward positive relationship between larger openness and faster economic growth has not been detected in developing countries (for example, Rigobon and Rodrik, 2004)

- Inequalities are also increasing in the LDCs trading with the US, whereas the simplest trade and globalization explanations predict a decline in inequality in relative skill-scarce economies, like the LDCs.

Contrarily, trade and globalization might still exert some direct effect, affirm other economists. As trade influences what types of technologies are more profitable to develop, there is an inclination for trade to create a tendency for the price of skill-intensive products to increase. Via the price effect, the incentives for the introduction of new skill-biased technologies are strengthened. Simply, trade and globalization induce further skill-biased technical changes. Finally, to the extent that the LDCs are using technologies developed in the US and in other developed countries, there will be a force toward increasing inequalities in the LDCs as well, counteracting the equalizing effects of trade in economies with relative skill scarcity.

Technology between Industrialized Countries and How it Aids Management of Multinational Managers

The technology between industrialized countries is very important in many ways. Information technology can play a strategic role at micro- as well as macro-organizational and national levels. At the organizational level, this technology is rapidly changing the business environment, practices, and relationships. For instance, competition has become global—customers and suppliers are no longer restricted by national boundaries, but span the world. Just-in-time inventory management has become a strategic tool for efficient employment of resources. Locking in customers and suppliers has become a viable strategy to gain a competitive advantage. Only information technology makes this possible (Azad et al., 1998). With this type of technology, industries are fast-moving so the competition is going to be very strong. International managers need to know what is going on in the world as well as with their competition in order to keep ahead of, or with, other international managers.

Communication, Teleconferencing, and E–mail

Communication via teleconferencing, e-mail, and videoconferencing is one of the most important technical tools for managers in industrialized countries. Competition among industrialized countries is immense. These instantaneous ways to communicate allow for cost savings, immediate feedback, virtually eliminate time zones, and offer the linking of people that yesterday's meeting provided.

However, one should be mindful of the trade-offs that technology creates, such as the decrease, or complete loss, of contact, which can subsequently result in a lessened understanding of other cultures.

With today's technology, international managers have to be continually aware of their surroundings. Companies with great technology are able to handle and deal with short-term/short-notice orders; they are able to contact the company, purchasers, and suppliers and are able to complete the customer's orders in a very efficient manner.

With the technology that we have today, managers are able to adapt quickly to the many situations facing them.

New Markets

There are going to be many new markets in technology in the years to come. Because external networks will be with us for the near future, and will play an increasingly important role in the global management of technology, organizations should have long-term strategies for external network participation. Such strategies should envision what the networked world of the future will be like, and consequently, planning and decision-making should move companies toward a form that will be compatible with that vision. Unfortunately, much of what has been written about network management tends to see it primarily as a process of building out from, or adding on to, current management practices. This approach has its validity, for experience is a valuable teacher. However, it should not preclude a sense of working toward a vision of the future.

The Economist Intelligence Unit (EIU) (2006) reported in its business information section of *The Economist* that Denmark has overtaken the US to become the leading nation in terms of e-readiness. E-readiness is defined as the extent to which a country's business environment is ready for Internet-based commercial opportunities.

Ranking is based on a number of factors including connectivity and technology infrastructure, business environment, consumer and business adoption, social and cultural infrastructure, and legal and policy environment and support services.

The US had enjoyed the top position in the early 2000s; however, the downturn in the US economy has meant that other nations have gained ground. Denmark, Sweden, and Switzerland along with the US held the top four positions.

According to the EIU, what sets Scandinavia apart is the extent to which the Internet has pervaded the marketplace and reshaped business transactions, and the eagerness with which citizens have incorporated Internet technology into their daily routines.

The US was second in the rankings, with the UK in fifth position. Hong Kong and Finland tied for sixth place, while the Netherlands came eighth and Norway ninth. Australia was in tenth spot.

In contrast to their northern European neighbors, Southern Europeans regard the Internet skeptically and are reluctant to move business online, according to the EIU. Among the region's stragglers are Spain (23rd), Italy (24th), Portugal (25th), and Greece (27th).

The above research indicates that most countries have improved, thanks to continued roll-out of broadband services, uptake of mobile telephony, and a spate of Internet-related legislation and government programs (Economist Intelligence Unit, 2006).

Technology will always be a part of our lives and will continue to grow in the future. International managers need to continually watch and see what new companies, old companies, and other countries are doing and what kind of technology they are using.

Changes in the Organization of Production

In a world in which skilled workers are scarce, firms are more inclined to hire, train, and employ them in relatively low-paid jobs. Today, the increase in the supply of skilled workers induces firms to be more selective in recruiting people and design jobs specifically for them. This increases the productivity and pay of more skilled workers, thereby excluding low- and medium-skilled workers from well-paid jobs. This factor also explains the decline in the relative wages of low-skilled workers, that pure technological theories have difficulties explaining (theories say that even with a technological change and skill bias, the wages of low-skilled workers should increase).

Conclusion

Information technology is a fundamental segment of international business in the global marketplace. From the creation of new products to the transfer of knowledge from one source to the next, information technology is an important base for economic growth and development. The old way of doing business internationally has been replaced by new methods that are sometimes complex, but potentially vigorous. For US businesses that compete globally, they must effectively control their destiny by remaining current with foreign information technology. In addition, US businesses need to form partnerships with foreign firms as a means of identifying new opportunities while at the same time sharing financial resources and new information technology advancements. It is also the hope that government legislation will continue to encourage technical growth and advancement through political tactics that are contingent with the businesses in mind. With the added security of market share for global competition, the e-business industry is expected to take a dramatic hold of the reins well into the future of the information age. Regardless of all else, international managers should be prepared to address the potential benefits that could arise from the expanding information technology industry.

Case Study

Adapted from Outsourcing: Jobs in Jeopardy

Workers at a Kettering health insurance call center did not understand why their office was closing. Weeks after the announcement was made, a message posted on an internal website said company trainers would be teaching new hires in Bombay, India, for 10 to 13 weeks. "Please congratulate the trainers on this global assignment; it will be a great opportunity to support the company initiatives," the announcement said. Offshoring—serving American customers with overseas labor—is disrupting workers' lives as more and more companies trim jobs, cut pay and require those who remain to work efficiently with people they have never seen in countries they know next to nothing about. Moreover, there is a fear felt by those who witness the rain of lay off notices: Will I be next?

No one knows exactly how many white-collar jobs that serve the American market are done outside the United States. Nevertheless, most estimate that 2 to 4 per cent of computer jobs and 5 per cent of call center work is done in India, where about 80 per cent of the overseas white-collar jobs go. The numbers will undoubtedly increase if smaller employers start moving office jobs to the developing eorld. A *Dayton Daily News* survey of Ohio's 30 largest employers found more than half are offshoring. In addition, that may not be the full measure of the trend.

The topic is so radioactive that an information technology employee at Kroger said he could not talk about how Kroger offshores, because he would lose his job. Companies have reasons for their reticence. Nearly one-third of consumers say they would stop buying from a company if they knew it was sending calls to another country, according to a survey by *Convergys* (NYSE: CVG), a Cincinnati-based call-center provider that has 10,000 employees in India and 1,000 in the Philippines.

Call center work in India is growing fast—a 100 per cent growth rate last year alone, according to Rafiq Dossani, a senior research scholar at Stanford University's Asia–Pacific Research Center. In July, Dossani met in India with executives of companies that provide call centers for US companies. They told him that their American clients have started to ask them to keep their contracts secret. "They don't want their company in the news," Dossani said. "Especially in sensitive states like Ohio, where job losses are a key elective issue."

Offshoring took off in the 1990s, but the seeds were planted more than a century ago through American and British colonization. The most popular offshoring sites are in former English or American colonies because they have many fluent English speakers.

Seventeen companies in the *Dayton Daily News* survey of Ohio's 30 largest employers said they send work for the American market overseas—and every one that disclosed where the work goes uses India.

Smaller companies are also getting into the game. Last year, Mridhul Prakash, 32, and Doug Dodson, 45, founded Strategix, a Dayton firm whose motto is "The India Advantage–Delivered." The consultants started the business to help mid-sized companies save money by automating and offshoring their back-office work.

So far, Strategix has not dislocated any American workers—they moved a small telemarketing center for a Florida client from Chennai, India, to the suburbs of New Delhi. But Dodson said his dad asked him, "So, you're going to take jobs offshore?" "This is going to happen, I might as well participate," Dodson replied. "Once you open up borders, figuratively and literally, you can't stop the flow."

The labor rate differences are dramatic. The salary for a computer call-center worker is $200 a month, compared to about $2,000 in the United States. However, added electricity, transportation, and management costs make offshoring more expensive than the difference in labor costs would suggest, and some companies have not realized any savings. Still, LexisNexis Chief Technical Officer Allan McLaughlin said the savings for getting computer work done in India is about 50 per cent.

When offshoring began, no one worried much about it because the job market was strong. That changed when IT unemployment began to rise, though the increase was due mostly to the recession and the bust of the dot.com bubble. During the mid- to late-1990s, companies imported computer workers on temporary visas—two-thirds of them from India—because of the huge demand for programers. Arun Mehta, 30, came to LexisNexis in June 2000 on one of those visas to manage one of its computer systems.

Mehta, who spent four years in Dayton as a contractor from HCL Technologies, just returned to New Delhi, India, where he hopes to manage computer work for LexisNexis. When Mehta arrived in Dayton, he took over a job that had been done by a LexisNexis employee. That man, who trained Mehta, was initially given more creative work, and then lost his job after the recession hit. "Suddenly, when 9/11 happened, future projects didn't have enough budgets," Mehta said. Between 100 and 200 employees were laid off in December 2001, he said—including the man he replaced as system owner.

Every time Procter & Gamble's Damon Jones files for reimbursement for business travel, he fills out the expense report, sticks it in an envelope, and sends it to San Jose, Costa Rica, where clerks process his check at a fraction of the cost of Cincinnati salaries.

That one small economy is just one of thousands that has enabled P&G to save $500 million in four years. P&G streamlined its global operations by consolidating administrative work in three regional offices—Costa Rica, England and the Philippines. Cheap labor, automation, and software standardization helped the company meet its cost-cutting goals a year early. Jones, a company spokesman, said the corporation then asked itself, "How do we take shared services to the next level?"

Domestic outsourcing was their answer. For instance, 2,000 Cincinnati IT workers now work for Hewlett Packard. IBM (NYSE: IBM) took over some HR duties. "Basically, 3,500 have moved in the last year," Jones said. They make the same wages at their new companies, and even have the same benefits for the first two years. If their new employers lay them off in the first couple of years, P&G will pay severance. "What you read about outsourcing/offshoring is job loss," Jones said. "We really wanted to do something different." The result—P&G has half as many employees as it did five years ago.

It is not just routine office and computer tasks that are sent abroad. Some companies have begun scientific research in Asia. They say globalization brings a fresh perspective from countries that could become lucrative future markets. GM Science Labs Executive Director Alan Taub likes to call GM Research and Development "an idea factory."

In September 2003, General Motors (NYSE: GM) decided to add to its arsenal of PhD brainpower, concentrated in Michigan. However, it did not build an office park near MIT or Princeton. It opened a Research and Development center in Bangalore, India. Taub gave a PowerPoint presentation there that linked the India Science Lab all the way back to Charles Kettering, the Dayton inventor who founded GM's Research and Development division in 1920. The Indian researchers do all the sophisticated work that scientists in Michigan do—from short-term projects for particular models, to exploratory programs, such as the possibility of running engines on solar power. Some of the work in Bangalore will be for the Indian market, but very few Indians can afford to buy cars. The vast majority of the work in Bangalore will be collaborating with Michigan researchers. Eventually, almost every engineer in Michigan will have a partner there, Taub said. In GM R&D, 46 per cent of employees have PhDs, 20 per cent have master's degrees, 14 per cent have bachelor's degrees, and 19 per cent have associate's degrees. So far, GM has hired about 35 researchers in Bangalore, a third of the way to its goal of 100. About a dozen of them were hired after they graduated from American universities.

"We're still the brain trust of the world," Taub said.

Reprinted with permission: M. Lee (2004), *Dayton Daily News*, August 23.

Case Questions

1. Based on your prior knowledge, what kinds of activities do firms outsource to lower-wage countries like India? Besides lower wages, what factors make India especially attractive as a country to which a company should outsource their activities?
2. What do other countries offer that is fundamentally different from the US when it comes to outsourcing? What new twist is the company giving to outsourcing strategies, and why?
3. Do you think a substantial number of young Americans might be willing to sign up for such job assignments in foreign countries? If you did it yourself, what would be the benefits to you and your resume or CV?
4. Can you think of other industries and other low-wage countries where outsourcing could be applied?

Chapter Review

This chapter focussed on current technology as a world system of operation in society and the impact that it has had in the way we conduct our business. For an international manager, it is critical to recognize the different technologies that affect how people communicate and to examine globalization by thinking about communication technology and its implications on culture, society, and trade.

From Europe to Asia to Canada, nations recognize the importance of information technology innovations, economic growth, and international competitiveness. The competitors are making ever-increasing investments in basic and applied information technology, strategies of government, and industry collaboration to stimulate technology-based growth, trade, and investment. Information technology has contributed to almost half of the nation's long-term economic growth since the Second World War. In addition, information technology is the most important enabling technology in the world today. Today, the business environment for information technology product and service producers is having a significant effect on management approaches to the recruitment, retention, and training of highly skilled information technology workers.

With the development of commercial computers, new information technology industries began to play important roles in the labor markets for highly skilled technical workers. At the same time, the computer and data processing services industry, consisting of software producers and information technology consultants, is experiencing a remarkable period of growth, with staggering employment growth. Time is one of the most critical competitive factors for companies whose information technology is their core business. While product and technology life cycles have decreased markedly across all industry sectors, time pressures are most intense for these information technology products and service producers. The pressures of time, product, and service proliferation play an important role in the labor market of the information technology industry. Product proliferation creates the need for information technology workers to specialize in particular technical skills and their applications.

Some major impacts that information technology has made on the world today are very crucial, such as the impact on less developed nations. Today's technology is linked together by several factors. Information technology can play a strategic role at micro as well as macro organizational and national levels. Only information technology makes this possible. With today's technology, international managers have to be always aware of their surroundings.

Chapter Questions

1. What role does technology play in a global organization?
2. What advantages or disadvantages does the technology hold for a company?
3. How did the proliferation of computers have productivity-enhancing effects?
4. What is the value of technology to a global organization?
5. What are the issues involved with technology and, specifically, innovations?
6. What determines the timing of technological innovations? Can these timings be forecast?
7. How does technology affect competition?
8. Are new technologies and technical innovations increasing demand for high-skilled workers, or vice versa?

Chapter 7

International Service Management

Service Management

International service management has become a top priority in today's society as organizations realize the importance of customer service. With new technological advancements, organizations are learning how easy it is for services to cross international borders to deliver their products to other customers. Organizations are learning that if they do not take care of their customers, both internally and externally, their business will not succeed.

There are important factors that organizations look at to determine if they are complying with the needs and wants of today's customer. Service standards, service quality, the service process, and technological advancements have helped to make service management a fundamental tool for organizations. Euro Disney is an example of an organization that has incorporated the tool of service management and has succeeded because of it. The success of Euro Disney will be discussed in detail later in this chapter.

International Service Standards

As succinctly stated by Aldous Huxley (1932), "Experience is not what happens to a man; it is what a man does with what happens to him." With this in mind, service standards are hard to define, because they are based on the perception of the individual customer. Therefore, having one set definition is not possible, but having guidelines and benchmarks is possible, and they are necessary. Each type of organization must meet and/or exceed their customer's needs, and in order to do so they must first be knowledgeable of their product and their customer. An example of this would be how British Airways turns negative situations into positive opportunities.

British Airways had a three-hour delay, due to fog, that the crew on the plane made a memorable experience for all of the passengers. They not only made the time pass by telling jokes and making light of the whole situation, but they also gave out prizes for a game that the crew made up as a way to pass the time. The passengers on the flight could have been very upset, but the service of the crew saved what could have been a negative experience and turned it into a positive experience.

An organization must know their product and/or service and customers inside and out or they will fail. This is the first step to becoming successful as a manager. It sounds easy enough, but is it that easy? If so, why are so many organizations all over the world struggling with their services? Almost all organizations can define their product, but what is it about service that makes it so hard to define? According to James L. Walker (1995), service has two aspects. One is the technical aspect and the other is the functional aspect. If you were to ask ten people to define what service is to them, they would each give you a different answer. That is because they each have a different perception of what is happening around them, so they will internalize the information differently than the person next to them. How do managers meet and exceed the needs of several people who are their customers?

First, they must know these customers expectations. Walker defines expectations as "predictions about what is likely to happen during the impending exchange, are used as a reference against which one can compare performance and assess disconfirmation" (Walker, 1995). Once the expectations of the customers are determined, managers must then perform to that level and above.

To perform to their expectations, some simple questions need to be answered: what service are they receiving? How are they receiving it? Why are they receiving it? In addition, where and when are they receiving the service (Walker, 1995)? These questions are especially important when the customer only receives value from the service, due to no tangible object (Samiee, 1999).

If we look at service to another country from the United States, we have to realize that that country does not have the same points of view and does not practice business the same way. Therefore, that country's standards of service will depend on the economy, government structure, and the beliefs or culture of the people in that country (Stauss and Mang, 1999).

Once an organization has its standards in place, it must keep working at them to make them better. When an organization has found a standard that works for it, it needs to continue to improve on that standard. Once it has made the standard the most effective it can be, its competition will pale in comparison.

Service Quality

Service quality and customer satisfaction are qualities customers expect everywhere they go. It does not matter if the business is a restaurant, hotel, gas station, or a grocery store. In today's society, customers (internal and external) demand a high level of quality service. If they do not feel they have received the quality of service they have demanded, they will not return to that particular place of business. For that reason alone, it is important that organizations realize the need and importance of improving their service quality. Quality service is a competitive advantage that an organization can use to draw customers to use its services.

Service quality has emerged as an irrepressible, globally pervasive strategic force, as well as a key strategic issue in the organization's agenda, according to Rapert and Wren (1998). Service quality can be defined as the relationship between the customer's expectations of a service and the perception of the service after it was received according to Edvardsson, Thomasson and Ovretveit (1994).

Because service quality is based on expectations and perceptions, service quality changes with every customer. Along with expectations and perceptions, quality of the product or service is included in how a customer views service quality.

Organizations need to be able to adapt their services to each customer they deal with in order to survive in today's society. If they are able to do this, customers will realize that the organization is focussed on treating customers with the service and respect they desire.

There are strategies that organizations can use to achieve a high level of service quality and customer satisfaction:

1. The first strategy is to have an objective that is clearly defined. This objective should include the organization's definition of service quality and what goals that organization is trying to meet for its customers.
2. The second strategy is to improve basic conditions within the organization. It is important that all employees understand that they can be successful. Show employees that the organization is committed to them and that they are what makes the organization a success.
3. The third strategy is to pay attention to what customers and employees are saying. The organization needs to have open ears to listen to suggestions, compliments, and complaints that internal and external customers may have. It is important that the goals and objectives are clearly understood by both the customer and the employee, especially when it comes to international customers. By listening, the organization will be able to see perceptions of the services that are provided.
4. The fourth strategy to achieve service quality is to implement training and education for employees and for customers. By training the customer and the employee, the organization will continue to be successful. The employee will learn new techniques to provide quality service to customers, and the customer will be able to see that the service is reliable because the organization cares about the customer.
5. The fifth and last strategy is to stress the need for continual improvement. Everyone must work together to achieve a high level of service quality. Service quality is a way of life for the organization as well as for the customer (Stamatis, 1996).

Two unique approaches of service quality need to be looked at carefully by organizations that strive for a high level of service quality. The first approach is the customer-perceived quality and the needs of the market. This approach looks at the external customers and is income-oriented. This approach is centered on the expectations and experiences that are related to the customer. Because the quality in this approach is perceived, it is centered on the customers' background characteristic features.

The second approach is directed toward quality control within the organization. This approach is directed toward the internal customers, the employees, and management staff. The internal customers need to understand and fulfill what is expected of them to attain a high level of service quality throughout the organization (Edvardsson, Thomasson and Ovretveit, 1994). Employees need to understand the importance of doing it right the first time, every time. Rework just adds additional costs and frustrations for the organization that are not necessary.

There are actions that an organization can take to make quality an integral part of the way they run their business:

- Keep a friendly atmosphere between management, employees, and customer.
- Maintain lines of communication that are open to all ideas that are suggested.
- Everyone should know what is going on and it is important that every voice be heard.
- Focus on win-win situations. By doing this, everyone works together and everyone succeeds. Everyone is involved and feels that they are important and that the work that they do is actually for a purpose.
- Keep procedures simple and short. By doing this, there will be less communication problems that will interfere with the quality of service being given (Stamatis, 1996).

The following study on hotel service will illustrate the influence of the customer's perception of quality on an organization. Due to China's great growth in the tourism industry since the early 1980s, international tourism hotels in China have experienced dramatic growth accordingly. This fast speed of hotel construction brought with it the challenge of customer service. The hotel industry suddenly found that it had the inability to produce qualified personnel quickly. In the context of hotels, personal service is a major factor in customer satisfaction (King and Garey, 1997). Therefore, measuring current personal service quality in hotels was an important criterion for improving total service quality and customer satisfaction.

As previously stated, the quality of a service is measurable as the gap between the qualities perceived by guests and that which they expect. According to the article, "Measuring Hotel Service Quality: Focusing on Personal Service by Hotels in the People's Republic of China," intangible service attributes are used to measure the international customers' satisfaction and the perceived importance of personal services during the service encounters. Personal service includes things such as attitude, interactions between employees and customers, and behavior. The subject of the article was a study titled, "Measuring Personal Service Quality: An Analysis of Hotels in the People's Republic of China." In the study, guests in six international tourism hotels in different categories (two 3-star, two 4-star, and two 5-star) in Beijing, China were chosen to participate. Three hotel departments were included— the reception department, the food and beverage department, and the housekeeping department. These departments were selected since they represented the operations where customers have most of their service encounters (Wang and Pearson, 2002).

The questionnaire went through rigorous testing and validity processes, and included the final version being printed in multiple languages, with questions regarding personal service attributes and questions concerning the respondent's demographic and travel-related information. Personnel from each of the identified departments to be studied reviewed the questionnaire, and professors and graduate students of the Department of Hotel and Tourism Management of Purdue University were sought for advice and confirmation. Finally, the survey was pre-tested by 20 guests staying at a major hotel in Beijing, with adjustments to content and wording changed based on the suggestions. The service attributes studied were:

- Accuracy in work
- Courtesy in service
- Efficiency and quickness in service
- Foreign language ability
- Friendliness to guests
- General service quality
- Knowledge about hotel services
- Knowledge about the foods offered
- Personal appearance
- Professional appearance
- Services at convenient times
- Skills in providing service
- Support for special guest needs
- Willingness to provide service.

Of the 472 respondents, 15.5 per cent (73) of them chose service as the most important factor in selecting a hotel in China, ranking it number one in all the factors listed, followed by accessibility (14.2 per cent, 67), location (12.1 per cent, 57), safety/security (11.4 per cent, 54), and price/value relationship (10.8 per cent, 51) as the leading factors (Wang and Pearson, 2002).

In general, the most important personal service attributes in the three departments were friendliness and willingness to serve. Foreign language ability was ranked among the least important attributes in both the food and beverage department and the reception department. Knowledge about hotel service was more important in the reception department, as compared to the food and beverage department and the housekeeping department. Courtesy was identified as the second most important service attribute in the food and beverage department, while services at convenient times was regarded as very important in the housekeeping department. Personal appearance was of medium importance in all three departments.

Most of the guests (73.5 per cent) were aged between 25 and 54; a large number of them (41.6 per cent) held professional or technical positions, and a comparatively large proportion of them (28.8 per cent) were managers or executives. Thus, it is not surprising that as many as 62.3 per cent of them finished their four years of college or graduate school, and another 22 per cent of them had some college education. These travelers are well aware of international hotel service standards. Accordingly, specific characteristics of these customers should be carefully studied to ensure that their special needs are met. More than half of the respondents claimed that this was the first time they had traveled to China. This brings a special challenge to the hotel frontline employees, since they are usually the first people whom the customers encounter, and the first impression of the customers is very important in affecting guest overall satisfaction and whether they will turn into repeat customers in the future (Wang and Pearson, 2002).

A comparison between the three hotel categories showed that hotel guests were more satisfied with personal services provided by 4-star hotels in comparison with 3- or 5-star hotels. This may be explained by the customer's price–value perception as well as their expectation of service quality in each hotel category. Customers would have higher expectations from the 5-star hotels, since these hotels usually charge high prices owing to high management fees and operation costs, as well as the intention to maintain their image and repute. On the other hand, 4-star hotels could compete with their 5-star competitors in providing price flexibility and various discounting programs, while still maintaining high quality service so that customers can see more value for their choice.

Likewise, customers might not be so critical about service quality in 3-star hotels considering their low expectations. This finding indicates that 5-star hotels should pay special attention to improving their service quality in order to meet the customer's high expectations, and anything short of standard could produce negative effects on the customer's overall quality evaluation. However, 3-star hotels should not make any compromise in their service quality just because they charge less, since that will lead the customers to the low-price low-quality perception, which is detrimental to these hotels in the long run (Wang and Pearson, 2002).

Since employees play an integral and important part in how consumers rate service quality, the employee's personal service skills are an important aspect in delivering quality service. This study examined the Chinese international tourism hotels' personal service quality as reflected by the international hotel customers' satisfaction level and their perceived importance attached to the personal service items in three hotel departments. These findings provided great insights and guidelines for the Chinese hotel industry to find their strengths and weaknesses in their service delivery, be aware of the customer's service expectations during the service encounters, and enhance and refine their personal service standards to ensure that every customer's need is satisfied.

Service quality needs to be the responsibility of every employee in the organization. From top management down, everyone in the organization should want to provide the customer with the highest possible service. The initial process of changing the old culture of an organization to the new service-oriented may take time and patience, but in the end, the customer loyalty that will be achieved is worth the effort. The pursuit of service quality may be time consuming, but as shown in the following example, the results show that the time is well spent.

Throughout the past decade, a great deal of interest has focussed on how to measure service quality in libraries. There have been a number of articles written regarding academic libraries and their pursuit of quality. Publications describing empirical research on the application of SERVQUAL in libraries include:

- Susan Edwards and Mairead Browne (1995), "Quality in Information Services: Do Users and Librarians Differ in Their Expectations?" *Library and Information Science Research*, 17, 163–82.
- Francoise Hébert (1994), "Service Quality: An Unobtrusive Investigation of Interlibrary Loan in Large Public Libraries in Canada," *Library and Information Science Research*, 16, 3–21.

- Danuta A. Nitecki (May 1996), "Changing the Concept and Measure of Service Quality in Academic Libraries," *The Journal of Academic Librarianship*, 181–90.

A recent New Zealand study titled "Surveying Service Quality within University Libraries," found in the *Journal of Academic Librarianship*, focussed on reducing the gap between customer expectations and the actual service that is provided in libraries. The study used a conceptual framework created by Peter Hernon and Ellen Altman. This framework measured service quality in academic libraries. The research, which was conducted in the seven university libraries of New Zealand during 1996, as expected, intended to provide university librarians in New Zealand, and hopefully elsewhere, with a flexible tool for analyzing and measuring customer expectations of service. They could then determine priorities, measure progress towards meeting customer expectations, review service policies, and reassess resource allocation (Calvert and Hernon, 1997).

The first stage of the research included using the Hernon and Altman framework as a basis and developing a set of statements, each one describing one aspect of service quality in a university library. The list was refined by pre-testing postgraduate students of the Department of Library and Information Studies of the Victoria University of Wellington, arranging focus groups comprised of 69 library staff, Assistant Librarian level or above, and creating, reviewing and revising the content at all seven New Zealand universities. The final questionnaire included 61 different items, some of which were subdivided so that, in total, there were 101 different statements of service.

Next, the survey was conducted separately at two sites, Victoria University of Wellington and Lincoln University just outside Christchurch. Students were recruited as research assistants to administer the survey, and they were paid a small sum in return. They were asked to visit their respective libraries at different times of the working day, including evenings, and ask customers to complete the questionnaire. Assistants were instructed to approach all customers—including academic staff, general staff, and external borrowers, but not internal customers (that is, library staff)—in a given area of the library and ask them to participate. In total, there were 459 respondents, 306 at Victoria University, and 153 at Lincoln University.

The findings agreed with intuitive expectations of what statements would be ranked most highly:

- Number one was "The library furniture is available (e.g. can find a seat or study desk)" and had a mean of 6.23653 and a standard deviation of 1.16594.
- Number 50 was "The online catalogue shows me materials I have requested." This had a mean of 5.65228 and a standard deviation of 1.42975.
- Number 100 out of 101 was "The library has an attractive interior" and had a mean of 4.38863 and a standard deviation of 1.87004.
- Finally, the least in importance was number 101, "Library staff take me to where the material is shelved instead of just pointing or telling me where to go." This had a mean of 3.93627 and a standard deviation of 1.89552 (Calvert and Hernon, 1997).

Other questions addressed lighting equipment, rest room facilities, staff, and wait time. This is an example of an area of service quality that has been studied for several years, and shows how time consuming it is to conduct reliable research in order to provide adequate service to customers.

There are instances when customer participation is needed to make the level of service quality acceptable. An example of this is a wedding coordinator. The customer is interacting with the coordinator on a regular basis to input the wants and desires of the wedding party. When this is the case, it is harder to control the result of the service. According to Kunst and Lemmink (1995), participation, cooperation, and satisfaction go hand in hand. Participation by a customer relies wholly on the customer. If the customer is not willing to make the service advantageous to both him and the organization, the quality of the service will be low. If a customer is enthusiastic regarding the service, the service will be a great success for everyone involved. When there is a service that requires the cooperation of a customer, the service will only succeed when the customer is willing to do the necessary requirements to fulfill his end of the service. It is important for an organization, when the service they are providing requires either participation or cooperation from a customer, that the definitions of their operations are clearly stated where the customer could view them. When there is active participation and cooperation, the satisfaction will be high and the efficiency level will be increased.

As an organization implements service management, it is important to measure the effectiveness. The measurement process can be difficult because there are so many factors that affect the perception of service quality (Johnson, Tsiros and Lancioni, 1995). Each customer has different needs and wants. Customer surveys, interviews, and audits are measurement tools that organizations can utilize to measure their service quality. McDonald's includes in their audits, three aspects of their service that they measure: evaluation of physical facilities and other service production resources, customer–employee interactions and the end result (Johnson, Tsiros and Lancioni, 1995). It is important that all aspects of the organization are included in the audit.

One methodology developed to improve the quality of customer service was the SERVQUAL methodology. This was originally developed by leading customer satisfaction researchers A. Parasuraman, Leonard Berry and Valarie Zeithaml (1990). SERVQUAL was developed as an instrument to improve the management of service quality (Kunst and Lemmink, 1995). This measurement tool follows five underlying dimensions: tangibles, reliability, responsiveness, assurance, and empathy (Johnson, Tsiros and Lancioni, 1995).

- Tangibles include physical facilities, equipment, and the appearance of personnel.
- Reliability is the ability to perform the pledged service dependably and accurately.
- Responsiveness is the willingness to help customers and provide prompt service.
- Assurance is the knowledge and courtesy of employees and their ability to inspire trust and confidence.

- Empathy is the individualized caring attention the organization provides its customers (Stafford, Stafford and Wells, 1998).

According to Kunst and Lemmink (1995), there is some overall reliability of this measurement tool when used in a variety of service industry contexts. There is, however, some variance among studies when looking at individual service quality dimensions. As with any type of measurement tool, the results rely on how well the test was administrated. Every organization will have different results because every organization has its own qualities.

Another well-known quality management system is the International Standards for Quality Management Systems (ISO 9000). ISO 9000 is a set of standards for quality management systems that is accepted around the world. Over 90 countries have adopted ISO 9000 as national standards. If a company is registered as an ISO certified company, one has guarantees that the goods or services will be of superior quality. In addition, there is a continual monitoring of customer satisfaction and continual improvement being performed at these organizations that provides the customer with increased assurances that their needs and expectations will be met. ISO 9000 registration is rapidly becoming necessary for any organization that does business particularly in Europe, and there is a growing trend toward universal acceptance of ISO 9000 as an international standard.

The Service Process

Today many international organizations have similar service processes. The international service managers who run these organizations overseas need to understand the different cultures that he or she will be living and working in. The most important thing for international service managers to do is keep their customers. Service process is one of the most fundamental areas of service management. It is described as the method and design of how service-operating systems work. Service process involves transforming input from the customer to output of the product or service. A service process is a list of steps an organization follows to reach its main goal of "satisfying its customer." "If you are not serving the customer, your job is to serve somebody who is" (Albrecht, 1990). Service processing can be categorized in four different areas such as people processing, possession processing, mental stimulus processing, and information processing.

People processing involves tangible actions to the customer. These tangible service items are physically present while the service is going on. Such items include transportation, machines, or technologies. The customer has to be physically present to absorb these benefits throughout the service. If customers want the benefits of the people processing service, they must cooperate with the service operation. For instance, their involvement in traveling from one place to another requires them physically to take a car, bus, train, or airplane. The output of this is that the customer reached their destination and is satisfied with everything that happened along the way, from the beginning to the end. This is where the decisive moment sets in. It is very important for organizations to have an international service manager to think about these processes and outputs. The last thing an international service manager wants is to lose customers, just because the process was not beneficial to the customer. "Do not do unto others, as you would have them do unto you: their tastes may not be the same" (Albrecht, 1990).

The next area of service process is possession processing; taking a product the customer already has and keeping it in operational condition. Examples of this are cleaning, improving, painting, restoring, or anything that would add value to the product. Customers are rarely involved in this stage. For example, when a customer travels, they drop off their luggage. They do not see where it goes or how it is delivered. If a customer has a product that is too heavy to move, the service provider will assist such a customer. Possession processing involves customers trusting the organization providing the service.

After the possession process, international service managers need to focus on the mental or psychology aspect of the service process. In some countries, services that interact with people's minds have to be very careful in what they provide for the customers. The reason for this is that many countries have different religious backgrounds. Some countries have ethical standards to live and go by. This is a big problem for many US organizations looking into the international marketplace. Many US organizations see this as a reason for not going global. However, for some they find it necessary to go after foreign markets.

Receiving a mental service takes time on the customer's part. For instance, education and entertainment are examples of services dealing with a customer's mind and behavior. Television and seeing an event in person are components that translate information to the customer. This leads service managers to use the information processing service area.

Mainly computers, the Internet, and many other technologies have developed the area of information processing service. Customer involvement in information processing is low, based on tradition or personal desire to use this service. The banking and insurance industries focus mainly on this. Customers can get all the information over the Internet about the service needed. Some customers prefer to use the telephone or e-mail to build strong relationships with their service provider. Another way for customers to receive good service is through ATM machines. Information processing is a way of getting the product or service to the customer quickly and efficiently.

The most important thing about the service process is whether you can deliver the service. Many international organizations use the Internet as a way of dealing with customers. Other organizations use call centers as a way of getting information, which will better serve their customers. Call centers have become an interactive tool that organizations can use to communicate efficiently and effectively with their customers. Organizations are realizing that customers need a place to call when they have questions or when they have compliments and/or complaints. Customers today do not want to speak to machines and voice mail; they prefer real people with real voices.

The service process is a unique way of establishing good solid relationships with customers. Without the service process layout, an organization could find itself left in the dark. Many organizations strive to have good service but do not have a process of achieving it.

Conclusion

Service management focusses on the management of both the strategic and operational aspects of business, as well as improving service quality and the efficiency and effectiveness of these processes. It includes understanding how new technologies can be integrated into service operations to help achieve maximum objectives. Service managers must have qualities such as business and financial management skills, relationship and communication skills, and the knowledge and commitment to focus on the needs and expectations of customers. Services include all internal and external activities of organizations aimed at customer acquisition, retention, and care. Customer service is required in all business sectors and is so important that no business can succeed without it. Concentration on service management and proper customer service will yield strong customer loyalty for businesses of the twenty-first century. International service management will need to incorporate the elements of cultural differences to all the aforementioned since what is considered good customer service in one country could be a disaster in another.

Case Study

Euro Disney

The Walt Disney organization has been very successful in the past with their movies, theme parks, and merchandise. They own and operate amusement parks in California, Florida, Tokyo, Paris, and Hong Kong. In the mid-1980s, the organization started to look at Europe for their fourth amusement park sight. The Disney Park and Resort opened April 12, 1992. It opened in northern Europe right outside of Paris. Euro Disney employed 12,000 people and had a forecast of 11 million visitors in the first year. Euro Disney included the park, six hotels, and an entertainment and retail center. Despite all the publicity and excitement, the first season was not up to everyone's expectations. They failed to reach target levels in attendance (50,000 showed instead of the projected 500,000), food and souvenir purchases were low, occupancy rates in the hotels were low, and the organization simply could not capitalize on their enormous land holdings. The situation did not improve the following year.

The international market for services grew to $1.2 trillion in 1995 and had been growing at double-digit rates (Samiee, 1999). An organization must be aware of what they will be dealing with in another country. They have to understand that culture's service expectations and cater to it. The Disney organization was behind in this area, most probably because of language barriers and cultural differences. For instance, in Hong Kong, Feng Shui has played a significant role in the park's design. It does not have the unlucky number four in its elevators, has moved its main gate so it was facing the right direction, and had put a bend in its walkway so that "chi" or energy does not flow into the South China Sea. Thus, because Disney was bringing a service to France, some levels of human resources were involved. With the use of human resources, the likelihood of cultural incompatibility lessened significantly (Samiee, 1999).

Euro Disney was armed with some huge strengths. First of all the Disney organization had been around since 1955. There were many years of experience and success behind it. Next, the Walt Disney name is internationally recognized. Its movies and merchandise are all constant reminders and advertisements for the organization on a daily basis. Another strength of Euro Disney was the support it had. It had backing from the Disney organization and from financial institutions all over the United States and Europe.

Euro Disney's weaknesses included critics, low knowledge of French culture, and high prices. French critics called it the "new beachhead of American Imperialism" (Lovelock, 2005). They said it "exemplified all that was wrong with American culture—namely size, money, and Hollywood" (Lovelock, 2005). The mass media highlighted difficulties and accentuated negative stories, including labor problems (during the first four months over 1,000 employees left). Euro Disney was using the same handbook (The Look Book) that was used in the American Disney theme parks. It did not fit in with the French culture and that upset many people. High prices were another weakness of the park. It was high by European standards but also higher than Disney's two American parks.

Euro Disney had several opportunities to make the park a success. One of the best things they did was change from ethnocentric staffing to polycentric staffing. Euro Disney had first opted to practice ethnocentric staffing. Ethnocentric staffing involves sending one of the organization's "own" abroad to manage. American management was not familiar with the French culture and it was hard for them to adapt to it. The organization lost nearly $1 billion in 1992 and 1993 because of this. The next season the organization decided to try polycentric staffing. Polycentric staffing is a concept where local managers from within the country are hired to fill management positions. Disney decided to hire a French chief executive named Philippe Bourguigonn, who lowered admission prices and realized a profit for Disney the next year.

The new French executive knew that in order to make the theme park successful, it needed to be catered more towards the French. The French thought that Euro Disney had too much of an American orientation. For example, it was too much for the French to celebrate Halloween, so the new management decided to place more accent on events familiar to Europeans. In addition, Euro Disney employees (who were mainly French) were using the exact same handbook that their American counterparts were. This caused a controversy because the French do not have the same customs or ideas of beauty that the Americans do. The handbook stated that female employees wear "clear nail polish, very little, if any, make-up, and flesh-colored stockings" (Lovelock, 2005). They were also required to smile at customers within 60 seconds of their entering the theme park, which was an immediate problem because "the French are not known for their hospitality" (Lovelock, 2005). The handbook was quickly changed to cater to the French employees. They were allowed to wear colorful nail polish and different colored stockings. Because they were allowed to be more themselves, staff turnover went way down.

The decision was made early on that French would be the first official language at Euro Disney. Some attractions would be named in French and others would keep their original American name. Signs would be in both English and French. Frontline employees would have to know two or more languages. Audio receivers would also be available in a choice of English, Spanish, German, and Italian at the movies.

Things did not work out as planned though. Workers ended up not being as fluent in the languages that they said they knew. Not all the signs were half-French and half-English. Most of them were English, which led to a lot of confusion when people were trying to find rides or restrooms. Eventually, better and more visible signs were implemented. In addition, interpreters that were more competent, and technology that allowed an employee to find quickly an interpreter for a language that they did not understand, were brought in (Lovelock, 2005).

Complaints about high prices for admission and hotels were another problem. It was cheaper to fly to Florida at $115 a day for travel, hotel, and park entry than it was for a similar package at Euro Disney. The French management broke another Disney taboo by introducing cut-rate entry and room rates for the off-season. They also decided to have lower price tickets after 5.00 p.m. and price reductions for school groups (Lovelock, 2005). This is also very similar to the problems in Hong Kong. There are some who have decided that Hong Kong Disneyland may not be worth its entry fee of anywhere from $37.90 to $45, compared to Ocean Park, a 29-year-old marine-themed park which costs $23.80. Ocean Park is also more centrally located than Disneyland, and is located on the green and luxurious Lantau Island, only 30 minutes away from downtown Hong Kong.

Waiting in line or "queuing" is a huge part of customer service. At Euro Disney, even the lines that looked short seemed to take forever to get through. Ride conductors were only filling the rides half-full and there were no employees around to control the lines and intruders, which led to many conflicts. In the service business, an organization needs to be able to give the customer the feeling that they are getting something for their money, although the product is not tangible. When the customer is waiting in line, they are being let down.

There are three characteristics that a service organization needs to know about queues. First, unoccupied time feels longer than occupied time. If the customer is kept occupied during their waiting time for service, the time will go faster and the customer will be less agitated. Euro Disney management could have had a Disney movie playing while people were waiting in line. Next, unexplained waits are longer than occupied waits. Management needed to go out to where the customers were waiting and explain to them why it is an unusually long wait. The customer needed to be offered something to calm them (like a free lunch). Third, unfair waits are longer than equitable ones. If employees are standing around instead of helping customers, it is an unfair wait. The manager needs to ensure that the employees are not standing around and that they are helping the customer efficiently. Managers should try to be creative and look for ways to make waiting more enjoyable for customers. There should be comfortable temperatures and restful music while customers are waiting for service. At Euro Disney, customers complained about the rides only being half-filled and about the fact that they had no one come out and explain why they were waiting for so long. Many just left the line (Lovelock, 2005). Eventually, management implemented the above practices, waiting time was lowered, and customer satisfaction returned.

Because customers usually derive value from services without obtaining permanent ownership of any physical object, the service organization has to work extra hard to impress the customer (Stauss and Mang, 1999). Euro Disney had to get the customer back up on a pedestal. They did this by changing management, lowering prices, orientating more towards the French culture, implementing better interpreters, and lowering the waiting time in lines. Euro Disney had a bad start but with some changes, all has ended well. In 2003, Euro Disney was the number one theme park in Europe. Over ten million people visit the park a year. Disney may have learned from its park in France in that it began small in Hong Kong, so that it could become profitable with 5.6 million visitors a year. Disney must be doing something right; the park in Tokyo, which opened in 1983, has since become the most-visited amusement park in the world, with more than 16 million visitors expected this year.

International organizations are beginning to understand the importance of service management across the board from their internal and external customers. The understanding that customers are top priority is extremely important. If a customer's expectations are not satisfied, they will lose the loyalty of that customer. By catering to the customer's wants and needs, the organization will be successful. This will mean listening to what the customer wants and finding the processes to achieve it.

Case Questions

1. What problems resulted from the following factors:
   a. Wrong assessment of the market situation
   b. Economic development considerations
   c. Guest awareness of high prices
   d. Cultural problems?
2. Were any of the characteristics of the traditional Disney theme park transferred to Euro Disney? Would you expect them to be?
3. Do you think Disney's assumptions in the planning process overlooked some key cultural differences in the market? How about in Europe and areas where Disney had had previous experience?
4. How did Euro Disney's change from ethnocentric staffing to polycentric staffing affect its service to its customers?

Chapter Review

International service management has become a top priority in today's society as organizations realize the importance of customer service. Service standards, service quality, the service process, and technological advancements have helped to make international service management a fundamental tool for multinational organizations. Service quality and customer satisfaction are qualities that customers expect everywhere they go. In today's society, customers (internal and external) demand a high level of quality service. Quality service is a competitive advantage that an organization can use to draw customers to use their services.

Service quality is defined as the relationship between the customer's expectations of a service and the perception of the service after it was received. Because service quality is based on expectations and perceptions, service quality changes with every customer. Along with expectations and perceptions, quality of the product or service is included in how a customer views service quality. Because of this, there are strategies that organizations should use to achieve a high level of service quality and customer satisfaction.

Service quality needs to be the responsibility of every employee in the organization. Customer surveys, interviews, and audits are measurement tools that organizations can utilize to measure their service quality. Responsiveness is the willingness to help customers and provide prompt service. Today many international organizations have service processes. Service process is one of the most fundamental areas of service management and the most important thing about service process is whether a company can deliver the service.

Chapter Questions

1. Identify the key concepts essential to becoming effective international managers in service organizations.
2. Discuss ways to improving international management skills in service sector companies.
3. Explain why understanding one's own leadership and influence style is important in order to improve one's effectiveness as a leader, as well as a team and organizational member.
4. How would you characterize international service management in terms of both service and product organizations?

Chapter 8

Culture Defined

Travel is fatal to prejudice, bigotry, and narrow-mindedness and many of our people need it solely on these accounts. Broad, wholesome, charitable views of men and things cannot be acquired by vegetating in one corner of the earth all one's lifetime.

Mark Twain

What is Culture?

One of the definitions of culture in *The New Webster's Dictionary and Thesaurus of the English Language* (1993, 235) is the social and religious structures, and intellectual manifestations that characterize a society. Thinking about people who belong to a cultural group, we might define culture as a group of peoples facing similar challenges and a common environment and who work together to create meaningful ways to survive and experience life.

The one thing that seems certain when trying to define culture is that there is no agreement on a single definition of the term. In fact, Kroeber and Kluckhohn (1952) identified over 160 different definitions of culture. One of the earliest widely cited definitions, offered by Sir E. B. Taylor (1871) over a century ago, defined culture as "that complex whole which includes knowledge, belief, art, morals, law, custom, and any other capabilities and habits acquired by man as a member of society."

Culture is everything that people have, think, and do as members of their society. The three verbs in this definition (have, think, and do) can help to identify the three major structural components of culture. In order for a person to *have* something, some material object must be present. When people *think*, ideas, values, attitudes, and beliefs are present. When people *do*, they behave in certain socially prescribed ways. Thus, culture is made up of 1) material objects; 2) ideas, values, and attitudes; and 3) normative or expected patterns of behavior. Also important to note is the final part of this definition, "as members of their society." This should serve to remind each of us that culture is shared.

Describing Culture

As Harris and Moran (1999) describe, culture comes in layers, like an onion. To be able to understand it you have to unpeel it layer by layer. On the outer layer are the products of culture, like language, food, or dress. As you peel away the layers, you will discover expressions of deeper values and norms in a society that are not directly visible, and are more difficult to identify.

There are three predominant layers to culture: the outer layer, explicit products; the middle layer, norms and values; and the core layer, assumptions about existence:

1. The outer layer, or explicit culture, is the observable reality of language, food, houses, architecture, agriculture, markets, fashions, art, and so on. This symbolic and observable level is where prejudices usually start. An important thing to remember is that each opinion we voice regarding explicit culture (what is symbolic and observable) usually says more about ourselves than it does about the community or person we are judging.

2. The second layer reflects the norms and values of an individual group. Norms are the shared sense a group has of what is right and wrong. Norms can develop on an official level as written laws, and on an informal level as social control. Values, on the other hand, determine the definition of good and bad, and are therefore closely related to the standards shared by a group. A culture is relatively stable when the norms reflect the values of the group. While norms, consciously or subconsciously, give us a feeling of "this is how I should behave," values give us a feeling of "this is how I desire to behave." A value serves as a measure to determine a choice from existing alternatives.

3. The third layer reflects the core of the individual, the center or essence of their assumptions about their existence. It is their individual harmony with the world. For instance, it reflects their gods, idols, or individuals, which are the source of their values.

In addition, culture must be studied indirectly by looking at the behavior, customs, material culture, and language. All of these areas are very important to concentrate on when researching culture because they greatly influence how each culture is different. Culture can be broken down into four different areas that help understand the meaning:

1. The first area is learned. Since culture is learned rather than inherited, it is evident that each one of us has the ability to learn about multiple cultures. Although our own culture will be the most comfortable, it is understandable that other's lifestyles will be acceptable. This process is called enculturation, or the acceptance of the behavior patterns of the surrounding culture.

2. The second area of understanding culture is the share value. There is absolutely no culture of an individual; members of the group share the culture. For example, what we all say and do must conform to a set of underlying linguistic and cultural rules that allows us to be in agreement with other members in our society. Otherwise, the differing behaviors would be idiosyncratic and not cultural. People in a society live and think in different ways that form definite patterns of that culture and society.

3. Thirdly, culture is dynamic rather than static. This means that it is always changing or adapting to the environment conditions. It also changes through the process of social interaction. For example, back when conquests and trade

contracts happened, there was a mixing of new ideas and artifacts among the human culture. That shows that everyday interactions are mixing and changing the cultures to better the world and society that we believe in.

4. Lastly, culture is a systemic or universal whole, and should not be broken down into high and low culture. The music heard on the street, the value of currency, and the rate of divorce is a part of each culture and are different in every culture. Within cultures, the beliefs, values, and attitudes are generally the same.

If one has to compare culture to something, the analogy of an iceberg is ideal. Culture seems to come before awareness in that even though we all have difficulty in defining what it is, and no one bothers to verbalize it, it still forms the roots of our actions—it is part of everything we think, say, and do. Like the iceberg, with its largest implicit part beneath the water, the essence of culture is not what is visible on the surface.

Overall, we need to remember that every country looks at culture and values differently. When you look at Americans, they value independence, competition, and individual success, while Arabs value family security, compromise, and personal reputation. Being able to recognize and understand each culture will give a manager a greater advantage of being a good international manager (Rodrigues, 2002, 6).

Understanding Culture

Understanding cultures different from one's own or from the mainstream culture is important in at least five situations in international management:

1. In communicating, transacting business, and negotiating with colleagues from other countries. Today, the integration between cultures has become an everyday occurrence.
2. In working for a foreign-based company. As international businesses continue to grow and unite people and cultures, the most important element of successful business results may be the appreciation and respect for cultural differences in the host country.
3. In managing human resources in another country, whether the employees are indigenous to that country or hired from yet another country. It is important for HR to understand the impact of cultural, political, and economic differences produced by the globalization of organizations. Whether sending an expatriate employee overseas, or merely communicating with a foreign office, there are conditions that affect companies with international personnel, and HR needs to be aware of these obstacles to cultural adaptability and the impact that cultural variations have on the organization.
4. In managing foreign-born or culturally diverse workers in the domestic company. Foreign national employees assigned to the US company face the same challenges that Americans would face in a foreign country, thus it is important to understand the effect of the American business culture on them

and recognize that there may be adjustment periods necessary. In addition, in managing those of another culture, an international manager must be cognizant of the beliefs, values, and attitudes of those he or she is managing.

5. In accommodating international guests. When hosting those of another country, one must be mindful of the fact that the "fish is now taken out of the pond" hence needing all necessary supports. It is necessary to introduce one's culture to the guest in a non-threatening way starting from what is common with the two cultures and move to what makes the cultures different.

Professor Geert Hofstede (1983), Emeritus Professor, Maastricht University, the Netherlands, has proposed that there are four dimensions of culture. Using these dimensions, it is possible to identify differences in management styles, organizational preferences, and motivation patterns. These dimensions explain how differences can affect the way in which managers from different cultures behave and perform individually and in a team. Often, multinationals see the cultural diversity within their operations as an area of difficulty rather than as an opportunity to build competitive advantage. However, it is important not only to understand differences between cultures, but also to identify the potential advantages and disadvantages likely to be brought to a team by managers of different cultures. The managerial implications are detailed in the following descriptions.

The dimensions of culture that may affect generic strategies are:

1. *Power Distance Dimension.* This dimension is defined as the extent to which members of organizations accept that power is distributed unequally. In other words, power distance is the degree in which employees interact freely with their superiors. The most common types of power distance are large and small. In large power distance situations, the employees are unequal compared to the boss, and only the boss is independent. In small power distance situations, the employees are equal compared to the boss and everybody is encouraged to be independent.

2. *Individualism/collectivism Dimension.* Individualism focusses on the degree the society reinforces individual or collective achievement and interpersonal relationships. A highly individualistic ranking indicates that individuality and individual rights are dominant in the society. Individuals in these societies may tend to form a larger number of looser relationships. A lower individualism ranking characterizes societies of a more collectivist nature with close ties between individuals. These cultures reinforce extended families and collectives where everyone takes responsibility for fellow members of their group (Hofstede, 1980).

3. *Masculinity/femininity Dimension.* Masculinity is the dimension that refers to the degree of assertiveness, materialism, and lack of concern for others. The cultures that scored high have a tendency to have very different expectations of gender roles in society. The more feminine cultures have a greater ambiguity in what is expected of each gender. Masculinity and femininity are two more dimensions that play a role in how to plan for a specific culture. Masculine cultures primarily deal with men being the most powerful gender in the

workplace, while feminine cultures have more integration in allowing women to hold the same position of power as men.

4. *Uncertainty Avoidance Dimension.* Uncertainty avoidance is another key dimension in planning for a specific culture. Uncertainty avoidance refers to how comfortable people feel towards ambiguous situations. Cultures that ranked low feel more comfortable with the unknown. High uncertainty avoidance cultures prefer strict laws; formal rules and any uncertainty can express itself in higher anxiety than those from low uncertainty avoidance cultures. Cultures that have strong uncertainty avoidance tend to be more aggressive and harder working, while cultures that have weak uncertainty avoidance tend to be laid back and virtually stress free.

In later research, using an international study developed with Chinese employees and managers, Hofstede and Bond (1988) added a fifth dimension, Confucian Dynamism. The final dimension that plays a role in planning for a specific culture is long-term orientation and short-term orientation. Long-term orientation would be a culture that is planning for the non-immediate future, while short-term orientation is planning for the immediate future.

These dimensions show how country differences and values are all very diverse. As an international manager, one needs to be cognizant of why people act as they do. There is not a correct way to behave. Many countries feel the manager is the ultimate authority, yet there are some countries that are much more casual in this regard. Several countries prize individualism (US, Australia) where achievement is highly valued; however, Pakistan and Panama feel quite the opposite. Additionally, Japan and Africa are collective, making decisions as a group, whereas most of Europe is more individualistic. These examples demonstrate how differences between countries, their values and customs, are ultimately their society's ideas of what is right and acceptable in their culture and environment.

Culture is a shared, learned, symbolic system of values, beliefs, and attitudes that shapes and influences perception and behavior. It is an abstract, such as, a blueprint or mental code. This means that culture is instilled in us when we are born, and culture changes and develops as we grow older. We are all born into a human culture, and it is culture that shapes our self-awareness and understanding of other individuals. It also reflects, depending on the cultural teaching, customs, or patterns of behavior in relating to other cultures.

Cultural Ethnocentrism

Most sociologists see culture as a social construction, meaning that the members of the group believe that it is real and that their culture is the best way. This is obvious in the fact that parents do not teach their children that someone else's way of doing things is better. It does not make sense to do so, thus the culture is passed on to their children (called socialization), and they pass it on to their children, and on and on for generations.

Table 8.1   Hofstede's Dimensions

Region/Country	Individualism–Collectivism	Power / Distance	Uncertainty/Avoidance	Masculinity–Femininity
North America	Individualism	Low	Medium	Masculine
Japan	Collectivism and Individualism	High and Low	High	Masculine/Feminine
Europe:				
Anglo	Individualism	Low/Medium	Low/Medium	Masculine
Germanic: West Slavic, West Urgic	Medium Individualism	Low	Medium/High	Medium/High Masculine
Near Eastern: Balkanic	Collectivism	High	High	Medium Masculine
Nordic	Medium/High Individualism	Low	Low/Medium	Feminine
Latin Europe	Medium/High Individualism	High	High	Medium Masculine
East Slavic	Collectivism	Low	Medium	Masculine
China	Collectivism	Low	Low	Masculine / Feminine
Africa	Collectivism	High	High	Feminine
Latin America	Collectivism	High	High	Masculine

Source: Raghu Nath and Kunal K. Sadhu (1988), "Comparative Analysis: Conclusions, and Future Directions," in Raghu Nath (ed.), *Comparative Management: A Regional View* (Cambridge, MA: Ballinger Publishing Company), 273.

Table 8.2   Cultural Dimension Scores for Ten Countries

	Power Distance	Individualism	Masculinity	Uncertainty Avoidance	Long-term Orientation
USA	40L	91H	62H	46L	29L
Germany	35L	67H	66H	65M	31M
Japan	54M	46M	95H	92H	80H
France	68H	71H	43M	86H	30L
Netherlands	38L	80H	14L	53M	44M
Hong Kong	68H	25L	57H	29L	96H
Indonesia	78H	14L	46M	48L	25L
West Africa	77H	20L	46M	54M	16L
Russia	95H	50M	40L	90H	10L
China	80H	20L	50M	60M	118H

Source: Raghu Nath and Kunal K. Sadhu (1988), "Comparative Analysis: Conclusions, and Future Directions," in Raghu Nath (ed.), *Comparative Management: A Regional View* (Cambridge, MA: Ballinger Publishing Company), 273.

The natural inclination to evaluate other cultures in terms of one's own is called cultural ethnocentrism. Ethnocentrism is a term created by William Graham Sumner, Professor of Sociology at Yale University. It is simply the view that one's ethnic group is the center of everything, against which all other groups are judged. Ethnocentricity can misrepresent one's views of other cultures because it views other cultures in terms of their own culture. In doing so, it causes one to overlook important human and environmental differences among cultures.

Perhaps all individuals and cultures attempt this challenge of "stepping out of their skin" and "walking in another's shoes." However, this concept of temporary detachment from one's beliefs is a significant piece of understanding the culture of another individual and nation.

International business projects can be damaged by ethnocentricity when a company's employees are insensitive to cultural distinctions. Projects can fail because companies may disregard something fundamental to another culture. For instance, a major US airline once painted a beautiful mural of white lilies inside its international aircraft, not realizing that white flowers symbolize death in the Chinese culture. This well-meant gesture, instead of portraying the beauty of the culture as intended, put a fear of flying into the minds of the Chinese community. Significant oversights and missteps can occur within a business relationship as a result of lack of host country research, selecting inappropriate colors and symbols for advertising, product packaging, or design.

Consideration and attentiveness of another's culture and beliefs is analogous to the consideration and attentiveness in any relationship. Each individual perceives things differently and understands them to be based on what they believe is natural. For example, in a high context culture, one person may value the form of communication, so much so that they explain things in great detail to ensure the receiver has heard each word clearly, even if it necessitates repeating the same sentence in different ways. They feel this detail is necessary, and it is not communication without it. However, the receiver in a low context culture may not maintain this same value for explicit form of communication. Culture is not only a "thing," it is a behavior, and once the international manager masters this concept of placing value, importance, and respect on all beliefs, not just his or her own, it will make understanding other cultures almost simple.

Cultural Comparisons

It is interesting to note how some cultures that seem similar are not. Americans often view the Canadians as "American" by most standards. After all, they speak English, eat what Americans eat, listen to similar music, live in similar dwellings, and dress as Americans do. However as noted below, there are dissimilarities, and thus it is important to remember that even those who we perceive to be similar to us may not be:

- Canada has been described as being a mixture of cultures where individual differences are celebrated, compared to the US "melting pot" where differences in culture are tolerated much less.
- English is the principal language other than in Quebec where French is the main language.
- All official Canadian government publications and signs throughout Canada are in both English and French.
- Canadians are inclined to use British English spelling rather than US English spelling.
- To Canadians, calling them American is an offense.

In addition, the chart below depicts the differences in the three countries that make up North America. Although they are physically close, they all have cultural differences. Mexico, for instance, has a different history and thus a different culture and ways of doing and looking at things. It is inaccurate to assume that geographically adjacent nations have similar cultures, as shown below.

Not only is it important to compare national cultures, but it is also important to understand the concept of a nation's subcultures. There may be a tendency to think of the nation as a whole when speaking of culture. For instance, by referring to British, Nigerian and Indonesian cultures as if all Britons, all Nigerians, and all Indonesians were culturally identical, is an example. This concept is a generalization since British cultures include the English, Scottish, and Welsh, while in the Nigeria

Table 8.3   Comparing Cultural Differences: Mexico with Canada and the United States

CULTURAL COMPARISONS		
Aspect	**Mexico**	**Canada/USA**
Family	Family is the first priority Children are celebrated and sheltered Wife fulfills domestic role Mobility is limited	Family is usually second to work Children often minimally parented; are independent Wife often fulfills dual roles Mobility quite common
Religion	Long Roman Catholic tradition Fatalistic outlook. "As God wills"	Mixed religions "Master of own life" outlook
Education	Memorization Emphasis on theoretical Rigid, broad curriculum	Analytical approach Emphasis on the practical Narrow, in-depth specialization
Nationalism	Very nationalistic Proud of long history and traditions Reluctant to settle outside Mexico	(US) Very patriotic Proud of "American way of life" Assumes everyone shares his or her materialistic values (Canadian) Less than US. Often has more "World" view
Personal Sensitivity	Difficulty separating work and personal relationships Sensitive to differences of opinion Fears loss of face, especially publicly Shuns confrontation	Separates work from emotions/personal relationships Sensitivity seen as weakness Tough business front Has difficulty with subtlety
Etiquette	"Old world" formality Etiquette and manners seen as measure of breeding	Formality often sacrificed for efficiency "Let's get to the point" approach
Personal Appearance	Dress and grooming are status symbols	Appearance is secondary to performance
Status	Title and position more important than money in eyes of society	Money is main status measure and is reward for achievement
Aesthetics	Aesthetic side of life is important even at work	No time for "useless frills"
Ethics	Truth is tempered by need for diplomacy Truth is a relative concept	Direct Yes/No answers given and expected Truth seen as absolute value

Source: Passaic County Community College, Patterson, NJ. Retrieved March 2004 from http://www.pccc.cc.nj.us/library/asrc/reading/Cultural%20differences%20Chart%20RD004%20week%206.htm

case, you have three principal cultures, namely, Yoruba, Igbo, and Hausa. Their languages and cultures are significantly different.

Specifically, there are often subcultures within a culture. Subcultures are groups of people who share a unique way of life within a larger, dominant culture. Subcultures share in the dominant culture but also have a unique and distinctive set of attitudes, values, and behaviors that differ in varying degrees from the dominant culture and from other subcultures within the culture. Subcultures can also extend beyond national borders, such as with the Arab nations.

Culture is Learned

Culture is transmitted through the process of learning and interacting with one's environment rather than through the genetic process. According to Ferraro (1994), culture can be thought of as a storehouse of all the knowledge of a society. The child who is born into any society finds that the problems that confront all people have already been solved by those who have lived before. For example, material objects, methods for acquiring food, language, rules of government, forms of marriage, and systems of religion have already been discovered and are functioning within the culture when a child is born (Ferraro, 1994, 18).

To look at this further, imagine two children growing up in different parts of the world. Although both of these children will grow up and behave quite differently, there is one basic principle regarding culture that holds true. Both of these children were born into an already existing culture. Once each of these children has learned the various solutions to basic human problems that his or her culture has set down, behavior becomes automatic. Culture is not inborn, or instinctive, but is passed on from one generation to another within a society.

Despite the large variations in cultures throughout the world, all people acquire culture through the same process—learning. Understanding that culture is acquired through the process of learning has several important implications for the conduct of international business.

First, such an understanding can lead to greater acceptance of cultural differences, which is a requirement for effective intercultural communication within a business setting.

Second, the learned nature of culture serves as a reminder that since we have mastered our own culture through the process of learning, it is possible (albeit more difficult) to learn to function in other cultures as well. Thus, cross-cultural expertise for Western businesspeople can be accomplished through effective training programs.

And finally, the learned nature of culture leads us to the inescapable conclusion that foreign workforces, although perhaps lacking certain job-related skills at the present time, are perfectly capable of learning those skills in the future, provided they are exposed to culturally relevant training programs.

It is sometimes easy to fall into the trap of thinking that since the Australian Bushman and the Central African Pygmy do not know what we know, they must be childlike, ignorant, and generally incapable of learning. These primitives, the argument goes, have not learned about calculus, Shakespeare, or the Los Angeles Dodgers because they are not as intelligent as we are. Yet, there is no evidence whatsoever to suggest even remotely that people in some cultures are less efficient learners than people in other cultures. What the comparative study of culture does tell us, however, is that people in different cultures learn different cultural content— that is, different ideas, values, behavior patterns, and so on—and they learn that content every bit as efficiently as anyone else does.

Intercultural Communication

Businesses, like other organizations, require effective communication to operate efficiently to meet their objectives. A company must communicate with its workforce, customers, suppliers, and host government officials. When one thinks about it, effective communication among people from the *same* culture is often difficult; moreover, it is extremely difficult when attempting to communicate with people from a different culture who do not speak English, and have different attitudes, ideas, assumptions, perceptions, and ways of doing things. One's chances for miscommunication increase enormously.

Cultures vary in terms of how explicitly people send and receive verbal messages. In the United States, for example, effective verbal communication is expected to be explicit, direct, and unambiguous. Good communicators are supposed to say what they mean precisely and as straightforwardly as possible. One could say that Americans speak frankly, and "tell it like it is." On the other hand, speech patterns in most cultures are different.

For example, as previously noted, Americans overwhelmingly speak clearly. Speakers and writers are urged to keep messages short and simple, use concrete vocabulary, and get to the point quickly. Clarity is stressed because of an underlying supposition that clear communication will be easier to understand and translate into clearer messages in the target language. However, clarity is not a universally appreciated quality. Asian cultures are often cautious of words and the misunderstandings they can provoke. Communicators must become much more skilled at interpretation and translation, at understanding ambiguity, silence, and absence, which may actually convey much of the meaning of the messages. This is important because indirectness and silence may be signs of politeness, calculation, foresight, and wisdom.

Japan is a high-context communication country (Hall, 1976) and the Japanese use the high context traits of ambiguity and indirectness as a tool to save face and give instructions politely. People using high-context communication communicate in ways that maintain harmony within their groups. Personal information is not used to predict behavior in high-context communication. Rather, group-based information is required (Gudykunst, Nishida and Chua, 1986). Gudykunst's (1983) study revealed that members of high-context cultures were more cautious during initial interactions with strangers, and made more assumptions about strangers based upon their backgrounds, compared to members of low-context cultures.

Because high-context cultures place emphasis on non-verbal communication, they need to know whether others understand them when they do not verbally express their ideas and feelings. They also need to know if they can understand others under the same circumstances, in order to reduce uncertainty. Sources of uncertainty in high-context cultures include: knowledge of social background, knowledge whether or not people will behave in a socially appropriate manner, understanding the feelings of individuals, means of communication, or whether others will make allowances for individuals when they communicate.

The Japanese culture is also a high uncertainty avoidance culture. Deviant behavior is not acceptable in cultures that are high in uncertainty avoidance, because there is a strong desire for consensus. In high uncertainty avoidance cultures "what is different, is dangerous," (Hofstede, 1991).

Gudykunst and Kim (2003) affirm that the uncertainty avoidance concept is useful in understanding differences in how strangers are treated. Interaction with strangers in high uncertainty avoidance cultures is characterized by the presence of rules and rituals that govern every situation, as these cultures try to avoid ambiguity. People from high uncertainty avoidance cultures need clear rules when they interact with strangers; otherwise, they may ignore the strangers, treating them as though they did not exist.

The purpose of communication in many Eastern cultures is to promote harmony and social integration, rather than enhance the speaker's individuality through the articulation of words. Many Western cultures tend to place a great deal of power in words while Asian cultures are more withdrawn and reserved. In societies with restricted codes, this cautious approach to words could be seen in the general suppression of negative verbal messages. Because of this, Eastern cultures have many indirect or non-verbal ways to say "no" without simply saying that word. This has caused many misunderstandings when people with an American cultural background try to communicate with the Japanese. For this reason, Japanese often say "yes" because they are expressing that they understand what is being said, not that they are agreeing with what is being said.

Listening is a vital aspect of communication for managers in a multicultural environment. This does not mean simply learning the language. It also means developing behaviors and sensitivities that enable the manager to understand accurately not only the words, but also the person speaking. Managers spend more of their day listening than engaging in any other communication activity. When a cross-cultural dimension is added to the already difficult task of listening, it is easy to understand how miscommunication may occur. If managers do not listen, employees become hesitant to talk. This type of atmosphere fosters high turnover, low job satisfaction, and less employee commitment and participation. Managers must strive to listen with objectivity and to view the problem from the viewpoint of the other person. If managers are successful at this, they can encourage employees to communicate their concerns upward, to participate in decision-making, and to collaborate with their colleagues. This creates an environment of trust and becomes a key to gaining and sharing information, which is a critical management function.

Effective communication requires the understanding of how people think, feel, and behave. It involves knowing something about the cultures' values, attitudes, and patterns of behavior. One of the best ways to gain cultural awareness is with language. Learning a second language is very important since it enables people to get inside the other culture. Communicating effectively involves proficiency in sending and receiving messages.

The vast majority of US business people continue to operate abroad without knowing the language of the opposite culture. Most of the explanations for not knowing the other language are that it is too hard to learn another language in a short period. The English language is rapidly becoming the international language of business. This makes it easier for Americans to avoid learning other languages.

Because communication is one of the most important components of international business, the level of importance attached to it cannot be overemphasized. Managers communicate at different levels and through different forms, depending on their culture. They may communicate either through their staff, by verbal or written methods. Finland is a country that prefers communication either through its staff or verbally. The United Kingdom prefers communication in a written form. It is also evident that managers experience different types of communication with different types of employees. In addition, some countries use a combination of communication techniques. For example, France is very interactive in both verbal and written forms when dealing with communication. The ability to communicate within a culture and an organization is one of the key skills an international manager must possess when working in the business environment.

Master of Destiny

There is a concern in adopting integrative strategies by some nationalities more than others. Studies tend to show that American business people show trust more willingly and more spontaneously than other cultural groups, and have a stronger tendency towards a problem-solving and integrative orientation. The concept of integrative strategy is strongly and culturally influenced by the American tradition of experimental research in social psychology applied to commercial negotiation. It is also based on master of destiny orientation, which feeds attitudes of problem resolution. The problem-solving approach appears to make sense to the American negotiators, but his or her framework may not work in all cases when applied to foreign negotiators. Americans tend to see it more as a creation of God. However, to our knowledge, there is no empirical study that has shown that, for example, Arabs from the Middle East have a tendency to be more distributive and less problem-solving oriented than Americans.

Issues of Environment

Five major areas of attitudes toward a nation's physical characteristics and natural resources are likely to result in cultural environmental presuppositions. These are:

1. Climate
2. Topography
3. Population size
4. Population density
5. The relative availability of natural resources.

These five sources of environmental difference surface when people communicate on a wide spectrum of business-related subjects. Notions of transportation and logistics, settlement, and territorial organizations are affected by topography and climate.

Population size and the availability of natural resources influence each nation's view toward export or domestic markets. The United States and China, for example, both have gigantic domestic markets and are rich in natural resources. Both nations export out of choice, and have a tendency to internalize their views of foreign markets. Foreign markets in such countries may be culturally reinforced as being secondary markets, as a result, with a cultural emphasis on domestic markets.

Population density and space usage influence the development of different cultural perceptions of how space and material are used. Thus, how people lay out or use office space, domestic housing, and buildings in general, shifts from nation to nation. For example, in many nations the size, layout, and furnishings of a business office communicate a message. The message communicated, however, varies from nation to nation.

Such differences may be subtle or overt. For example, the distinctions between the US and French upper-level executive's office may be quite subtle. In both France and the United States, the size of an office, the lushness of its furnishings, and the location in the building (corner office or top floor of the building) reflect the status of the office's owner. In France, however, the individual esthetics of the office decor convey an important statement about the office owner, while in the US office the wall decorations and furnishings are often selected by a designer with little input from the office's occupant.

Education's Role in Developing International Competency

At the same time that we are faced with an ever-increasing need for international competency, the resources that our nation is devoting to its development are declining. This problem is not limited to the area of business. It is a national problem that affects many aspects of American life, including national security, diplomacy, scientific advancement, economics, and international political relations. Future generations of American businesspeople, however, must be drawn from society, and it is this society, through its educational institutions, that has not in the past placed central importance on educating the general populace for international competence (Ferraro, 1994, 13–14).

Several national reports on international education, namely by the National Governors' Association, 1989 (Merryfield, 1995) and the Council on International Educational Exchange, 1988, indicate that there is significant shortfall in our international competence:

- The United States continues to be the only country in the world where it is possible to earn a college degree without taking any courses in a foreign language.
- Less than 1 per cent of the US military personnel stationed abroad can use the language of their host country.
- Only 17 per cent of US elementary schools offer any form of foreign language instruction.
- More than one-half (53 per cent) of US undergraduates take no foreign language courses whatsoever during their four years of university education.

Our national inability to handle foreign languages is paralleled by our less than adequate understanding of foreign affairs:

- Approximately one-half of all American adults are not able to locate the Republic of South Africa on a world map.
- A United Nations study of 30,000 students (age 10–14) in nine countries found that US students ranked next to last in their understanding of foreign cultures. In a recent survey, only 30 per cent of American adults could locate Holland on a map of Europe.
- A recent survey found that Americans watching television news programs understood the major points of only one-third of the international stories.
- One in every four high school seniors in Dallas, Texas, could not identify the country bordering the United States to the south.

When you take into account the low priority that international competency has had in our educational institutions, it is not surprising that those Americans that are expected to function successfully in multicultural environments are so poorly prepared for the task. It is not just in our general education programs that the international dimension is weak, but also in our business school curricula. According to a report of the Task Force on Business and International Education of the American Council on Education, "Over 75 per cent of the graduating Doctorate of Business Administration (DBA), or PhDs in business, have had no international business courses during their graduate studies ..." (Nehrt, 1977, 3.)

While graduate schools in business have increased their international offerings since the 1970s, courses on the cultural environment of international business have received relatively little attention. This general neglect of cross-cultural issues in business education is reflected in the attitudes of the international business community. To illustrate, in a study of 127 US firms with international operations, respondents showed very little concern for the cultural dimension of international business. When asked what should be included in the education of an international businessperson, respondents mentioned—almost without exception—only technical courses. There was, in other words, almost no interest shown in language, culture, or history of one's foreign business partners (Reynolds and Rice, 1988, 56).

In whatever way we choose to measure it, there is substantial evidence to suggest that as a nation our people are poorly equipped to deal with the numerous challenges of our changing world. If our nation is to continue to be a world leader, we must build deep into our national psyche the need for international competency—that is, a specialized knowledge of foreign cultures, including professional proficiency in languages, and an understanding of major political, economic, and social variables affecting the conduct of international and intercultural affairs.

Importance of Cultural Awareness

Why is it so important to be aware of cultural environments and their impact when involved in management, and especially in international management? Because the more you look at case studies, the more you will find that failure to consider the cultural context in the home organization can, and has, led to misunderstandings, miscommunication, lawsuits, and generally a deflation of the goals of the organization. When considering international business, the need to be aware of cultural environments becomes even more critical. Here the degree of the cultural differences is much greater, and consequently, breakdowns of communication usually increase dramatically.

Whether dealing with issues of selling, managing, or negotiating, the success or failure of a company overseas depends on how effectively its employees can implement their skills in a new location. That ability will depend on both their job-related expertise and the individual's sensitivity and responsiveness to the new cultural environment. One of the most common factors contributing to failure in international business assignments is the mistaken assumption that if a person is successful in the home environment, he or she will be equally successful in a different culture.

Books and articles on international business are filled with examples of business miscues when US corporations attempted to operate in an international context. Some might be mildly amusing, while others are simply embarrassing. However, all of them, to one degree or another, have been costly in terms of money, reputation, or both. For example, when American firms try to market their products in other countries, they often assume that if a marketing strategy or slogan is effective in the home country, it will be equally effective in other parts of the world. However, problems can arise when changing cultural contexts. Following are some examples according to former US Senator Paul Simon (1980):

- *Body by Fisher*, describing a General Motors product, came out "Corpse by Fisher" in Flemish, and that did not help sales.
- *Come Alive with Pepsi* almost appeared in the Chinese version of the *Reader's Digest* as "Pepsi brings your ancestors back from the grave."
- A major ad campaign in green did not sell in Malaysia, where green symbolizes death and disease.

Another area that international managers need to consider is the fact that insensitivity to the cultural realities of foreign workforces can lead to disastrous results. Lawrence Stessin (1979) reported on a North Carolina firm that purchased a textile machinery company near Birmingham, England, in hopes of using it to gain entry into the

European market. Shortly after the takeover, the US manager attempted to rectify what he considered a major production problem, the time-consuming tea break. Stessin recounts:

> In England, tea breaks can take a half-hour per man, as each worker brews his own leaves to his particular taste and sips out of a large, pint-size vessel with the indulgence of a wine taster. Management suggested to the union that perhaps it could use its good offices to speed up the "sipping time" to ten minutes a break. The union agreed to try but failed. Then one Monday morning, the workers rioted. Windows were broken, epithets greeted the executives as they entered the plant and police had to be called to restore order. It seems the company went ahead and installed a tea-vending machine—just put a paper cup under the spigot and out pours a standard brew. The pint-sized container was replaced by a five-ounce cup imprinted as they are in America with morale-building messages imploring greater dedication to the job and loyalty to the company. The plant never did get back into production. Even after the tea-brewing machine was hauled out, workers boycotted the company and it finally closed down (Stessin, 1979, 223).

It has become a cliché to say that the world is shrinking or developing into a "global village." Rapid developments in technology, transportation, and communication in recent years have brought people all over the world closer together in a physical sense. But in doing research, many factors seem to point to the realization that if the United States is to remain a leader in world economic affairs, America needs to become more involved in cross-cultural understanding. American managers must realize that despite what may have been true in the past, the product will no longer sell itself. Since there are so many good products on the market today, the crucial factor in determining who makes the sale is not so much the intrinsic superiority of the product but rather the skill of the seller in understanding the dynamics of the transaction between himself or herself and the customer. Unfortunately, because of our relative success in the past, Americans are not particularly well equipped to meet the challenges of the international economic arena during the twenty-first century.

The more we look at the data that is available, the more we realize that the inescapable conclusion from what we find is that the US is not selling their goods and services to the world as successfully as they did during the expansionist past. The important thing now is to look at what has changed and why this is true.

Paul Simon (1980) of Illinois gave a good example of the need for international businesspeople to become better attuned to other languages and cultures:

> The international market is, in some respects, similar to the domestic market. For several years, I was in the newspaper and job printing business, publishing weekly newspapers in small communities, and printing everything from business forms to funeral notices. I bought newsprint from Pioneer Paper Company because they had the best price, and envelopes from the Roodhouse Envelope Company for the same reason. However, for most supplies, competitive prices were fairly close, and then I bought the salesperson rather than the product. The salesperson that knew about my family and me as a customer. If someone had come to my office speaking only Japanese, he might have had the best product in the world but I would probably not have bought from him. The world market is no different. To sell effectively in Italy, speak Italian (Simon, 1980, 31).

Statistics on the premature return rate of expatriate Americans (that is, those returning from overseas working assignments before the end of their contracts) vary widely throughout the international literature. Estimates of attrition rates in the late 1970s ran as high as 65–85 per cent for certain industries (Edwards, 1978, 42; Harris, 1979, 49). Recent figures, while not as high, still serve to illustrate how difficult it is for Americans to live and work successfully abroad. For example, Caudron (1991, 27) cites premature returns of Americans living in Saudi Arabia to be as high as 68 per cent; 36 per cent in Japan; 27 per cent in Brussels; and 18 per cent in London, a city that one would expect most Americans to adjust to easily. Regardless of whether we are dealing with attrition rates of 68 per cent or 18 per cent, the costs are enormous. Considering that it costs a firm between three and five times an employee's base salary to keep that employee and his or her family in a foreign assignment, the financial considerations alone can be staggering (Van Pelt and Wolniansky, 1990, 40).

America's leaders from both the public and private sectors have recognized the seriousness of the trade deficit. However, when looking at the recommendations that various groups made up of leaders in American business, government, and labor have put forth in their reports, there seems to be a common oversight—the relationship between expanding exports and stimulating language and cultural studies in our own country. Since Americans are not taking the time to study other languages and cultures, we simply are not getting to know our international customers, and in return, we are not selling abroad as well as we could.

The Impact of Culture on Business Practices

The reason why people think and act the way they do in a culture are important determinants of how a company negotiates with locals, markets its products, and supervises employees. Understanding a culture's language helps managers to understand a culture. In addition, understanding a culture's unspoken language helps managers avoid sending unintended or embarrassing messages.

For instance, Americans prefer a wider distance from those with whom they are involved in face-to-face communication, unlike those in Arabian cultures, who prefer a very short distance between themselves and those with whom they are communicating. Egyptians tend to speak at a much closer distance than Americans do as well. However, even if one is unaccustomed to this level of contact, it is best not to shy away, since if you keep your distance, the perception might be that you find the corresponding person's physical presence distasteful or that you are a very cold, unfeeling person.

Cultures vary in several ways. Perception of space and time is another way. For instance, Mexican and Italian cultures are very casual about time whereas in Asia and the United States, people arrive promptly for meetings, keep tight schedules, and work long hours. Americans strive toward workplace efficiency but may leave work early if their work is done because they value individual results. However, the Japanese look busy even when business is slow to demonstrate dedication—an attitude grounded in cohesion, loyalty, and harmony.

The importance of hierarchy within a culture, the importance a
gender roles, the nature of authority and humans' relationship to the
are a few more examples. Culture refers to many elements that ar
therefore not evident and can influence professional interactions. For more
may be uncertain whether completing a task or building a relationship will take
precedence. It might not be clear whether the written word or the spoken word is
more trusted. Often, negotiations are not based on facts, but rather on the reputation
of the individual.

Therefore, some general guidelines for working interculturally are important. Do
not assume that the actions are different or counterproductive. Listen, observe, and
discuss the differences, but be respectful of the other members, especially if they are
not comfortable discussing them.

Managers working in international business must develop a detailed knowledge
about a culture so the manager is able to function effectively within it. This knowledge
and education will improve the ability to manage employees, market products, and
conduct negotiations in other countries.

The Impact of Culture on Staffing—The Case of Brazil

Culture is an important factor in staffing in Brazil. Culture has been defined as "a way
of life of a group of people … which is handed down from one generation to the next
through the means of language and imitation" (Toft and Reynolds, 1994, 119). This
culture provides people with a set of explicit and implicit guidelines for thinking,
doing, and living. The way people *think* includes their values, beliefs, myths, and
folklore. The *doing* refers to the laws, statutes, customs, ceremonies, and etiquette
that fashion their daily life. The *living* refers to the tools, food, clothing, and materials
available to them. Culture also looks at ideology, technology, communication, and
language (Toft and Reynolds, 1994, 120).

The cultural environment is often influenced by factors that interact with each
other. These factors form the unique culture that affects the nature and form of
staffing procedures needed in a country, in this case, Brazil. These factors are:

1. History
2. Religion
3. Learning and education
4. Family
5. Class structure
6. Language
7. Economics.

History

The culture of modern Brazil has been transformed through time, as early Portuguese
settlers combined their customs with the original Native Americans. The colonization
of Brazil was the work of Portuguese settlers that came to the area to log the great

orazilwood, which gave the new land its name. Later, the colonists started plantations of sugar cane. Slavery was common for many European countries at that time and Portugal was no exception. An African element was introduced during the colonial period when millions of black African slaves were brought into Brazil. According to Clissold (1996),

> Historians tend to dwell on the patriarchal character of the master-and-slave relationship (and the records contain no lack of evidence of its harsher side). There can be no doubt that it produced a distinctive society, well adapted to the tropical environment in which

Map 8.1 Brazil

Source: CIA–World Factbook
https://www.cia.gov/cia/publications/factbook/geos/br.html

the disparate elements of European, Indian, and Blacks were mellowed, and to a certain extent fused, by a gradual process of miscegenation.

The Portuguese colonization led to a new race in Brazil because of the interbreeding of the native Indians with the African Negro. This resulted in a new race that is typified by a somewhat dark skin tone and blue eyes. This African strain gave a special flavor to the Brazilian culture which is most noted in its folklore and music.

In 1822, following three centuries under the rule of Portugal, Brazil became an independent nation (CIA Factbook, 2004). Portugal had tried to keep Brazil closely linked to the mother country both culturally and economically. It was not allowed to build schools or even to have newspapers. However, the new land was far away from the motherland and began to develop its own character. The Portuguese language was enriched with a new vocabulary appropriate to the flora and fauna and the peculiar mode of life of the New World, and was gradually modified in structure and pronunciation by the colored population who spoke it (Clissold, 1996, 124). The idea of slavery became unpopular in the nineteenth century, and Portugal was pressured to abolish slavery by the other European countries. They were threatened to have supplies cut off and other sanctions. The government also began to realize that a slave-holding Brazil could never take its place among the other civilized nations as long as it had slaves; hence, abolition was achieved in 1888.

Religion

Religion helps to establish the beliefs and norms of a culture and determines whether a population sees themselves as good or evil, and whether they can control or will be controlled by the environment, and what is truly important in life. Religion can affect how a person should eat, dress, relate to others, and work. Brazil is 70 per cent Roman Catholic, 19.2 per cent Protestant, and 10.8 per cent other religions, which include Jewish, Mormon Church of Latter-Day Saints and Jehovah's Witnesses. Custom of folk religions and Afro-Brazilian cults based on the belief in spirits and slave and Indian traditions—such as Umbanda and Candomblé—is widespread among all ethnic groups (Nyrop, 1983). Many Catholics combine worship of African deities with their Christian religious practices. The Protestant population has been growing steadily in the last few years due to the availability of satellite television and the promotional evangelical programs they now have access to. The Protestant religion offers more personal freedom than the more traditional Roman Catholic religion, yet most Native Americans follow traditional religions. There is a distinct separation of church and state. The Roman Catholic cultural tradition pervades their history and their ways of life and thinking. The early explorers and conquerors brought the missionaries with them to convert and civilize the pagan inhabitants. At first, the clergy protected the Indians and helped, through their missions, to educate them. The church eventually became part of the establishment. The church played a role in supporting nationalism and opposing birth control, divorce, and social change. In 1960, Pope John XXIII encouraged the church to promote social justice and to make it a priority in Latin America (Harrison, 1983, 379). The church has since been very active in trying to eliminate the existing violence and to improve human rights for the lower classes.

Education

Learning is important to a society, as it provides the means of transmitting knowledge, skills, and attitudes necessary to live in that society. The teaching style may be authoritarian or participative. The style of teaching will form the attitudes of the student that will transfer into their work and life styles.

Brazil's education system is organized on three levels—eight years of primary education, three years of secondary education, and higher education. The states and municipalities are largely responsible for primary education, with the states controlling secondary education, while private institutions largely oversee higher education, except for federal universities.

Primary school is free and compulsory for children between the ages of seven and fourteen. An average student in the Brazil public school receives four hours or less of class time per day, although national guidelines suggest six hours per day. Primary and secondary schools enroll approximately 90 per cent of Brazil's children. Only about a third of students enrolled in primary school finish the eight-year mandatory schooling. There are an estimated 5 million children and 25 per cent of the poorest children who do not attend school.

There are 68 major universities in Brazil—35 are federal, 20 are private or church-related, two municipal, and 11 are state-supported. About 800 other colleges and institutions of higher education grant degrees in areas such as engineering, medicine, agriculture, law, economics, and business administration. Three military academies train officers of the Brazilian Army, Navy, and Air Force, granting diplomas equivalent to a BA degree (Nyrop, 1983).

Population and Family Members

The population of Brazil consists of 26.6 per cent of its population from 0 to 14 years, 67.6 per cent from 15 to 64 years, and 5.8 per cent aged 65 years and over (CIA Factbook, 2004). Although nearly half of Brazilians are in their mid-20s, the fraction under 14 years of age has fallen from 43 per cent to 34 per cent, while the fraction over 60 years of age has risen from 4 per cent to 8 per cent. The median age is 24.3 years of age.

The citizens of Brazil receive a wide range of benefits that include health insurance and old age pensions. Workers, employers, and the government fund the benefits. The 1988 constitution provides for a 40-hour workweek, maternity leave of 120 days, and paternity leave of five days. Average life expectancy at birth has increased from 46 years to 71 years since the 1950s. The expected number of adults entering the workforce is expected to create a need for 1.6 million new jobs every year.

The ethnic make-up of Brazil consists of the Portuguese, who began colonizing in the sixteenth century, and various European immigrant groups—mainly Germans, Italians, Spanish, and Polish, mixed Caucasian, African, Amerindian (principally

Tupi and Guarani linguistic stock), Japanese, and other Asians and Arabs. Sao Paulo has ther largest Japanese community outside of Japan, except for Hawaii (US Department of State, Background Notes: Brazil, 2005).

The concept of family can range from the nuclear family (immediate parents and children) to the extended family, which includes grandparents, cousins, aunts, and uncles. The power or influence the family has over the individual will affect those members' actions in society. The Brazilian culture has an extended family structure and places a high respect on family and relationships. Historically, the family has been perhaps the single most important institution in the formation of Brazilian society (Nyrop, 1983, 108). The traditional upper class family is patriarchal and characterized by "taciturn father, submissive mother, and cowed children" (Nyrop, 1983, 108). According to historians, a woman's place is in the home and, according to a common proverb, the ideal woman was to leave home only for her baptism, her marriage, and her funeral (Nyrop, 1983, 108). Women, however, are placed on a pedestal and a man's *machismo* (see *Class Structure*) is to protect and impress them. Authority is centered on the father. The husband owes his wife and children protection and will provide it to them. They, in turn, owe him obedience and respect. Children are expected to care for their parents when they are old. Parents will help their children in any way possible to help them get started in life. It is common for several generations to live together.

There are also extended families known as *parentelas*, which are made up of close relatives as well as very distant cousins and cousins of cousins. These *parentelas* influence their social life. There are continual family-oriented events such as weddings, baptisms, funerals, and others. The *parentela* is a very strong support system and provides social interaction as well as help when needed. Loyalty to family is considered the individual's highest duty, and failure to help a family member is frowned on. Nepotism in Brazil is encouraged and thought to be the family member's first obligation (Nyrop, 1983, 109).

However, some of these traditions are changing as the country is becoming more industrialized. There is an increasing need by larger organizations to go into international markets and as they do so, they need to look at the skills and abilities of those people needed to accomplish these objectives, which means that transcending the family boundaries may be the most economically wise thing to do. Businesses would, of course, only hire relatives if they were skilled in the right areas; they would be reluctant to hire relatives if they could not do the job. Old habits and traditions are more difficult to break, and whether or not these practices actually change may be more difficult in smaller, more traditional organizations.

The forces that have been driving this family transition evolved in conjunction with the introduction of industrialization, science, and technology. With the growth of specialized wage labor, economically productive work moved beyond the reach of the family compound. Individualized remuneration and liability led to a redefinition of kinship obligations. The family that was engaged in farming or crafts could be expanded because extra hands could produce extra food and other products. Its boundaries were elastic (Lasch, 1977).

Even without significant industrial growth, the expansion of global markets, the mass media, the civil service, and other services such as healthcare, education, and transportation led to the formation of modern families in developing countries.

Class Structure

Brazil has what is described as a closed class society. It is described as a society where one's position is determined by who you are; that is, by birth rather than individual achievement. The concepts of class and status are strong in Brazil, influencing many other aspects of Brazilian life. Brazil is a predominantly European-formed society, settled largely by the Portuguese, Italians, Germans, and Spaniards. They were the founders of Brazilian family life as we know it today. As previously mentioned, they have a patriarchal family structure. The societies are divided between the wealthy and the poor, with a small middle class. Jobs are accorded a particular status, and an upper or middle class person would not perform a lower class job. Differences in language, dress, and behavior are often attributed to class. People are placed in the social hierarchy by such things as color, income, education, family connections, and even personal charm and special aptitudes (Harrison, 1983, 4).

Brazil inherited this highly stratified society from the colonial system and from its history of slavery, which persisted for nearly three generations after independence in 1822. During the post-war period, poverty continued to be widespread—most prevalent in the rural parts of the north-east—but also including areas of urban poverty in the largest cities in the developed regions. In 1990, the number of indigents suffering from extreme poverty was estimated to be approximately 32 million, about one-fifth of the country's total population. Currently, the socio-economic disparity in Brazil is evident with the wealthy living in attractive neighborhoods, usually centrally located, with their children attending private schools, having the luxury of driving or riding in cars, and shopping at malls. The poor in the city live in *favelas* or distant housing projects, take long bus trips to work, go to public schools, or drop out, and shop at smaller supermarkets or local shops. The rural poor in the country's inner region are almost undetectable to the urban upper and middle classes (US Library of Congress, 2005).

Contrary to the dualistic stereotypes of other Latin American societies, Brazilian class structure cannot be limited to the wealthy elite versus the poor peasants and workers. The middle sectors or classes have been significant at least since the nineteenth century. Sectors of Brazil's population that were neither slave owners nor slaves began to grow in the colonial period, when craftsmen, shopkeepers, small farmers, freed slaves, and persons of mixed racial origin began to outnumber slave owners and, eventually, slaves. During the twentieth century, the middle sectors continued to grow. Although the present middle class does not own large properties, industries, or firms, they are also not destitute. This class consists largely of a workforce of clerks, professionals, teachers, salespersons, public servants, and highly skilled workers. The middle class social structure is based more on knowledge and skills than on property. A surge of upward mobility strengthened the middle class during the "economic miracle" in the late 1960s and early 1970s. At the same time, blue-collar workers with middle to low levels of skills constitute a lower middle class that is numerically very significant (US Library of Congress, 2005).

There are jobs that Brazilians will not do if the job is thought to be below their level, such as making coffee at the office, cleaning, and manual labor. These tasks are thought of as demeaning, which stems from the early slave days and is continued in their class structure. Upper class and upper-middle class Brazilians employ women as housecleaners to do the cooking and the heavy housework, and may employ a male gardener as well. A housecleaner is considered a low-status occupation in Brazil. The Brazilian blacks have been stereotyped into the lower class and have had a difficult time breaking through that barrier (Harrison, 1983, 89).

In addition to those formally employed, many workers are in the so-called informal economy, which includes self-employed businesspeople and workers who do not have the legal protection of labor legislation. In 1990, the informal sector accounted for nearly half of the economically active population. The informal sector grows in times of recession because of unemployment and during times of prosperity, when opportunities for making money are more readily available.

Women have also had to endure hardships with their stereotype. Brazilian men boast about their *machismo*. *Machismo* relates back to their patriarchal nature. The men are expected to be the head of the family and all others are to respect them and not question their authority, thereby putting women in an inferior role. Brazilian men do not expect to see women in executive and managerial positions. The woman who does business with a man must be particularly careful not to appear too aggressive, but to establish rapport and, if possible, let the suggestions come from the man, or at least appear to come from the man. A man's image is extremely important in Brazil. Businesswomen and wives may drink, but they should choose wine and hard liquor rather than beer and should never be drunk in public. Businesswomen and wives should simply not press the issue of women's rights and should not present a liberated front in Brazil (Harrison, 1983, 79).

Differences are seen in Brazil among social classes and geographical locations. Certain families may be more traditional than others. There is a desire for change, and economic realities have dramatically altered the picture in Brazil. The majority of women have college degrees and work outside the home. Women are getting more involved in politics in the larger cities, and daughters are sometimes taking over their father's businesses. New divorce laws, changing attitudes towards single or separated women, and extended maternity and paternity leaves are very positive steps to equal rights.

These social inequities are solemn and thought-provoking. Research has shown the relationship between social class and health, crime, and mortality in Brazil. For instance, according to an article in the *International Journal of Epidemiology*, social inequality is viewed as an important factor in the distribution of illness and death in Brazilian society. To demonstrate the extent of social differentials in mortality in Brazil, deaths in men aged 15–64 years of age, residing in Sao Paulo from 1980 to 1982, were linked in occupationally driven categories to estimates of population size based on the 1980 Brazilian national census. The occupational categorizations utilized a Brazilian classification scheme and additionally that of the British Registrar General, whose function is to provide information regarding registration of births, deaths, and marriages, among other statutory items; the Brazilian scheme was a method used to categorize the stated population in certain occupational categories. The results showed that mortality was 3.8 and 2.9 times greater when comparing the least to the most socially favored occupational category in each of the two classification systems, respectively. Independent of the system, mortality decreased approximately 1.1 per cent for each 1 per cent increase along the occupationally defined social gradient. This decrease was 48 per cent greater than the equivalent calculated decrease for men of England and Wales. These data support the contention that mortality for Brazilian adults, even more so than for adults of the world's more economically developed nations, is inextricably bound to the issue of social equity (Duncan et al., 1995).

In addition, according to the article, *Inequality, not Poverty, Begets Crime in Brazil*, Irene Lobo (2004), who works for Agência Brasil (AB), the official press agency of the Brazilian government, states that the inequalities between the upper and lower classes of Brazil is the main reason for so much of the youth violence that occurs in Brazil. This fact is noted by Ipea (Instituto de Pesquisa Econômica Aplicada—Applied Economic Research Institute). "Social inequality is the major cause of youth violence. It is the context of that violence, the setting where these youths between the ages of 15 and 24 live out their lives in the midst of the problem," says Luseni Aquino, who wrote the study together with Enid Rocha.

One of the factors is the extreme poverty that 4.2 million (12.2 per cent) of these 34 million young Brazilians live in. They come from families with a monthly income of slightly more than US\$22 (one-fourth of Brazil's minimum wage). Sixty-seven per cent of these youths have not concluded elementary school and are considered illiterate, plus over 30 per cent have no employment and do not go to school. Tragically, the numbers get even worse as one's skin gets darker. The Ipea study found that among blacks, the illiteracy rate rose to 73 per cent, and 71 per cent of them have no employment and do not go to school. This is clear evidence that it is not the poverty but the social inequalities that drive youth violence (Lobo, 2004).

The social classes in Brazil are striking, and these examples show the relationship between social inequality and health and crime. One can only hypothesize that this social inequality eventually leads to strong polarization, and excludes people from social and material opportunities.

Language

The words and grammar available in a language strongly affect a culture's values, beliefs, relationships, and concepts. Body language is also important in Brazil. Brazilians are known for their public displays of affection. It is customary for them to hug and kiss acquaintances when they meet. A newcomer should understand that it is customary to, at a minimum, shake hands and not to be surprised if they are hugged. Part of this is due to the need for affiliation and to preserve harmony. In Brazil, you are dealing with people who can be highly emotional. The national language in Brazil is Portuguese with some areas that speak German and Italian. All but a few isolated Amerindians, who retain their languages, and any immigrants who have not yet acquired proficiency in the language, speak Portuguese. There are no official regional dialects. Brazil is the only Portuguese-speaking country in South America (US Library of Congress, 2005).

Brazilians will always answer a question when asked, as they do not want to be rude and not have an answer. Unfortunately, they sometimes answer a question to which they do not know the correct answer! They may also say yes sometimes when they actually mean no. They do this because they do not want to disagree with you. This can be a difficult situation at times, and individuals need to be aware of this Brazilian characteristic. When you are addressing others, you need to use their proper name and title. The main difference in Brazil is that they generally go by their first name instead of their last name, because last names are often too difficult to pronounce. Common greetings begin with *Senhor* for the man, *Senhora* for a married or older woman, and *Senhorita* for a single or younger woman.

Economics

Economics includes production and distribution. The extent to which a country is either a free market or controlled by the government will tend to shape the citizens behaviors and actions of that country.

Brazil is a mixture of government control and free market. As noted, Brazil has become the tenth largest economy in the world. Brazil's economic activity has surpassed that of all the other developing countries. Since 1964, the federal authorities have undertaken a comprehensive program to overcome obstacles that were caused by inflation. They also provided an economic environment conducive to renewed expansion of the industrial public and private business sectors. Brazil has established technologically sophisticated industries in the fields of telecommunications, electronic data processing, biotechnology, and new materials. The four key sectors responsible for this expansion are steel, auto, petrochemicals, and utilities.

Economic power is primarily in the hands of a few people in Brazil. Brazil's leading industries in value of production are textiles and clothing, machinery and transportation equipment, chemicals and food processing. The basic unit of currency is the *real*, which was introduced in 1994 to replace the *cruzeiro real*. The transportation system of Brazil is very extensive with 18,275 miles of railroad, 1,071,821 miles of highway roads, and a vast waterway system. There are also 40 major harbors along the Brazilian coast to serve regional as well as international commerce. The information technology structure is a key area of development for Brazil. The current telephone structure is inadequate and represents a challenge and a large growth opportunity for the information systems companies. The continued development of this industry is critical to Brazil's economic growth and ability to compete in global markets, to educate its population, and to link remote communities across a country with a landmass greater than the contiguous United States.

Brazil has been experiencing difficulty with inflation since the 1980s. This trend slowed significantly in the 1990s, with inflation at 3.87 per cent in October 2002, up from 2.40 per cent in September 2002 (Emerging Markets Economy, 2002). The good news is that the economy has been growing at double-digit rates. This has created a global interest in Brazil as the country is showing great potential. It has enormous natural resources and a population that can support a growing economy.

The government has been working hard to eliminate some of the social inequalities that have existed due to their culture. Some of the changes that have been introduced in the 1988 Constitution involve eliminating child labor and discrimination, and protection of minority and women's rights. These changes are outlined in Chapter II, Social Rights, Articles 6–11, of the Federal Republic of Brazil Constitution. Brazil became known as the "miracle economy" in the late 1960s, during a time when the country was recording double-digit growth rates and military rule had produced some political stability. During this time, the country expanded its industries, and people flocked from the countryside to the cities to find work. By the early 1980s, Brazil had become one of the leading industrial nations, boasting the tenth largest GNP in the world.

Impact of Culture on Human Resource Development Implementation and Staffing

The role of human resource development is influenced by several of the cultural factors mentioned and need to be considered when setting up the staffing function and necessary policies. There are also elements such as power distance, individualism, uncertainty avoidance, masculinity, and Confucian Dynamism from Hofstede's Cultural Dimension Model that will be examined as well.

Staffing in Brazil

A US company that plans to recruit for general indirect labor positions as well as managerial and support levels in Brazil should employ the following issues, factors, and methods:

Skills Needed The general labor positions will vary according to job category and each job category will have a job classification. Brazil has a number of large labor unions in the general labor industry. Brazil is rated as medium to high in power distance. This would indicate that it would be best to have a structured workforce with a designated supervisor to lead the group. The leadership qualifications are discussed later. The labor market is growing on a national level and, generally, a US-based firm should not anticipate any problem filling these positions.

Strengths and Weaknesses of Labor Market Brazil has increased its emphasis on education recently and there are more students completing the general classes. After the age of 14, students are not compelled to attend school and are legally of age to work. Although these young adults are willing, it is of concern what their motivation and maturity level is. Males or females can accomplish most general labor jobs since there are no physical limitations. Most companies have automated their processes and provide on the job training for those positions, although many of the local businesses in Rio de Janeiro overlook minorities and women. The Brazilians have a paternalistic nature and expect the company to take care of them. In return, they will be loyal and devoted to the company they are employed by. This could create the type of workforce that a company needs, as training can take as long as six months and a company will want to retain the workers after they are trained. However, this can also have its problems. According to an interview with Jim Meinert, Director of International Management, Snider Mold Company (1997), it is extremely difficult to fire anyone in Brazil. The company is required to offer some type of severance package for anyone that they terminate, which is a financial setback for the firm.

Work Ethic The work ethic varies throughout the country. Sao Paulo and Rio de Janeiro are much more industrialized than the interior of the country. The cities are very much like large cities in the United States. One of the factors associated with Brazilians is their attitude about time. The traditional view was that Brazilians had a much more relaxed view of schedules and appointments. Brazilians are classified as people who value people and problems over schedules and often deal with things simultaneously. Training and workshops might have a start time of 7.30 a.m. and a coffee break at 8.30 a.m. Business interactions involve a process of socializing in order to establish a comfortable social climate before starting to discuss business. They also use intermediaries to help introduce the individuals and begin the socialization. There is a need to have a contact person, according to Harrison (1983), because "if you know somebody, that's the key to everything in Brazil." Research conducted in publications from the 1970s and 1980s showed this traditional view of time as changing in the larger cities. Business is conducted similarly to the United States, where a person is expected to meet and come ready to talk directly about the subject. Time is very important. Harrison (1983) also goes on to say that the north-eastern part of Brazil has a different style and people will want to get to know you first.

In some companies, employers may hire friends and family over outsiders, regardless of skills or experience. Status is defined in Brazil by your position or rank and salary as well as the length of time one has spent with the job or with the company. This is typical of a higher power distance index. This also affects how you are treated in business. The senior person is always given the respect of the group. Higher status people tend to arrive at work earlier and to stay at work later than the standard workday hours. Having a secretary reflects a high status. A higher status person will not be as punctual and a person that is of less status will be expected to be punctual and not keep the senior person waiting. The senior person is seldom disagreed with. Higher position people will have larger private offices, the higher the status the better the office. Doors on offices also reflect privacy and high status.

Conflict Conflict within the organization is seen as a threat to harmony. This is frowned on as it violates their cultural tendency to be high in the Confucian Dynamism. Use of authority is, therefore, justified to subsume conflict and maintain a peaceful work climate (Rahim and Blum, 1994, 136). Mediators play a crucial role in conflict management because of the cultural aversion to face conflict (Rahim and Blum, 1994, 137). The roots of the difficulty with direct confrontation may perhaps be found in the socialization process and the power distance relationship of their society. The belief is that the father has absolute authority over his family. An authoritarian climate that begins at home is reinforced through the education system where compromise and negotiation are reinforced. In the work area, labor unions are also used as a third party in settling disputes.

Recruiting Methods   A US company may desire to utilize the United States Department of Commerce in Brazil and the US Embassy in setting up their firm. These organizations have resources available to help search for the needed staff and may do the screening and testing of candidates. One of the concerns that a company will need to address is the language barrier. The Department of Commerce is also able to help the company locate bilingual support staff that help to strengthen the ties between the parent company and the subsidiary. There is a preference for speaking Portuguese versus Spanish or English. English is fast becoming a second language as it motivates people in Brazil to learn English as a second language. Nevertheless, for business purposes, and to be more in harmony with their culture, Portuguese is best. Interpreters can also be used, but often times are not as effective, as the people expect the leaders to talk directly to them because of their power distance preference.

Other Aspects to Consider in Recruiting   The Brazilians have a tendency to be in harmony with nature. Hofstede and Bond (1988) also verify this when you consider their very high Confucianism rating. A high rating in harmony or Confucianism indicates that there is a belief in preserving the family and places high value on group harmony and in saving face with others. People that have these qualities would find it difficult to disagree with someone or to do the necessary evaluation and action that is necessary when recruiting for ability not affiliation. Good communication and interpersonal skills would still be very important as well as being decisive and having critical decision-making skills.

Interview Process   Key team members of a Brazilian human resource team and some management positions should be determined with the help of the US Department of Commerce. The Department of Commerce could help supply the parent company with the applicable laws and regulations that are current as well as be a resource in locating reliable employment agencies and advertising assistance. According to Meinert (1997), officials in Brazil are very concerned with helping an American business succeed in Brazil. The Brazilian HR staff should do the initial screening and interviewing. This process is very important to try to verify actual educational achievements and personal references. It is assumed that all personal references will be good, due to the Confucian nature of the society. People will be very reluctant to give any negative feedback about a friend and the potential employee will probably only put down potential good references anyway. The educational verification may not be very revealing as well. The current record system is poor and may not give us the information that is needed.

Screening the Candidates   A prospective company should also work with the Department of Labor to determine an acceptable entrance exam that will help to qualify individuals by general math, language, and motor skills. If the labor market shows a general weakness in any of these areas, the company will have to consider subsidizing this skill or area with in-house training classes. The minimum working age in Brazil is 14. The minimum wage is 240–260 *reals*, roughly US$ 80–87 per month. The company policy will be to use the entrance exam as a sorting tool, and will factor in the results of the interview, which will focus on determining their communication skills, previous experience, and willingness to learn.

Performance Evaluation and Compensation   Once employed, the employee's supervisor should conduct the performance evaluation. The supervisor should conduct a subjective performance review, which focusses on the positive attributes of the employee. According to Meinert (1997), Brazilians are extremely sensitive about evaluation and criticism. The people are very relationship-oriented and it is important to respect that in order to keep their loyalty and trust. The successful evaluation should be informal but very constructive and appeal to their Confucian tendency. Brazilians tend to blame the process not the person when there are problems. They also tend to bend the rules and do whatever is necessary to get the job done. It is very difficult to disqualify an individual in Brazil, so the manager will have to learn to deal with performance problems in a constructive fashion versus the American method of corrective action. The American method generally follows specific warnings to the employee that can lead to termination if the problem is not corrected. Americans seldom make allowances for an employee's failure to correct a problem and will most often terminate with little concern for the employee's future or current situation.

Leadership Style

Brazilians prefer an authoritarian style of management. Brazilians prefer a person who is a decisive, clear, and charismatic leader. They like to be identified with a successful leader and will be loyal to him as a person. Leadership style is somewhat determined by Hofstede's power distance ranking. Brazil is rated as medium to high (Hofstede, 1980, 115). The higher power distance indicator is characterized by direct communication from the boss. "Upward communication is neither expected nor encouraged. In these countries, the paternalistic employer appears to develop in the working forces a feeling of gratitude and dependence mingled with resentment" (Hofstede, 1980, 115). There may also be low personal trust and lack of cooperativeness among the workers. A higher power distance indicator looks at power and wealth as something that is inherited versus earned.

Close supervision is positively evaluated by subordinates (Hofstede, 1980, 119). The manager will gain best results by directing and controlling the employees instead of utilizing a team-concept. A manager that needs feedback and consensus to make important decisions will not do well in Brazil. The employees want and expect a leader that will tell them what to do and make decisions for them. They expect a manager to be authoritative and paternalistic. "Decisions must be made by the one in authority. Authoritarianism does not allow for questioning." These viewpoints were also verified in the interview with Meinert (1997).

The power distance dimension also reflects a lack of participative style on the part of managers and a relatively low preference for participative managers by the employees. The employees will also be reluctant to disagree with the manager. Hofstede (1980) has also found strong uncertainty avoidance in Brazil, which reflects a need for rules and employment stability.

Brazil has an individualism score of 38, which is low (Hofstede, 1997). Virtually all the Latin countries are considered collectivist societies as compared to individualist cultures. This is manifest in a close long-term commitment to the member group, be that a family, extended family, or extended relationships. Loyalty in a collectivist culture is paramount, and overrides most other societal rules. A low score in this dimension shows a local as opposed to a cosmopolitan attitude, emphasizing loyalty to organization rather than personal achievement. Brazil is ranked as medium to low in the masculinity range, which puts it more into the feminine value side. This dimension measures work values that stress challenge, advancement, and earnings (masculine values) as opposed to relations, security, and location of employment (feminine values). This combination of characteristics tends to create a warm but autocratic organizational climate. This climate fosters a benevolent autocratic management style, which fits the employee's expectation of their manager. Top managers find that it is difficult to generate discussion and get new ideas. Attempts that would require team building and group decision-making are practices that are at odds with an emphasis on status and power differentials between superiors and subordinates (Rahim and Blum, 1994, 140).

Strong managers are the main mechanism of control and coordination. Little emphasis is placed on various informal means of coordination that may threaten the formal authority of the manager. Managers treat authority as belonging to their person rather than position alone. A manager's effectiveness is seen as closely tied to respect received from subordinates (Rahim and Blum, 1994, 140).

Brazilian managers prefer collaborating significantly more often than communicating and compromising when dealing with conflict. The preferred style is one of dominating toward subordinates, obliging toward superiors, and avoiding toward peers. A concern for face-saving is a factor in the undesirability of obliging. Obliging is the only style that is used significantly more when a manager is in conflict with a superior, which reflects an employee's fear of expressing disagreement with their manager and lack of participation in decision-making. When encouraged to participate, subordinates expect top managers to make propositions and then limit their participation only to identifying possible problem areas without, however, directly contradicting their executives.

Domination reflects the prevalent authoritarian tone in Brazil. Most managers believe that to be in control, they have to be firm toward disagreeing subordinates. To preserve the authority relationship, any concessions made to a subordinate must come after the superior has asserted himself and an obliging response has been secured.

Compromising is seen as representing a lack of principles or integrity of position and is only used to preserve harmony. "The primary focus of role evaluation is placed on the ability to control others, rather than on the ability to achieve the goals of the organization" (Rahim and Blum, 1994, 149).

Leadership Studies

Empirical studies involving the Brazilian nursing practice show the confident, controlled, and self-assured Brazilian leadership style, which validates the warm but autocratic climate in their organizational environment.

In the article, "The Changing Focus of Nursing Practice in Brazil," the authors used both a historical and a social perspective. Nurses were analyzed in the areas of supervision and leadership throughout the history of Brazilian nursing from 1930 to 1995. The empirical material was separated into four historical time frames. In the first period (1930–49), preliminary expressions of nursing were of organization and control. In the second period (1950–69), the concept of human relations in the nursing profession emerged, and in the third period (1970–79), concern about staffing structures and changes in the health sector emerged as important to the nurse as a leader. In the latest period studied (1980–95), a new perspective was established, that being nursing as a social practice related more to supervision rather than leadership. Based on this historical search, and in conjunction with opinions of health practice and the changes in Brazilian society, supervision and leadership in the nursing field became concepts located within the management ideas and practice of the profession. These concepts demonstrate a close relationship with control of workers or the work process and its effects in the health sector, especially in nursing (Silva et al., 1998).

Secondly, in support of the above, a subsequent study involved 14 Brazilian nurses who were chosen for their leadership skills. These nurses were asked about their view on leadership issues and about their perceptions of the relationship between nursing and leadership. The data provided by the professionals managing the study showed that the interviewed nurses had an unambiguous and clear view of these issues and of their important role in the nursing profession. They saw leadership as a group process through which people or behaviors are influenced, and that such a process is carried out aiming to reach a goal. The conclusions realized a close relationship between leadership and nursing (Lourenco and Trevizan, 2001).

These data illustrate that Brazil is a society whose leadership is based on authoritative decision-behavior, close supervision, loyalty to the company, collaboration, and domination, and in the field of nursing, these traits are exhibited strongly, yet with the humanity and kindness requisite in their profession, and evident in the Brazilian social class. These attributes suggest that Brazilian culture, in general, falls into Hofstede's large power distance cultural dimension, moderate-to-low individualism (collectivist) cultural dimension, moderate-to-strong uncertainty avoidance cultural dimension as well as moderate-to-strong masculine cultural dimension.

Summary

The above description is a guideline that can assist individuals in understanding the differences that exist between a US business anticipating a presence in Brazil and the new Brazilian division. There are differences as well as strengths and weaknesses on each side. By recognizing these, they can be stronger as a shared company and use this information to their advantage. Brazil has an outstanding market potential and a diverse workforce that is eager to work. Both organizations will struggle with these differences at times, but will ultimately learn from them and become stronger as new solutions to old problems are found. Change can be difficult, but understanding what lies ahead can help prepare individuals so they can better understand why people act and think as they do.

Case Questions

1. Describe the role national cultures play in defining effective leadership styles and performance. Summarize Brazil's culture according to the above description using Hofstede's dimensions. Is there another country to which you can compare Brazil?
2. Education is only compulsory to age 14. Discuss this law in relation to work ethic, motivation, and loyalty to the company.
3. Would the process of writing a job design or description be different for Brazil from other countries, and vice versa? Why or why not?
4. Explain why networking would be important in Brazil.
5. Discuss career development as a critical human resource element in South America.
6. Since local law hinders the severing of employees, and encourages long-term employment, discuss the impact, if any, this would have in a department where a US expatriate also worked.
7. How would you establish performance standards for a department mixed with local employees, Third County Nationals, and expatriates?
8. Describe the advantages and disadvantages of monetary incentive programs in Brazil.

Conclusion

Stereotyping can have extreme negative effects on people, especially when managers make fewer attempts to engage those of other cultures because they do not realize that there may be a reason why an employee of a different ethnicity makes little eye contact with them. When managers interact with others of different cultures, receptiveness to interpersonal feedback, good observation skills, and effective questions are important. It is highly beneficial to observe how people of the same culture interact with each other. Do not hesitate to ask questions, as most people respond very positively to questions about their culture. Making a genuine effort to explore the historical and cultural contributions of a society, and also learning a few polite expressions in another person's language, can have particularly encouraging effects.

Differences between cultures and peoples are real and can add fullness to all other cultures. People everywhere have things in common, such as a need for relationships and love, participation, and contribution. When the exterior is peeled off, there are not as many differences as it might seem.

Case Study

Counselors Now Target Japanese Overseas

The growing number of Japanese nationals residing abroad—expected to surpass 1 million by 2006—is being matched by the need for specialist counseling agencies that help with the stress of living in an alien culture. Many Japanese expatriates have been sent abroad by their companies, so some of the stress they suffer is work-related. All too often, their employers offer little or no help.

The Industrial Safety and Health Law states that employers must make efforts to ensure their employees' workloads are not excessive, and a 2000 health ministry guideline says firms must try to care for their workers' mental health. Neither, however, is binding.

Work-related stress is meanwhile exacting a toll. Japan, in 2003, saw a record 1,878 suicides out of 34,427, which were directly related to work, according to the National Police Agency. Company employees who killed themselves, including those posted overseas, also hit a record 9,209 for the year, although the suicides may not all be directly linked to work.

Labor experts say these figures are related to the increased burden placed on workers amid Japan's prolonged economic slump, and they note there is a pressing need for mental health care, especially at small firms and companies' overseas offices.

While the number and age of employees sent abroad per company are declining to keep costs down, their overall mental health-care needs are not.

Career Management Consulting President Junichi Yoshida believes, however, that only major companies really attempt to address such needs. "Only global corporations that are aware of the legal consequences of someone dying from overwork want to seek contracts with us. Other high-risk firms are totally uninterested," Yoshida said, citing general contractors with offices in the Middle East involved in Iraq's reconstruction whose employees might need such care.

Tokyo-based Peacemind Inc., which has offered counseling to people both in and out of Japan since 1998, last month opened its first overseas office in New York, naming Motoaki Ibano, former president of the information conglomerate Recruit Inc.'s US unit, as the representative.

New York was chosen as its first overseas office because of a large number of Japanese companies operating there, but Peacemind plans to open offices in Los Angeles, London, Hong Kong, Singapore, and other cities.

Peacemind President Kunihiro Ogiwara said Ibano, who worked for 13 years at Recruit's US unit, is ideal for the job because he is well aware of the troubles Japanese expatriates often encounter, including the work ethics of locally hired staff that often differ greatly from that of Japan.

Locally, hired staff in many cases value their private lives much more than their jobs, unlike typical Japanese workers, and some are extremely competitive and uncooperative, Ogiwara said. Some locally hired staff also feel their expatriate colleagues benefit from an unfair double standard, including housing allowances and higher salaries, he said.

Japanese transferred overseas are often accorded higher living standards than local hires, and when the latter complain, this becomes a source of serious stress for Japanese used to workplace harmony back home, Ogiwara said. He added that expatriates ordinarily prefer to consult with fellow Japanese who understand what it is like living abroad, but this can be difficult because they fear that confiding to colleagues or superiors back in Japan may lead to a poor evaluation, and their usually small overseas Japanese communities are often gossip mills.

Sachiko Harada, 27, operates Quality Life Consulting Ltd., an online agency in Sydney that caters only to individual female clients. Harada, who herself experienced a fear of people and an excessive appetite while on a working holiday in Australia, came up with an original self-help training aid for women suffering mental problems. Harada observed that women who live abroad and seek her help are typically in three social positions with three typical problem types.

"The first are expatriates who feel they have missed out on women's happiness by solely pursuing their careers," Harada explained. "The second are expatriate's wives suffering an identity crisis who want to shut themselves in because they feel they aren't good for anything, and the third are students who study abroad because there are no jobs in Japan but have lost confidence trying to cope with a foreign language and culture."

She gave the example of a woman in her late 30s who was sent to Shanghai by a Japanese TV production agency. Although she always liked her job, fatigue began to set in from the stress of working in a land with a very different culture. She soon began to resent that the other expatriates around her, all men, had happy family lives outside of work, while she was all alone. The constant reminders by her family back home that she needed to think about her biological clock only made matters worse, Harada said, noting the woman was in a serious state when she finally sought counseling.

Harada said she managed to gradually convince the woman that what she had accomplished was very special and not something other women were able to do, and that helped the client see her life in a wider perspective. "The choices for women are rapidly expanding. We want to keep helping women overseas who are in all kinds of situations," Harada said.

Reprinted with permission: Y. Wijers-Hasegawa (2004), "Counselors Now Target Japanese Overseas," *The Japan Times*, August 19.

Case Questions

1. Discuss the difference between the American and Japanese cultures. Why will the Japanese expatriates find their jobs more stressful than the comparable jobs that the Americans fill?
2. What can US companies do to diminish an inpatriate's anxiety and increase the chance of success of an assignment in America? What should be done in advance of the assignment and during the assignment?
3. To what degree does a US organization benefit from an inpatriate or foreign national experience?
4. What should a prospective US expatriate learn from an inpatriate?

Chapter Review

Since every culture has its own perceptions about roles, values, attitudes and beliefs, there is nothing innately natural when it comes to managing an international enterprise. Individual culture shapes the ideas and norms for all groups and there are real possibilities that it will cause a conflict. Each thinks his or her style is correct, and they may not know any differently. Workers from different countries often find themselves responding to and being managed by individuals from other ethnic or cultural backgrounds, and employees from different cultures generally have different values and feelings about their companies, jobs, and relationships. International managers are often viewed as important business leaders. To be successful, international managers are expected to have personal contact with members of the staff— as such behavior inspires loyalty and trust—as well as good interpersonal skills and a willingness to invest time with each employee. The manager is often viewed as a facilitator whose role is not to take charge but to improve the initiatives of others and nurture an environment in which employees work together for the good of the company.

Today's managers are challenged to create work environments that address the needs of a culturally diverse workforce. For that to happen, managers need to be involved and move beyond their own cultural frame of reference to a multicultural one. Effective managers must also be strong intercultural communicators in the workplace.

In international business, questions arise regarding what is proper by which culture's values, what is wise by which culture's view of the world, and what is right by whose standards. Attitudes toward accents and dialects create barriers in international business planning and communication. The ways in which people use the resources available to them often shifts drastically from culture to culture. One major communication obstacle among those from control cultures is the belief that other cultures wish to be more like them. Control cultures tend to describe themselves as the industrialized nations. No two cultures share the same level of contexting. As a result, high context cultures tend to favor a business communication approach based on indirection and politeness; low context cultures follow more of a confrontation strategy and use a direct plan approach to business communication. High context cultures view indirectness as honest and showing consideration, while low context cultures view indirectness as dishonest and offensive.

Behaviors such as respect (conveyed through eye contact, body posture, voice tone and pitch), interaction posture (the ability to respond to others in a descriptive, non-evaluative, and non judgmental way), orientation to knowledge (recognizing that one's knowledge, perception, and beliefs are valid only for oneself and not for everyone else), and interactive management are critical elements to the success of an international collaboration. Creating an environment of trust and information sharing becomes a key management function.

Cultural differences can be a significant barrier to the success of a business. Becoming aware of what these differences are and being able to employ culturally sensitive management and communication approaches can greatly improve a company's chances for success.

Chapter Questions

1. Norms are beliefs that group members share about appropriate and inappropriate behaviors. What are the norms for living in an Islamic country such as Saudi Arabia?
2. What behaviors are acceptable? What behaviors are unacceptable?
3. Explain how culture affects international business relationships.
4. Identify the advantages/disadvantages of culturally diverse workplaces. How does this build effective multicultural work teams?
5. What are the skills needed to communicate effectively in cross-cultural settings?
6. What are some variables of culture's core values?
7. Discuss Hofstede's cultural framework within the scope of a place of employment where you have worked.

Chapter 9

The Impact of Culture on International Management

If one manages to extricate oneself from the culture that he or she is a product of, one would be extremely surprised to see how different the same world appears to be from another perspective. One should not dare offer beef to a Hindu or pork to a Muslim or an Orthodox Jew. Yet, some people in the Far East butcher dogs and consider their meat a delicacy. The same dogs are considered impure and not even touched by most Muslims, are badly treated and abused by people in many countries, kept as a strict necessity in most of Africa, respected as a unique form of life in India, and treated almost as members of the family by many Americans. India holds approximately one-third of the world's livestock in their country. India assigns such strong social and economic values to its cattle that they are seen as religious symbols. One can see the relationship between the Indian people and their cattle in the high regard they hold for the cattle; they treat them almost as individuals, and definitely as vital family-providers. Hence, there is a strong opposition to both killing and eating such animals.

There are currently over 160 independent countries in the world, hundreds of major ethnic groups, and even greater diversity of cultures, and at least 3,000 spoken languages. At the same time, immediate communication virtually everywhere, rapid transportation, global trade, worldwide political interaction, and universal interdependence are ever growing and expanding. Understanding each other and communicating across linguistic, political, religious, and other cultural barriers have become necessary in today's world for one to succeed. It was estimated that in 1987 there were about 10,000 Japanese business executives in the United States, virtually all of who spoke English and had a good understanding of American culture. However, in this same period, there were only 1,000 American executives in Japan, only a handful of who spoke Japanese (Nicholas, 1990, 9). Knowing the poor performance of US businesses in Japan, one can only wonder how many of those American executives had a good grasp of Japanese culture and business behavior.

To understand Japan's economy, it is important to study its history. Due to the destruction caused by the war, Japan's population had not changed from 1940 to 1946; however, as the Japanese began arriving from Manchuria and Korea, the number began increasing. Japan was becoming aware that it would not be a military power; its limited resources were realization that the hope of success through victory was over. Japan was dependent on goodwill and trade, and with the realization that the US would supply the military needed for protection, it could now concentrate on developing peace and reconstructing its economy. Throughout the subsequent 20 years, Japan achieved developed status as a country, and in the late 1960s, its economy developed to become the second largest in the world, with the US being number one.

According to the Embassy of Japan, the number of Japanese citizens living in cities almost doubled between 1950 and 1970, which increased the demand for services. Agriculture and light manufacturing used to be the strongholds of the economy; however, now it had shifted to heavy industry and services. The dominant players in the industrial sector were iron and steel, shipbuilding, machine tools, motor vehicles, and electronics. Even though high growth rates were predicted for the 1970s, inflation and the oil crisis in the Middle East contributed to a recession, which in turn decreased the expectation for future growth. In spite of the crisis, Japan's major export industries remained competitive by reducing costs and increasing efficiency. This reduced the demand for energy, and the automobile industry was able to improve its global position by manufacturing vehicles that were more economical. In 1979, yet another oil crisis created a change in Japan's industrial structure and the importance moved from heavy industry to computers, semiconductors, and other technology and information-intensive industries. This contributed to a time of rapid and needed growth for Japan (Embassy of Japan, 2004).

In the late 1980s, the Yen rose sharply in value to three times its value in the 1970s. With the increase in the price of Japanese exports, competitiveness was decreased overseas, while government financial measures increased demand domestically.

In order to suppress the high value of assets such as land, the government tightened its monetary policies. However, higher interest rates sent stock prices downward. Steeply dropping land prices burdened financial institutions with bad debts and some of them even went bankrupt. In 1993, the recession reached its low point, but has been recovering slowly since then.

In part, Japan's technological innovation has enabled them to regain a sturdy market position, in spite of the US's stand at the front of the computer and computer software industries. Information technology will be the engine that will power Japan's recovery. Although the US is making a comeback in its automobile industry, Japan has retained its position as a leader in the semiconductor and automobile industries.

Another factor in the recovery of Japan's economy was the marked rise in the value of the Yen. Even though the Yen had decreased since it was at its highest in 1995, the rise caused any company in the important import industries to transfer their production to overseas locations. This was seen mostly in the automobile industry.

A future concern of Japan's is the elderly. The workforce will be reduced as the population ages in future years and this will inevitably mean an increase on the social system as well as an increase in the tax burden that younger workers will be expected to bear. Japan feels that a low employment force may be a factor in their future growth potential. Japan's prolonged economic troubles are often attributed to its long post-war economic system. Currently the Japanese government is taking direct measures to deal with problems in order to concentrate on industrial globalization. The government is attempting to steady the financial system and revitalize its economy. While the collapse of what is termed the "bubble economy" in the early 1990s has slowed the growth in GDP, the government is currently encouraging deregulation of numerous profitable sectors to promote a more efficient economy (Embassy of Japan, 2004).

American businesspeople, students, diplomats, and military personnel are involved with other countries virtually all over the world. Their success depends to a large degree on their understanding of these cultures, on their knowledge of American interests and obligations in the area, and on their communication skills. An equally important factor often ignored is a good understanding of American culture and values, which are often taken for granted. Most of the time we judge others by our own value system; by what we believe is right or wrong, good or bad, normal or different, and so on. The truth is that such basic values may differ from society to society, and we become aware of our culture only when separated from it, and find ourselves in a strange environment. Only when we are confronted with another culture do we develop a better understanding of our own, and possibly of others.

Imagine yourself taking a job in China as an international manager. You do not know a thing about China, how they live, the way they do business procedures, or even the Chinese language. The only thing you know is what you were taught in your international management classes at university. You were only taught how managers in the United States conduct business. Do you think you would survive in China?

Before traveling to another country, one needs to be able to distinguish and understand that culture. This gives an advantage to an international manager. The impacts of culture on international management are tremendous. Culture is very different from one country to another. Knowing different cultures is very important for an international manager to succeed. One might not always agree with the cultures and beliefs of people in certain countries; however, it is necessary to know how to handle a situation one does not approve of. This chapter will discuss the procedures and training of recognizing and understanding how to handle such situations.

Because culture has such an impact on international managers' activities, it is important to be well versed on several issues relating to culture.

How Culture Impacts Planning and Implementation of Goals and Objectives

A large part of management is not only to get highly skilled workers, but also to keep them highly motivated. This can make it hard to maintain different cultures within a culture. Many work environments have different cultures and they tend to stick together as a group because they are familiar with their ways of life, behavior, and how they see the world. Some examples are as follows:

- In Bolivia, South America, approximately 95 percent of the population is Roman Catholic. Time is not as important as their significant feelings toward friendship are kindness, gentleness, and concern for another's welfare. An important point for visitors from the United States is that visitors should avoid saying "In America..." but should use "In the United States."
- A woman visiting Brazil for business or vacation should know that people in Brazil are outgoing. Men tend to stare at and make comments about woman passing by. However, this is not considered rude and generally is ignored by the woman.
- Different gestures can mean very different things in other countries. For instance, in Quebec, Canada, the US sign of thumbs-down (meaning "no" or that something is bad) is an offensive gesture and should be avoided. It is also offensive to burp in public,

even if one excuses oneself.

- In France, slapping the open palm over a closed fist is vulgar. In addition, it is impolite to sit with your legs spread open or even with your legs crossed. Ones feet are not to be placed on the table or chairs, and it is improper to speak with hands in the pockets or to chew gum in public.
- In Finland, the fashion standards are very high and internationally recognized. It is important to know that men remove their hats when entering a building or elevator, or when speaking to another person.
- Lastly, in Jamaica, Jamaicans take a flexible approach to time. If a manager were going to be assigned to Jamaica to work, it would be good to inform the person of the following: A common good-natured answer to life's challenges is "No problem man," even if there is no solution at hand. In addition, events and meetings do not necessarily start on time (Coon and Tyler, 1984).

How Culture Impacts the Competitive Environment of Organizations

International business would be a lot easier if everyone was alike. However, as we know, not everyone is the same. Different cultures believe and act differently. The following pages will analyze the differences in cultures and how these cultural differences have an influence on the competitive environment of organizations.

Different regions of the United States maintain their own ways of working, speed, time, and place. The United States is just one continent. Now imagine seven different continents with millions of different people on them. As increasingly more corporate mergers cross regional boundaries, avoiding clashes of cultures becomes increasingly important. Not only must CEOs and top executives learn about other cultures, but they will also have to decide who will be in charge of their firms in other parts of the world. Even the simplest things such as vacations, to answering the phones after 5.00 p.m. in different time zones may be a factor. Some examples of different ways of doing business just in America are listed below:

- In Austin, Texas, visitors have to be prepared to do business over huevos rancheros.
- In Mexico, foods that include the main colors of the flag (green, white, and red) are popular on the Mexican table. Huevos rancheros, a classic Mexican dish, with avocados, sour cream and salsa, is a good example of this.
- In Memphis, Tennessee, deals can be closed on the golf course—a common practice in the rising economy of the new South and Sun Belt.
- In Seattle, dinner remains the finest business meal.

If you were traveling for a company, how would this affect your home life? If you were moving to a different state, the dress code may also be different. Here are some examples of different American dress codes:

- In Boston, dress conservatively. For example, men should be in shirts, ties, and business suits. If they are going to a meeting, their jackets must be worn. Otherwise, they may work at their desks without their jackets on.

- Casual in Chicago—khakis and a polo shirt—is very different from casual in Los Angeles where everything from jeans to flip–flops and cutoffs fly during casual days.

From an international perspective, Italy has fashion as its trademark. When doing business in Italy, clothing is a sign of success, therefore men should wear high quality suits, and women should likewise wear dresses and suits with Italian labels or expensive taste. Also influential are quality accessories. Alternatively, in Canada, men wear dark conservative suits, with classic lines and a traditional lapel, in conservative colors of navy and gray, with shirts in white and light blue. Women, also very conservative, wear a business suit or dress, again with classic lines and colors of navy, gray, or ivory. Unlike Italy, new or trendy clothing is a poor choice, while classic clothing that is clean and neat is more valued.

Another way that cultural differences influence the competitive environment of organizations is in the speed of the workplace and the technology level of the locations and cultures. The level of technology that is available or has been learned by an individual can determine how competitively such an individual will perform in a different technological environment. If an employee is from an advanced technological company that is or has expanded to an underdeveloped country, it could affect the business as a whole. Other factors, such as cigarette smoking, have an impact on an organization's performance. Consider a country where cigarette smoking is very prevalent—Greece for instance. With many employees who may smoke, the business might have to allow additional smoke breaks to keep their employees happy. If an employee from Greece moves to Norway, for instance, where cigarette smoking is not as common, that person might not be happy with the rules. This is because smoking is addictive and he or she may not be able to handle going all day with only their scheduled breaks. The businesses may find that he or she will try to sneak out for smoke breaks when the employee feels a cigarette is needed.

Considering other negative factors such as suicide, there is speculation as to whether some countries have higher numbers of suicides because of work-related stress or other reasons. In comparing countries, it can be observed that although life expectancies are generally the same, other aspects of life such as birth out of wedlock or alcohol intake have drastic variations in different countries. This briefly describes how all things, no matter how relevant or irrelevant they seem, must be considered when managing an international team.

Effect of Culture on International Planning

Planning is a systematic decision process that an individual, group, or organization pursues to set objectives. In some way or another, all businesses in all cultures have to do some kind of planning to succeed; the way each culture plans differs immensely. The extent to which cultural norms in one country differ from those in another country, also named cultural distance, can affect the success or failure of the business.

International Planning

Planning is defined as setting an organization's goals and deciding how best to achieve them. International planning is affected by the various ideas on which normative cultural concepts are based, including the master-of-destiny versus the fatalistic viewpoint, and the never-ending quest for improvement. Planning also enables management to affect rather than accept the future. Management sets objectives and charts a course of action to be proactive rather than reactive to the dynamics of the business environment. Management believes that through its continuous guidance it can enhance the future state of the business.

There are many different benefits that planning provides. First, planning provides a means for dynamically involving personnel from all areas of business in the management of the organization. Second, employee involvement increases their overall understanding of the organization's objectives and goals. Involvement in planning fosters a great personal commitment to the plan and to the organization. These positive attitudes improve overall organizational morale and loyalty. Lastly, planning benefits managerial performance. It focusses the energies and activities of managers in the use of scarce resources in a competitive and demanding marketplace. In addition, planning is a mental exercise from which managers accomplish experience and knowledge. Planning can prepare managers for the challenges of the business world by encouraging them to think ahead and predict future contingencies, strategies, and profit-making ideas.

Although there are different management styles, all management applies the same steps to planning. The basic steps are the following and completion of each step is a prerequisite of the next:

- Set objectives
- Use those objectives to provide direction
- Perform a self-review process that will determine the company's capabilities
- Establish goals
- Forecast market environment
- State actions
- Determine and obtain resources
- Institute procedures
- Finalize and execute plan.

Strategic Planning

One type of planning used today is strategic planning. Strategic planning, or, strategy making, is a technique that chief executives of any size business can use to identify and deal with concerns that they have about the future of their business. To some, strategic planning is a glorified repacking of old-fashioned business planning, and to others, it is just a modification of long-range planning. While it includes both elements, strategic planning is really a management system that allows managers to focus more clearly on the most important aspects of their business.

From an overall perspective, the strategic planning process integrates elements of three management-planning concepts: the annual business plan, diversification planning, and long-range planning. Long-range planning usually consists of straight-line extrapolations of existing data to meet acceptable growth rates and financial ratios. The typical result is a growth rate for the next five years equals at least twice that of the last five years. A strategic plan eliminates much of this artificial growth projection by requiring an objective assessment of the business.

Management must both ask and answer tough questions about all aspects of the business. Diversification planning is an activity separate from the annual business plan. In most cases, it turns out to be a relatively unorganized search for new products, new technology, new processes, and new businesses.

The first form of strategic planning was a combination of the annual budget and long-range plan. The result seemed to be very confusing and the exercise seemed to take forever. However, it forced planners to ask more questions about the sense of the exercise. Over the last several years, this combination has been refined into a sophisticated planning process, and is being used by all different sizes of businesses, even Fortune 500 companies.

For strategic planning to be successful, it needs the support and involvement of management. This includes anyone from the CEO to junior managers. If everyone works together, there are considerable positive results.

The strategic planning process benefits a business in many different ways. First, it assembles an effective management team. Second, it points an organization's resources toward very specific goals, giving little amounts of resources to be wasted. Third, it generates a thorough analysis of business strengths and weaknesses. Lastly, it forces managers a needed discipline that makes them better managers in the company.

There are four common benefits strategic planning provides for a company. The first is that the value of teamwork is greatly enhanced and creates a task-oriented, organizational flexibility. Second, entrepreneurial drive is reborn in a common commitment to make things happen. Third, open communications create a healthier climate. Lastly, a feeling that a company can create its own future instead of external forces doing so is inspiring. Combining these positive attitudes with a good strategic plan enables a business to concentrate on its strengths, keeping its weaknesses to a minimum.

Operational Planning

Another type of planning is operational planning. As the word suggests, this type of planning involves the operations of the organization. In other words, it is what the organization intends to accomplish, how and when it will operate to fulfill that intention, and who will be responsible for the operations. This is also the type of planning by which an organization's strategic plan is carried out. Generally, top-level management determines the goals that are required to carry out the mission of the organization, thus the senior executives start the planning process, and the process is assigned to the appropriate departments. This is the key difference between operational and strategic planning. Strategic planning is primarily handled at the upper levels; operational planning involves every manager and employee. It is important for every organization to have a strategic plan; however, it is even more important for every unit to have its own operational plan to support the strategic plans. These plans work vertically and horizontally with the other. Operational planning requires understanding, involvement, simplicity, and methods.

Operational planning needs to address not only all managerial levels, but also all key employees if possible. If all these subjects agree, then the operational planning process will be very effective. In operational planning, there are two separate considerations, the plan and the process. An operational plan is a document identifying specific results to be achieved within a given period, and contains six distinct elements:

1. Operational analysis
2. Key results areas
3. Indicators of performance
4. Operational objectives
5. Action plans
6. Budgets.

Together, these six elements form an important management tool for determining specific short-term results to be achieved and fixing accountability for those results. The involvement of operating executives, managers, and key employees in producing operational plans for the total organization are all parts of operational planning. A particular strength of operational planning is its emphasis on team planning through many well-organized meetings. This aspect gives a company belief and commitment to the operational plan.

There are many reasons why you need an operational plan. The first reason is to achieve short-term operating results. These include financial results, sales performance, new product development, new markets/customers, and people development. The results are most often more specific and detailed than those in a strategic plan. The second reason is the implementation of the current year's portion of the organization's strategic plan. The operational plan is the primary means by which the strategic plan is carried out, thus the two must be carefully integrated. Third, an operational plan ensures that all parts of the organization are pulling together. Lastly, it involves and gets commitment of all key people in meeting organizational objectives. The operational plan depends on contributions of key people at all levels. It also serves as a communication device for involvement of all people in the business. It is as necessary to the success of any organization as its people, financial resources, products, and technology. No organization can continue to succeed and grow without operational planning.

Cross-cultural Planning

Business is not conducted in an identical fashion from culture to culture. Consequently, business relations are enhanced when managerial, sales, and technical personnel are trained to be aware of areas likely to create communication difficulties and conflict across cultures. Similarly, international communication is even further strengthened when business people can anticipate areas of communication. Finally, business in general is enhanced when people from different cultures find new approaches to old problems, creating perspectives and examining the problem at hand from each other's different cultural perspective.

Problems in business communication conducted across cultures often arise when participants from one culture are unable to understand culturally determined differences in communication practices, traditions, and thought processing in planning.

Ethnocentrism is the belief that one's own cultural group is somehow innately superior to others. Problems can occur when one or more of the people involved adhere to an ethnocentric view of how to conduct business. Since members of any culture perceive their own behavior as the most accepted and logical, and since that behavior works for them, ethnocentrism can be misleading. Each culture has its own set of values, which are often different from those values in other cultures. These differences can be slight or they can be marked. In international business, it is indistinguishable about what is right or wrong, which culture's values should be upheld, what is right by whose standards. Internationally, businesspeople must be cautious in conducting business communications across cultures, since no one individual is liable to recognize the subtle forms of ethnocentrism that shape who he or she is. One needs to understand how the perception of a given message is regarded, depending on the culturally determined viewpoint of those communicating:

- Language—this is the deepest and richest expression of a primary social culture. It reflects and interprets the culture, providing vital insights into how it operates.
- Context—the elements that surround and give meaning to a communication event. In a scale of high to low, low context communication holds information in the single message or event objective, and high context communication is more subjective and distributes the information within the person. The meaning of the event is deeply colored by elements, including relationships, history, and status.
- Time—cultural attitudes toward time are generally monochronic (one event at a time) or polychronic (many events at one time). Polychronic time is a state of being, monochronic time is a resource to be measured and managed. Concepts of time differ in interrelationships between past, present, and future.
- Equality/power—the distance and types of relationships between people and groups as regards the degree of equality, status, and authority.
- Information flow—how messages flow between people and levels in organizations and how action chains more toward communication or task completion. The general flow patterns can be sequenced or looped.

The above illustrates that each variable is holographic, meaning that each exists in a dynamic relationship to all others, which results in cultural patterns. Aspects of each variable are reflected in all the others. Culture directly affects the international planning process in the following ways.

Language

One of the most frequent barriers to conflict-free cross-cultural business is the use of different languages. It is important not to underestimate the importance that an understanding of language plays in international business. Difficulties with language can range from serious translation problems, the difficulty in conveying subtle distinctions from language to language, and culturally based variations among speakers of the same language.

Gross translation errors, though frequent, may be less likely to cause conflict between parties than other language difficulties for two reasons. First, they are generally the easiest language to be detected; only those errors that continue to be logical in both the original meaning and in the mistranslated version pose a serious concern, and even when easily detected, gross translation errors waste time and wear on the patience of the parties involved. For some, such errors imply a form of disrespect for the party into whose language the message is translated.

The subtle shadings that are often crucial to business negotiations are also weakened when the parties do not share similar control of the same language. In English, for example, the mild distinctions between the words "misinterpret" and "misunderstand" can prove significant in a sensitive situation. To a touchy negotiator, to say that he or she "misunderstands" may imply that he or she is dimwitted. In such a situation, the term applies more objectively to the matter at hand than to the specific negotiator. To a non-native speaker with inadequate control of the language, however, such subtle distinctions might be lost.

Dialectical difference within the same language often creates gross errors. One frequently cited example of how variations within a single language can affect business occurred when a US deodorant manufacturer sent a Spanish translation of its slogan to their Mexican operations. The slogan read, "If you use our deodorant, you won't be embarrassed." The translation, however, which the Mexican-based English-speaking employees saw no reason to avoid, used the term "embarazada" to mean "embarrassed." This provided much amusement to the Mexican market, as "embarazada" means "pendant" in Mexican Spanish.

Attitudes toward accents and dialects create barriers in international business planning and communication. The view that a particular accent suggests loyalty or familiarity to a nation or region is widespread in many languages. Regional ties in such nations as Italy, France, or Germany, among others, can be suggested by the dialect a native speaker uses. Finally, national prejudices and class distinctions are often reinforced through sociolinguistics—the social patterns of language. For example, due to regional prejudice and racism, certain accents in the United States are associated with urban areas or rural regions, or race may reinforce negative stereotypes regarding business ability, education level, or acumen among certain

US subgroups. Similarly, some cultures use sociolinguistics to differentiate one economic class from another.

Environmental and Technological Considerations

The ways in which people use the resources available to them often shifts drastically from culture to culture. Culturally ingrained biases regarding the natural and technological environment can create communication barriers. Most people are accustomed to ways of looking at the environment and the use of technology particular to their own culture. This, in turn, may make it difficult to accept or even to understand those views held by other cultures.

The failure of businesses to modify their communications to accommodate environmental differences often develops from an ethnocentric rigidity toward other culturally learned views of technology. Generally, cultures have three attitudes toward technology:

- Control—in control cultures such as those of northern Europe and North America, technology is usually viewed as an essentially positive way of controlling the environment.
- Subjugation—in subjugation cultures such as those of central Africa and southwestern Asia, the existing environment is also viewed as instinctively positive, and although technology is viewed as innately positive, it is viewed with some skepticism.
- Harmonization—in harmonization cultures, such as those common in many Native American cultures and some East Asian nations, a balance between the use of technology and the existing environment is attempted. In these cultures, neither technology nor the environment are innately good and the people of these cultures see themselves as part of the environment in which they live, being neither subject to it nor master of it.

One major communication obstacle among those from control cultures is the belief that other cultures wish to be more like them. Control cultures tend to describe themselves as the industrialized nations. Their members are often acculturated to believe that the way in which people in less industrialized nations use their resources results from inherently inferior technology. Often, though, the reason people use the resources available to them in the manner that they do is that it makes good business sense to use them in that fashion within their own cultural views.

Social Organizations

Social organization, as it affects the workplace, is often culturally determined. One must take care not to assume that the view held in one's own culture is universal on such issues reflecting the culture's social organization. Examples of this are nepotism and kinship ties, educational values, class structure and social mobility, job status and economic stratification, religious ties, political affiliation, gender differences, racism and other prejudices, attitudes toward work, and recreational or work institutions.

All of these areas have far-reaching implications for business practice. Choosing employees based on resumes, for example, is considered a primary means of selection in the United States, Canada, and much of northern Europe—all nations with comparatively weak concepts of familiar relationships and kinship ties. In these cultures, nepotism is seen as subjective and likely to protect less qualified workers through familiar intervention. By contrast, it would seem anywhere from mildly to highly inappropriate to suggest to members of many Arabic, central African, Latin American, or southern European cultures to skip over hiring relatives to hire a stranger. For people in these cultures, nepotism both fulfills personal obligations and ensures a predictable level of trust and accountability. The fact that a stranger appears to be better qualified based on a superior resume and a relatively brief interview would not affect that belief, as it might, for example, in the United States or Sweden.

The nature of praise and employee motivation can be socially determined. For example, the promotion of a single member of a traditional Japanese work group may cause the productivity and morale of both the group and the promoted employee to fall. A similar promotion in the United States, by contrast, might be seen as a reward for the promoted employee and might even be viewed as encouraging the remaining members of the group to work harder for a goal that they too might attain. Thus to communicate such a promotion openly may prove to be a poor policy in Japan, but a good policy in the United States.

An individual may personally believe that a country's social system is inefficient or incorrect. Nevertheless, in the manner that individual conducts business on a daily basis, it is necessary to work within the challenges of that culture to succeed. One may choose not to do business with people from such a culture, but one cannot easily impose one's own values on them and expect to do well.

Contexting and Face-saving

Communication depends on the context in which the communication is set. The more information the sender and receiver share in common, the higher the context of the communication and the less necessary to communicate through words or gestures. In high context cultures, how something is said matters more than what is actually said. By contrast, in low context cultures, the actual words matter more than the intended meaning. What is actually said—and especially what is actually written—matters more than the context in which it was said. Communication, then, can be seen as being high or low in contexting.

In a high contextual situation, much of what people choose not to say is essential to understanding the transmitted message. Even though a person may not have said anything directly, others are still expected to understand the unspoken message. Edward T. Hall (1976) was the first person to coin the term contexting. Hall observed:

> The matter of contexting requires a decision concerning how much information the other person can be expected to possess on a given subject. It appears that all cultures arrange their members and relationships along the context scale, and one of the great

communication strategies, whether addressing a single person or an entire group, is to ascertain the correct level of contexting of one's communication ... the rules vary from culture to culture, so that to infer by the level of contexting that they do not understand may be an insult, even though your assumption is correct.

No two cultures share the same level of contexting. Thus, in any cross-cultural exchange, one party will act as the higher contextual and one the lower contextual. As a communicator in an international business setting, it is important to assess the level of contexting inherent in the communication of the culture in which one conducts business in order to clearly understand what has been conveyed.

A correlation exists between face-saving and contexting. Cultures with high contexting are more concerned with face; that is, preserving prestige or outward dignity. Low context cultures are less concerned with face since words are more likely to be taken without underlying implied meaning. As a result, high context cultures tend to favor a business communication approach based on indirection and politeness; low context cultures follow more of a confrontation strategy and use a direct plan approach to business communication. High context cultures view indirectness as honest and showing consideration while low context cultures view indirectness as dishonest and offensive.

Authority Conception

Different cultures often view distribution of authority in their society differently. Geert Hofstede (1980), the Dutch international business researcher, has called this dimension of cultural variation power distance, defining this as the degree to which a society accepts that power in institutions and organizations is distributed unequally.

The view of authority in a given society affects communication and planning in the business environment, as significantly as it shapes the view of how a message will be received based on the relative status or rank of the message's sender to its receiver. Thus, in a relatively decentralized business environment—as exists even in many centralized US companies—people generally pay attention to a person based on how convincing an argument he or she puts forth, regardless of that person's rank or status within the organization or society. By contrast, in a highly centralized culture, a relatively high-ranking individual's communication is taken very seriously, even if one disagrees.

Non-verbal Communication Behavior

Among the most markedly varying dimensions in inter-cultural communication is non-verbal behavior. Knowledge of a culture conveyed through what a person says represents only a portion of what that person has communicated.

Much of non-verbal communication may be broken down into six areas: dress; kinesics, or body language; oculesics, or eye contact; haptics, or touching behavior; proxemics, or the use of body space; and paralanguage. Any one of these areas communicates significant information non-verbally in any given culture.

One of the most apparent differences is how dress is interpreted. Even when cultures share similar forms of dress, the message inherent in the choice of clothing is not always the same. For instance, the selection of a conservative tie for a formal negotiation might well be shared by several cultures, but exactly what a conservative tie is (even when all parties belong to cultures in which men generally wear ties) remains to be determined by the standards that prevail in that particular culture. Thus, what is a conservative tie in one culture may seem unconservative or flashy in another, giving a different message altogether.

Just as importantly, people often bring to a cross-cultural meeting ethnocentric prejudice regarding what they believe to be proper dress. Thus, a European or an American may condemn as somehow less than civilized, a Saudi or Iranian in traditional garb. Conversely, a Saudi or Iranian may well consider as flagrantly immoral the bare face, arms, and legs of a European or an American woman in business attire.

Non-verbal behavioral differences in kinesics may be less obvious than dress differences. How people walk, gesture, bow, stand, or sit are all, to a large part, culturally determined. In many cases, a kinesic sign well understood in one culture is totally unknown in another culture.

Some kinesic behavior may carry distinctly different meanings in more than one culture. In such cases, all parties recognize the gesture, but interpret it differently. During George H.W. Bush's visit to Australia while he was president, he held up two fingers in a V sign. In both countries, the symbol is widely understood—in the United States, the "V" emblem is a sign of goodwill, victory, and solidarity, while in Australia it carries a lewd, sexual meaning.

Oculesics, or the use of eye contact, also varies significantly depending on the culture involved. In several cultures, for example, it is considered disrespectful to prolong eye contact with those who are older or of higher status. In many cultures, it is considered improper for women to look men in the eye. While steady eye contact in the United States may indicate the listener's interest and attentiveness, intense eye contact may prove disconcerting.

Proxemics, how far apart people stand when speaking or how far apart they sit in meetings, carries significant information to people who share the same culture. Personal space is culturally determined. In many Latin American, southern European, central African and Middle Eastern cultures, comfortable conversational distance would be much closer. Indeed, in many parts of the world, friendly or serious conversations are conducted close enough to feel the breath of the speaker on one's face. The US or northern European communicator unaware of this may face a very discomforting situation, with the speaker literally backing his or her US or northern European counterpart into a corner as the speaker continues to move closer to the retreating listener. The result in a business situation could be disastrous.

Time Conception

International business communication and planning is also affected by cross-cultural differences in temporal conception or the understanding of time. Most US and northern Europe businesspeople view time as inflexible; a thing to be divided, used, or wasted. This is not, however, a universal view. The manner in which one uses time, consequently, may profoundly affect the way in which business is conducted in various parts of the world. While it is dangerous to overgeneralize, most cultures fall with varying degrees into two types of temporal conception—a monochronic system or a polychronic system.

In a monochronic system, personal feelings are rarely allowed to flourish on the job precisely because personal involvement must not be allowed to affect preset schedules if the system is to function smoothly. Personal relationships are determined by the terms of the job. Multiple tasks are handled one at a time in a prescheduled manner. People in authority are, in contrast to those in polychronic societies, available by scheduling appointments.

In a polychronic system, time conception differs significantly from the monochronic one. For example, in a polychronic system, one should be aware that people distinguish between insiders and those outside the existing personal relationships. One must, therefore, try to establish an inside connection to facilitate the effectiveness of a given message. By contrast, in a monochronic society, one needs only to schedule a meeting with the appropriate people. One should not expect people in a monochronic system to give preference to those they know over complete strangers. The outsider is treated in exactly the same fashion as the close associate.

The influence of temporal conception on communication is extensive. This is further complicated by the fact that no culture is exclusively polychronic or monochronic. Members of any culture lean to one direction or the other, although the cultures as a whole may organize their thoughts and conceive of time more one way or the other. The central issue here is to keep alert in the planning process to communication differences that would indicate that one culture was more monochronic or polychronic in orientation, and to adapt one's communication strategies accordingly.

As the world has seen businesses increasingly evolve to an integrated world market, the world has realized the need to communicate at a global level. Misunderstandings deriving from ethnocentrism or unawareness of other cultures will accelerate to unproductive conflict between employees and negotiators. In the ever-increasing competitive environment, there is a decreasing chance of doing business within the confines on one's culture. Consequently, the need to learn, accept, and understand intercultural differences has grown as well and will continue to do so.

The cross-cultural issues suggested provide a framework for asking the right questions when preparing for business affairs with those from other cultures. By asking the way in which each of these factors is likely to affect people of that specific culture, many of the communication barriers and cultural variables between people of different cultures can be anticipated, and the planning process will be more successful.

Effect of Culture on International Controlling

Controlling means evaluating the progress and correcting it when needed. Controlling is a difficult thing to accomplish from culture to culture. One of the hard parts of controlling is determining what needs to be corrected. Culture plays a big part in controlling, in that the measure of one thing usually differs from one culture to the next. Controlling has a lot to do with the management style and the guidelines set by the company. A strategy that MNEs could be influenced by is the national culture of the country in which they are based. It has been argued that MNEs which are based in high power distance yet low uncertainty avoidance culture countries, may have a natural preference for full power of their foreign affiliates.

If the management style is the type that allows for a large power distance, controlling will be cut and dried. In this case, if you do not meet the required standard, you probably will not work at the company for much longer. If there is a small power distance, controlling might be a little more difficult. In this case, the manager is open-minded and more of a friend than a boss. It could be easier or harder, it all depends on the employees and their cultures.

Guidelines set by companies could be easy to follow in all cultures, if the guidelines are culturally adjusted. In this case, if something or someone is not meeting the predetermined guidelines, a decision is not hard to make dealing with company guidelines.

Effect of Culture on International Organizing

Organizing means designing a structure that will allow an individual, a group, or an organization to meet its goals. Organizing is a necessary ingredient for success in every culture. Organizing is a very important part of international management, because guidelines need to be set for any organization to function. These guidelines will differ from culture to culture due to differing societies' viewpoints and beliefs. For example, some cultures organize workers to work in groups while others organize their employees to work on individual assignments. Culture influences the title given to employees. For instance, in Thailand, the title on one's business card is very important. Most organizations in Thailand have titles such as VP (Vice President), SVP (Senior Vice President), or GM (General Manager) even when an employee does not have any people to manage. It is important for the Thai to appear important in the eyes of others; thus, this type of structure, title and arrangement is very important.

Organizing encompasses the division of labor, span of control, delegation of authority and the rules put in place for authority in an organization. Rules such as time must be considered. Societies that have a slack approach towards time should not have strict guidelines dealing with punctuality. Viewpoints are another factor that deals with the way a company organizes. A large part of this is the way the culture feels about personal relationships versus the company's objectives. If this is the case, roles of the employees should be adjusted so that the employees do not feel overwhelmed with work and have time to interact socially. The same holds true in the culture that views the company over personal relationships. In this case, the company should adjust the workload so that employees do not run out of work to do.

Culture is important when organizing the human resources of an organization. The ideal way to have people working together would be to group people of the same cultural beliefs together. Since we do not live in an ideal world, it is necessary to provide training to give people the cultural understanding of the people they are working with, especially on a very important project. A case in point is the construction of the tunnel from England to France.

Chunnel Case: British Isles and Continental Europe

In mid 1994, the British Isles and continental Europe were joined together for the first time. The Channel tunnel, or Chunnel as it is better known, is Europe's biggest infrastructure project financed completely by private capital. Although the project had many financial difficulties brought about by unexpected production costs, it must be considered a success on several levels. Eurotunnel, the company in charge of tunnel operations, has succeeded in connecting England and France, an idea that has been around for centuries. As a result, consumers, the tourism industry, commercial trade, and the coastal towns are all expected to prosper. Additionally, if projections were correct, the environment would benefit through reduced air pollution.

The desire to link Britain and France dates back more than 200 years. It is told that a French farmer referencing "A Dissertation on the Ancient Link between England and France" stated that the two countries should be linked by tunnel, bridge, or causeway. Many years later, Napoleon approved a French mining engineer's plan for twin tunnels with chimneys, which reached the surface for ventilation. However, England and France went to war a year later and the plan died. The first serious construction attempt took place in the early 1880s. Tunneling had actually begun from both the British and the French coasts, but after a mere 2,000 yards, the British became uncomfortable with the potential success of the project and called it off (Grimes, 1990).

Over the next 100 years, studies were done and proposals were written. It was not until late in 1984 that the British and French governments finally reached an agreement to build the tunnel. The tunnel has been said to be perhaps the greatest example of international collaboration in transportation. This is due to the cooperation fostered between British and French companies. Eurotunnel is the British company serving as the operator, and Trans–Manche Link is its French partner—a construction company. The European Passenger Services and the French and Belgian rail companies, SNCF and SNCB, which run the Eurostar services between London, Paris, and Brussels, have also been noteworthy (UK Department of Transportation, 1995).

The Chunnel connects Folkestone, England and Calais, France. The Chunnel consists of two parallel tunnels, allowing traffic to move in both directions, and is linked by a third tunnel, which provides air conditioning and other technical services. Passengers are able to exit the highway on either side of the Channel, pick up a ticket at a tollbooth, and drive to Le Shuttle, which will take them to the other side. Crossing the Channel via the tunnel takes a mere 35 minutes compared with 75 minutes by ferry.

While all these statements reflect a positive attitude toward tunnel construction, it cannot be said that its completion was entirely smooth; rather it was filled with safety and environmental concerns, management regulations, and cultural tensions.

Culture has long been a division between England and France—symbolically, much wider than the water that separates them. The thought of linking the island with the continent strikes at the center of the British belief that those of the island nation are better off alone. This attitude is reflected in a general abhorrence of the European Union, which they joined in 1973 merely out of fear of being left behind. To much of the British public, the tunnel is the symbol of everything negative looming on the mainland. They fear invasion, if not by foreigners, then by the French foxes, which British tabloids suggest are moving toward Calais. Nevertheless, locals see the light at the end of the tunnel as a train moving full steam ahead (Wells and Revzin, 1990).

France, on the other hand, welcomed the project with open arms. The French took on the tunnel with visions of growth and success. It is a platform of its technical expertise and a source of national pride. The French tunnel workers even personalized their digging machines with nicknames, which the British, not surprisingly, did not!

On a positive note, the younger generation in Britain is more accepting of the Chunnel. To them, the Chunnel to Europe makes access to their beloved travel and shopping in Paris, Vienna, or Berlin that much simpler.

The actual construction project was coordinated between Britain and France, but the potential and real benefits of the tunnel can be experienced internationally.

Case Questions

1. Describe the similarities or differences in the British and French cultures.
2. Discuss the cultural considerations that should have been anticipated in this project.
3. How should the dissimilar cultures be handled throughout the project?
4. Is it possible to lessen the division of cultures in a situation such as this? Would it be better to work with the differences, or try to educate or influence each culture accordingly?
5. How did British and French history contribute to this cultural clash?

Effect of Culture on International Leading

Leading means directing people in the right way to accomplish specified goals. All members of an organization should share the responsibilities and privileges of leadership. The scope of these will vary greatly, as will the material rewards. Still, ideally, leadership is systemic and the challenge is how to accomplish this so that the leaders contribute to the organization's overall success.

In different cultures, the role of the leader stands for different things. Extreme fusion of core values and competencies may render them indistinguishable, as in the case of reproduction; a value and competency shared by the top 1 per cent of leaders may produce other leaders. It is important to infuse core values into people so that they may clearly differentiate right from wrong. In some cultures, the leader is to be feared and respected. In other cultures, the leader is looked upon as a friend or equal. In the culture you are working with or involved in, it is very important to know the role of the leader. If you display the wrong type of leadership in the culture you are in, you may easily lose the respect of your workers.

In some cultures that Hofstede (1980) referred to as large power distance, such as Russia, Spain, Poland, and many African countries, leaders are to be distant, unapproachable, and very demanding. In cultures like this, the type of management is usually along the lines of a dictatorship. A dictatorship might seem a little bit harsh to people from the United States, but in some cultures, they feel this is the best way to manage. In this type of system, the manager will make all the decisions, and employees will follow the decisions.

In other cultures that Hofstede (1980) termed low power distance, such as the United States, Germany, and Australia, leaders are approachable, easy to get along with, and open-minded. In these cultures, management is usually along the lines of a democracy. With this type of system, the employees will interact with the manager freely and help determine the best solution. This type of management is becoming a common practice worldwide.

A Study of the Impact of Culture on Leadership: The Case of Ghana

Social, Political, and Geographical Background of Ghana

In a discussion of globalization, Africa is often the forgotten continent. Few people, especially Americans, seem to recognize or understand the business practices in the African countries. In a business sense, Ghana is one of the principal countries of Africa. Throughout the world, national culture influences leadership. This is also true in Ghana, where deeply held values regarding the rights and duties of citizens form the core of national culture and constitute their professional views. Leaders in all countries, including Ghana, must lead, motivate, and make decisions; their cultural background often determines the way in which they approach these managerial behaviors. In addition, culture also determines both the leadership variables and the leadership theories that can be applied.

One thing that can often form a foundation to a culture is the geographic location in which a population lives. Ghana is located in West Africa on the Greenwich Meridian. It is a rectangular shaped country, about the size of Oregon, that is surrounded by Cote d'Ivoire to the west, Togo to the east, Burkina Faso to the north, and the Atlantic Ocean to the south. A tapered grassy plain stretches inland from the coast, widening in the east, while the south and west are enclosed by dense rainforest. The north holds forested hills, and beyond the hills is open woodland. In the far north is a plateau. In the east, the Aduapim Togo hills run inland from the coast along the Togo border. The Black and White Volta Rivers go through Ghana from Burkina Faso, merging into the largest man-made lake in the world—Lake Volta. Ghana's coastline is sprinkled with sandy palm-fringed beaches and lagoons (Coon and Tyler, 1984).

Map 9.1 Ghana

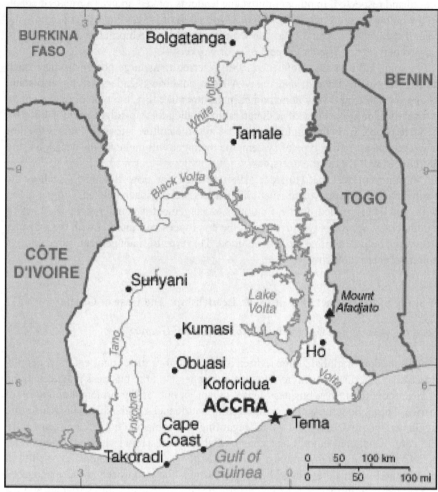

Source: CIA–World Factbook. https://www.cia.gov/cia/publications/factbook/geos/gh.html

History of Ghana

Historically speaking, Ghana takes its name, though not its modern boundaries, from one of the great inland trading empires that flourished in West Africa from the fourth to the eleventh centuries A.D. The fabled university city of Tombouctou (now in Mali) was part of ancient Ghana. Because of the diversity of the ethnic groups, the history of the country is varied. Modern history began with contact of the Portuguese in 1470. They developed gold mining and slave trading in the area. The area is the Gold Coast, named after one of the ancient Sudanese Empires, which flourished between the fourth and tenth centuries. Control of the Gold Coast fell into British hands in the nineteenth century and after 74 years of battles with the Ashantis of the interior, the British gained control of the present-day Ghana in 1901.

Ghana gained independence from British colonial rule on March 6, 1957. Three years after independence Ghana became a Republic with Dr Kwame Nkrumah, leader of the Convention Peoples Party (CPP) as the first President. Under Dr Nkrumah, Ghana made extraordinary and fast progress in education, industrial, and infrastructural development, and in the provision of social services. Simultaneously, the country played a leading role in international affairs, particularly in the struggle for the liberation of dependent countries in Africa, and African unity. The country also played an active role in a number of international organizations including the United Nations and its specialized agencies, the Commonwealth, the Organization of African Unity, and the Non-Aligned Movement. However, on February 24, 1966, the Ghana armed forces, in cooperation with the Police Service, conquered the CPP government in a coup led by Colonel Emmanuel Kotoka (Brake, Walker and Walker, 1995).

Since independence, Ghana has had four civilian governments and five military regimes. Today, Ghana, divided into ten regions, is a multi-party democracy, although in practice the country is still in transition from a dictatorship to a democracy. The last military-turned-democratic head of state was Flight Lieutenant Jerry John Rawlings. The current, true democratically elected leader is John Agyekum Kufuor.

Ghanaian Population

Ghana's diverse population also has a significant impact on the culture of this West African country. The population of Ghana is more than 16.7 million and is growing rapidly at 3.1 per cent a year. The population density rate is 110 people per square mile. While 99.8 per cent of the population is Black African, it is divided into more than 100 different ethnic groups, each with its own language and cultural heritage. Some major groups include the Fante in the coastal areas, the Asante in the south–central area, the Ga-Adangme and Ewe in the south, and the Hausa and Moshi-Dagomba in the north. The 0.2 per cent non-black population is mostly European, with some Lebanese merchants and communities of Indians and Chinese (Coon and Tyler, 1984). The largest city is the capital of Accra, with more than one million people.

While the official national language is English, languages spoken in Ghana include Ga, Twi, Ewe, Fante, Akan, Ga-Adangme, and Mole-Dagbani. In addition, although more than 60 per cent of the population is Christian, culturally, Ghana is a mix of other religions as well, including Muslim and traditional beliefs. All forms of religion have a strong influence on Ghanaian life. Because of this, many Ghanaians find themselves caught in a strange mixture of Western values and ancestral, religious, and tribal loyalties and obligations.

Ghanaian Economy

The Ghanaian economy is primarily based on agriculture, which employs more than 60 per cent of the labor force. Cacao, from which coca is made, is the most important cash crop, accounting for about 70 per cent of the country's export. Other chief products include corn, root crops, sorghum, millet, and peanuts. Mining is also an important part of the economy in Ghana. Ghana is the fifth largest producer of diamonds and the seventh largest producer of gold. Manganese, bauxite, and aluminum are also minerals that are mined as an important part of Ghana's economy. Industry employs only about 17 per cent of the people in Ghana. Key industries include fishing, light manufacturing, and timber. Since the completion of two hydroelectric projects, Ghana has been able to develop some heavier industry as well, including an aluminum smelter. Oil and gas exploration have been given a high priority by the government, but as yet, no commercially exploitable quantities have been discovered.

The United Kingdom is Ghana's largest trading partner. Nigeria, the United States, Germany, Japan, and the Netherlands are other important trading partners. However, despite the financial resources that are earned from these countries, great financial strain and economic difficulties may still result from Ghana's economic growth, being dependent as it is on world prices for exports.

To combat this vulnerability, Ghana is a member of the Economic Community of West African States. It has been a test bed for a new economic development program arranged and supervised by the International Monetary Fund (IMF) and the World Bank. Termed the Structural Adjustment Program, the program involves measures to liberate the economy and remove trade barriers and state intervention to industry, and maintain firm budgetary control. Despite the perceived success of the program and steady economic growth since its introduction, economic recovery has proved elusive since the introduction of the program, and the population at large has seen few material gains.

Characteristics of Ghana's Culture

The view of time on Ghana is focussed on the past. The future has little place in Ghanaian thought. The linear concept of time in Western thought, with an indefinite past, present, and indefinite future, is practically foreign to Ghanaian thinking. The future is virtually absent because events which lie in it have not taken place; they have not been realized and cannot, therefore, constitute time. Actual time is, therefore, what is present and what is past. It moves backward rather than forward; and people set their minds not on future things, but chiefly in what has taken place.

The culture in Ghana is, in general, more "being" than "doing" oriented. Ghanaians are very warm, friendly, and sociable people. They are polite and open, even with strangers. They tend to live life at a more relaxed pace, viewing time as a series of events rather than a matter of hours or minutes. In other words, people are more important than schedules (Brake, Walker and Walker, 1995). Traditionally, change has not been valued for its own sake. Work is done after sincere, trusting friendships, have been established. Today, many Ghanaians are experiencing the transition from village to city and, consequently, are losing some of their reliance on close relationships. However, for most, the importance of relationships is still paramount. An aggressive focus on the task at hand is often perceived as trying to demonstrate superiority. Work is not the central component of a good life in Ghana. Alternatively, leisure and family are extremely important.

Communication in Ghana is high context, indirect, and inexpressive. Free expression is not given a high value. Ghanaians rarely reveal their inner emotions or talk about their beliefs in more than superficial terms. As often as not, they will tell you what they think you want to hear rather than risk offending you with an opinionated view. Politeness and protocol are highly valued, and hospitality is generous. With this in mind, it is clear that in Ghana, loud and boisterous behavior is disliked.

In Ghana, personal space is closer than in the United States. Space is more oriented to being public than private. This fits with the collective nature and reliance on friendship and trust that Ghanaians prioritize. Friendly touching is also common in Ghana.

The Ghanaian culture is highly based on collectivist ideals. These values of the society are reflected in organizations, in the high regard managers have for their subordinates as people. Managers in Ghana view workers as a network of people rather than as human resources. The emphasis is on maintaining relationships rather than on providing opportunities for individual development, and on highly ritualized interpersonal interactions that often place greater value on the observance of protocol than the accomplishments of work-related tasks. This is also shown by the desire of workers to have a close relationship with their boss and by the reluctance of managers either to accept individual blame for mistakes or to criticize individual subordinates in a direct manner.

Finally, in Ghana, the culture, specifically in the business environment, is based on moderately formal ideals. Ghanaian dress is modest, neat, and generally conservative. Punctuality, efficiency, and rational thought processes are not high priorities in the Ghanaian culture.

Ghana's Leadership Style

These cultural aspects, history, governmental structure, population characteristics, and economy all combine to form the foundation of the country's leadership variables. People in cultures throughout the world behave in dissimilar ways regarding management and organizational structure, and differ in how they view their environment. Thus, national boundaries make a substantial difference in a manager's goals, inclination for taking risks, pragmatism, interpersonal skills, and leadership style. This is because, overall, the environment that affects leader–subordinate relations varies across countries and cultures due to variances in the cultural foundation upon which the leadership variables are based.

In Ghana, the dominant mode toward nature is one of subjugation. This may be expected due to the history of colonialism over the past five centuries and the predominance of subsistence farming and extreme poverty. Low per capita income, minimal education opportunities for much of the population, the lack of adequate administrative and physical infrastructures, the dependence on foreign aid, and the relatively small middle class on the continent hinder the emergence of control orientation. Understanding this, it is not surprising that the majority of the population cannot help but see their lives as governed by external forces—the climate, foreign government, internal (often, authoritarian) government, and so on.

Power in Ghana is based on a clear system of hierarchy. Authoritarian leaders are common and authority is rarely questioned. In the Ghanaian culture, absolute objectives exist only with God. In the world, persons in authority positions represent God, so their objectives should be followed. Furthermore, organizations in Ghana tend to be viewed by society as having a wider mission than is generally understood in the United States. Leaders are often expected to provide benefits such as employment, housing, and transportation.

Organizational structure in Ghana is very high. Ghanaian managers regard security as an important factor in their work, to be reinforced by unchanging structures, detailed procedures, and close supervision of subordinates. Leadership plans are very consistent, with very few risks taken. Even today, organizations tend to retain the major characteristics of structures developed in the colonial era, namely, rather rigid bureaucratic, rule-bound hierarchies. Leaders in organizations provide both the structure and the details for the organizations.

These leadership variables represent the values and beliefs of cultures and strongly affect the methods that managers and other leaders must use to lead and motivate employees. Because there is such a strong connection between culture and effective managerial techniques, it is clear that managerial behavior that works well in one culture will not necessarily work well in another. There are several organizational leadership theories that have been developed in the United States as well as other developed countries, that ask universal questions about effective leadership styles, but the answers to these questions are culture-specific. Rather than being applicable worldwide, many theoretical models are only effective within specific contexts.

Leadership Theories

Douglas McGregor developed a concept of leadership that was explained in the United States more than three decades ago, in his book *The Human Side of Enterprise* (1960). This concept of leadership theory is called Theory X and Theory Y. This concept proposes that managers must adhere to one of two opposing theories about people. Theory X posits that the average human being has an inherent dislike for work and will avoid it if he or she can. This theory goes on to claim that the only way for a leader to motivate this type of person is with the use of force, threats, or punishment. Conversely, Theory Y puts forth that the outflow of physical and mental effort in work is as natural as play or rest (Rodrigues, 1996). This theory claims that force and punishment are not needed as motivators. People will seek out responsibility and self-direction of their own will.

Fundamentally, these theories propose the notion that participative leadership behavior is more effective than authoritarian leadership behavior. Although this may be true in small power distance cultures, such as the United States, in large power distance cultures such as Ghana, employees tend to expect authoritative leadership. The Theory X and Theory Y leadership ideals would, therefore, not apply in the Ghanaian culture.

With this in mind, Professor Hofstede (1987), a European professor, proposed another concept, Theory T and Theory T+. This theory is based on the collectivist, large power distance nature of the Asian cultures, which coordinates well with the nature of Ghana. Professor Hofstede proposed that people should find their rightful place, in peace and harmony with their environment.

Theory T advocates that tradition is a source of wisdom; therefore, the average human being has an inherent dislike of change and will rightly avoid it if he or she can. Conversely, Theory T+ supports that change is a natural function, and resisting it will lead to negative consequences. Unlike the Theory X and Theory Y of the United States, which are opposites of one another, Theory T and Theory T+ fit harmoniously together and, particularly Theory T, are much more compatible with the Ghanaian culture.

A further comparison of the leadership styles that are developed in the United States to those that are developed in Asian cultures can be made when considering Abraham H. Maslow's Hierarchy of Needs Theory and I-Ching. The Hierarchy of Needs Theory was based on the United States individualistic culture where people work toward self-actualization as an end, whereas the I-Ching is based on the collectivist ideals of Asian cultures where self-actualization is viewed as a means to an end—to serve the group better.

Specifically, the Hierarchy of Needs includes five progressive stages of needs including basic needs, safety needs, social needs, esteem needs, and, finally, self-actualization needs. The I-Ching expands these stages to better accommodate the Asian's desire for betterment of society. To accomplish this they have added the stages of social awareness, social contribution, social altruism, and multi-dimensional development to the original Hierarchy of Needs. Because of the collectivist nature of the Ghanaian cultures and their concern for relationships with others, the I-Ching is better suited to the leadership needs of Ghana than the individualistic-based Hierarchy of Needs (Adler, 1991).

Another theory that is often recognized in the United States is the Relationship-Oriented and Task-Oriented Leadership Theory. This theory focusses on leader–subordinate relationships. It states that some leaders are, by nature, relationship-oriented, while other leaders are task-oriented. It is clear that culture would have a strong impact on these types of leadership styles. In Ghana, although the culture has a large power distance, they are also collectivists, indicating that relationships are still a strong priority. For this reason, relationship-oriented leaders would undoubtedly be more effective in Ghana than task-oriented leaders.

Another theory that is based on nearly the same principle as the United States Relationship-Oriented and Task-Oriented Theory is Japan's PM Theory of Leadership. There is one fundamental difference, however, in that Japan's PM leadership theory emphasizes groups and the United States theory emphasizes individuals. In this theory, the P stands for performance, or forming and reaching group goals, and the M stands for maintenance, or preserving group social stability.

Although Japan's PM Theory of Leadership is focussed on groups, which would be more compatible with Ghana's collectivist nature than the United States Relationship-Oriented and Task-Oriented Leadership Theory, the PM Theory was developed under Japan's small power distance environment, which contradicts with the large power distance environment of Ghana. For this reason, this theory would also not be successful in the Ghanaian culture.

Initiating Structure and Consideration is also a leadership theory that is often used in the United States. This theory compares leadership styles as either focussed on structure, which would be concerned with organizing and getting things done, or on consideration, which is more concerned with building trust and relationships. Once again, Ghana's collectivist ideals would no doubt classify their leaders as more closely related to the consideration aspects of this theory.

Effect of Culture on Leadership

The leadership characteristics that are necessary in an organization may vary depending on a specific situation. The United States has developed three types of leaders, each with their own leadership qualities. The first is called an innovator. This type of leader introduces new ideas, controls their subordinates, and is most commonly used during a crisis. A second type of leader, an implementer, specializes in developing structure and providing a stable working environment. The third type of leader that the United States has identified is the pacifier. This type of leader provides only general guidance to subordinates, allowing them freedom and independence within the organization.

Of course, a nation's culture has a strong impact on the type of leader that is most appropriate in that country. A country with a small power distance nature, such as the United States, would probably work best with a pacifier-type leader. Whereas, a country with a large power distance nature, such as Ghana, would require the strong leadership style that an implementer-type leader could provide.

It is also clear that the values of the political system of a country affect the organizational leadership. Political structures usually reflect central national culture values, including ideas about the most appropriate and effective type of leadership. Countries with democratic political values and system of government, such as the United States, prefer participative leadership in the workplace. However, countries that have had autocratic political regimes and limited experience with democracy, such as Ghana, have low expectations for worker participation in organizational decision-making, and use non-participatory management philosophies.

Conclusion

Ghanaian organizations function in an environment of acute resource scarcity, economic uncertainty, and highly centralized political power. In addition, Ghanaian leaders tend to view their authority, professional competence, and information as personal possessions, rather than impersonal concomitants of their organizational role, and as a source of status and prestige. However, with improvement of their leadership skills, the economic standing of Ghana may continue to improve over time. After all, it would be a critical mistake to believe that conditions cannot improve. People's thinking does not remain static from generation to generation.

Cultural factors do change gradually over time as new technologies are introduced into the society.

Case Questions

1. Discuss the cultural aspects that, according to this case study, form Ghana's leadership style.
2. Using Hofstede's analysis of culture, describe the culture of Ghana in all dimensions.
3. Discuss the economic/political factors that may contribute to its leadership style.
4. What roles have outside powers such as the United Nations, the United States, and so on, played in the development of Ghana?
5. Research Ghana's leaders and compare three of them in reference to political and personal backgrounds, and leadership style.

Effect of Culture on International Staffing

Staffing means finding and hiring the necessary qualified people for the necessary job. Staffing internationally can be a tricky subject. Sometimes it is better to staff people in the host country, due to their knowledge of the culture and co-workers. Other times it is better to staff people outside of the culture, due to their technical knowledge, knowledge of the firm, and work ethic.

This challenge is made more difficult by a lack of information or the extent to which various practices are universal versus culture specific. Although there have been a few comparisons of national differences in approaches to selection, these have been limited in scope to only a few countries. Typically, these selections stem from the same region, which have not involved a large sample size, and have provided little in the way of a theoretical framework for explaining differences when they are found (Ryan et al., 1999).

As stated earlier, hiring people locally is probably the most common practice of staffing. This is a popular practice because the local people know the culture and usually do not need any special training to adapt to the new culture. Another plus to hiring locally is that the new employees do not tend to get home-sick. In addition, by hiring people locally, the wages tend to be low compared to bringing someone in from abroad. Hiring host-country workers has its advantages and disadvantages. Some advantages include:

- Being familiar with the local environment and culture—they know their language already, their culture, and customs.
- Host-country workers can sometimes be productive right away—they do not need to adapt to the local environment and can sometimes be productive from the beginning of the assignment.
- Knowing local business subtleties—they possess knowledge of the subtleties of the local business situation.

- Goodwill—they may enhance the company's image, that they appreciate working for someone of the same nationality.
- Usually less expensive to employ—salaries are often lower.
- Broadens and influences the local talent pool while bringing new perspectives to the firm.
- Promotes a polycentric (many centers of authority and control) philosophy.

Some disadvantages include:

- Loyalty may be to the country, not to the company—host-country managers may favor national policy over the company's interest.
- Often it is difficult to find qualified people at the local level who possess the right skills for the assignment.
- More difficult to assess abilities—it is usually more difficult to assess locals' skills and abilities than to assess someone who is working for the corporation.
- Workers may not understand the corporation's culture—the local most likely does not possess sufficient knowledge of the firm's policies and culture, including the informal decision-making network in the home office.
- May not be mobile or may not want to move once they are at a job until they retire.

Cultural Impacts on Employee Motivation

Employee motivation and job performance are important because every culture is different when it comes to what motivates people to be productive in their jobs. Cultural differences need to be noticed to avoid problems that might occur. Some of the ways to alleviate such problems might include training and preparation, study of language, current issues within the countries, and daily life interactions.

Culture affects employee motivation in many different ways. For example, in any culture, an employee's job performance will improve if the company implements goal-setting, reward programs and a performance rating and feedback system. In the United States, people are high on being individualistic and overseas employees are communitarianism- or group-orientated. When a person is in the situation of being put into an environment that they are not familiar with, it causes tension and can decrease job performance. That is why Americans have seen a growing emphasis on teamwork in organizations. In a constantly changing and competitive global business environment, it is necessary for organizations to increase efficiency, productivity, and profitability through these practices.

Another difficulty with culture is communication. Employee motivation will decrease if they do not understand what their boss, peers, or subordinates are trying to communicate to them. Not being able to understand what a person wants or why they want it done a certain way is a major problem when you look at culture and motivation. This will ultimately lead to miscommunication, employee resentment, and poor morale. When these characteristics are put together, it is easy to find a major decrease in employee motivation and increase in tension among employees.

For instance, as stated in the *Journal of Management Development* ("Developing Expatriates' Cross-cultural Sensitivity," 1997) when conducting business, people in high context cultures, including the Chinese, Korean, Japanese, Vietnamese, Arab, Greek, and Spanish cultures, prefer to establish social trust first, develop personal relations and goodwill, and make agreements based on general trust, and are likely to conduct slow and ritualistic negotiations. People in these cultures prefer that messages not be structured directly. Instead, they prefer that a message be indirect, building up to the point, and stating conclusions last. Individuals in low context cultures, including Italian, English, North American, Scandinavian, Swiss, and German cultures, get down to business first, value expertise and performance, like agreement by specific, legalistic contracts and prefer to conduct negotiations as efficiently as possible. Individuals in these cultures prefer that messages are structured directly; that they get immediately to the point and state conclusions or bottom lines first ("Developing Expatriates' Cross-cultural Sensitivity," 1997).

Observing cultural differences and respecting them is not usually enough. Being able to come up with approaches to solve problems arising from cultural differences and helping the organization achieve common goals is usually a necessity.

Some ways that can aid in avoiding cultural differences are to have thorough training and preparation, a good hiring process, a study of the language, and be familiar with current issues and daily life interactions. If all these are integrated into an organization, it will help the organization to avoid a disastrous situation. Many adjustment factors such as personality, expectations, motivation, and prior international experience can affect how an employee's motivation will be when they enter into a new and different culture. Personality factors such as flexibility, open-mindedness, interdependence, risk-taking, and inquisitiveness need to be looked at. This will have a direct impact on how a person will react and adjust to being in a new environment. As a manager, it is necessary to look at all of these different factors in order to choose the right employee who could be motivated for the international assignment.

Overall, an employee's cultural values, beliefs, and norms will increase and decrease motivation. For example, Americans put a major emphasis on time while other countries do not.

Reward and Punishment

When dealing with reward and punishment, it is hard to distinguish between what is right or wrong. For example, in the United States, rewards are given to people by promotions or opportunities because of what they did to deserve it. Meaning, with good, hard work, people can make more money or even get a better job in the business they work at. In some societies, rewards can be in the form of trophies, food, and promotion. When rewarded, you feel that you have been appreciated and that is what reward is all about. It states in *The New Webster's Dictionary and Thesaurus of the English Language* (1993, 852), that reward means "something given or promised in recognition of service rendered." Understanding what motivates employees in different cultures is essential to the success of US corporations doing business globally. The following are some of the issues companies should look at when considering ways to motivate, recognize, and reward employees in different cultures.

Table 9.1   How to Reward your Global Workforce

Country	
Japan	Individual recognition programs have not worked well because Japan has a collectivist culture and workers do not want to be conspicuous. Individual pay-for-performance is considered potentially disruptive to pleasant working relationships and is not used. Instead, year-end bonuses should be given based on loyalty, years of service and one's family situation. Team awards have been more effective—including salary increases and an allowance system—as incentives for outstanding performance.
Russia	Money is the most important factor in determining whether a Russian will take and keep a job, but it is not the only one. Russians want benefits such as pension plans, healthcare, regular performance reviews, and lunch! In Soviet times, most offices had a cafeteria, which offered a modest midday meal for a pittance.
Scandinavia	Employees have a voice in management decisions, particularly those that relate to compensation, safety, and capital expenditures. It is important to incorporate new employees into the corporate culture.
Korea	The Korean government has a long tradition of prize and discipline incentive systems to enhance productivity. Few group incentives are used. Employees who have served more than 20 years can receive a special award of 10 days' paid leave.
Sweden	Workforce management is based on the premise that employees are willing and able to do a good job. A Swedish manager is thought of as a good listener and a coach—motivating staff and leading employees through principles of cooperation and agreement. Sweden has a high rate of employed women and a reputation for having a high ratio of family-friendly men who are seeking a better integration of work and family. Therefore, there is a broad acceptance of home-based telecommuting.
Latin America	Companies are very concerned about the family and family values. When companies hire a person, it is as if they are hiring the entire family.

Reprinted with permission: Bob Nelson, "Motivating Workers Worldwide," *Global Workforce*, November 1998. Bob Nelson, PhD, is president of Nelson Motivation Inc., and author of *1001 Ways to Reward Employees*, *1001 Ways to Energize Employees*, *Managing for Dummies*, and *The 1001 Rewards and Recognition Fieldbook: The Complete Guide*. For more information, please visit www.nelson-motivation.com.

Promotion

Promotion is the act or fact of being raised in position or rank. Promotion means success in something we have accomplished. The dissatisfaction perceived by local managers in foreign subsidiaries of Japanese firms appears to be largely due to the failure to promote and delegate authority. The issue of promoting local employees to higher-level management positions is a great concern for foreign firms of any nationality where there are both expatriate and local managers. When comparing the Japanese to the United States, the complaints with regard to the lack of promotion are documented by a number of lawsuits filed by American management personnel against Japanese companies.

In American society, the business atmosphere is more laid back and easy-going; Americans do not want to have to work quite as hard to be promoted. In Singapore, on the other hand, a promotion is hard work. The Singaporeans are very hard workers, and much more serious. The turnover rate for Americans is higher, unfortunately, because they are not afraid to take new chances, such as switching jobs. Because there are so many jobs available for them to choose from, Americans tend to take the risk in their jobs for others with more opportunity. Unlike America, Japanese have limited work due to having so many workers. Therefore, they cannot take as many chances and they usually stay at the same job their whole life.

Furthermore, in Canada and Australia, promotions are based on merit, where the tendency is for people to look after themselves and their immediate family. In China and the South American culture, where the tendency is for people to belong to groups and to look after each other in exchange for loyalty, they have a weaker work ethic and promotions are based on seniority.

Managing a Culturally Diverse Workforce

For a manager to be able to manage effectively with a culturally diverse workforce, he or she must examine the organization culture. The manager will have to identify the elements of the culture and the basis from which behaviors develop, and also determine whether the roots support or hinder aspirations for managing diversity. Finally, the manager has to support the beliefs that facilitate managing diversity.

To manage diversity is to provide an environment where all employees feel that they are valued by and contributing to an organization. Externally this means that organizations are flexible about changes occurring in world markets. Being able to manage a diverse workforce has become a very critical management skill. Corporations that can maintain such a workforce in an encouraging environment can save the upset and costs of bias and discrimination lawsuits. An even greater incentive is that corporations that encourage diversity among their employees are better positioned in both differentiated domestic and global markets. It will provide an organization with an inside track on cultures to motivate and help workers in fulfilling organizational and personal goals. This will promote social accord among employees. Therefore, if a manager is looking to become effective at managing a diverse workforce, he or she needs to observe the cultures, employees, and the company's culture to develop the best way to have success in their organization.

Conclusion

As we have seen, being an international manager has many challenges. Culture affects employee motivation, planning, and implementation of goals and objectives, organizing, staffing, leading, controlling, communication, and promotion.

All international managers need to be aware of the implications that culture has on the different aspects of managing in the international environment. With employee motivation, international managers need to remember to implement goal-setting, performance feedback, and valued rewards. This will help the increase of employee's job performance. In addition, to help avoid cultural differences, managers need to implement training and preparation, the study of language, current issues, and daily life interactions.

With the planning and implementation of culture, many businesses will look for highly skilled and motivated individuals to work for their company. One issue international managers may encounter is the Affirmative Action Law in America. This law covers a set of public policies and initiatives designed to help eliminate past and present discrimination based on race, color, religion, sex, or national origin. Affirmative action could be handled in different ways depending on the culture. Knowing this law for an international manager will be of great help.

Organizing, staffing, leading, and controlling are very important for an international manager. As shown, organizing is designed so you can meet your goals. For an international manager to staff the business, you need to look for the most qualified and educated worker so these goals will be met. To accomplish these goals you need to direct the workers. Once you have completed your process of organizing, staffing, and leading, you need to take control and change whatever needs to be corrected to make the business succeed.

Looking at the whole prospect of culture, communication is the most important process. To be a good international manager, you need to get within the culture so that what you are trying to communicate can be understood. Without understanding, the communication process is not accomplished.

When dealing with reward, punishment, and promotion, it varies from culture to culture. This may be difficult for international managers to deal with because this may not be what they believe in. Good international managers can put their beliefs aside and do what is best for that culture.

To become a good international manager, you need to be able to incorporate all of these concepts before being put into the job. You will also need to get to know the culture inside and out. If you are open-minded and able to accept a new culture, then you could be a step ahead in becoming a good international manager.

Case Study

Adapted from "Transplanting Corporate Cultures Globally"

Because corporate culture is the language that communicates a company's mission, the ability to transplant that culture from one country to another is critical to the success of an international company. You do not have to speak different languages to need an interpreter. The USAir–British Airways partnership is an example of that. What happens when two English-speaking groups get together and have to learn each other's way of doing business? Culture shock.

In January 1993, London-based British Airways and Arlington, Virginia-based USAir formed an alliance designed to benefit both companies financially and operationally. USAir wanted an international presence over the long term, but lacked the resources to purchase international routes. The airline was looking for a strategic partner. The alliance allows USAir access to the strong international presence and markets of the British company, while giving British Airways entry to the US domestic market, so that it can continue its expansion throughout the world.

Now, the Britons and Americans have to transmit their values and blend their corporate cultures as well as their workforces. "The mission we have essentially is winning the hearts and minds of our employees—at both companies—with respect to the benefit of the alliance," says Ollie Lawrence Jr., vice president of employee communications at USAir (and previously assistant vice president of employee relations). "We need to develop an understanding of each other's cultures."

The companies are in the process of doing that. First, there is an exchange program in which management personnel from one company shadow a counterpart at the other company to learn how they do business, make decisions, and manage employees. For example, an individual from British Airways will work side by side in Washington, DC with USAir's director of employee relations, learning how the company makes key personnel decisions. In turn, the USAir individual will then go to London to spend several weeks at British Airways' headquarters. It is one way for people to begin to understand and be sensitive to the internal workings of the other company.

Second, there will be corporate training programs so that key individuals will be able to recognize cultural differences and deal with them. Third, they are developing working committees within major departments of both companies, such as operations, marketing, and sales, to hammer out programs and procedures by which both carriers can work as partners.

"We recognize there are some cultural differences between the two companies in the way they operate and manage," says Lawrence. "By recognizing those differences, we'll be more successful as we work together."

One of the more surprising differences is language. Although both groups speak English, vocabulary and style can cause problems. Cautions Lawrence, these can be very subtle but can contribute to creating stubborn barriers. For example, he says, the British tend to be more conservative and straightforward than the Americans are. They are deliberate in the way in which they communicate and do business.

"We want to identify those significant cultural differences so they don't get in the way of our being able to manage this alliance effectively," he says. "With respect to this partnership, each company has to appreciate that the other has its own culture. We are not a merger. But we also want to recognize the shared vision that created the alliance and identify mutual values so both groups of employees will rally behind that vision."

Once management establishes a clear vision statement, the staff will create a focused message to communicate with employees. Already, both companies use the weekly employee newsletters and e-mail to tackle corporate-culture issues head-on. Internal company handouts detail the benefits of the USAir–British Airways alliance to passengers, to local communities and to USAir and British Airways workers. A handout of Interesting Facts underscores the independence and interdependence of each carrier in the alliance.

The way in which each enterprise communicates the alliance to its workforce is different. "At USAir, we believe this alliance is going to help the long-term future of the airline. Ultimately, by entering into a strategic alliance to be part of a global airline network, it will help with the job security of our employees," says Lawrence.

British Airways will have to communicate its rationale a little differently since it already is an international carrier. It wants to be a predominant international carrier through the development of partnerships around the world.

In addition to the more formal communications, the companies are developing a line of apparel for employees that will heighten awareness of the alliance. They are also co-hosting special events, such as fish and chip parties.

How do the companies know if the cultural communications are working? By measuring employee reaction. USAir conducts random telephone interviews and leads focus groups. An outside consultant meets with a cross section of employees to learn about their understanding of the alliance. The feedback provides management with information about where to put more emphasis or provide more explanation.

Equally important, simply by concentrating on these questions, it reinforces the message that management is trying to convey to the workers. In other words, employees know that the company does not measure something that is not important. "I think managers need to recognize that messages are sent not only through formal communications. They are sent through management action or inaction—how an organization rewards its employees, what is rewarded, and what is not. It's reinforced through what's measured," says Lawrence. "If the company measures productivity, that tells employees that the company is concerned about how many units get out. If it measures service, that tells employees service is important."

What the managers communicate and how it communicates the message builds an understanding of the company mission. That is one reason these business partners stress personal communication along with the more formalized ways. Executives have adopted cities that they must visit three or four times a year. They reinforce the alliance, answer questions, and explain some of the specifics of the partnership in employee meetings.

Reprinted with permission: Charlene Marmer Solomon (1993), "Transplanting Corporate Cultures Globally," *Personnel Journal*, 72(10), October, 78–88.

Case Questions

1. What is the strategic reason for the USAir–British Airways partnership?
2. What in the case are specified as value and corporate culture differences?
3. What is the specific mission of the strategic alliance?
4. What are the three-prong approaches used to achieve set objectives?
5. What is the communication style used to achieve the strategic alliance objective and how do the companies know if the cultural communications are working?

Chapter Review

The literature on international business is filled with examples of business miscues when US corporations attempted to operate in an international context. Often the managers were not prepared for the cultural environment of international business. Involvement in planning fosters a great personal commitment to the plan and to the organization. One type of planning used today is strategic planning. To some, strategic planning is a glorified repacking of old-fashioned business planning, and to others, it is just a modification of long-range planning. From an overall perspective, the strategic planning process integrates elements of three management-planning concepts: the annual business plan, diversification planning, and long-range planning. The strategic planning process benefits a business in many different ways. The second type of planning used today is operational planning. The primary difference between strategic planning and operational planning is that in a strategic plan it primarily concerns the upper management, but in operational planning every manager and key employee within the organization must understand the operational plan and determine the results for which he or she is held accountable. The involvement of operating executives, managers, and key employees in producing operational plans for the total organization are all parts of operational planning. The operational plan depends on the contributions of key people at all levels.

Culture is very different from place to place and country to country. Knowing different cultures is very important to succeed as an international manager. Effective communication among people from different cultures is often difficult because cultures vary in terms of how explicitly people send and receive verbal messages. The English language is rapidly becoming the international language of business. Managers experience different types of communication with different types of employees.

Culture influences the manager's decision in the areas of planning, organizing, staffing, leading, and controlling. Conducting international business would be a lot easier if everyone acted and believed similarly. However, different cultures act and behave differently based on their values and beliefs. Beliefs are opinions that people feel strongly about, and they differ from culture to culture, making a unified system of managing impossible. Like beliefs, values differ from one person to the other and obviously from culture to culture. Culture underpins strategy, affects communication process elements, and influences strategic relationships.

International business communication and planning is also affected by cross-cultural differences in temporal conception or the understanding of time. In the complicated world of business, many different variables make business very complex and confusing. Each culture has a different way of dealing with planning and has different values, ethics, and goals. Culture distinguishes the members of one group of people from another. Individual culture profile is not only shaped by national culture, but also by family, religion, neighborhood, education, profession, corporate culture, social class, gender, race, generation. Business is not conducted in an identical fashion from culture to culture. Similarly, international communication is even further strengthened when business people can anticipate areas of communication. Problems in business communication conducted across cultures often arise when participants from one culture are unable to understand culturally determined differences in communication practices, traditions, and thought processing in planning.

Culture affects employee motivation in many different ways. For example, an employee's job performance, in any culture, will improve if the practices of goal-setting, performance feedback, and valued rewards are implemented. When considering promotions, rewards and discipline, the first thing that a manager needs to do is examine the organization culture. With employee motivation, international managers need to remember to implement goal-setting, performance feedback, and valued rewards. When dealing with reward, punishment, and promotion, it varies from culture to culture. Good international managers can put their beliefs aside and do what is best for that culture.

Chapter Questions

1. What is culture? Discuss culture in the context of individuals, nations, and organizations.
2. Discuss the cultural perspectives of international management.
3. What are ways to encourage motivation and productivity among Asians? Europeans? Africans?
4. How do cross-cultural communications affect the methods and outcomes of international business?
5. What are the basic skills in operating, managing, and controlling a global business?
6. What are some contemporary issues in the global business arena?
7. Discuss the concept of face-saving and describe a country, and its culture, specific to this concept.

Understanding Culture Exercise

Think of all the people from different cultural backgrounds that you interact with on a daily basis, for example, co-workers, friends, student peers, neighbors, retail and restaurant employees, gas station attendants, and so on. Think of an interaction you have had with one of them that puzzled you or left you with an unusual impression.

1. Note your impression(s) of the person's behavior to which you had a reaction.
2. What aspects of the behavior (that is, cultural background) were positive?
3. What aspects of the behavior (that is, cultural background) were negative?
4. In what way(s) do you feel their behavior goes against or coincides with your own implicit cultural norms and values?
5. Describe what cultural norms and values their behavior(s) could be based on.
6. What significance does being of a particular nationality (for example, Hispanic, Italian, African American, Israeli, American, Hmong, Taiwanese, and so on) have in how the behavior was demonstrated?

Chapter 10

Cross-cultural Training and Expatriate Assignments

Selecting the wrong person for a job can lead to failure and be an unexpected and unbudgeted cost for a company. The risk is even higher for expatriate assignments. Mendenhall et al. (1995) define expatriate as anyone who is "living or working in a country of which he or she is not a citizen and who can be classified as possessing skills critical to the success of the performance of foreign subsidiaries." As Groenewald and Neubeiser (2000) indicate, the term expatriate generally refers to an employee who is on a long-term assignment outside their home country (Mayerhofer et al., 2004). According to Forster and Regnet (2000), an expatriate assignment involves relocation of their family and personal lives to a different environment and, as such, it has been recognized as a difficult and strategically significant aspect of international human resource management (Mayerhofer et al., 2004). Regardless the definition, it is widely known and agreed upon that international assignments require extra treatment when considering the employees, families, different culture of the country, politics, and business practices of the mixed organization.

Increasingly, since the 1980s, the matters associated with selection, training, appraisal, and compensation have been reconsidered in the context of expatriate appointments, as well as the general difficulties and costs of the expatriation and repatriation development (Bennett et al., 2000), hence it is important for the company to learn some key predictors of success, as well as common mistakes that lead to failure for expatriate assignees. In addition, the increasing number of international assignments creates many challenges to international human resources (IHR) departments and to those who are moving to work abroad. According to Hechanova et al. (2003), apart from changes in job responsibilities, expatriates typically need to adjust to a different climate, a new culture, and a variety of language barriers.

Planning an Expatriate Assignment

At the start, an expatriate assignment takes considerable planning and preparation. In planning, the following are points to consider:

- The package should appropriately support the employee's financial, family, and career needs
- The company should provide cross-cultural preparation
- There should be a plan in place for repatriation opportunities.

Time, money, and resources are wasted if management training for functioning in a multicultural environment is less than satisfactory. Cross-cultural orientation programs are designed to teach members of one culture ways of interacting effectively, with minimal interpersonal misunderstanding, in another culture. This general definition can be applied to most cross-cultural orientation programs. Specific training objectives must be developed according to specific needs and purposes of the organization.

Cross-cultural preparation helps to alleviate two concerns for the expatriate; the culture shock that a new country can produce, and unsuccessful communication on the job. Whether or not a company has a formal cross-cultural training program in place, it is clearly an advantage to become familiar with the host country's history, customs, and etiquette. Regardless of the cross-cultural preparation or how often an employee has visited the host country, there is still a difference between theory and reality. When the assignee finally begins living and working abroad, the common trait that seems to be shared among successful expatriates is their ability to be flexible and adaptable. Companies should recruit only those who see an overseas posting as an opportunity, not an obligation. Expatriates who try to recreate their home country lifestyle overseas will not be able to adjust enough into their new culture.

Cross-cultural Business Etiquette and Sensitivity

Sensitivity is important when working with different cultures, and international managers must be aware of the cultural differences versus stereotypes and view these differences as resources rather than as constraints. The valuing of culture and diversity is no longer merely a social goal. With globalization changing so rapidly, managers realize that they are now required to learn new techniques and skills for understanding, motivating, and empowering each employee regardless of race, gender, or religion. We are a world of diverse populations and groups, and the success of international business depends largely on our ability to effectively communicate, reach mutual understandings, and to realize that in diversity there is strength.

According to Ethnic Harvest (2001, July 5), a multicultural resource organization, one can take ten steps toward cultural sensitivity:

1. Take the initiative to make contact with the "international," the "outsider," the "foreigner," even if language is a problem at first.
2. Show respect for their culture and language. They may be in culture shock and grieving over the "loss" of their culture or at least the fear of losing their cultural identity.
3. Learn how to pronounce names correctly. Their name is as important to them as yours is to you. Practice saying it until you pronounce it as closely as

possible.

4. Be sensitive to their feelings about their homeland. Developing nations are not as poor, backward, or uneducated as North Americans tend to think.

5. When speaking English, do so slowly and clearly. Remember, raising your voice does not make English more understandable.

6. Show that you care about them as people and that you honestly want to help.

7. Take time to listen. If you do not understand, or, likewise, you are not understood, take time to find out why. Explain or ask questions. A key question might be, "Would you help me understand?"

8. Be careful about promises. In English, we express the subjunctive (possibility, probability, or contingency) in a way that is sometimes misunderstood by internationals.

9. The key to developing and maintaining a long-term relationship with internationals is a friendship built of mutual respect and a desire for understanding.

10. Do not allow cultural differences (or preferences) to become the basis for criticism and judgments. Differences are neither good nor bad. What we do with them is the key.

Familiarization with cultural characteristics, history, values, belief systems, and behaviors provides the knowledge of that culture. Americans may see the French as arrogant and conceited, who do not want to speak English and who are rude to tourists. Alternatively, the French may see Americans as people who are arrogant and righteous, people who only think about money and people who do not take criticism well (Rochefort, 2004). Developing sensitivity and understanding of another culture involves changes in terms of attitudes and values. Knowing that cultural differences as well as similarities exist, without assigning values to those cultural differences, is the epitome of cultural sensitivity.

If employees are not properly trained in culture, it has negative consequences on the business. A company who can afford to become a global firm should be sensible when it comes to international and cross-cultural training. Here are some guidelines for employees who deal with people from different cultures:

- Know and understand your own culture.
- Study why one culture values certain things and behaves in certain ways. Know the other culture.
- Make an effort to understand why the other culture holds the values they do and behaves as they do.
- See the strengths in the other cultures.
- Respect the other culture. It is the ability to create relationships and work through others that leads to effectiveness.
- Recognize your ethnocentric thoughts and behaviors.
- Listen actively to others for guidance that you and the organization will benefit from.

Managers should also be aware of some cross-cultural communication guidelines. They are as follows:

- Understanding the home and host countries cultural preferences—nature, time, action, space, and so on.
- Do not assume the other culture is similar to your own until you have received confirmation. Beware of jokes. They may not communicate well.
- Speak at a comfortable pace for your foreign associates. Do not raise your voice. Use visuals and print to support what you say.
- Break information into small pieces and present one piece at a time.
- Repeat what was said, summarize, confirm, and clarify.
- Do not prejudge or rush into hasty evaluations. Respect differences. Listen, observe, and describe rather than evaluate.
- Do not settle for the surface meaning. Patiently, search for what is really being communicated.
- Respect the appropriate level of formality in the other culture.
- Avoid taboos and pay particular attention to your non-verbal behavior.
- Above all, work at making relationships not just deals.

Communication is a very important factor in any type of management; however, as stated in previous chapters, it should be a priority in international endeavors. Below are some ways to limit any barriers when communicating with another culture.

Language

Use simple and slow-paced speech; avoid jargon, slang, and unusual idioms. Check for understanding and attempt to learn at least the basics of the other language. Avoid negative reactions such as, "That does not make sense," "What a strange idea," or "We do not do that here or where I come from."

Assumptions

Be clear of what certain statements mean in the culture you are dealing with. "Soon," "in a minute," "just a moment," "I am on my way," "no problem" and "yes" may mean different things in different cultures. Be realistic with expectations. Seek to learn all you can.

Stereotypes

Be curious about the new culture. In addition, be alert to the fact that the other side may be working with stereotypes of you. An example of this may be "the arrogant Frenchman" or "the winning American."

Hasty Judgment

Check for correct interpretation of statements before reaching a conclusion or opinion. Keep an objective frame of mind.

Place/Time

Be aware of time differences and utilization of time in different cultures. Relax, and do not rush. Take time to learn the rules of the culture. Build relationships over time.

Gesture

Certain gestures mean different things in different cultures. Learn those of the culture that you will be joining. Keep hold of your sense of humor. Be personable. Reach mutual understandings. Maintain confidence in your own abilities and strengths.

Status

Observe status differences in most cultures in the world. Differences to ranks and hierarchical levels are important in Latin American, Asian, African, and European cultures.

Enough time should be allowed for managers to be cross-culturally trained. This is not something that can be rushed or that a corporation should expect a manager to learn on his or her own. The impact on a corporation of cross-cultural training depends on the manager and on the corporation itself. If they choose the proper training and allow enough time for the manager to learn, then the results should be positive. If the corporation does not provide effective training and the manager does not have enough time to learn properly the other culture, then the results could be unsuccessful, such as losing clients and money or even a whole branch or division of the corporation that is located in a foreign country.

Importance of Cross-cultural Training

Implementing a cross-cultural training program is an integral part of the international assignment process. Cross-cultural training enhances the capabilities of personnel on international business assignments (Weaver, 1998a, 1998b, 188). Often expatriates going overseas, as well as foreign national employees coming to the US, experience what has come to be termed as "culture shock." Culture shock develops from the anxiety that results from losing the familiarities of the home culture while living in a host location.

Many things can hasten culture shock, such as loss of familiar surroundings, activities, and comforts, a diminished ability towards interpersonal communication and the personal loss of identity as the employee knows it. These three causes are interrelated; however, they may not be directly obvious to the employee.

The initial time in a new culture is exciting for the expatriate; however, as time progresses, they begin to feel the stress of adjusting and can begin to feel low, depressed, and even physically ill. In time, this adjustment process eases. Finally, they adjust and adapt to the new culture by learning how to cope and operate in the new environment (Weaver, 1998a, 1998b, 187). It is apparent that the confusion of a cross-cultural adjustment to a new culture can cause unneeded concern for a person on international assignment. It will influence the effectiveness of an employee, on and off the job, as well as affect their families. In fact, human resource personnel indicate that assignment failure is most commonly due to expatriates and their families not adjusting successfully to the host culture.

Thus, one goal of cross-cultural training programs is to give international assignees the tools that will help them through this adjustment period. In addition to helping the assignee adjust, training will also provide information about the culture they will be residing in, develop his or her skills for cross-cultural negotiation and interaction, and learn about one's own culture and preconceived perceptions of others.

A point often overlooked is that training should also be provided to family members who will be accompanying the expatriate. The employee will have the support and structure of his or her work and other expatriate workers in the office, while the family members often have a more difficult time in the cultural adjustment process, since they may have greater daily contact with the host society.

Types of Cross-cultural Training

There is a multitude of organizations providing cross-cultural training, utilizing many different methods in their programs. Weaver (1998b) has identified four areas that training should assist expatriates in:

1. Anticipating the stress of cross-cultural adjustment.
2. Facilitating the development of coping strategies.
3. Helping the expatriate feel confident that they will be able to adjust successfully to the new culture.
4. Assisting the expatriate in understanding the process of cross-cultural adaptation.

Additionally, Gudykunst, Guzley and Hammer (1996, 66) have outlined four basic categories of training methods:

1. Didactic culture general
2. Didactic culture specific
3. Experiential culture general
4. Experiential culture specific.

The didactic approaches emphasize lectures and other types of presentations, whereas the experiential approaches utilize more role-plays and simulations that require active participation from the trainees. The culture general approach emphasizes overall cultural concepts in lieu of specific information about a particular culture, which is used in the culture-specific training methods.

James Downs (1970) lists four models of training as:

1. The intellectual model
2. The area simulation model
3. The self-awareness model
4. The cultural awareness model.

The intellectual model consists of readings and lectures about the host culture. The area simulation model is a culture-specific training program. It involves simulation of future experiences and practice in functioning in the new culture. The self-awareness model is based on the assumption that understanding and accepting oneself is critical to understanding a person from another culture. Sensitivity training is a main component of this method. Lastly, the cultural awareness model assumes that for a person to function successfully in another culture, he/she must learn the principles of behavior that exist across cultures. These programs prepare individuals to work with people who think and behave differently, and hold different beliefs and values. Other sources of widely used cross-cultural training methods are noted here.

The Culture Assimilator

The culture assimilator is an area simulation program that is culture-specific. The basic goal of this program is to prepare managers to respond to specific situations in a particular country. It is a programmed learning experience designed to expose members of one culture to the basic customs and values of another country. Some problems may arise when using this method, such as the lack of field assessment, long-range evaluation of assimilator-trained persons, and that the program focusses on the foreign culture and that culture's particular characteristics and differences.

The Contrast-American

The contrast-American method of cross-cultural training is a technique that was developed to simulate psychologically and culturally significant interpersonal aspects of the overseas situation in a live role-play encounter. An example of this would be the American wanting to get the work done, while the contrast-American's desire is to preserve the status relation between the manager and the employees. Following the role-play, the trainees receive feedback from the trainers. One difficulty with this method is that if the role-players are not well trained, the technique is less effective. Another problem is the culture general approach and the applicability and transfer of concepts to a particular situation.

The Self-confrontation Training Technique

The self-confrontation training technique uses a videotape—a trainee plays a role with a person from another culture in a simulated cross-cultural encounter, and the situation is videotaped. Following the encounter, the tape is played for the trainee, and the trainer points out strengths and weaknesses in both the verbal and non-verbal behavior of the trainee. The trainee can observe responses and evaluate behavior for improved performance in future role-play situations and for actual performance in a different culture. This is a culture general approach, although the situations can also be specific to a particular culture. Retention and application of these skills over a long period have not been demonstrated. Another problem concerns the videotaping of the experimental and the control group. The experimental group may have done better during the encounter because they are at ease with the videotape equipment and the control subjects may not have been thus, resulting in a difference in performance.

As noted above, several methods and models can be used to train an employee before his or her assignment. An organization should choose the best cross-cultural training that suits their needs, and will most adequately prepare their managers.

Effectiveness of Cross-cultural Training Programs

Cross-cultural training gives expatriates and assignees a chance at succeeding in the host culture. In the case of an international employee, there is little question as to the assignee's technical qualifications and skills needed to fulfill the assignment; companies go to extreme lengths to find the proper candidate for these assignments, often mentoring them in the home country for years before actually assigning them overseas. Since the technical skills are present, training acts as an enhancement to the position, facilitates the entry into another culture, and focusses on easing the adjustment in a foreign country for both the assignee and his or her family.

There have been many studies of cross-cultural training and its impact upon how effective and successful an expatriate is. Each study indicated that cross-cultural training has a very beneficial effect on the expatriate in terms of success and employee satisfaction factors. It was also determined that careful training led to a lower failure rate of international assignments.

A 1971 study by Richard D. Hays (1971, 40–46) asked American expatriates in Mexico City to evaluate four factors as the primary influences upon assignment success or failure. Hays (1971) found that job ability, defined as technical skill, organizational ability, and belief in mission, was seen as a prerequisite for the assignment and therefore crucial to its success. If the expatriate does not have the skills necessary to do the job, they cannot succeed. Relational abilities, defined as the ability to deal with local nationals and cultural empathy, was viewed as necessary for success. Hays (1971) identified a third factor, family situation, as one that can avoid failure. Family situation was defined as the level of adaptability and support from family members for the assignment. The family situation can have either a neutral or a negative effect upon the assignment. A fourth success factor, according to Hays (1971), is that of language skill, where a high skill level will assist with the assignment, but a low level may not necessarily have an adverse effect upon the assignment.

A study by Rosalie Tung (1981, 68–78) also identified several success factors that can be evaluated. The study's factors for success included: technical competence on the job; personality traits or relational abilities; family situation; and environmental variables. This study includes the success factors as discussed by Hays (1971), with the addition of environmental variables. Tung (1981) described environmental variables as the political, legal, and socio-economic system of the host country, which may be very different from what the transferee is used to, and will require adjustment. This might also be described as the cultural environment of the host location. Bhagat and Prien (1996) have also set forth several factors that affect the success of international assignments. They include individual, family, and job-specific attributes as well as the host country cultural environment.

The Expatriate Assignment and the Role of Human Resources

An international HR program means more than personnel management, training, and utilization; it should also offer more options in individual lives through learning. This will allow personnel to become more effective in their positions.

To assist in achieving a successful assignment, human resources will determine an expatriate compensation package that will meet the employee's personal, financial and quality of life goals. Components of a package include relocation assistance, compensation with protection against currency rate fluctuations and tax disparities, allowances for housing, education, hardship, danger pay, home leave, expatriate clubs, automobiles, and occasionally security guards and housekeepers. Home healthcare benefits should carry abroad and include the option of returning to the home country for major medical needs as well as annual well care examinations. Lastly, tax impactions include foreign tax and tax equalization obligations, which generally the company is responsible for while the employee is on assignment, but it is still important to explain the process to the expatriate to lesson his or her anxiety.

Finally, knowing the language of the host country helps enormously in expatriate assignments, but is not a necessity. English is the language of business, so an English speaker should be able to communicate in most places. However, expatriates should try to learn some of the host country's language, if different from their own. Such efforts contribute to establishing good relationships with staff and business partners (Schumacher, undated).

Of lesser, but certainly not less significant, importance are these suggestions. Self-nomination for the position is an indicator of success. If someone is interested in a country and a culture, then that is one of the best people to send. They are appreciative of being sent and are not looking for other kinds of perquisites to make it worthwhile to go. Nevertheless, it is important to remember that desire itself is not a guarantee of success. Certain personality traits, such as flexibility, willingness to learn, openness, sense of humor, adaptability, and ability to handle ambiguity, are helpful characteristics to those working abroad.

In addition to those core traits, there should be a good match between the management style of the person and the way business is conducted in the country. The differences between business cultures in the US and some regions abroad can be dramatic. There could be a top salesperson in the US who is aggressive and a high achiever, but who will fail in Korea for the very reason he is a success in the United States. In addition, even when an employee has one successful expatriate assignment, it does not mean he will find similar success in a different location. Each place is different, and just because someone did well in Korea does not mean he or she will do well in China (Poe, 2002).

Genuine consideration of the above will lead to success; disregard for any of the above can lead to expatriate failure. Overwhelmingly, family matters are still one of the major reasons cited for assignment failure. It is a big distraction if the family does not want to be there and one that can be disruptive to the company. To help in these circumstances it may be a good idea to invite the spouses of candidates in for interviews and to have the family travel to the location before committing to the candidate selection. The cost of the trip is nothing compared to a failed assignment. Failing to screen a spouse can have a major impact on the success of an assignment.

The process for staffing expatriates is complex and can be quite lengthy. There can be stressful negotiations between the employee and employer to make the package fit both the financial needs of the company and the employee and his or her family. Filling an assignment with the right employee with the hopes of a successful assignment is a challenging, but not impossible, task. Getting clear answers and commitments to all of these issues are important to ensure a smooth transition abroad.

Table 10.1   Mercer Human Resource Consulting, Cost of Living Survey—Worldwide Rankings 2006

| Rankings | | | | COL Index | |
March–06	March–05	City	Country	March–06	March–05
1	4	Moscow	Russia	123.9	119.0
2	5	Seoul	South Korea	121.7	115.4
3	1	Tokyo	Japan	119.1	134.7
4	9	Hong Kong	Hong Kong	116.3	109.5
5	3	London	United Kingdom	110.6	120.3
6	2	Osaka	Japan	108.3	121.8
7	6	Geneva	Switzerland	103.0	113.5
8	8	Copenhagen	Denmark	101.1	110.0
9	7	Zurich	Switzerland	100.8	112.1
10	10	Oslo	Norway	100.0	105.3
10	13	New York City	United States	100.0	100.0
12	15	St. Petersburg	Russia	99.7	99.5
13	11	Milan	Italy	96.9	104.9
14	19	Beijing	China	94.9	95.6
15	22	Istanbul	Turkey	93.1	93.8
15	12	Paris	France	93.1	102.2
17	34	Singapore	Singapore	92.0	88.0
18	13	Dublin	Ireland	91.8	100.0

Table 10.1 continued

| Rankings | | | | COL Index | |
March–06	March–05	City	Country	March–06	March–05
19	20	Sydney	Australia	91.3	95.2
20	30	Shanghai	China	91.2	90.4
21	17	Rome	Italy	89.8	97.3
21	54	Kiev	Ukraine	89.8	84.5
21	16	Vienna	Austria	89.8	97.8
24	39	Tel Aviv	Israel	89.7	87.6
25	20	Helsinki	Finland	87.8	95.2
25	73	Dubai	UAE	87.8	77.8
27	22	Douala	Cameroon	87.6	93.8
28	29	Taipei	Taiwan	86.8	90.6
29	44	Los Angeles	United States	86.7	86.7
30	64	Abu Dhabi	UAE	86.0	81.0
31	96	Lagos	Nigeria	85.5	72.8
32	52	Beirut	Lebanon	85.4	84.6
32	50	Hanoi	Vietnam	85.4	84.9
34	119	Sao Paulo	Brazil	85.0	66.6
34	50	San Francisco	United States	85.0	84.9
36	18	Stockholm	Sweden	84.8	96.8
37	56	Ho Chi Minh	Vietnam	84.2	83.8
38	52	Chicago	United States	84.1	84.6
39	57	Miami	United States	83.9	83.3
40	124	Rio de Janerio	Brazil	83.5	65.4
41	123	Lusaka	Zambia	83.4	65.6
41	24	Amsterdam	Netherlands	83.4	93.3
43	45	White Plains	United States	83.2	86.6
44	63	Shenzhen	China	82.9	81.3
45	26	Abidjan	Cote d'Ivoire	82.8	93.0
45	36	Dakar	Senegal	82.8	87.9
47	82	Toronto	Canada	82.6	76.2
48	71	Jakarta	Indonesia	82.4	78.9
48	31	Bratislava	Slovak Republic	82.4	89.9
50	28	Prague	Czech Republic	82.1	90.8

Note: Exchange rates used in attached table of cost comparisons: 1 GBP = 1.75 USD, 1 GBP = 1.46 EUR

Source: Mercer Human Resource Consulting (2006), "Worldwide Cost of Living Survey 2006—City Rankings." Available at http://www.mercerhr.com/pressrelease/details.jhtml/dynamic/idContent/1142150;jsessionid=QN31H2M4FPL4SCTGOUGCHPQKMZ0QUJLW

Female and Minority Expatriates

In the world of international assignments, it seems that there may be fewer female and minority expatriates compared to their counterparts. Dr Rosalie Tung (1996), Professor of International Business at Simon Fraser University, British Columbia, Canada, conducted an extensive study of expatriates. Dr Tung's study was sponsored by Arthur Andersen's International Executive Services practice. According to the survey, 75 per cent of international assignees are white, well-educated males who identified themselves as senior or middle management. Women represent 14 per cent of the expatriates working for US companies, and minorities comprised 11 per cent of the population. This clearly shows the lack of women and minorities in expatriate positions. Whether this is a trend or not, there may be some reasons for this and perhaps some suggestions for reversing the trend.

The Society of Human Resource Management states that the first reason may be that some organizations have the same challenge at the front door to their main office—the challenge of increasing diversity in their own managerial and professional ranks. Internationally, companies should manage the number of diverse expatriates, but before they can do this, they need to ensure a diverse workforce within a domestic context. If a company is inattentive to its home population, it will naturally carry over to the expatriate ranks. Some of the key drivers for any organization are:

- There should be both women and minorities reporting directly to senior managers, and both should receive their fair share of promotions into senior-level jobs
- All organizations should have certain jobs that are platforms for learning and can benefit a career path. Women and minorities should have a share in all assignments.
- Employers should identify and place both female and minority candidates into management pipelines—that is, succession planning.
- If turnover rates for female and minority managers are higher than those for white male managers, something must be amiss (Leonard, 2002).

The second possible reason involves the issues of safety, barriers such as discrimination and racism, and cultural differences. Although these concerns are valid, a company's misconception of these issues may cause them to withdraw from sending a woman or a diverse employee overseas, which may be to the detriment of the company.

There are many myths and misconceptions about what happens to women and minorities sent abroad—from the belief that they are crime targets, to the assumption that some cultures will not accept them in business. These illusions may prompt managers to overlook these people when filling international assignments. Most often employees, whether male or female, find out about assignments from their immediate supervisor. If the supervisor perceives that women or minorities are less willing to go on international assignments, there lies the dilemma. It is not always true that women are less inclined to disrupt their families, or that a minority candidate is fearful of discrimination or racism. Good managers, with the most honorable intentions, can make the wrong assumptions about their employees (Tyler, 2001).

Although they fear these employees working overseas could become crime victims and they believe that some societies' cultural prejudices against them could hamper their effectiveness on the job, is that true? Consider the Philippines. It does not matter if you are a man or a woman, white or black, it is a dangerous country, and it is dangerous for whomever. Also, in some cases, women working abroad may actually be safer than men because women are less likely to underestimate risks. Women take more precautions. Men do not feel as at risk, which exposes them to the danger more readily than they think.

A third reason that minority and females may not be sent on international assignment as often as their male counterparts is that managers may feel that these groups might have difficulty being accepted in business because of prejudices against them in the host countries. Cultural prejudice can be subtle or pronounced. In some countries, workers may refuse to acknowledge women or minorities during meetings, question their decisions, or make derogatory comments. In some cultures, women may be forced to change the way they dress as well as their habits, such as going out in public only with their husbands because the local culture prohibits women from being seen with other men. While such limits can affect them, they do not necessarily prevent them from succeeding as expatriates.

Suggestions to reverse this trend, and thus increase the number of women and minorities in expatriate assignments, are straightforward and fair. The most important proposal is that companies should not make assumptions about an employee's interest or willingness to go abroad. Human resource departments need to be resourceful in recruiting more diverse candidates for these positions. Sometimes it is as easy as having the company initiate the conversation. There may be many candidates who would want to embark on an international assignment, and will succeed, but they do not consider it themselves. Do not assume that a woman's personal life will prompt her to turn down an assignment, and do not assume a minority candidate may fear racism or discrimination. In particular, a company should do the following:

- Create a system for identifying employees willing to take these assignments—surveys, conversations during performance reviews, referrals from colleagues
- Use successful minority and female expatriates to recruit others
- Be flexible about timing
- Address social needs
- Provide mentors
- Plan for the employee's return.

Differences in the workplace can be a powerful means for international business success, allowing the organization to better understand and meet the needs of global customers. However, these differences can also cause confusion and frustration. As has been stated numerous times throughout the chapters, people are brought up in different cultures and relate in very different ways to other people and cultures. Managing and collaborating amongst these different cultures can be challenging and susceptible to misunderstandings. Global business is an established fact for many companies, but most find themselves struggling to staff appropriately and effectively on a global scale. A diverse global workforce requires managers to accept the anxiety created by working toward both commonality and difference. Amazingly, a company can obtain a competitive edge and advantage from the energy that this tension generates. This collaboration and sharing of thoughts and ways of operating enables a company to liberate the creative potential inherent in heterogeneous teams made up of individuals with different outlooks, thought processes, and experiences.

Expatriate Adjustment

The adaptation to a foreign environment is difficult for many expatriates and their families; in fact, research literature has demonstrated in recent findings that the failure rate of expatriates was high enough for concern. Black and Gregersen (1991) report that about 80 per cent of midsize and large companies have employees working abroad, and 45 per cent anticipate increasing their expatriate workforce in the future. Generally, 10 to 20 per cent of people sent on expatriate assignments return early, and about one-third of those who remain do not perform up to their supervisor's expectations while in these assignments, both of which are extremely costly for the organization.

However, Tung (1998) indicates that a premature return is not the main measure of failure (Black et al., 1991). It has been argued that under certain conditions a premature return could be seen as success, whereas completing the scheduled stay might be a failure (Varner and Palmer, 2002). In this argument the important thing is not the length of stay, but rather: how effective the expatriate was during his/her stay (Caligiuri, 2000; Tung, 1998); what knowledge the expatriate gained and how the company is institutionalizing and using that knowledge (Varner and Palmer, 2002); and how long the expatriate stays with the company after repatriation. If the expatriate leaves the firm within a short time of completing the assignment, one could argue that the assignment was not successful because the company might lose the knowledge (human capital) that the expatriate gained at the company's expense (Varner and Palmer, 2002).

Each of these criteria is important to the overall success of an expatriate and suggests the inherent relationship among the aforementioned elements of expatriate success. If employees are unable to adjust to their new surroundings, they may be unable to perform their job activities competently (Varner and Palmer, 2005). For example, an expatriate who does not adjust to interacting with host nationals may not be able to obtain the information needed to perform effectively or to adjust to daily life in the new culture (Black et al., 1991).

According to Tye and Chen (2004), expatriate success has at least three aspects: adjustment, performance, and turnover. Additionally, Caligiuri and Di Santo (2001) identified three areas that determine expatriate competence, which may lead to successful assignment: ability, knowledge, and personality. Results of their study indicate that ability and knowledge can be trained; however, personality is more innate and, therefore, more difficult to manipulate. Black and Gregersen (1991) found that, in general, MNCs emphasize the following characteristics in their expatriates:

- A collaborative negotiation style
- An international orientation
- Broad-based sociability
- Cultural flexibility
- Drive to communicate.

According to Black and Gregersen (1991), companies that manage their expatriates successfully tend to concentrate on creating knowledge and developing global leadership skills and to ensure that candidates have cross-cultural skills to match their technical abilities (Ali, 2003). Surprisingly, a Global Relocation Trends Survey by Windham International and the National Foreign Trade Council in 1994 revealed that with respect to the criterion that are most valued in an expatriate in a global management position, professional skills ranked in importance after flexibility and having an international perspective (Ali, 2003).

In discussing the problems associated with expatriate assignments from an organizational point of view, HR has a restricted role, meaning that they are restricted largely to providing administrative support and not that of a full strategic partner (Anderson, 2005). The limited role of HR is also highlighted by Swaak (1995). According to Anderson (2005), the results of a National Foreign Trade Council (NFTC) survey, carried out in conjunction with Selection Research International (SRI), attributed assignment failures to a number of causes, including an urgent need to fill a position overseas, which may lead to the selection of the "best available candidate" and line management overriding HR's advice.

For some time, human resources professionals and academic researchers have been conscious that employees who are transferred abroad need to achieve adjustment in order to successfully complete their overseas assignments (Anderson, 2005). In addition, Ali (2003) identified that expatriate success has most usually been determined by examining cross-cultural adjustment, performance, and completion of the international assignment.

It has been demonstrated that adjustment comes neither quickly nor easily, and anecdotes and reports of managers struggling during their international assignments document that a transfer abroad can create substantial risks for the expatriate employee as well as for the multinational firm (Anderson, 2005). In addition, they tend to stick to the home culture; for example, spending more time with other expatriates from their home country whenever possible. These findings on international personnel transfers have consistently demonstrated that there is an important risk that managers who embark on foreign assignments may initially not possess the required skills to fulfill the requirements of their jobs abroad.

Expatriate Failure

The success of an international employee's assignment is scrutinized more than almost any other in the company, since a failed assignment can cost anywhere from three to five times an assignee's annual salary. According to Black, Gregerson and Mendenhall (1992), it is estimated that the direct household shipping costs alone can exceed US$100,000 for a failed assignment (Ali, 2003). In addition, a study by Black and Gregersen (1991) revealed that the total cost to corporations of premature returns is approximately US$2 billion per year (Ali, 2003). These costs are the direct costs. The indirect costs could be equally negative to both corporations and individuals. Naumann (1992) argued that the indirect costs of a failed international business assignment may include reduced productivity and efficiencies, lost sales, market share and competitive position, an unstable corporate image and damage to international networks (Ali, 2003). Tung (1988) added that withdrawal from international assignments can also be costly for expatriates and their families, in terms of diminished self-esteem, impaired relationships, and interrupted careers (Ali, 2003). Incorrect selection resulting in expatriate failure is disruptive to employees and families and has both a financial and operational impact on business.

A study performed in the United Kingdom by Forster (1997) exposed that an average of 8 per cent of expatriate employees return home before the agreed end of the assignment (Ali, 2003). When the definition of expatriate failure was expanded to include the negative effects, stresses, and strains of an international assignment on expatriates and their families, the failure rate increased to 28 per cent, an increase of 20 per cent. Such breakdowns often constitute a personal setback to the expatriates' self-esteem and ego. According to Tung (1987), the "failed" expatriates may take some time before they regain confidence in their own abilities (Ali, 2003).

The fact that many expatriates do not complete their assignments is not surprising in the opinion of Mendenhall et al., who acknowledge the numerous cross-cultural obstacles confronting expatriates as including "culture shock, differences in work-related norms, isolation, homesickness, differences in health care, housing, schooling, cuisine, customs, sex roles and the cost of living, to name but a few (1987, p. 331)" (Anderson, 2005). According to the investigations of Thomson (1986), the problems facing expatriate partners include marital strain, managing servants and children, loss of privacy and identity, children's education, a new culture, the local environment, security requirements and uncertain infrastructure (Anderson, 2005).

As the Global Relocation Trends Survey (2003) reports, spouse and family issues continue to cause assignment failure as, 15 years later, the Global Relocation Trends (2002) Survey Report indicated that senior HR professionals identified that the related issues of spouse/partner dissatisfaction (94 per cent) and family concerns (94 per cent) were often or sometimes responsible for assignment failure (Anderson, 2005).

The Role of Outside Organizations

Many human resource departments today, suffering from increased workload and decreased staff, simply cannot recruit, staff, orient, consult, benchmark, tackle legal and labor issues, and still find the time to provide cultural training to its expatriates. This is an unfortunate thing, because when a company considers the expense of an expatriate, cultural training should be an element of the package that is a priority. However, often, the HR department relies on colleague expatriates to welcome them and to orient them to the new country.

Fortunately, several well-informed and comprehensive outside organizations or consultants are emerging that can help with an expatriate's cultural transition. For instance, the International Center of Indianapolis (ICI) is an organization that offers services for all citizens, domestic and international. They offer educational programs for those relocating overseas on an expatriate assignment as well as opportunities for the assignees to receive valuable interaction with international visitors and interns. For international citizens making Indiana their new home, the ICI offers services in the home search, and they provide an orientation program for international employees, short-term assignees, and the spouses of both. Not only does ICI assist in an overwhelming transition, the Center is committed to its community to offer these services as a way to respond to the needs of an international Indianapolis.

Conclusion

The acceptance of cross-cultural training by businesses is an important piece of international business. The implementation of cross-cultural training will provide a high level of support to international employees and their families, which will in turn enhance the effectiveness and success of the assignments to their sponsoring organizations.

Training is an effective tool to improve the chances of assignment success. It is common for HR to be considered in the strategic planning process for overall corporate strategy. The same belief should be applied to cross-cultural training; that it merits the same consideration as one of several strategic elements of international assignment support. It has significance not only for the individual but also for developing cross-cultural competencies within the business organization.

In today's global market, multinationals must make their expatriates aware of the cultural differences surrounding them. In order to retain a position among stiff competition from other multinational companies, companies must start investing in their employees. Companies should seriously weigh the cost of failure among expatriates in relation to the benefits of cross-cultural training. The key for tomorrow's success is in today's cross-cultural awareness.

Case Study

Placing a US Firm in Germany

Geographic Location Germany has a population of 82 million people. Germany is considered the heart of Europe. Germany is densely populated, highly urbanized, and culturally united. Qualified workers are more concentrated in the bigger cities such as Bonn, where the education is higher. When talking about international staffing, foreign workers and their families play a major role in Germany. During the late 1960s, workers from Mediterranean countries were recruited in large numbers to meet labor shortages, and a growing number of illegal immigrants from Central Europe were becoming a serious problem. Thus, for an example, if a company such as Mills Fleet Farm were to open a store in Germany, in order to locate qualified workers they must move to highly populated areas first, like Bonn or Berlin.

Background The staffing department's duties are to help the enterprise's management recruit, develop, train, and place the right people in the right spots. One of the problems is selecting managers to staff the firm's foreign operations. Three options for international businesses to select staff to manage their foreign operations are to send someone from the home country, hire someone in the host country, or hire someone from a third country. Numerous factors influence the choice of whether to use an expatriate, a host-country national, or a third country national. The factors include the top management-staffing outlook, perceived needs, corporation's characteristics, characteristics of the personnel available at home, and the host country's characteristics. A company's view of international business corporations can be ethnocentric, polycentric, regiocentric, or geocentric. Other factors that have an influence are staffing strategies, level of technology, and market influences. In international managerial staffing, one must look at the organizational structure of a company, the dependence on international business, a firm's experience, cost benefit factors, and the style of management. All of these listed above need to be considered when deciding on which route to take in human resource development internationally.

Political and Legal The history of Germany's political stability has an impact on the labor force today. The political definition related to the staffing department deals with German government policy and the stability of their legal environment. After national unification, eastern German industrial output collapsed to about 40 per cent of its 1989 level, leading to high unemployment in the new states. Reunification strained German public finance, hurt the labor market, and eventually exposed structural weaknesses in the economy. 1995 growth was unexpectedly low at 1.9 per cent though eastern Germany maintained growth of over 5 per cent. 1996 GDP growth was an even lower 1.4 per cent due mainly to a drop in construction investment and lower private consumption. Growth forecasts for 1997 ranged from 1.5 to 2.4 per cent, not enough to reduce unemployment. Exports continued to drive growth in 1997 as private consumption remained low, because of the modest nominal wage gains, higher contribution to the social security system and the postponement of tax relief measures (Country Commercial Guide: Germany. Report prepared by US Embassy Bonn, released August 1997). Growth from 2001 to 2003 fell short of 1 per cent. The modernization and integration of the eastern German economy continues to be a costly long-term process, with annual transfers from west to east amounting to roughly $70 billion. Currently, in 2005, the fall in government revenues and the rise in expenditures have raised the deficit above the EU's 3 per cent deficit to GDP ratio (CIA Factbook, 2004).

German–American political, economic and security relationships continue to be based on close consultation and coordination at the most senior levels. High-level visits take place often and the US and Germany cooperate actively in international fora. Standard work permits are required among the foreigners seeking employment.

As two of the world's leading nations, the US and Germany share a common pledge to an open and expanding world economy. Germany is the second-leading trading nation in the world. It is the fifth largest trading partner to the US. Personal ties between the US and Germany include immigration, foreign exchange programs, tourism, and the presence in Germany of large numbers of American military personnel and their best dependants.

Economics Economic issues relating to the staffing department deal with the foreign investment climate and any sort of labor restrictions that are in Germany. Germany ranks among the world's most important economic powers. From the 1948 Currency Reform Act until the early 1970s, West Germany experienced almost continuous economic expansion, but real growth in gross national product slowed and even declined from the mid-1970s through the recession of the early 1980s. The economy then experienced eight consecutive years of growth, then ended with a downturn beginning in late 1992 (*Germany Labor Trends*, 1997).

The German government and industry actively encouraged foreign investment in Germany. One measure of the openness of the German system is that the chairperson of one of Germany's most prestigious business organizations, the Bundesverband der Deutschen Industrie (BDI), was formerly associated with a US-owned subsidiary.

In the event of expropriation, German law provides that private property would be confiscated for public purpose only, in a non-discriminatory manner, and in accordance with established principles of international law. There is due process and transparency of purpose, and investors and lenders to expropriated entities receive prompt, adequate, and effective compensation.

German employee performance requirements and incentives are available for foreign employees. A comprehensive package of federal and state investment incentives is available to domestic and foreign investors. Particular emphasis has been placed on investment in eastern German states. Many of these programs and incentives were scheduled to expire in 1998 and 1999. Efforts were made in 2005 to modify and extend, although at a modestly lower level, many of these programs. Vacations range from three weeks, minimum by law, to around six weeks. With Germany's economic position, it is a key place for a US firm to move to (*Germany Labor Trends*, 1997).

Availability of Labor Availability of labor is the amount of qualified workers and managers available for a particular company. While employers complain that wages and fringe benefits are high, the German labor force is well educated, well trained, and well disciplined. High unemployment remains the key economic problem. The highly acclaimed dual system of combined on-the-job training for apprentices produces the skills needed by employers. Legislation is designed to protect workers' limits; the ability to lay off redundant workers discourages flexible hiring practices. As a part of its 50-point reflation plan to encourage growth, employment, and investment, in 1996 the government weakened the protection of workers by raising the threshold of companies covered by the strictest protection regulations from the former level of five employees to more than ten employees. This change is estimated to have affected about 10 per cent of the gainfully employed, or roughly three to four million people (*Germany Labor Trends*, 1997).

Germany has no minimum wage law. Wages and salaries are determined by either collective bargaining agreements or individual contracts. Collective bargaining agreements are legally binding and are enforced through the courts. It is strongly recommended that a US company use the large diverse labor force that exists in Germany to establish their workforce within their stores. This applies to all employees up to top management positions.

Staffing Factor Discussion and Analysis All of the issues that have been discussed lead up to the international staffing of a company in Germany. Many factors can influence the decisions that need to be taken into account. For this company, the most important issues are the availability of labor and Germany's investment climate. Germany offers a large and diverse labor force. Germany is similar to America in many aspects relating to work issues, which would make it easier for this company to be placed there.

From these important facts, it is recommended for successful management staffing to hire someone in the host country, Germany. Because there is a large amount of qualified workers and managers that exist in Germany, it is recommended that a business hire their employees from the German workforce. One reason for this is the language barrier would not exist between manager and employee. With Germany's availability of skilled labor, it would not be difficult to find good quality management.

In Germany, there is a demand for a very high level of quality, for both materials provided and the work performed. There is an enormous market of knowledgeable people in this particular area and regulations concerning the workforce are similar to the US; therefore a firm such as Mills Fleet Farm would find a high rate for successful placement of staff in Germany. With all this considered, it is easy to see the potential. With the German background and knowledge of the home improvement industry, there is an excellent chance of success in Germany.

Case Questions

1. What are the legal, political, social, cultural, and economic implications of a global company locating in Germany?
2. There is a long tradition of German collective bargaining practice. Explain the impact this will or will not have on employees if expatriate managers are assigned to this location.
3. Discuss any conditions that may affect a firm's success in Germany, such as barriers against or support for cultural adaptability.
4. With what particular advice, feedback, or suggestions should a manager be provided in order to be successful in Germany?

Chapter Review

An expatriate assignment takes considerable planning and preparation and should appropriately support the employee's needs. Cross-cultural orientation programs are designed to teach members of one culture ways of interacting effectively, with minimal interpersonal misunderstanding, in another culture. Implementing a cross-cultural training program is an integral part of the international assignment process. Cross-cultural training enhances the capabilities of personnel on international business assignments. Cross-cultural training undoubtedly affords assignees a better chance at succeeding in the host culture. Many studies have examined cross-cultural training, and its impact upon the effectiveness/success of the expatriate. Each study indicated that cross-cultural training has a positive effect upon the expatriate in terms of success and employee satisfaction factors. Cross-cultural preparation helps to relieve two concerns for the expatriate; the culture shock that a new country can produce, and ineffective communication on the job.

Some tips for international managers who deal with people from different cultures are to know the other culture, respect differences, be aware of time differences and utilization of time in different cultures, and observe status differences in most cultures in the world. Enough time should be allowed for managers to be cross-culturally trained. Knowing that cultural differences as well as similarities exist, not assigning values to those cultural differences is the epitome of cultural sensitivity.

The planning for international assignments and the acceptance of cross-cultural training by businesses is a critical piece of international enterprise. Training is an effective tool to improve the chances of assignment success and the key for tomorrow's improvement in cross-cultural awareness.

Chapter Questions

1. What are the business implications for achieving cross-cultural competencies?
2. To what extent can the contributions of human resources play a role in preparing an employee for an overseas assignment?
3. How do your underlying beliefs, assumptions, and socialization influence your world view and interactions with others who are different from you? How can training assist in this process?
4. Compare and contrast two of the training models discussed in the chapter, explaining any similarities or differences between the two. How does each facilitate the international cultural training process?

Chapter 11

Toward New International Business Conditions and Opportunities

Global management, internationalization of trade, global finance, transnational entrepreneurship, have never been as significant as they are today. It is paradoxical that such phenomena could be so revered by some while dispersed by others. We have seen that there are dozens and dozens of definitions of globalization and how this phenomenon interrelates with customers and local cultures. In this context, multinational corporations see globalization and the related concept of global management as producing a wide spread of democratization and development for underdeveloped nations, and, of course, good trends for business and profit-makers. Antiglobalists purport that globalization manifests the worst and to them, the only good thing about it is boosting profits for transnational corporations who are indeed undemocratic. Global management would be the most terrific aspect of this global issue.

In contrast to this view, entrepreneurial enterprises and competition among them had an important role in fostering economic growth regionally and globally, providing a significant addition to real economic growth and employment opportunities.

World Oil Peak and Oil Reserves

The oil industry is a contemporary example of an industry scrutinized a great deal in today's world. For instance, there is the Hubbert Peak and the discussion that arose after it. Hubbert's Peak is named after Marion King Hubbert, a Shell Oil geologist who made an effort in 1956 to come up with a simple way to predict the lifetime of a natural resource. He would have to find out when oil output in the United States would peak, thus to begin declining thereafter. Hubbert realized that the trajectory of oil discovery in the continental United States could be a classic bell-shaped curve, for the decades from 1910 to 1970 and he also saw that there would be a second bell-shaped curve that would represent petroleum extraction. Hubbert, using what he knew in 1950 about the history of discoveries and consumption, predicted the year 1970.

After him, experts have tried to calculate this peak for world production. It would be disastrous if these resources dry up, which some believe will happen sometime soon. Speculation about the doomsday era is common today. Although doomsdays were prophesied three times in the past century, they never occurred. The situation worldwide is quite undetermined but the world is not really running out of these resources. In all, we must have good expectations for a significant reserves increase.

Leonardo Maugeri (2006) provides accounts for this and the more pessimistic of experts' projections about how declining global reserves are unsound, and we do not have problems of scarcity or upcoming oil blackmail. BP (2006) shows that the world's known crude oil reserves are 163.6 thousand million tonnes as of the end of 2005. So simplistically, we could say that as the world is pumping out of the ground a given amount of barrels a year, we have some 40.6 reserves-to-production ratio, although the issue is more complex. Concerning the world petroleum peak and the current world oil consumption of 1,000 barrels per second, it has been estimated as somewhere between 2000 and 2015 (see, for example, Deffeyes, 2005; Roberts, 2004; Kunstler, 2005). Goodstein (2004) predicted the age of fossil fuels will end sometime in this century and recently Tertzakian (2006) makes a case that the end of oil is nigh and will reach a production peak during the next five to ten years. Even optimistic experts guess oil peak will come around sometime in the next 30 years; therefore, in case of a peak around us, one should foresee the end of the age of oil and be prepared for rising oil prices and market volatility, as well as structural changes. Turning to natural gas to replace diminishing supplies of oil, the Hubbert Peak for natural gas has been calculated only a decade or so behind oil; nevertheless, worldwide, BP (2006) reports that the world's known natural gas reserves are 179.83 trillion cubic meters as of the end of 2005, of which 26.6 per cent would belong to Russia and 14.9 per cent to Iran.

However, it is not certain when the Hubbert Peak will materialize, or whether the world's petroleum production is at its maximum right around now. If scientists estimate that we had 2.1–2.2 trillion barrels oil in the ground before we ever started pumping it (Goodstein, 2004), the total amount of petroleum that ever existed tends to increase with time for a variety of reasons. Both the starting quantity of oil and proven reserves today are only partially reliable and few statistical figures prove it, although too much pessimism is unjustified, as Maugeri (2006) and others believe. Proven oil reserves were calculated at 770.4 thousand million barrels in 1985, 1,027 in 1995, and 1,220.7 by 2005! As for the gas proved reserves, they were 99.54 trillion cubic meters in 1995, rising to 143.42 in 1995, and estimated to be 179.83 in 2005, BP (2006) reports.

New technology and recent discoveries, mounting oil and gas advance recovery techniques would make investing in new fields available and pulling these commodities out of the ground convenient. There are several recent examples, but the most recent is that of the summer of 2006. Through using advanced technology, a mega oil field has been discovered in the Gulf of Mexico, 430 km south-west of New Orleans, some 2,000 meters below the seabed: this would enjoy some 3 billion barrels of reserves, perhaps up to 15 billion barrels, which would be more than 50 per cent of current Unites States' reserves. Additionally, ENI, the Italian hydrocarbons giant, has made a new gas discovery located in the US deepwater of the Gulf of Mexico, 195 km south-east of New Orleans.

Although developing alternative sources and enhancing energy efficiency are also ways to benefit the environment, the analysis build up on Hubbert's Peak is conceivably exaggerated. Without considering the aforementioned concerning technology and the capacity to explore additional fields, let us bear in mind that the country has huge world proved reserves: 6.2 per cent of oil, 26.6 per cent of natural gas, and 17.3 per cent of coal (BP, 2006).

Increasing knowledge about specific deposits and advances in technology for recovering the oil led to the discovery of additional reserves. Maugeri (2006) says that proven reserves exceed one trillion barrels and that overall, the world would retain more than three trillion barrels of recoverable oil resources (yearly consumption is about 28 billion barrels) and no one knows the exact amount of reserves available in Russia.

Thanks to new exploration, drilling, and recovery technology, the cost per barrel of oil has declined over the last 20 years, from an average of about $21 in the late 1970s to less than $6 in the late 1990s, just when the recovery rate from world oil fields has increased from about 22 per cent in 1980 to 35 per cent today.

Global Management and Global Culture in Fast Growing Regions

Global management and culture provide more opportunities than threats for entrepreneurs to expand their business opportunities worldwide. This has been so in the past and will increasingly continue in the future. Just look at what changes China and India have realized in their political and cultural history. They have been a part of the global economy for centuries. Once isolated, each country began gradually to trade with the Middle East and Europe. Originally prized for such natural resources as spices and tea, each in time became valued as a market for Western products. In addition, each experienced the rigors of colonial exploitation, industrial development, and, ultimately, political independence (see Table 11.1).

Toward A New Concept of Global Entrepreneurship

Global management and local entrepreneurship are the comprehensive solution that many companies are now exploring. Many of the world's largest firms are truly global, and even their smaller counterparts increasingly participate in cross-border activities by subcontracting, having customers and joint venture partners collaborate with them around the globe.

In actuality, the arena of international management and global entrepreneurship has never offered so many opportunities and challenges to individual managers, businesses, governments, and the academic community alike. The expansion of the global market has created a need for managers who are familiar with the problems of international trade such as culture, political structure, foreign exchange, geographical terrain, time, food, and technology, which indeed is a paradox in itself.

There is no country or even region in the world today, including the United States, which is economically self-sufficient without some sort of interdependence with other countries. Society has quite often divided the world into north and south, rich and poor, communist and capitalist, and many other convenient stratifications. Splitting the international community again finds continuity around the process of globalization and its institutions, which some perceive as both positive and negative simultaneously, that is, rightful versus sinful international regulatory institutions.

Table 11.1 Timeline Featuring Some of the Significant Historical Developments in China and India

Year	Event
2600 BC	Trade between the Indus Valley and Mesopotamia
25–21 BC	The Silk Road (really numerous routes) connects China with Indian oases and Arabian Sea ports.
650 AD	Arab traders establish outposts in China's coastal cities.
712	Arabs invade India, and trade begins between the two regions.
1229	The Mongol conquest of China furthers commerce and development.
1500s	A Chinese trading community spreads across Asia. The Portuguese are the first Europeans to restore trading links to India that were blocked by the Ottoman Empire; the Dutch and British soon follow.
1600	Britain grants a monopoly over the India trade to the British East India Trading Company, which focusses on spices, cotton, silk, and sugar. The East India Company ships opium to China in exchange for tea.
1700s	The sale of Asian silks and printed or dyed cottons is banned in England. A highly developed pre-industrial Indian textile industry collapses due both to the embargo and to industrial competition. India is becoming an agricultural colony of Britain.
1759	Chinese merchant families centered in Guangzhou (Canton) are commissioned by the government to act as brokers with European companies.
1800s	In China, urban areas and handicraft workshops flourish.
1842	Britain's victory in the Opium War leads to the opening to trade of Guangzhou and four other ports. China cedes the barren island of Hong Kong to Britain.
Mid-1800s	The British introduce irrigation canals, railroads, modern banking, and a system of commercial law in India. The export trade sees a steady rise.
1869	The new Suez Canal lays the basis for the integration of the Indian economy into the world market.
1890s	Japan, Britain, Germany, Russia, and France carve up China.
Early 1900s	Constitutional reforms allow India an increasing level of fiscal independence, including tariffs that encourage industrialization. In 1912, Tata Co., financed and controlled by Indians, begins to produce steel, hydroelectric power, textiles.
1914–20	WWI allows a wave of industrialization in China, and an annual growth rate of 13.8 per cent. Modern banking begins.
1940s	Indian industry grows rapidly during WWII.

Year	Event
1947	British rule comes to an end in India. Under Congress Party rule, the public sector dominates in manufacturing and banks are nationalized. Corporate dynasties such as Tata, Birla, and Bajaj grow to account for 15 per cent of the economy.
1949	The Communists win China's civil war and initiate land reform and a collectivization of agriculture. Major advances take place in healthcare and education.
1950s	Civilian space research begins in India.
1958	The Great Leap Forward, a mass mobilization to effect economic transformation, proves disastrous. Millions die amid famine.
1960	US aid helps Taiwan develop. Production for export soars, especially in consumer electronics, steel, computers, and military hardware.
1970s	The Communists' economic program allows some free-market activity, small-scale rural industry. After Mao Tse-Tung's 1976 death, leaders including Deng Xaioping begin emulating the market economies of China's Asian neighbors.
1979	The Open Doors Policy is actually started. Foreign investment is legalized; Special Economic Zones are established along the Southeast coast and Yangzi River.
1980	The first stock exchange since 1949 opens in Shanghai. Capitalism begins changing the face of Shenzhen.
1982	Beginning as a 12-person outfit, Infosys Technologies develops software for global corporations. The outfits grow at a rate of 40 per cent per year for a decade.
1984	Rajiv Gandhi, Prime Minister from 1984–89, encourages high-tech development.
1991–97	A balance-of-payments crisis—due largely to Gulf War-related oil-price shocks—leads to borrowing from the IMF and World Bank. Economic reforms follow, including opening state-controlled sectors to private investment and a liberalized trade policy. Between 1993 and 1997, economic growth averages 6.8 per cent per year.
1997	The Communists announce that state-owned industries are to be phased out. China's economy is growing faster than almost any other in history, says the World Bank. A transition to Chinese rule begins in Hong Kong.
2000	Indian software firms blossom as the Y2K scare ends. General Electric and other multinationals build R&D facilities in Bangalore, which becomes a global hub. The auto parts industry, pharmaceuticals, and chemicals become major exporters.
2001	China enters the World Trade Organization, committing itself to sweeping liberalization in virtually every industry.
2003	A fourth generation of Communist leaders takes over, led by Hu Jintao and Wen Jiabao.

Source: "China and India–From Then to Now," Business Week Online. Available at: http://www.businessweek.com/magazine/toc/05_34/B3948chinaindia.htm.

However, even a judicious observer would discern definite verdicts about global management and a cultural approach to it as we have done in this book. Because globalization is producing additional waves of competition, the international environment has been creating enormous challenges for managers. Therefore, the paradox of something perceived to be so beneficial could be problematic about obtaining the necessary skills to manage while maintaining cultural and national identity. What is more important, international management demands a contingency approach to the ever-changing environment. This means the choice of management system and style depends on the nature of the country and the people involved. So, is a Lithuanian or Nigerian manager, for example, ready to sacrifice cultural and national identity in the interest of globalization? On the other hand, has an American or Japanese manager relinquished his or her identity in pursuit of a global management approach?

Globalization is problematic to small and medium-sized firms who are planning to enter the international market. They face a difficult decision regarding the choice of governance methods. The options available to a firm include internalization and externalization. Existing theories contradict each other about the strategic benefits of these options. This book has compared existing theories and resorted to case studies in the context of a variety of enterprises involved in global management. The merits of internalization and externalization vary with market contexts and the resources under the company's control. Under certain conditions, one theory can be more powerful than the other.

In view of this and from another context, Great Britain Prime Minister Tony Blair (2005) stated, "In this modern world there is no security or prosperity at home unless we deal with the global challenges of conflict, terrorism, climate change, and poverty." Mr. Blair went on to say, "Self interest and mutual interest are inextricably linked." As Tony Blair put it in his speech about globalization,

> It all happens as a result of what people themselves are doing. Occasionally we debate globalization as if it were something imposed by governments or business on unwilling people. This is wrong. It is the individual decisions of millions of people that is creating and driving globalization. Globalization is not something done to us. It is something we are, consciously or unconsciously, doing to and for ourselves.

In a political context, to borrow from Tony Blair's speech again, "Nations are deeply connected at every level, of course, economically, but also now through communication, travel and technology." Mr. Blair also stated, "This is a world integrating at a fast rate, with enormous economic, cultural, and political consequences." The trend toward a single global economy is expanding markets and providing unlimited opportunities for international managers. To remain parallel and compatible to other technologies, for example, countries need to work together as more of a global economy. The course of the globalization paradox could not have been very far-fetched from the impact of culture and ethical issues. Culture, as observed, is the sum of beliefs, rules, techniques, institutions, and artifacts that characterize human populations. When considering the ethics of a company, one can view the conduct of an international organization to decide if they neglect the correct procedures to gain an ethical consensus on the mainstream programs they realize in less advantageous economies.

The new economy is built on information technology and the sharing of knowledge and intellectual capital as we have seen in previous chapters. This process of global management and cultural approach to local and international trends also relates to the new knowledge economy, though it is fundamentally different from the social and economic contexts of the past two centuries. In a knowledge-based economy, those countries that have the capacity to deliver quickly will achieve a competitive advantage and have innovative forms of work organizations that raise productivity. In such an environment, small and medium-sized enterprises have tremendous opportunities. Technological, organizational, and marketing hurdles are also making it more difficult for small enterprises to succeed in knowledge-based economies. To be a player in this competitive arena, they require a large investment in personnel, infrastructure, and a full awareness of culture.

When it comes to global management and global cultural entrepreneurship, there are many questions to ponder, and also paradoxes. This book has tried to give answers to all possible relevant aspects. Should the balance between the freedom to operate and the accountability to shareholders and the international community be the same everywhere? Alternatively, should we allow managers/insiders more leeway in less efficient markets? Should we insist on compliance with international best practices or does this delay world economic growth? The international community is slowly becoming divided regarding the benefits of globalization. Should there be universal rules or is it more important to preserve national and cultural values? A single global model may be inappropriate due to differences in cultural, social, and economic levels of development in the developed countries versus those in less developed countries. As the concept of global management and global entrepreneurship impresses on a society's choices and alternatives between their native values and the values of global policies, the difficulties can swing from developing dynamism to absolute inconsistency that leads to economic stagnation, social dysfunctions, and less cultural value in some parts of the world. Herein lays the challenge of participating in an international system while keeping one's national interests at heart.

Finally, yet importantly, we cannot ignore the impact of culture while dealing with global trends, since it drives the concept and the process.

Conclusion

This book represents a major attempt in the field of study of global business and the impact of culture on development in both economics and business realms. We have combined business evolution with several economics aspects while considering the larger realities surrounding this field of interest and its ever growing impact worldwide. With this instrumental approach in mind we wanted to serve a very specific purpose, which is to offer and combine case studies and a variety of examples drawn from the business realities all round the world—both from the past and today—to several purposes. Our intent it to service reading students in their understanding of business culture that goes beyond mere economic and business theories and the business community, to starting or enlarging business activities by going into the implications of business culture in its wider possible interpretations and forms. This aspect, supported by cases studied from the growing Asian region, China, India, Europe, the Americas, and the future of African nations. together with the very recent trends in political business attitudes will help students and business makers comprehend realities better, grasp the intimate logic of why certain trends appeared in one way and not in others, and set better strategies for the future. Above all, what our work wants to show is that economic and business decisions may change over time due to different and ever-changing business opportunities at the national level, but national culture or even regional cultures and attitudes will always be extremely important benchmarks in doing global business. The interconnectedness of trade and financial issues, coupled with increasing trade flows, will make the approach adopted in this book even more challenging.

Chapter Questions

1. What is the Hubbert Peak?
2. What should we intend for proven oil reserves?
3. Why do some experts believe that there would be a huge difference between proven oil reserves and reserves actually available but not discovered yet?
4. By referring to statistical data freely available to all (for example, www. bp.com), discuss how oil supply from different regions or countries (for example, the Middle East, Russia, Venezuela, and so on) is important for international business.
5. Does international politics serve to explain the market for oil, the price per barrel, and so on?

Case Study

Ford, GM Fight over Brightest Labor Market–Car Makers Ford and GM Plan Expansion in China

Summary As China's market and economy grow, automakers like GM and Ford are developing a variety of strategies for expanding their market shares. The rivalry is intensifying between Ford and GM (according to this article), as Ford develops new initiatives to catch up. GM is enjoying the benefits of its first mover advantages when it forged an alliance with the government automaker years ago when the Chinese market was small for this industry. Both companies have plans for expanding operations bearing in mind the increasing competition from other manufacturers.

Fighting to catch up with rivals in China, Ford on Friday unveiled an agreement that will allow the automaker to boost its manufacturing capacity in China to 150,000 vehicles a year from the current 20,000.

GM China Group, which posted the widest profit margins of all the automotive businesses within GM last quarter, will introduce a flurry of new products and expand capacity in China next year.

Fresh from a Wednesday announcement by GM that profits in the Asian-Pacific region nearly doubled in the third quarter, GM China's top executives said this week that the company will introduce a minimum of at least one new model a year into China.

On Friday, Ford announced in Beijing that it and its partner in China, Changan Automobile Group, would invest more than $1 billion over the next few years as part of ambitious expansion plans in China.

Ford Chairman and Chief Executive William Clay Ford Jr. has been touring Asia this week, touting a new strategic plan to grab a bigger share of Asia's auto market. Earlier this week, Mr Ford announced that his company and its Japanese affiliate, Mazda Motor Corp., are investing $500 million in their joint-venture plant in Thailand over the next several years to expand its manufacturing capacity of 135,000 vehicles a year to more than 200,000.

In China, Ford said the investment announced Friday will initially go toward adding new products and expanding production capacity at a plant Ford runs jointly with Changan in Chongqing. Ford began producing a version of the Fiesta small car at the plant in January and is expected to produce 20,000 vehicles this year and 50,000 in 2004.

Ford also said it and Changan would establish a second car plant and new engine plant over the next few years. Ford did not share details about locations of the new plants or the products that will be manufactured at the new plant.

The expansion would be a critical steppingstone for Ford to boost its presence in China's burgeoning passenger vehicle market over the next several years, said Nick Scheele, Ford's president and chief operating officer.

Under the plans, Ford is expected to begin full production of its Mondeo at the Chongqing plant next year. According to people familiar with the plans, production of the Focus and a station wagon based on the Mondeo also may soon follow. Already, Ford is selling the Mondeo and the Maverick compact sport utility vehicle in China by importing largely assembled "knockdown" kits for the vehicles from Taiwan and assembling them at the Chongqing plant.

"China is clearly going to be pivotal" to Ford's future, Mr Scheele said. Ford is playing catch-up in China after fumbling its entry to the country a decade ago. Cross-town Detroit rival GM has worked more than a decade to build its presence there and is reaping benefits of its foresight. GM said earlier this week that it earned $162 million in its Asian auto operations during the third quarter, or about $1,200 per vehicle sold, compared with net income of $128 million in North America, or $102 per vehicle sold.

In China, by far Asia's hottest market, Ford executives said the company wants to eventually grab 10 per cent of the passenger vehicle market, with mostly locally produced vehicles. Having a 10 per cent share is a threshold level of penetration that an automaker needs "to be a player" in China, said a top Ford executive.

Ford lost to GM a decade ago in a competition to forge an alliance with a Chinese automaker—the only government-approved way for a foreign automaker to set up shop and sell vehicles in the country. That defeat meant little when the Chinese auto market remained small. Then, over the past two years, consumer demand for passenger vehicles began surging as China's middle class amassed more purchasing power.

Ford's rivals, most notably GM and Volkswagen AG of Germany, have multiple alliances and have passenger vehicle manufacturing plants on the country's eastern seaboard, where people are more prosperous. Both VW and GM have a significant market share advantage over Ford, which is expected to sell about 20,000 passenger vehicles in China this year. That is tiny in a market in which passenger vehicle sales totaled some 1.2 million last year. Sales rose more than 80 per cent in the first half of this year and are projected to hit as many as four million vehicles by 2006. Industry executives say China is likely to finish this year as the third-largest single-country market in the world, behind the US and Japan.

GM China, in a bid to meet growing demand, will soon expand its Chevrolet portfolio and begin selling Cadillacs in China sometime early next year. GM Chairman and Chief Executive Phil Murtaugh offered few details about which Cadillac models would be introduced and where they would be manufactured.

Ideally, the Cadillacs would be manufactured in China through Shanghai General Motors Co., the 50–50 joint venture GM formed in 1997 with Shanghai Automotive Industry Corp. However, GM is currently unsure as to how such an arrangement would work, GM China officials said.

On top of new competition from a wide range of formidable competitors, GM also is facing uncertainty about how it will offer and enforce financing to consumers in China's relatively unrefined credit environment.

With 85 per cent of consumers in China paying cash for vehicles, GM and its competitors are waiting for the Chinese government to roll out the new regulations needed to establish a reliable framework for extending and enforcing financing in China.

Shanghai GM now has annual production capacity of about 200,000, since recently stepping up production efforts to three-shifts, 24 hours a day in Shanghai. The new capacity will enable GM to begin producing as many as 40 vehicles a day from the facility by March.

GM is betting that the luxury market in China will continue to flourish. While the average per capita income in China is less than $5,000 a year, GM will depend on a smaller, disproportionately wealthier segment of the market for a significant amount of its growth.

For example, almost one-third of the cars GM sold last year were priced at more than $30,000. That reality helped influence GM to seriously consider selling Cadillacs in China, GM executives said.

Meanwhile, the other half of Shanghai GM, SAIC, also is betting that China will continue to show promise. "China's economy is still powering ahead in recent years," said Chen Hong, vice president of SAIC and president of Shanghai General Motors. "It is unlikely to derail the growth trend in the foreseeable future, even if the development of the global economy slows down."

"All famous auto makers have realized the huge potential of the China market, and they are bringing the latest products and technology to China, trying to secure and expand their market share," Mr. Hong said. "The competition in China will be more severe."

Reprinted with permission: N. Shirouzu and L. Hawkins, Jr (2003), "Ford, GM Fight over Brightest Labor Market", *The Wall Street Journal*, October 17, A9.

Case Questions

1. Discuss the current climate for doing business in China. Compare this climate to the past, especially for the auto manufacturers.
2. What are the advantages of a joint venture operation for both GM and Ford in China?
3. Discuss the potential arrangement (organization structure) for GM for the purposes of manufacturing and/or selling Cadillacs in China.
4. What are the market potentials for Cadillac sales in China? Explain.

Appendix

International Metaphors

International metaphors, clichés, expressions, and proverbs are word pictures of truth about a culture's values and beliefs. Values like ambition, virtue, generosity, and patience are addressed in sayings from almost every culture. Each culture has proverbs that are unique to it. To assist in understanding a culture, knowing their proverbs may be helpful. For example, sayings from various Native American tribes often reflect their view of the land as sacred. Japanese proverbs often refer to morals, and Mexican proverbs reflect the thinking and values of rural people or the average person on the street, and hope is a common theme. Multicultural workplaces are becoming increasingly important, as this text has shown. We can learn about a people through its culture's sayings. Sharing these proverbs can be one way to learn about other cultures, their similarities and differences compared to ours.

African

- A child's fingers are not scalded by a piece of hot yam, which his mother puts into his palm.
- A man who pays respect to the great paves the way for his own greatness.
- A proud heart can survive a general failure because such a failure does not prick its pride.
- A wise man who knows proverbs, reconciles difficulties (Yoruba).
- As the dog said, "If I fall down for you and you fall down for me, it is playing."
- Do not look where you fell, but where you slipped.
- If a child washes his hands, he could eat with kings.
- If you do not stand for something, you will fall for something.
- The lizard that jumped from the high iroko tree to the ground said he would praise himself if no one else did.
- The mouth that eats does not talk.
- The sun will shine on those who stand before it shines on those who kneel under them.
- Those whose palm-kernels were cracked for them by a benevolent spirit should not forget to be humble.
- When a man says yes, his *chi* (personal god) says yes also.
- When the moon is shining, the cripple becomes hungry for a walk.
- You can tell a ripe corn by its look.
- You must judge a man by the work of his hands.

Arab

- Examine what is said, not him who speaks.
- When God wanted to doom the ant, he gave it wings.

Armenian

- To be willing is only half the task.
- You do not water a camel with a spoon.

Belgian

- Experience is the comb that nature gives us when we are bald.

Czech

- Do not protect yourself by a fence, but rather by your friends.

Chinese

- When the student is ready, the master will appear.

Danish

- God gives every bird its food, but does not always drop it into the nest.

Dutch

- Everything of value is defenseless.

Estonian

- Where you find fault with something, come, and give a hand.

Ethiopian

- He who conceals his disease cannot expect to be cured.

French

- A bare foot is better than none.

- A dead man fights not, we say; a dead dog bites not.
- A fool and wealth cannot possess each other.
- A woman laughs when she can, and weeps when she will.
- Adversity makes wise.
- After the love, the repentance.
- Borrowers we say beggars are no choosers.
- Chance (luck) passes science.
- Don't sell the bear skin before you kill the bear.
- Each one is a craftsman of his own fortune.
- Enough there is where too much is not.
- Even small things matter.
- Everyone makes his or her own destiny.
- Everyone should have a mentor.
- Fools pass for wise men while they silent are.
- For lack of the ox, one plows with one's donkey.
- Friend of many, friend of none.
- Good things come in small packages.
- He that asks more than he should, hears more than he would.
- He that will go barefoot must plant no thorns.
- Hunger makes anything taste well.
- In old times, the greatest women were the greatest housewives.
- In small field, good corn grows.
- In the small boxes, the good ointments.
- It is better to lose a witty remark than a friend.
- Long absence changes love: looses friendship and alters affection.
- On a lengthy journey, even a small burden weighs.
- One cannot have too many friends.
- One does not believe in grass on a trodden path.
- One learns while failing.
- One should not judge the tree by the bark.
- Reason lies between the bridle and the spur.
- Science can be proven and luck there's always a chance.
- The allouette in hand is better than the goose that flies. A bird in the hand is worth two in the bush.
- Greed is a bad fault.
- The money hammer opens the iron door.
- The purse opens the mouth.
- The road less traveled; people do not take chances.
- When need comes, one know one's friend.
- Where you lead is how you get there.
- Who was born a cat pursues the mice.
- Wine tells the truth, and should not be believed.
- With many friends, you do not really have one great one.
- With a young hunter, one needs an old dog.
- You cannot have your butter for free.
- You must not put the plow before the steer.

German

- When he has to, the devil eats flies.

Greek

- The heart that loves is always young.

Hebrew

- He who spares the whip hates his son.

Italian

- A fool and his money are soon parted.
- A friend to all and a friend to none is one and the same.
- Better one day as a lion than a hundred as a sheep.
- Do not judge a book by its cover.
- Every rule has an exception.
- He who finds a friend, finds a treasure.
- Love is blind.
- Love rules without rules.
- Not all those who are learned are wise.
- Once a thief always a thief.
- One who makes his bed must lie in it.
- People in glass houses should not throw stones.
- Since the house is on fire let us warm ourselves.
- The liar needs a good memory.
- The tongue has no bone but it breaks bone.
- When the chess game is over, the pawns, rooks, knights, bishops, kings, and queens all go back into the same box.
- You catch more flies with honey than a barrel of vinegar.

Japanese

- A single arrow is easily broken, but not ten in a bundle.
- Fall seven times, stand up eight.
- The rich man thinks of next year, the poor man of the present moment.

Korean

- A stranger nearby is better than a far-away relative is.

Latin

- If there is no wind, row.

Libyan

- Instruction in youth is like engraving in stone.

Malay

- Do not think there are no crocodiles because the water is calm.
- Like a frog underneath coconut shell.

Native American

- If you see no reason for giving thanks, the fault lies in yourself (Minquass).
- It is impossible to awaken someone who is pretending to be asleep (Navajo).
- Man has responsibility, not power (Tuscarora).
- Talk to your children while they are eating; what you say will stay even after you are gone (Nez Percé).

Nigerian

- He who is being carried does not realize how far the town is.
- Not to know is bad; not to wish to know is worse.

Norwegian

- For someone to become a good hook, he or she must be bent early (in childhood).
- For someone to become a good mother, she must be amused early.

Romanian

- Adversity makes a man wise, not rich.
- If you wish good advice, consult an old man.

Russian

- A bird may be known by its flight.
- A drop hollows out a stone.
- A fly will not get into a closed mouth.

- A man is judged by his deeds, not by his words.
- A man should not be struck when he is down.
- A priest's beard is always soaked in butter.
- A sparrow in the hand is better than a cock on the roof.
- A wolf will not eat wolf.
- After a storm (comes) fair weather, after sorrow (comes) joy.
- All are not cooks that walk with long knives.
- All cats are grey at night.
- All is not gold that glitters.
- An empty barrel makes the greatest sound.
- Any fish is good if it is on the hook.
- Any sandpiper is great in his own swamp.
- As is well that ends well.
- As you cooked the porridge, so must you eat it.
- Better a dove on the plate than a woodgrouse in the mating place.
- Better to stumble than make a slip of the tongue.
- Beware of a quiet dog and still water.
- Cut down the tree that you are able to.
- Do not carry rubbish out of your hut.
- Do not cut the bough you are sitting on.
- Do not dig a hole for somebody else; you yourself will fall into it.
- Do not make an elephant out of a fly.
- Do not measure (others) by your own yardstick.
- Do not plant a tree with its root upward.
- Do not play with fire—you will burn yourself.
- Do not praise yourself while going into battle. Praise yourself coming out of battle.
- Do not teach a pike to swim; a pike knows his own science.
- Eggs cannot teach a hen.
- Every sandpiper praises its own swamp.
- Every seed knows its time.
- God gives to those who get up early.
- God takes care of the one who takes care of himself.
- He would exclaim "Ah" looking at himself.
- Idleness is the mother of all vices.
- It is a bad workman that has a bad saw.
- It is good to be visiting, but it is better at home.
- Not everyone who has a cowl on is a monk.
- Once burned by milk you will blow on cold water.
- One does not go to Tula with one's own samovar.
- One does not look for good from good.
- One does not sharpen the axes after the right time; after the time they are needed.
- One fisherman sees another from afar.
- One is one's own master on one's own stove.
- One may make up a soft bed (for somebody), but still it will be hard to sleep in.

- One who sits between two chairs may easily fall down.
- One would like to eat fish, but would not like to get into the water.
- Stormy weather cannot stay all the time; the red sun will come out, too.
- Stretch your legs according to your clothes.
- Tell me who is your friend and I will tell you who you are.
- The appetite comes during a meal.
- The devil is not as frightful as he is painted.
- The end is the crown of any work.
- The one who draws (a cart) is urged on.
- The peasant will not cross himself before it begins to thunder.
- The sun will shine into our yard too.
- The tongue speaks, but the head does not know.
- There is no evil without good.
- There will be trouble if the cobbler starts making pies.
- There will come a time when the seed will sprout.
- We do not care of what we have, but we cry when it is lost.
- Where something is thin, that is where it tears.
- You can get to the ends of the world on a lie, but you cannot return.
- You cannot break through a wall with your forehead.
- You cannot pull a fish out of a pond without labor.
- You do not need a whip to urge on an obedient horse.
- You do not swap horses while crossing the ford.
- You need a sharp axe for a tough bough.
- You need not be afraid of a barking dog, but you should be afraid of a silent dog.
- You will reap what you will sow.

Scottish

- What may be done at any time will be done at no time.
- With lies you may go ahead in the world, but you can never go back.

Spanish

- A tree that grows crooked will never straighten its trunk.
- After all, to make a beautiful omelet you have to break an egg.
- Do not postpone until tomorrow what you can do today.
- Do not speak unless you can improve on the silence.
- He who gets close to a good tree, will have a good shade.
- Once you build a bad/good reputation it stays forever.
- One that does badly will pay before he/she dies the same way.
- One that portrays to be good and his intentions are bad.
- What the eyes do not see the heart does not feel.

Swedish

- Do not throw away the old bucket until you know whether the new one holds water.
- Go often to the house of a friend, for weeds soon choke up the unused path.
- Shared joy is a double joy; shared sorrow is half a sorrow.

Turkish

- Kind words take the snake out of his hole.
- Measure a thousand times and cut once.
- No matter how far you have gone on a wrong road, turn back.

Welsh

- Adversity brings knowledge and knowledge, wisdom.

Yiddish

- Everyone is kneaded out of the same dough, but not baked in the same oven.
- If all men pulled in one direction, the world would topple over.
- If you sit in a hot bath, you think the whole town is warm.

Source: Proverb Resources (2003).

Bibliography

"10 Years Down the Line" (May 2004), *Black Economic Empowerment*, Business Map Foundation.

"100 Best Corporate Citizens" (Spring 2004), *Business Ethics Magazine*.

1988 Educating for Global Competence: The Report of the Advisory Council for International Educational Exchange (1988), Council on International Educational Exchange.

Acemoglu, D. (1998), "Why Do New Technologies Complement Skills? Directed Technical Change and Wage Inequality," *Quarterly Journal of Economics*, 113(4), 1055–89. [DOI: 10.1162/003355398555838]

Adekola, A. and Sergi, B.S. (2007), "The Significance and Paradox of Globalisation in the 21st Century: The Role of Three Major Global Institutions in Selected Areas," *International Journal of Management and Enterprise Development*, 4(3), 354–71.

Adhikari, R. and Yang, Y. (2002), "What Will WTO Membership Mean for China and Its Trading Partners?" *Finance and Development*, 39(3), 22–5.

Adler, N.J. (1991), *International Dimensions of Organizational Behavior*, 2nd edn (Boston: PWS-KENT Publishing Company).

Albrecht, K. (1990), *Service Within: Solving the Middle Management Leadership Crisis* (Homewood, Ill.: Dow Jones-Irwin).

Al-Ghamdi, S. (2006), "The Impact of Globalization on Saudi Arabian Dairy Industry: A Case Study Approach," *Journal for Global Business Advancement*.

Ali, A.J. (2003), "The Intercultural Adaptation of Expatriate Spouses and Children. An Empirical Study on the Determinants Contributing to the Success of Expatriation." Available at: http://dissertaitions.ub.rug.nl/FILES/faculties/management/2003/a.j.ali/titlecom.pdf.

Al-Otaibi, M.M. and Robinson, R.K. (2002), "The Dairy Industry in Saudi Arabia: Current Situation and Future Prospects," *International Journal of Dairy Technology*, 55(2), 75–8. [DOI: 10.1046/j.1471-0307.2002.00048.x]

Anderson, B.A. (2005), "Expatriate Selection: Good Management or Good Luck," *International Journal of Human Resource Management*, 16(4), 567–83.

Anderson, J.E. and van Wincoop, E. (2004), *Trade Costs*, NBER Working Paper No. 10480.

Antràs, P. (2003), "Firms, Contracts, and Trade Structure," *Quarterly Journal of Economics*, 118(4), 1375–1418. [DOI: 10.1162/003355303322552829]

Artis, M.J. (2002), "The Stability and Growth Pact: Fiscal Policy in the EMU," in Breuss, F., Fink, G. and Griller, S. (eds), *Institutional, Legal and Economic Aspects of the EMU* (Wien and New York: Springer), 101–15.

Azad, A.N., Erdem, A.S. and Saleem, N. (1998), "A Framework for Realizing the Potential of Information Technology in Developing Countries," *International Journal of Commerce and Management*, 8(2), 121–33.

Baldwin, R.E. and Krugman, P. (2004), "Agglomeration, Integration and Tax Harmonization," *European Economic Review*, 48(1), 1–23. [DOI: 10.1016/S0014-2921%2802%2900318-5]

Barysch, K. (2004), *Is Tax Competition Bad?* "CER Bulletin 37, August–September." Available at http://www.cer.org.uk/articles/37_barysch.htm.

Bennett, R., Anniston, A. and Coloquhon, T. (2000), "Cross-Cultural Training: A Critical Step in Ensuring the Success of International Assignments," *Human Resource Management*, 39(2/3), 239–50. [DOI: 10.1002/1099-050X%28200022%2F23%2939%3A2%2F3%3C239%3A%3AAID-HRM12%3E3.0.CO%3B2-J]

Bernard, A.B., Jensen, J.B. and Schott, P.K. (2003), *Falling Trade Costs, Heterogeneous Firms, and Industry Dynamics*, NBER Working Paper No. 9639.

Besley, T., Griffith, R. and Klemm, A. (2001), *Empirical Evidence on Fiscal Interdependence in OECD Countries* (London: London School of Economics).

Best, B. (1990), "Monetary Systems and Managed Economies." Retrieved June 1999 from http://www.benbest.com/polecon/monetaryhtml.

Bhagat, R.S. and Prien, K.O. (1996), "Cross-cultural Training in Organizational Contexts," in Landis, D. and Bhagat, R.S. (eds), *Handbook of Intercultural Training*, 2nd edn (Thousand Oaks, Calif.: SAGE Publications), 216–30.

Bhagwati, J. (1984), "Splintering and Disembodiment of Services and Developing Nations," *World Economy*, 7(2), 133–44.

Bhagwati, J., Panagariya, A. and Srinivasan, T.N. (2004), "The Muddles over Outsourcing," *Journal of Economic Perspectives*, 18(4), 93–114. [DOI: 10.1257/0895330042632753]

Black, J.S. and Gregersen, H.B. (1991), "When Yankee Comes Home: Factors Related to Expatriate and Spouse Repatriation Adjustment," *Journal of International Business Studies*, 22(4), 671–94. [DOI: 10.1057/palgrave.jibs.8490319]

Black, J.S., Gregersen, H.B. and Mendenhall, M.E. (1992), *Global Assignments: Successfully Expatriating and Repatriating International Managers* (San Francisco: Jossey-Bass).

Black, J.S., Mendenhall, M. and Oddou, G. (1991), "Toward a Comprehensive Model of International Adjustment: An Integration of Multiple Theoretical Perspectives," *Academy of Management Review*, 18(2), 291–317. [DOI: 10.2307/258863]

Blair, T. (2005), *Lord Mayor's Banquet at The Guildhall in London*, November 14.

Blankart, C.B. (2002), "A Public Choice View of Tax Competition," *Public Finance Review*, 30(5), 366–76.

Bohn, H. (1991), "Time Consistency of Monetary Policy in the Open Economy," *Journal of International Economics*, 30(3/4), 249–66. [DOI: 10.1016/0022-1996%2891%2990021-W]

BP (2006), *BP Statistical Review of World Energy, June 2006* (London: BP).

Brake, T., Walker, M.D. and Walker, T. (1995), *Doing Business Internationally: The Guide to Cross-Cultural Success* (New York: Richard D. Irwin, Inc).

Brazil Experience (1995), International Video Network (Videotape).

Broda, C. and Weinstein, D.E. (2004), *Globalization and the Gains from Variety*, NBER Working Paper No. 10314.

Brynjolfsson, E. and Hitt, L.M. (2003), *Computing Productivity: Firm-Level Evidence*, in MIT Sloan Working Paper No. 4210–01.

Caligiuri, P.M. (2000), "Selecting Expatriates for Personality Characteristics: A Moderating Effect of Personality on the Relationship between Host National Contact and Cross-Cultural Adjustment," *Management International Review*, 40(1), 61–80.

Caligiuri, P.M. and Di Santo, V. (2001), "Global Competence: What Is It, and Can It Be Developed Through Global Assignments?" *Human Resource Planning*, 24(3).

Calvert, P.J. and Hernon, P. (1997), "Surveying Service Quality within University Libraries," *Journal of Academic Librarianship*, 25(5), 408–15.

Caudron, S. (1991), "Training Ensures Success Overseas," *Personnel Journal*, 70(12), 27–30.

Caves, R.E. (1996), *Multinational Enterprise and Economic Analysis*, 2nd edn (Cambridge, UK: Cambridge University Press).

Center for Trade Policy Studies: the Cato Institute before the House Committee on International Relations Subcommittee on International Economic Policy and Trade (July 22, 1998), *America's Misunderstood Trade Deficit*. Testimony of Daniel T. Griswold, Associate Director.

Chatterjee, P. (1997), "Peru Goes Beneath the Shell," *Multinational Monitor*, 18(5), 14–17.

Cheah, C.W. (1987), *Calculus of International Communications: A Study in the Political Economy of Transborder Data Flows* (Westport, Conn.: Libraries Unlimited).

"China and India—From Then to Now," Business Week Online. Retrieved October 6, 2006 from http://www.businessweek.com/magazine/toc/05_34/B3948chinaindia.htm.

"China Urges the US To Narrow its Trade Gap with the Asian Country" (September 25, 2003). Retrieved March 2005 from http://en.cappma.com/news/readnews.asp?r=7.50751593026671&svr=4&newsid=4388.

CIA Factbook (2004). Retrieved November 2004 from http://www.cia.gov/cia/publications/factbook/.

Clissold, S. (1996), *Latin America Cultural Outline* (New York: Harper & Row).

Cnossen, S. (2003), "How Much Tax Coordination in the European Union?" *International Tax and Public Finance*, 10(6), 625–49. [DOI: 10.1023/A%3A1026373703108]

Coon, D.L. and Tyler, V.L. (1984), *Culturegrams* (Provo, UT: David M. Kennedy Center for International Studies, Brigham Young University).

Culturegrams. Retrieved April 2005 from www.culturegrams.com. (London, UT: Culture Grams Axiom Press, Inc.).

Daniels, N.C. (1994), *Information Technology: the Management Challenge* (Reading, Mass.: Addison-Wesley).

David M. Kennedy Center for International Studies (1992), *Culturegrams: The Nations Around Us* (Garrett Park, MD: Garrett Park Press).

Davies, G. (2002), *A History of Money from Ancient Times to the Present Day*, 3rd edn (Cardiff: University of Wales Press).

De Grauwe, P. (2002), "Europe"s Instability Pact," *Financial Times*, July 25, 17.

de Haan, J. and Sturm, J.E. (2000), "On the Relationship between Economic Freedom and Economic Growth," *European Journal of Political Economy*, 16(2), 215–41. [DOI: 10.1016/S0176-2680%2899%2900065-8]

de Mooij, R.A. and Ederveen, S. (2003), "Taxation and Foreign Direct Investment: A Synthesis of Empirical Research," *International Tax and Public Finance*, 10(6), 673–93. [DOI: 10.1023/A%3A1026329920854]

Deaton, A. (2001), "Counting the World's Poor: Problems and Possible Solutions," *World Bank Research Observer*, 16, 125–47. [DOI: 10.1093/wbro%2F16.2.125]

Deffeyes, K.S. (2005), *Beyond Oil: The View from Hubbert's Peak* (New York: Hill and Wang).

Delors, J. (1989), *Report on Economic and Monetary Union in the European Community* (Brussels: European Community).

Desai, M.A., Foley, C.F. and Hines, J.R., Jr (2002), *International Joint Ventures and the Boundaries of the Firm*, NBER Working Paper No. 9115.

Desai, M.A., Foley, C.F. and Hines, J.R. (2003), "Chain of Ownership, Tax Competition, and the Location Decisions of Multinational Firms," in Herrmann, H. and Lipsey, R. (eds), *Foreign Direct Investment in the Real and Financial Sector of Industrial Countries* (Berlin: Springer).

Desai, M.A., Foley, C.F. and Hines, J.R. (2004), "Foreign Direct Investment in a World of Multiple Taxes," *Journal of Public Economics*, 88(12), 2727–44. [DOI: 10.1016/j.jpubeco.2003.08.004]

"Developing Expatriates' Cross-cultural Sensitivity: Cultures where 'Your Culture's OK' Is Really not OK" (1997), *The Journal of Management Development*, 16(9), 690–702.

Devereux, M.P. and Freeman, H. (1995), "The Impact of Tax on Foreign Direct Investment: Empirical Evidence and the Implications for Tax Integration Schemes," *International Tax and Public Finance*, 2(1), 85–106. [DOI: 10.1007/BF00873108]

Devereux, M.P. and Griffith, R. (1998), "Taxes and the Location of Production: Evidence from a Panel of US Multinationals," *Journal of Public Economics*, 68, 335–67. [DOI: 10.1016/S0047-2727%2898%2900014-0]

Devereux, M.P., Griffith, R. and Klemm, A. (2002a), "Corporate Income Tax: Reforms and Tax Competition," *Economic Policy*, 35, 451–95.

Devereux, M.P., Lockwood, B. and Redoano, M. (2002b), *Do Countries Compete over Corporate Tax Rates?* CEPR Discussion Paper No. 3400.

DFID (2000), *Eliminating World Poverty: Making Globalisation Work for the Poor.* (London: DFID).

Downs, J. (1970), "Understanding Culture: Guidelines and Techniques for Training," *Trends*, 3(2).

Duncan, B.B., Rumel, D., Zelmanowicz, A., Mengue, S.S., dos Santos, S. and Dalmáz, A. (1995), "Social Inequality in Mortality in São Paulo State, Brazil," *International Journal of Epidemiology*, 24(2), 359–65.

Dunn, R., Jr (1999), "An Easy Monetary Policy in the European Union," *Challenge*, 42(4), 29–43.

Dunning, J.H. (1993), *Multinational Enterprises and the Global Economy* (Wokingham: Addison-Wesley).

Duttagupta, R., Fernandez, G. and Karacadag, C. (2005), "Moving to a Flexible Exchange Rate. How, When, and How Fast?" (Washington, DC: International Monetary Fund) *Economic Issues* 38.

Economist Intelligence Unit. Retrieved May 2004 from http://www.nua.ie/surveys/.

Economist Intelligence Unit (2006), *Seventh Annual E-Readiness Rankings* (London: Market Wire), April 26.

Edvardsson, B., Thomasson, B. and Ovretveit, J. (1994), *Quality of Service: Making it Really Work* (Columbus, OH: McGraw-Hill).

Edwards, L. (1978), "Present Shock and How to Avoid it Abroad," *Across the Board*, 15(2), 36–43.

Egger, P. and Winner, H. (2004), "Economic Freedom and Taxation: Is There a Trade-Off in the Locational Competition between Countries?" *Public Choice*, 118(3–4), 271–88. [DOI: 10.1023/B%3APUCH.0000019904.30629.33]

Embassy of Japan (2004) "Japan's Economy Enters an Era of Globalization." Retrieved August 14, 2004 from: http://www.sg.emb-japan.go.jp/JapanAccess/economy.htm.

Emerging Markets Economy (2002), "A Decline in Brazilian Inflation Expected after Agreement with the Brazil's Petroleos Brasileiro (Petrobras)," by EMEconomy Reporters, August 11.

"EP Dairy Companies Plan Tie-up." Available at: http://www.arabnews.com?page=1&section=0&article=32546&d=25&m=9&y=2003&pix=kingdom.jpg&category=Kingdom.

Estabrooks, M. (1995), *Electronic Technology, Corporate Strategy, and World Transformation* (Westport, Conn.: Quorum Books).

"Estimated Volume of Investments in the Saudi Dairy Sector Exceeds SR 13 Billion" (July 2003), Saudi Economic Survey Available at: http://www.menafn.com/qn_news_story_s.asp?StoryId=25718. http://www.marketresearch.com/product/display.asp?productid=1063657&xs=r&SID=65262079-342785493-395160618.

European Commission (2001), "Company Taxation in the Internal Market," *COM* (2001), 582 Final (Brussels: Office for the Official Publications of the EC).

European Parliament (2004), *Hearing of Laszlo Kovacs, Taxation and Customs Union*. Available at: www.europarl.europa.eu/press/audicom2004/resume/041116-KOVACS-EN.pdf.

Executive Report (1999), *International Conference on Management of Technology, Technology Administration*. Retrieved January 2001 from: http://www.technology.gov/Reports/Compendium/intro.pdf.

Federal Reserve Bank of Richmond. Retrieved July 7, 2004 from: http://www.rich.frb.org/research/econed/museum/1a.html.

Feenstra, R.C., Heston, A., Timmer, M.P. and Deng, H. (2004), *Estimating Real Production and Expenditures across Nations: A Proposal for Improving the Penn World Tables*, NBER Working Paper No. 10866.

Feenstra, R.C. and Kee, H.L. (2004), *Export Variety and Country Productivity*, NBER Working Paper No. 10830.

Feld, L.P. and Reulier, E. (2005), *Strategic Tax Competition in Switzerland: Evidence from a Panel of the Swiss Cantons*, CREMA Working Paper Series 2005-19, Center for Research in Economics, Management and the Arts (CREMA).

Ferraro, G.P. (1994), *The Cultural Dimension of International Business*, 2nd edn (Englewood Cliffs, N.J.: Prentice-Hall).

"Future of Dairy Product Companies in the GCC" (2004). Visited June 2005 at: www.Zawya.com.

Germany Labor Trends (1997), National Trade Data Bank, November 11.

Gibson, J.L. and Gouws, A. (2002), *Overcoming Intolerance in South Africa; Experiments in Democratic Persuasion* (Cambridge, UK: Cambridge University Press).

Giddens, A. (1999), *Runaway World: How Globalization is Reshaping our Lives* (London: Profile).

Going Global (2004), *Country Export Issues*. Retrieved July 2004 from: home3.americanexpress.com/smallbusiness/resources/expanding/global/reports/11160090.shtml.

Goodstein, D.L. (2004), *Out of Gas: The End of the Age of Oil* (New York: W. W. Norton and Company).

Greider, W. (1987), *Secrets of the Temple: How the Federal Reserve Runs the Country* (New York: Simon & Schuster Inc.).

Griffin, M. (1999), "FAO's Involvement in the Promotion of School Milk," *Dairy Development Newsletter*, 5. Food and Agriculture Organization International Dairy Federation of the United Nations.

Grimes, W. (1990), "Chunnel Vision," *The New York Times Magazine*, September 16, 77.

Groshen, E.L., Hobijn, B. and McConnell, M.M. (2005), "U.S. Jobs Gained and Lost through Trade: A Net Measure," *Federal Reserve Bank of New York Current Issues in Economics and Finance*, 11(8).

Grubert, H. (2001), "Tax Planning by Companies and Tax Competition by Governments: Is there Evidence of Changes in Behavior?" in Hines, J.R., Jr (ed.), *International Taxation and Multinational Activity* (Chicago: University of Chicago Press), 113–39.

Grubert, H. and Mutti, J. (2000), "Do Taxes Influence where U.S. Corporations Invest?" *National Tax Journal*, 53(4), 825–39.

Gudykunst, W.B. (1983), "Similarities and Differences in Perception of Initial Intercultural Encounters," *The Southern Speech Communication Journal*, 49, 49–65.

Gudykunst, W.B., Guzley, R.M. and Hammer, M.R. (1996), "Designing Intercultural Training," in Landis, D. and Bhagat, R.S. (eds), *Handbook of Intercultural Training*, 2nd edn (Thousand Oaks, Calif.: SAGE Publications), 61–80.

Gudykunst, W.B. and Kim, Y.Y. (2003), *Communicating with Strangers* (Reading, Mass.: Addison-Wesley).

Gudykunst, W.B., Nishida, T. and Chua, E. (1986), "Uncertainty Reduction in Japanese–North American Dyads," *Communication Research Reports*, 3, 39–46.

Hale, D.D. (1998), "The IMF, Now More Than Ever: The Case for Financial Peacekeeping," *Foreign Affairs*, 77(6), 7–13.

Hall, E.T. (1976), *Beyond Culture* (New York: Anchor Press/Doubleday).

Hallak, J.C. (2004), *Product Quality, Linder, and the Direction of Trade*, NBER Working Paper No. 10877.

Hanmer, L., Healey, J. and Naschold, F. (2000), "Will Growth Halve Global Poverty by 2015?" *ODI Poverty Briefing* (London: ODI).

Harris, P. (1979), "The Unhappy World of the Expatriate," *International Management*, July, 49–50.

Harris, P.R. and Moran, R.T. (1991), *Managing Cultural Differences* (Houston, Tex.: Gulf Publishing Company).

Harris, P.R. and Moran, R.T. (1999), *Managing Cultural Differences: Leadership Strategies for a New World of Business*, 5th edn (Burlington, Mass.: Gulf Professional Publishing).

Harrison, P.A. (1983), *Behaving Brazilian* (Rowley, Mass.: Newbury House Publishers).

Hassan, A. (1999), *The Beef-Hormone Dispute and its Implications for Trade Policy* (Stanford, Calif.: Stanford Institute for International Studies).

Hastings, D.F. (1999), "Lincoln Electric's Harsh Lessons from International Expansion," *Harvard Business Review*, 77, 163–78.

Hastings, J. (2001), *Modern International Law: An Introduction to the Law of Nations* (Upper Saddle River, N.J.: Pearson Education).

Hays, R.D. (1971), "Ascribed Behavioral Determinants of Success–Failure Among U.S. Expatriate Managers," *Journal of International Business Studies*, 2(1), 40–46. [DOI: 10.1057/palgrave.jibs.8490729]

Head, K. and Ries, J. (2003), *Heterogeneity and the FDI v Export Decision of Japanese Manufacturers*, NBER Working Paper No. 10052.

Hechanova, R., Beehr, T.A. and Christiansen, N.D. (2003), "Antecedents and Consequences of Employees' Adjustment to Overseas Assignment: A Meta-analytic Review," *Applied Psychology: An International Review*, 52(2), 213–36.

Helpman, E., Melitz, M.J. and Yeaple, S.R. (2003), *Export v FDI*, NBER Working Paper No. 9439.

Henderson, D.R. (1989), "Are We All Supply-siders Now?" *Contemporary Policy Issues*, 7(4), 116–28.

Hodgetts, R. and Luthans, F. (2002), *International Management: Culture, Strategy, and Behavior* (New York: McGraw-Hill Education).

Hofstede, G. (1980), *Culture's Consequences: International Differences in Work-Related Values* (Thousand Oaks, Calif.: SAGE Publications).

Hofstede, G. (1983), "Dimension of National Cultures in Fifty Countries and Three Regions," in Deregowski, J.B., Dziurawiec, S. and Annis, R.C. (eds), *Explications in Cross-Cultural Psychology* (Lisse, the Netherlands: Swets and Zeitlinger), 335–55.

Hofstede, G. (1987), "The Applicability of McGregor's Theories in SouthEast Asia," *Journal of Management Development*, 6(3), 16–18.

Hofstede, G. (1991), *Culture and Organizations* (London: McGraw-Hill).

Hofstede, G. (1997), *Cultures and Organizations: Software of the Mind* (London: McGraw-Hill).

Hofstede, G. and Bond, M.H. (1988), "The Confucian Connection: From Cultural Roots to Economic Growth," *Organizational Dynamics*, 16(4), 4–21.

Hubbert, M.K. (1956), *Nuclear Energy and the Fossil Fuels*. Paper Presented before the Spring Meeting of the Southern District, American Petroleum Institute, San Antonio, Texas, March 7–9.

Hubbert, M.K. (1962), *Energy Resources: A Report to the Committee on Natural Resources of the National Academy of Sciences-National Research Council* (Washington, DC: National Academy of Sciences/National Research Council).

Huizinga, H. and Nicodeme, G. (2003), "Foreign Ownership and Corporate Income Taxation: An Empirical Evaluation," CEPR Discussion Paper 3952.

Hummels, D. and Klenow, P.J. (2002), *The Variety and Quality of a Nation's Trade*, NBER Working Paper No. 8712.

Huxley, A. (1932). Retrieved from http://www.quotationspage.com/quote/24956. html.

Ibrahim, S.E. (1995), The Third Nordic Conference on Middle Eastern Studies: Ethnic Encounter and Culture Change, Joensuu, Finland, 19-22 June 1995, "Management and Mismanagement of Diversity. The Case of Ethnic Conflict and State-building in the Arab World," Ibn Khaldoun Center, Cairo.

ILO (2006), *Global Employment Trends* (Geneva: International Labour Organization).

Internet Economy Indicators. Retrieved May 3, 2004 from: http://www. internetindicators.com/facts.html.

Internet World Stats Usage and Populations Statistics. Retrieved June 21, 2004 from: http://www.internetworldstats.com/stats1.htm.

Johnson, R.L., Tsiros, M. and Lancioni, R.A. (1995), "Measuring Service Quality: A Systems Approach," *Journal of Services Marketing*, 9(5), 6–19. [DOI: 10.110 8/08876049510100272]

Jorgenson, D.W., Ho, M.S. and Stiroh, K.J. (2004), "Will the U.S. Productivity Resurgence Continue?" *Federal Reserve Bank of New York Current Issues in Economics and Finance*, 10(13).

Jovanovic, M.N. (2005), *The Economics of European Integration: Limits and Prospects* (Cheltenham, UK: Edward Elgar).

Kapp, R.A. (1998), The China Business Review, Letter from the President. Common Sense on MFN for China. *US-China Business Council*.

"Kathie Lee Goes on Defense" (1999), *Multinational Monitor*, 20(9), no page available.

Kiely, R. (2005), "Globalization and Poverty, and the Poverty of Globalization Theory," *Current Sociology*, 53(6), 895–914. [DOI: 10.1177/0011392105057154]

King, C.A. and Garey, J.G. (1997), "Relational Quality in Service Encounters," *International Journal of Hospitality Management*, 16(1), 39–63.

Kroeber, A.L. and Kluckhohn, C. (1952), *Culture: A Critical Review of Concepts and Definitions* (Cambridge, Mass.: The Museum).

Kubicová, J. (2004), "Tax Competition in Today's World Affairs," in Sergi, B.S. and Bagatelas, W.T. (eds), *Economics and Politics: Has 9/11 Changed Anything?* (Bratislava: Iura Edition), 205–31.

Kunst, P. and Lemmink, J. (1995), *Managing Service Quality Textbook* (London: Paul Chapman).

Kunstler, J.H. (2005), *The Long Emergency: Surviving the Converging Catastrophes of the Twenty-First Century* (New York: Atlantic Monthly Press).

Lall, S. (2004), "Industrial Success and Failure in a Globalizing World," *International Journal of Technology Management and Sustainable Development*, 3(3), 189–214. [DOI: 10.1386/ijtm.3.3.189%2F0]

Lasch, C. (1977), *Haven in a Heartless World* (New York: Basic Books, Inc).

Lee, E. (1998), "Trade Union Rights: An Economic Perspective," *International Labour Review*, 137(3), 313–19.

Lemon, S. (2002), "Look to China for Outsourcing Services." Retrieved June 2004 from: http://www.cnn.com/2002/TECH/industry/01/21/outsourcing.china.idg/index.html.

Leonard, B. (2002), "Ways to Tell if a Diversity Program Is Measuring Up," *HRMagazine*, 47(7), 21.

Loayza, N., Schmidt-Hebbel, K. and Serven, L. (2000), "What Drives Private Saving Across the World," *The Review of Economics and Statistics*, 82(2), 165–81. [DOI: 10.1162/003465300558678]

Lobo, I. (2004), *Inequality not Poverty Begets Crime in Brazil*, Agência Brasil.

Lord, W. (1993), "Clinton and China's President Will Meet to Discuss Disputes," in a meeting in the White House on September 25, *New York Times*, October 2, 1993.

Lourenco, M.R. and Trevizan, M.A. (2002), "Líderes de la enfermería brasileña: su visión sobre la temática del liderazgo y su percepción con respecto a la relación liderazgo y enfermería," *Rev. Latino-Am. Enfermagem*, 9(3), 14–19.

Lovelock, C.H. (2005), *Services Marketing: People, Technology, Strategy*, 5th edn (Upper Saddle River, N.J.: Prentice-Hall).

Luengo, E.G. (1998), "Resurging Latin America Presents Global Technology Managers with New Markets and Venture Opportunities," *Research Technology Management*, 41(4), 2–4.

Luhnow, D. and Terhune, C. (2003), "A Low-Budget Cola Shakes Up Markets South of the Border," *The Wall Street Journal*, October 27, A1.

Mankiw, G.N., Forbes, K.J. and Rosen, H.S. (2004), "Testimony before the Joint Economic Committee, U.S. Congress: 'The Economic Report of the President,'" February 10.

Mason, H.R. (1987), *Management* (Homewood, Ill.: Irwin Publishing).

Maugeri, L. (2006), *The Age of Oil: The Mythology, History, and the Future of the World's most Controversial Resource* (Westport, Conn.: Praeger Publishing).

Mayerhofer, H., Hartmann, L.S., Michellitsch-Riedl, G. and Kollinger, I. (2004), "Expatriate Assignments: A Neglected Issue in Global Staffing," *International Journal of Human Resource Management*, 15(8), 1371–89. [DOI: 10.1080/0958 519042000257986]

McGregor, D. (1960), *The Human Side of Enterprise* (New York: McGraw-Hill).

McLuhan, M. (1960), *Understanding Media* (London, UK: Routledge).

Meares, C.A. and Sargent, J.F., Jr (1999), *The Digital Work Force: Building Infotech Skills at the Speed of Innovation* (Washington, DC: US Department of Commerce Technology Administration, Office of Technology Policy).

Meinert, J.L. (September 30, 1997), Testimony Before the Subcommittee on Trade, of the House Committee on Ways and Means Hearing on the Implementation of Fast Track Trade Negotiating Authority.

Meisler, A. (2004), "Where in the World is Offshoring Going?" *Workforce Management*, January, 45.

Mendenhall, M.E., Punnett, B.J. and Ricks, D.A. (1995), *Global Management* (Cambridge, MA: Blackwell).

Mendenhall, M.E. and Wiley, C. (1994), "Strangers in a Strange Land: The Relationship between Expatriate Adjustment and Impression Management," *American Behavioral Scientist*, 37(5), 605–20. [DOI: 10.1177/0002764294037 005003]

Mercer Human Resource Consulting (2006), "Worldwide Cost of Living Survey 2006—City Rankings." Available at: http://www.mercerhr.com/pressrelease/details.jhtml/dynamic/idContent/1142150;jsessionid=QN31H2M4FPL4SCTGOUGCHPQKMZ0QUJLW.

Merryfield, M. (1995, July), "Teacher Education in Global and International Education," ERIC Clearinghouse on Teaching and Teacher Education, Washington DC. *ERIC Identifier:* ED384601.

Miles, M.A., Feulner, E.J. and O'Grady, M.A. (2005), *2005 Index of Economic Freedom* (Washington, DC: The Heritage Foundation and *The Wall Street Journal*).

Miller, J.J. (1987), *Issues for Managers* (Homewood, Ill.: Irwin Publishing).

"Najran Dairy," (2004). Visited May 2004 at: http://www.najrandairy.com/.

Nath, R. and Sadhu, K. (1988), "Comparative Analysis, Conclusions and Future Directions" in Nath, R. (ed.), *Comparative Management—A Regional View* (Cambridge, Mass.: Ballinger Publishing Company), 273.

Naumann, E. (1992), "A Conceptual Model of Expatriate Turnover," *Journal of International Business Studies*, 23(3), 499–531.

Nehrt, L.C. (1977), *Business and International Education. International Education Project* (Washington, DC: American Council on Education Occasional Paper) No. 4.

Nelson, B. (1998), "Motivating Workers Worldwide," *Global Workforce*, 3(6), 25–7.

New Webster's Dictionary and Thesaurus of the English Language (1993), (Danbury, CT: Lexicon Publications, Inc.).

Nicholas, D. (1990), *Cross Cultural Communication* (McLean, VA: Institute for the Study of Man).

Nyrop, R.F. (1983), *Brazil, a Country Study* (Washington, DC: Library of Congress).

OECD (1998), *Harmful Tax Competition: An Emerging Global Issue* (Paris: Organisation for Economic Co-operation and Development).

Owens, J. (2005), *Fundamental Tax Reform: the Experience of OECD Countries*, Tax Foundation Background Paper No. 47.

Oxford English Dictionary, 2nd edn (1989). Retrieved May 2004 from: http://www.lib.umn.edu/.

Parasuraman, A., Berry, L.L. and Zeithaml, V. (1990), "An Empirical Examination of Relationships in an Extended Service Quality Model," Marketing Service Institute Working Paper, 90–112.

Petrazzini, B. and Kibati, M. (1999), "The Internet in Developing Countries," *Communications of the ACM*, 42(6), 31–6. [DOI: 10.1145/303849.303858]

Pierre, C. (1980), *Multicultural Managers* (Washington, DC: The Society of Intercultural Education, Training, and Research, SIETAR).

Poe, A.C. (2002), "Selection Savvy," *HRMagazine*, 47(4), 77–81.

Rahim, A.M. and Blum, A. (1994), *Global Perspectives on Organizational Conflict* (Westport, Conn.: Praeger Publishing).

Rapert, M.I. and Wren, B.M. (1998), "Service Quality as a Competitive Opportunity," *Journal of Services Marketing*, 12(3), 223–35. [DOI: 10.1108/08876049810219 539]

Redding, S. and Schott, P.K. (2003), *Distance, Skill Deepening and Development: Will Peripheral Countries ever Get Rich?* NBER Working Paper No. 9447.

Reynolds, A. and Nadler, L. (1983), *The Global HRD Consultant's & Practitioner's Handbook* (Amherst, Mass.: Human Resource Development Press, Inc.).

Reynolds, J.I. and Rice, G.H. (1988), "American Education for International Business," *Management International Review*, 28(3), 48–57.

Rigobon, R. and Rodrik, D. (2004), *Rule of Law, Democracy, Openness, and Income: Estimating the Relationships*, NBER Working Paper No. 10750.

Roberts, P. (2004), *The End of Oil: On the Edge of a Perilous New World* (Boston: Houghton Mifflin).

Rochefort, H.W. (2004), *French Fried: The Culinary Capers of an American in Paris*. Retrieved May 2004 from: http://www.understandfrance.org/France/Intercultural.html.

Rodrigues, C. (1996), *International Management: A Cultural Approach* (New York: West Publishing Company).

Rodrigues, C.A. (2002), *International Management: A Cultural Approach*, 2nd edn (Mason, OH: South-Western).

Romalis, J. (2005), *NAFTA's and CUSFTA's Impact on International Trade*, NBER Working Paper No. 11059.

Rugman, A.M. and Hodgetts, R.M. (1998), *International Business: A Strategic Management Approach* (Upper Saddle River, N.J.: Pearson Education).

Ryan, A.M., McFarland, L., Baron, H. and Page, R. (1999), "An International Look at Selection Practices: Nation and Culture as Explanations for Variability in Practice," *Personnel Psychology*, 52(2), 359–91. [DOI: 10.1111/j.1744-6570.1999.tb00165.x]

Samiee, S. (1999), "The Internationalization of Services: Trends, Obstacles, and Issues," *Journal of Services Marketing*, 13(4), 319–28. [DOI: 10.1108/088760 49910282574]

"Saudi Dairy Market to Reach SR 3.6 Billion" (May 2005), The Saudi Arabia Information Resource. Visited July 27, 2006 at: http://www.saudinf.com/main/y8175.htm. http://www.foodproductiondaily.com/news/news-ng.asp?id=27961.

"Saudi Milk Processors Merge" (2002), *Food Production Daily*. Visited July 2006 at http://www.foodproductiondaily.com/news/news-ng.asp?id=27961.

Schmidheiny, K. (2004), *Income Segregation and Local Progressive Taxation: Empirical Evidence from Switzerland*, CESifo Working Paper Series 1313.

Schumacher, M. (undated), *Effective Strategies for the First-Time Expatriate.* Retrieved February 14, 2005 from: http://www.expat-online.com/forum/bluesteps. cfm.

Seno'o, M. (1996) *Yamada Hagaki and the History of Paper Currency in Japan*, Bank of Japan, Institute for Monetary & Economic Studies.

Sergi, B.S. (1998), "External Inflationary Incentives in Europe: How and Why They Moved in the 1980s," *Economie Appliquée*, 51(2), 123–37.

Sergi, B.S. (2005a), "International Organizations and Global Affairs," *Global Economic Review*, 34(3), 345–54. [DOI: 10.1080/12265080500292625]

Sergi, B.S. (2005b), "Slashing Taxes on Corporate Profits. Does it Help Entrepreneurship?" *Transformations in Business and Economics*, 4(2)(8), 21–36.

Sergi, B.S. (2006a), "Economic Agents, Ethics and International Economic Organisations," *Managing Global Transitions*, 4(1), 63–78.

Sergi, B.S. (2006b), *Central and Peripheral Regions in Europe: Can Tax Competition Attract Foreign Direct Investment Forever?* (Washington, DC: American Consortium on European Studies (ACES), ACES Cases, No. 2006.3).

Shirouzu, N. and Hawkins, L., Jr (2003), "Ford, GM Fight Over Brightest Labor Market," *The Wall Street Journal*, October 17, A9.

Shyman, M. and Gough, N. (2004), "The Ties that Bind," *Time Asia*, 164(1).

Silva, M., Alves Rozendo, C., Laus Ribas Gomes, E. and Puntel de Almeida, M.C. (1998), "The Changing Focus of Nursing Practice in Brazil," *International History of Nursing Journal*, 3(4), 19–24.

Simon, P. (1980), *The Tongue Tied American* (New York, NY: Continuum Press).

Skoko, H. (2005), *Theory of Parallel Import and its Protection* (Belgrade: Andrejevic Endowment).

Smelser, N.J. (1998), "Social Transformations and Social Change," *International Social Science Journal*, 50(156), June, 173–78.

Solomon, C.M. (1993), "Transplanting Corporate Cultures Globally," *Personnel Journal*, 72(10), 78–88.

Sorensen, P.B. (2001), "Tax Coordination in the European Union: What Are the Issues?" *Swedish Economic Policy Review*, 8(1), 143–95.

Stafford, M.R., Stafford, T.F. and Wells, B.P. (1998), "Determinants of Service Quality and Satisfaction in the Auto Casualty Claims Process," *Journal of Services Marketing*, 12(6), 426–40. [DOI: 10.1108/08876049810242687]

Stahl, G.K. and Caligiuri, P.M. (2005), "The Effectiveness of Expatriate Coping Strategies: The Moderating Role of Cultural Distance, Position Level and Time on the International Assignment," *Journal of Applied Psychology*, 90(4), 603–15. [PubMed 16060781] [DOI: 10.1037/0021-9010.90.4.603]

Stamatis, D.H. (1996), *Total Quality Service* (Boca Raton, Fla.: St. Lucie Press).

Stauss, B. and Mang, P. (1999), "Culture Shocks in Inter-cultural Service Encounters," *Journal of Services Marketing*, 13(4/5), 329–46. [DOI: 10.1108/08876049910282583]

Stessin, L. (1979), "Culture Shock and the American Businessman Overseas," in Smith, E.C. and Luce, L.F. (eds), *Toward Internationalism: Readings in Cross Cultural Communication* (Rowley, Mass.: Newbury House), 214–25.

Strayhorn, C.K. (1995), *Trade with Cuba: Past and Future*, Window on State Government, State of Texas. Retrieved February 29, 2006 from: http://www.window.state.tx.us/comptrol/fnotes/dec95fn.html.

Streeten, P. (2001), *Globalisation: Threat or Opportunity?* (Copenhagen: Copenhagen Business School Press).

"Study Reveals Corporate Social Responsibility a Major Factor in Overseas Investment and Purchasing" (2004) *Ethical Corporation Magazine*, January 20.

Sullivan, M.A. (2005), "On Corporate Tax Reform, Europe Surpasses the US," *Tax Notes*, May 29, 992–5.

Swaak, R. A. (1995), "Expatriate Failures: Too Many, Too Much Cost, Too Little Planning," *Compensation and Benefits Review*, 27, 47–56.

Tertzakian, P. (2006), *A Thousand Barrels a Second: The Coming Oil Break Point and the Challenges Facing an Energy Dependent World* (New York: McGraw-Hill).

The Saudi Arabian Economy (2005), The Saudi Arabian Business Council. Visited June 2005 at: http://www.us-saudi-business.org/The%20Saudi%20Arabian%20Economy.html.

Toft, B. and Reynolds, S. (1994), *Learning From Disasters* (Oxford, UK: Butterworth-Heinemann).

Tokyo Stock Exchange. Retrieved May 2004 from: http://www.tse.or.jp.

Trefler, D. (2004), "The Long and Short of the Canada-U.S. Free Trade Agreement," *American Economic Review*, 94(4), 870–95. [DOI: 10.1257/0002828042002633]

Tung, R.L. (1981), "Selection and Training of Personnel for Overseas Assignments," *Columbia Journal of World Business*, 16(1), 68–78.

Tung, R.L. (1982), "Selection and Training Procedures of U.S., European, and Japanese Multinationals," *California Management Review*, 25(1), 57–71.

Tung, R.L. (1998), "American Expatriates Abroad: From Neophytes to Cosmopolitans," *Journal of World Business*, 33(2), 125–44.

Tye, M.G. and Chen, P.Y. (2004), *Selection of Expatriates: Decision Making Models Used by HR Professionals* (Colorado State: Human Resource Planning, Department of Psychology) 28.

Tyler, K. (2001), "Don't Fence Her In," *HRMagazine*, 46(3), 70–76.

UK Department of Transportation (1995), "Mawhinney Outlines UK Transport Policy in the International Arena," UK Government Press Release, March 8.

UNCTAD (2002), *The Least Developed Countries Report* (New York and Geneva: United Nations).

UNCTAD (2005), *World Investment Report 2005: Transnational Corporations and the Internationalization of R&D* (New York and Geneva: United Nations).

UNCTAD (2006), *World Investment Report 2006. FDI from Developing and Transition Economies: Implications for Development* (New York and Geneva: United Nations).

UNDP (2002), *Human Development Report* (Geneva: United Nations).

US Department of State, Background Notes: Brazil (March 2005) Bureau of Public Affairs Department of State Publication 7756.

US Department of State, Background Notes: Germany (1997), FY 1998, *Country Commercial Guide: Germany.* Report prepared by US Embassy Bonn.

US Saudi Arabian Business Council (undated). http://www.us-saudi-business.org/fdemo.htm.

US Library of Congress (2005), *A Country Study: Brazil.* Available at: http://lcweb2.loc.gov/frd/cs/brtoc.html.

Van Pelt, P. and Wolniansky, N. (1990), "The High Cost of Expatriation," *Management Review*, 79(7), 40–41.

Vanhonacker, W. (1999), *Asian Marketing Casebook* (Upper Saddle River, N.J.: Pearson Education).

Varner, I.I. and Palmer, T.M. (2002), "Successful Expatriation and Organizational Strategies," *Review of Business*, 23(2), 8–11.

Varner, I.I. and Palmer, T.M. (2005), "Role of Cultural Self-Knowledge in Successful Expatriation," *Singapore Management Review*, 27(1), 1–26.

Vernon, R. (1995), *Manager in the International Economy. Prentice-Hall Professional Technical Reference* (Englewood Cliffs, NJ: Prentice-Hall).

Victor, D.A. (1992), *International Business Communication* (New York, NY: Harper Collins).

Wade, R. (2002), "Globalization, Poverty and Income Distribution: Does the Liberal Argument Hold?" DESTIN Working Paper 02–33 (Development Studies Institute, London School of Economics).

Walker, J.L. (1995), "Service Encounter Satisfaction: Conceptualized," *Journal of Services Marketing*, 9(1), 5–14. [DOI: 10.1108/08876049510079844]

Wang, Y. and Pearson, T.E. (2002), "Measuring Personal Service Quality: An Analysis of Hotels in the People's Republic of China," *International Journal of Hospitality & Tourism Administration*, 3(2), 3–29.

Weaver, G.R. (1998a), "Understanding and Coping with Cross-Cultural Adjustment Stress," in Weaver, G.R. (ed.), *Culture, Communication, and Conflict: Readings in Intercultural Relations*, 2nd edn (Needham Heights, Mass.: Simon & Schuster Publishing), 187–204.

Weaver, G.R. (1998b), "The Process of Reentry," in Weaver, G.R. (ed.), *Culture, Communication, and Conflict: Readings in Intercultural Relations*, 2nd edn (Needham Heights, Mass.: Simon & Schuster Publishing), 230–38.

Wells, K. and Revzin, P. (1990), "As Britain-France Tunnel Gets Closer, Two Sides Couldn't Be Further Apart," *The Wall Street Journal*, October 25, A17.

Werner, P. (1970), *Report to the Council and the Commission on the Realization by Stages of Economic and Monetary Union in the Community* (Luxembourg: European Communities).

"What Does China's WTO Accession Mean for Foreign Industry." Retrieved September 2004 from: http://www.chinabig.com/en/market/wtochina/what01.htm.

Wijers-Hasegawa, Y. (2004), "Counselors Now Target Japanese Overseas," *Japan Times*, August 19, 5.

Wirth, L. (1998), "Women in Management: Closer to Breaking Through the Glass Ceiling?" *International Labour Review*, 137(1), 93–103.

Wolf, M. (2001), "A Stepping Stone from Poverty," *Financial Times*, December 19.

World Bank (2000/01), *World Development Report: Attacking Poverty* (New York: Oxford University Press).

World Bank (2001), *Global Economic Prospects and Developing Countries* (Washington, DC: World Bank).

World Bank (2002a), *Global Economic Prospects and Developing Countries: Making Trade Work for the Poor* (Washington, DC: World Bank).

World Bank (2002b), *Globalization, Growth and Poverty: Building an Inclusive World Economy* (Oxford: Oxford University Press).

World Bank (2004), *World Development Report 2005* (New York: Oxford University Press).

World Economic Forum (2006), *The Global Competitiveness Report 2006-2007: Creating an Improved Business Environment* (Geneva: World Economic Forum).

World Trade Organization (WTO) Visited July 28, 2006 at: www.wto.org.

Zaun, T. and Millman, J. (2003), "Japan, Mexico Hammer Out Final Details on Trade Deal," *The Wall Street Journal*, October 17, A9.

Zodrow, G.R. (2003), "Tax Competition and Tax Coordination in the European Union," *International Tax and Public Finance*, 10, 651–71. [DOI: 10.1023/A%3A1026377819946]

Index

Note: Bold page numbers indicate tables; italic page numbers indicate maps and illustrations.